The

CRIMES

of

PARIS

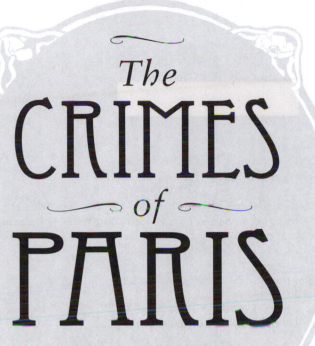

The
CRIMES
of
PARIS

A True Story of Murder,
Theft, and Detection

DOROTHY AND THOMAS HOOBLER

Little, Brown and Company
New York Boston London

Little, Brown and Company
Hachette Book Group
237 Park Avenue, New York, NY 10017
Visit our Web site at www.HachetteBookGroup.com

First Edition: June 2009

Little, Brown and Company is a division of Hachette Book Group, Inc.
The Little, Brown name and logo are trademarks of Hachette Book Group, Inc.

Library of Congress Cataloging-in-Publication Data

Hoobler, Dorothy.
    The crimes of paris : a true story of murder, theft, and detection / Dorothy and Thomas Hoobler. — 1st ed.
        p.   cm.
    Includes bibliographical references and index.
    ISBN 978-0-316-01790-9
    1. Leonardo, da Vinci, 1452–1519. Mona Lisa.   2. Art thefts—France–Paris.
I. Hoobler, Thomas.   II. Title.
    ND623.L5H66 2008
    364.16'2870944361—dc22   2008042646

10   9   8   7   6   5   4   3   2   1

RRD-IN

Printed in the United States of America

CONTENTS

CONTENTS

The
CRIMES
of
PARIS

THEFT

It was a Monday and the Louvre was closed. As was standard practice at the museum on that day of the week, only maintenance workers, cleaning staff, curators, and a few other employees roamed the cavernous halls of the building that was once the home of France's kings but since the Revolution had been devoted to housing the nation's art treasures.

Acquired through conquest, wealth, good taste, and plunder, those holdings were splendid and vast—so much so that the Louvre could lay claim to being the greatest repository of art in the world. With some fifty acres of gallery space, the collection was too immense for visitors to view in a day or even, some thought, in a lifetime.[1] Most guidebooks, therefore, advised tourists not to miss the Salon Carré (Square Room). In that single room could be seen two paintings by Leonardo da Vinci, three by Titian, two by Raphael, two by Correggio, one by Giorgione, three by Veronese, one by Tintoretto, and—representing non-Italians—one each by Rubens, Rembrandt, and Velázquez.

A stunning display, certainly. But even in that collection of masterpieces, one painting stood out from the rest. That very morning—August 21, 1911-as the museum's maintenance director, a man named Picquet, passed through the Salon Carré on his rounds, he pointed out Leonardo da Vinci's *Mona Lisa,* telling a co-worker that it was the most valuable object in the museum. "They say it is worth a million and a half," Picquet remarked, glancing at his watch as he left the room. The time was 7:20 A.M.

Shortly after Picquet passed through the Salon Carré, a door to a storage closet opened and a man (or men, for it was never proved whether the thief worked alone) emerged. He had been in there since the previous day — Sunday, the museum's busiest, as that was the only day most Parisians had off from work. Just before closing time, the thief had slipped inside the little closet so that he could emerge in the morning without the need to identify himself to a guard at the entrance.

There were many such small rooms and hidden alcoves within the seven-hundred-year-old[2] building; museum officials later confessed that no one knew how many. This particular one was normally used for storing the easels, canvases, and supplies of artists who were engaged in copying the works of Old Masters — a training exercise for those who wished to improve their technique. The only firm antiforgery requirement the museum placed on such students was that the reproductions could not be the same size as the original.

Emerging from the closet, the intruder might have been mistaken for one of these copyists, for he wore a white artist's smock. However, his garment had another purpose on this particular day: the museum's maintenance staff also wore such smocks, apparently a practice intended to demonstrate that they were on a higher plane than "ordinary" workers, and if anyone noticed the thief, he would likely be taken for another of the regular museum employees.

As he entered the Salon Carré, he headed straight for his intended target: the *Mona Lisa.* Only four sturdy hooks held it there, no more securely than if it were a framed print in the house of a bourgeois Parisian. Later, museum officials said that the paintings were fastened to the wall in this way to make it easy for guards to remove them in case of fire.

Even so, lifting down the *Mona Lisa* and carrying it into a nearby enclosed stairwell was no easy job. The painting itself weighs approximately eighteen pounds, for Leonardo painted it not on canvas but on three slabs of wood. A few months earlier, the museum's directors had taken steps to physically protect the *Mona Lisa* by reinforcing it with a massive wooden brace and placing it inside a glass-fronted box, adding 150 pounds to the weight. The decorative Renaissance frame contributed perhaps 30 additional pounds, bringing the total to nearly 200 pounds.

Once safely out of sight behind the closed door of the stairwell, the thief quickly stripped the painting of all its protective "garments"—the brace, the glass case, and the frame. Since the *Mona Lisa*'s close-grained wood, an inch and a half thick, made it impossible to roll up, the thief slipped the work underneath his smock. Measuring approximately thirty by twenty-one inches, the painting was small enough to avoid detection.

Though evidently familiar with the layout of the museum, the thief had made one mistake in his planning. The enclosed stairway led down to the first floor of the museum, but at the bottom was a locked door. The thief had obtained a key, but now it failed to work. Desperately, he used a screwdriver to remove the doorknob—but then heard footsteps coming from above.

Down the stairs came one of the Louvre's plumbers, a man named Sauvet. Later, Sauvet—the only man to witness the thief inside the museum—testified that he saw one man (only one), dressed as a museum employee. The man complained that the doorknob was missing. Helpfully, Sauvet unlocked the door with his own key and even produced a pliers to turn the mechanism to open the door. The plumber suggested that they leave it open in case anyone else should use the staircase. The thief agreed and went on about his business.

The door opened onto a courtyard, the Cour du Sphinx. From there the thief crossed through another gallery and into the Cour Visconti and then—probably trying not to appear in a hurry—headed toward the main entrance of the museum. Few guards were on duty that day, because it was felt they were only necessary when the public was admitted. However, there was one assigned to that entrance, the last barrier between the thief and the city. As luck would have it, he had left his post to get a bucket of water to clean the vestibule. He never saw the thief, or thieves, leave the building.

One person outside did: a passerby who noticed a man on the sidewalk carrying a package wrapped in white cloth (the smock that he had used to impersonate a workman). The witness recalled seeing the man throw a shiny metal object into the ditch along the edge of the street. The passerby glanced at it. It was a doorknob.

Inside the museum, all was serene and would remain so for quite some time. At 8:35 A.M. Picquet passed through the Salon Carré again and noted that the painting was gone. He thought little of it at the time, for the museum's photographers freely removed objects without notice and took them to a studio elsewhere in the building. Indeed, Picquet even remarked to his workers, "I guess the authorities have removed it because they thought we would steal it!"[3] His quip seemed less humorous later.

Incredibly, all through that day no one thought it alarming that there was an empty space where the *Mona Lisa* should have been. Not until Tuesday, when the Louvre again opened its doors to the public, did anyone express concern over the fact that the world's most famous painting was missing from its usual place. Louis Beroud, an artist, set up his easel in the Salon Carré. He was not there to copy a particular work. His intention was to create a genre painting that would show much of the room and the contents of its walls. (Sometimes Beroud's scenes included attractive young women viewing the museum's collection. His paintings, and others like them, were popular with foreign visitors who wanted something more than postcards as souvenirs of their trip to Paris.)

Beroud noticed at once that the centerpiece of his intended

work was missing. He complained to a guard, who shrugged. Like Picquet the day before, he assumed the *Mona Lisa* had been removed to the photographer's studio. Beroud persisted. His time was valuable. No one had scheduled a removal of the painting. How long would it take before it was returned?

To stop Beroud's badgering, the guard finally went to see the photographer, who denied having anything to do with the painting. Perhaps it had been taken by a curator for cleaning? No. Finally, the guard thought it wise to inform a superior. A search began and soon became increasingly frantic. The director of the museum was on vacation, so the unthinkable news filtered up to the acting head, Georges Bénédite: *Elle est partie!* She's gone.

THE CITY OF LIGHT

On April 14, 1900, French president Émile-François Loubet opened the Paris Exposition Universelle, whose goal was to "reflect the bright genius of France, and show our fair country to be, today as yesterday, in the very vanguard of Progress."[1] Spread across the city, from the place de la Concorde to the Eiffel Tower, was a fantastic array of Swiss villages, Hungarian Gypsy caravans, mosques and minarets and Arab towns, as well as reproductions of the great Basilica of San Marco in Venice, a temple at Angkor Wat, and the Imperial Palaces in Peking. The expo contained displays from fifty-eight countries in 210 pavilions covering 350 acres. From April to November of that centennial year, Paris welcomed fifty million visitors from all over the world.

The star of the event was electricity, newly harnessed by science. Every evening, with a flick of a switch in the Palace of Electricity, light from fifty-seven hundred incandescent bulbs flooded the pavilions, inspiring the nickname Ville Lumière, "City of Light," for Paris. Electricity also powered a train that circled the fair and a *trottoir roulant* (moving sidewalk) that allowed people to glide to the galleries. This newly harnessed invisible force propelled a giant Ferris wheel, carrying forty cars and twenty-four hundred people at full capacity, modeled after the original that had appeared at the Chicago World's Fair ten years earlier. The fair was seen as a herald of the exciting and unparalleled new gifts that science would bring to the modern age.

A visitor, Pierre Laborde, a university student from Bordeaux, wrote: "You could say I've touched with my finger this delicious century that's just begun. I've danced all the dances of the world from the Pont des Invalides to the Pont de l'Alma, and travelled by 'moving carpet' from a Venetian palazzo to Washington's Capital, from an Elizabethan manor to a Byzantine church. . . . I've seen moving photographs and electrified dancing: cinematography and Loie Fuller [a red-headed American dancer who used electric lights to make her costumes glow and attempted to buy radium as a decoration because she had heard it glowed in the dark. . . . Life on a screen [the movies] . . . isn't yet art, but it will be. And on a glass floor when the lights change color a woman becomes a flower, a butterfly, a storm, a flame from a brazier."[2] The fair was an affirmation of the new century's glowing promise, transformed by an energy that no one could see but all could experience.

i

The years in Paris from 1900 to the beginning of the First World War are often called the Belle Époque, the "beautiful time." It was the height of a great civilization, confident, prosperous, cultured, and creative. Paris was not only the seat of the nation's government but also the cultural focus of France—and, many felt, of the world. Within the city were the collected treasures of France—not only in museums, but within institutions of higher education, libraries, and archives. Paris was an international center for the arts of painting, dance, music, theater, and publishing. It had the foremost medical and scientific institutions of the day, and the most modern manufacturing facilities. The face of the future could be seen in Parisian leadership of such brand-new fields as motion pictures, automobile manufacturing, and aviation.

Visitors and wanderers were an essential component of this success. France's colonial empire in Asia and Africa (a "civilizing mission," as the French called it) brought to Paris examples of foreign cultures that understood the world in ways that were different from the European tradition. These in turn stimulated the imagination of the artists and scientists. Among the geniuses who lived in Paris in 1900 were Henri Matisse and Paul Cézanne in art, Claude Debussy in music, Henri Poincaré in mathematics, Marcel Proust in literature, and the Curies, Marie and Pierre, in science. The achievements in painting during the Belle Époque can only be compared with those of Renaissance Florence when Leonardo lived there.

Among the fifty million visitors to the Paris fair was the nineteen-year-old Spaniard Pablo Ruiz, who visited the Spanish Pavilion (which resembled a Castilian castle) to see his own painting on display. Pablo was entranced with the city, its freedom, its variety, its openness to what was new and different. Like so many others, he would return and forge a new identity for himself. In his youth in Spain, the young man had learned to paint anything he could see; in Paris, he would discover how to paint things that nobody but himself saw. Forging a new identity for himself, he took his mother's family name: Picasso.

A city of more than 2.7 million people in 1900, Paris had been the site of a settlement long before the Romans established a fort there around 300 C.E. Yet the twentieth-century city was in many ways quite new, the creation of Baron Georges Haussmann, the first and the most powerful representative of what today are known as city planners. Serving as prefect of the Seine from 1853 to 1870, Haussmann had been entrusted by Napoleon III with the task of modernizing the city, making it grander and more beautiful. He had acted ruthlessly to fulfill his mandate. He demolished much of the ancient center of the city, wiping out whole neighborhoods on the Île de la Cité and the banks of the Seine. Paris also expanded, adding suburbs in places previously occupied by mills, grape arbors, and fields. Haussmann filled such lightly populated areas with housing for workers who had been displaced from the central city.

Drawing bold lines across the existing map of Paris, Haussmann built wide, straight, tree-lined boulevards that, fortuitously, would eventually carry multiple lanes of traffic by an invention he had not yet seen: the automobile. New bridges across the Seine and the Île de la Cité bound the Left Bank and Right Bank together and further eased traffic circulation. Safe drinking water was carried to the city through aqueducts from as far as one hundred miles away, and the new underground canals of the sewer system were regarded as so extraordinary that they became tourist attractions despite their smell. The wide streets made police surveillance easier as well, and the police force expanded to monitor Paris's growing population.

Lining the boulevards were fine theaters, expensive restaurants, shops, cafés, and music halls. Elegant apartments with balconies offered housing to the very rich on broad avenues such as the Champs-Élysées. As dynamos brought electricity to all parts of Paris, it became possible to install electric-powered elevators in buildings, reversing the traditional Parisian order of living. Formerly the poor had to climb stairs to their upper-story apartments; now the rich could ride there in comfort to enjoy the beautiful views. Construction began on even taller buildings, called *à l'américaine* after the home of the skyscraper. Some people feared that these new outsize structures would destroy the proportions of the city and even hurt the tourist trade. "When Paris resembles Chicago and New York," a newspaper editor warned his fellow Parisians, "the American women we want so much to attract, won't come here anymore."[3] He needn't have worried. Paris was a shopper's mecca. Recently opened were huge department stores called *grands magasins*, such as Au Bon Marché and Galeries Lafayette, with multistory connected galleries that attracted shoppers from the world over.

The American writer Theodore Dreiser was in Paris at the turn of the century and described its mode of life: "He [the Parisian] lives by the way," he wrote, "out of books, restaurants, theaters, boulevards, and the spectacle of life generally. The Parisians move briskly, and they come out where they can see one another—out into the great wide-sidewalked boulevards and the thousands upon thousands of cafés, and make themselves comfortable and talkative and gay. It is obvious that everybody is having a good time, not merely trying to have it; that they are enjoying the wine-like air, the *brasseries,* the net-like movements of the cabs, the dancing lights of the roadways, and the flare of the shops. It may be chill or drizzling in Paris, but you scarcely feel it. Rain can scarcely drive the people off the streets . . . for there are crowds whether it rains or not, and they are not despondent."[4]

Indeed, after the theft of the *Mona Lisa,* many people joked that the woman in the painting had gone out for a night on the town. If she had, she would have fit right into the scenes on either bank of the Seine, for the French capital was a magnet for the beautiful, wealthy, talented, and creative from the world over. Gertrude Stein, an American who arrived in the city in 1903, wrote, "Paris was where the twentieth century was."[5]

ii

Many came to Paris because of the city's bohemian neighborhoods, where artists and writers congregated to be on the cutting edge. Though Paris was a rich city, it was possible to live quite cheaply, if one could endure hardship. In 1891, Maria Sklodowska (who would later become the wife and scientific partner of Pierre Curie) arrived in Paris from her native Poland, then under Russian control, to study at the Sorbonne. "The room I lived in," she recalled, "was . . . very cold in winter, for it was insufficiently heated by a small stove which often lacked coal. During a particularly rigorous winter, it was not unusual for the water to freeze in the basin in the night; to be able to sleep I was obliged to pile all my clothes on the bedcovers. In the same room I prepared my meals with the aid of an alcohol lamp and a few kitchen utensils. These meals were often reduced to bread with a cup of chocolate, eggs or fruit. I had no help in housekeeping and I myself carried the little coal I used up the six flights."[6]

Another of the city's residents was Guillaume Apollinaire, who was to become the great friend and publicizer of Picasso. Born out of wedlock in 1880 to a Polish woman in Rome (he himself spread stories that his father was a cardinal or perhaps even a pope), he formally bore an impressive collection of names: Guillaume Albert Wladimir Alexandre Apollin de Kostrowitsky. Along with a younger brother, he and his mother lived for a time in Monte Carlo, Cannes, Nice, and several other French cities, giving Guillaume a cosmopolitan air that would serve him well—although he recalled they frequently had to sneak out of hotels in the middle of the night when they could not pay the bill. Though Apollinaire was too poor to take the required courses for a university degree, he was able to find a job as a tutor with a wealthy family. A sojourn in Germany and then an unrequited passion for a young Englishwoman inspired him to begin writing poems. He settled in Paris, living in his mother's house in the suburb of Le Vésinet but spending his time in Montmartre, like so many other aspiring artists. Working as a bank clerk, he contributed poems and articles to small literary journals and even edited one himself. He also wrote two elegant pornographic novels, which brought an offer from a publisher to edit and write introductions to a series of classic erotic works. Carrying all this off with aplomb and dignity, Guillaume soon became a familiar figure in the cafés of Montmartre.

Another arrival who had invented her own identity in Paris was Gabrielle Chanel, later known to the world as Coco. Born in a poorhouse in the town of Saumur on the Loire River, she spent her teen years in an orphanage after her mother died and her father deserted his children. Chanel devoured romance novels, whose plots she later incorporated into her own life story. After she became a famous couturier, a friend suggested that psychotherapy might help her to be more honest about her humble origins. Chanel replied with a laugh, "I—who never told the truth to my priest?"[7] Like many who came to Paris, her life was a work of art, a blend of fact and fiction, assembled as she chose.

Not everyone found immediate success. Marcel Proust, the son of a doctor, spent hours on the bed of his cork-lined room on the second floor of 102, boulevard Haussmann, writing the mammoth six-part novel *À la recherche du temps perdu,* which many regard as the greatest French literary work of the twentieth century. In 1911, however, when he sent the first part of the book to a publisher, the editor emphatically rejected it, saying, "I may be dense but I cannot understand how a man can use up thirty pages to describe the way he turns over and moves about in bed before falling asleep. It makes me want to scream."[8] Proust later sent his work to André Gide, an editor of the *Nouvelle Revue Française* who would himself become famous as a writer. Gide, like Proust, was a homosexual and feared a public outcry over the frank depictions of sexuality in Proust's novel, which he rejected as "the worst thing possible for our magazine."[9] Proust was doing in literature what Picasso would do in painting: creating a world from the images inside his head, just as the narrator of his novel relates. But he had to publish the first volume of his long work at his own expense.

iii

Proust may have consoled himself at one of the homosexual brothels that he frequented. (He even made money investing in one.) By the dawn of the twentieth century, Paris was a center for sex tourism. In the 1890s there were thirty strip shows in Paris. A critic described Mlle. Cavelli, the star attraction at one of them, the Alcazar d'Été, "doffing her hat, her dress, her petticoats, her corset, her pretty white and pink underwear, with a decent interval between each stage of her undressing to allow the spectators to recover their sang-froid." [10] Fully nude dancers were not hard to find. The city's most famous bordello had been opened in time for the Paris Exposition of 1878; a favorite of the Prince of Wales, it had a special bathtub designed to hold his girth and reserved for him exclusively. A visitor at the time wrote, "The salons are sumptuous, each one represents a cabin in a pleasure yacht, and with elegant bathrooms. Visitors are received in a magnificent hall modeled from a courtyard of the Spanish Alhambra and are given an illustrated booklet of views of the best apartments in the eight-storied house. Every flat is divided into numerous rooms, neatly furnished in Louis XV style." [11]

Paris offered many pleasures even for those who were not royalty. The city's night life centered in the two well-known bohemian sections on either side of the Seine: Montmartre and Montparnasse. Montmartre, on the Right Bank, kept its rural charm well into the twentieth century. The highest point in Paris, it still contained vineyards and windmills and the narrow, winding streets that were characteristic of all Paris before Haussmann's renovations. Its cabarets and cafés attracted bohemians and working-class people alike; moreover, it was known as the haunt of criminal gangs. Aristocrats seeking adventure liked to go slumming there.

Rodolphe Solis, an artist and mathematician, boasted: "God created the world, Napoleon founded the Legion of Honor, and I invented Montmartre." [12] Solis opened Le Chat Noir in 1881; it was a cabaret that would forever influence entertainment in Paris. The waiters were dressed like members of the prestigious Académie française, with the headwaiter wearing the colorful uniform of the papal Swiss guards. The interior was decorated in the style of Louis XIII, with ornate, voluptuous lines and colors. Its entertainment ranged from *ombres chinoises* (Chinese shadow puppets) to barbed political humor and songs that commented on follies and scandals in the news. Avant-garde composer Erik Satie often accompanied singers on the piano, and another composer, Claude Debussy, was a regular patron. Stand-up comedians told dirty jokes and threw insults at members of the audience, bringing roars of approval. One performer whose act was so vulgar as to be beyond taste was Pétomane, the world's greatest farter, whose poster proudly proclaimed: "the only performer who doesn't pay composers' royalties."[13] Though Le Chat Noir had closed in 1897, its spirit and influence lived on through the Belle Époque, inspiring other entertainment venues throughout Montmartre.

Another option was the *café-concert,* a kind of music hall or nightclub. A contemporary described the raucous atmosphere: "In all of these halls, singing, dancing, and often shameless dramatic performances are given these days in front of princes, wealthy loafers, fashionable ladies, and those who act as if they were. This type of entertainment . . . manifests above all, a desire for uninhibitedness, spectacle, and debasement that is peculiar to our times. However low the [more formal type of] theater may have sunk, however little it demands from its audience in terms of behavior and intellectual effort, it still makes certain demands. One may not smoke or keep one's hat on there; moreover, one has to understand the play, or at least seem to understand it, and even the actors do not say or mime everything. In the *café-concert,* on the other hand, there are none of these limits! One smokes, drinks, comes and goes as one pleases, while watching highly suggestive acts and listening to incredibly risqué jokes. The *café-concert* is the paradise of libertinism and the more determined bad taste. On top of this the prices are low and the incitement of all the senses is practically free. For a few sous one gets everything that refreshes as well as excites. How then could one avoid coming here to still, or seem to still, the freely admitted or secret desire for dissolute excess that currently plagues the *peuple* as much as good society?"[14]

Montmartre became well known as a place where people went to abandon their inhibitions. At Le Rat Mort in place Pigalle, for example, women dressed in men's clothing and danced with one another. Guides to the city, such as one written in 1913 by the Englishman Frankfort Sommerville, raved about the area Parisians nicknamed the Butte. "Montmartre," he declared, "is the dwelling-place of the most curious collection of poets, painters, sculptors, bar-keepers, vagabonds, girls of the street, models, apaches, scoundrels in the world—the most gifted and the most degraded (and there is not always a very sharp line dividing them). Montmartre is just as remarkable a mixture of gaiety, strenuous work, poetry and mockery, artistic sense and irreligion." [15]

To outsiders, perhaps the best-known spot in Montmartre was the Moulin Rouge, which opened in October 1889 to take advantage of the Paris World's Fair of that year. Its moving windmill sails (and later, flashing electric lights), served as a beacon to attract visitors to its shows—revues and popular musical plays as well as dance routines. (One observer commented that the cabaret's "sails never ground anything but the customers' money." [16]) The Moulin Rouge was renowned for its professional female dancers performing the then-risqué cancan, and the first time Picasso visited Paris, he went there, as did many other tourists. Posters and paintings of the entertainers by the artist Henri de Toulouse-Lautrec added to the international fame of the cabaret. The chanteuse Yvette Guilbert charmed the audience with her sophisticated and touching songs, in which she invoked the pathos of lower-class suffering.

The cabaret scene in Montmartre provided entertainment for every taste, even the tantalizingly perverse. Picasso's companion Carles Casagemas wrote home that his favorite haunts were the next-door-neighbor cabarets named Ciel (Heaven) and Infer (Hell)—and a third named Néant, or Nothingness. At the Cabaret du Ciel, patrons entered gates lit by blue-tinted electric lights, with the action starting at 11:00 P.M. Inside, the ceiling was painted blue, with stars and clouds; paintings of saints and angels lined the corridors. Another visitor described his experiences here around 1910:

> The head waiter greets visitors with a blasphemous welcome that need not be set down. . . . Suddenly from among the clouds at the end of the room St. Peter appears, keys at girdle, a mysterious vessel in one hand; he sprinkles the nearest devotees with his imitation of

holy water and disappears. The waiters now assemble before a shrine at the end of the room, on which a gilt pig sits enshrined. They light candles and perform genuflections. From the pulpit at the other side of the café a man dressed as a preacher delivers an unprintable discourse. Then after a procession of Angel garçons the assembled guests, being duly santified, file out of the "Home of the Angels," St. Peter himself being in the passage to give out tickets. . . . You pass out to the street, meeting Father Time at the exit with his hourglass turned up to receive the contributions of those who wish to enjoy a long life.

In the Cabaret du Néant you can see a body put into a coffin and turn into a skeleton before your eyes, and return again to healthy life. You are attended by mutes, and the drinks supplied are called by the names of various hideous diseases. Outside the Cabaret of Hell you are greeted by a red devil with horns and trident, who bids you enter and be d——d, for Satan is calling for you. And if you care to go inside, Satan will be heard delivering a discourse, strange medley of morality and blasphemy.[17]

Cafés and cabarets also dotted Montparnasse, on the other bank of the Seine. Especially popular was La Closerie des Lilas,[18] a café on the boulevard Montparnasse, adjacent to the Latin Quarter, where many students from the University of Paris lived. Vladimir Lenin, then an exile from Russia, lived in Paris from 1901 to 1912. And though he much preferred London as a city (he described Paris as a "foul hole"), he did have drinks sometimes at the Closerie des Lilas.[19] Across the street was Bal Bullier, which held a weekly *grande fête* for students, artists, and workers, who danced in its backyard gardens under colored lights. In the spring, costumed art students paraded in the Bal Bullier. One who did so remembered "students and artists, handsome and merry in their stunning velvet suits and floppy slouch hats, and with their girls, some in their cycling bloomers, others in silk robes, and still others in summer blouses."[20] The Café Dôme's proprietors welcomed visitors and new arrivals, and it became a gathering place for foreign artists. The Cabaret de la Rotonde, which opened around 1911, was called "the navel of the world" at the height of its popularity.[21] It attracted such Russian revolutionaries as Lenin, Leon Trotsky, and Anatoliy Lunacharsky and was the favorite café of the Italian artist Amedeo Modigliani. Also to be found there were the Mexican painter Diego Rivera and the Russian artists Marc Chagall and Chaim Soutine.

Gino Severini, an Italian, arrived in Paris in October 1906. A friend of Picasso and Apollinaire, he was to become a leader of the Italian futurists, who pursued their own kind of modernism and sought to incorporate speed, energy, and force into their works. "Few have ever arrived in an unfamiliar city as penniless and hopeless as I was," he wrote. "I had no friends, no money (barring 50 francs I counted in my pocket that evening), only a scant knowledge of French. . . . I arrived at the Gare de Lyon in a lighthearted, ebullient frame of mind. I took the white tram . . . went straight to Montparnasse, and ordered my first café-au-lait at a little bar on the corner of boulevard Montparnasse and boulevard Raspail. The bar was called La Rotonde and years later would become a famous meeting place for modern artists. . . . Having arrived at six in the morning, by nine I was settled in, and could wander out to the boulevard Raspail, where a new building was going up in a wonderfully chaotic construction site that I could start to draw."[22] Paris, with its unmatched atmosphere of intellectual and artistic ideas, was a place where Severini, like others, could thrive.

iv

Paris at the turn of the century was the epicenter of modernism—the new artistic, social, cultural, and scientific revolution that was changing the way people looked at the world.

Rapid change was to be an essential part of modern life. Technological advances, such as automobiles, telephones, airplanes, electric streetcars, and urban railways such as Paris's Métro, were radically increasing the speed at which products and information could be exchanged. The dense urban concentration of populations made retail establishments such as department stores possible and gave rise to a new consumerism. Population density also fostered crime, for human relationships became increasingly random and impersonal and the gaps between the haves and the have-nots became more conspicuous. Meanwhile, Freudian psychology, physical studies of the human brain, and the experiments of French psychologists such as Jean Charcot were providing new theories of human behavior and motivation.

Above all, modern life was marked by speed. As the poet Octave Mirbeau said of the streetcar, "Life everywhere rushes headlong."[23] Nothing captured the imagination of people like the automobile. Between 1890 and 1904, France led the world in the production of motor cars, and in 1900 the wait could be as long as twenty-two months for delivery. Before the days of the assembly line, each coach was custom-built to each owner's specifications, and the height could vary along with the fashions in ladies' hats. The renowned *grande horizontale* (courtesan) known as La Belle Otéro had an automobile that was so high and narrow that it could overturn if rounding a curve too fast. Race car drivers became celebrities, and before World War I, some automobiles reached the phenomenal speed of eighty miles per hour. Even at lower velocities, however, an automobile made the world seem different. Mirbeau observed that riding in a car "put things into a new relief, giving me an impression that objects and persons were not just static but intensely active."[24] The poet strained to express the feelings that his automobile gave him: "I can contemplate without a tremor the dispersion of my books, my pictures, and all my collection, but I cannot bear the thought that a day may come when I shall no longer possess my magic charger, this fabulous unicorn that bears me so gently and swiftly, with a clearer and a keener brain, across the whole map of nature's beauties, the richness and diversity of the human scene."[25]

Even more thrilling than the automobile, though not so widely available, was the airplane. The realization of the dream of flight, one of the many obsessions that Leonardo had filled his notebooks with, was seen as a manifestation of the great power of modern science. At the 1900 Paris Exposition, Alberto Santos-Dumont, the son of a Brazilian coffee king, made ascents in his bicycle-powered balloon, using the handlebars to steer. By 1906, Santos-Dumont had constructed a biplane, which he flew a distance of 60 meters, the first powered flight in Europe. This set off a competition to build better engines and planes and increase the time in the air. In 1908, Léon Delagrange, a sculptor, flew a plane 854 meters, the first flight to be filmed.

The great hero of early flight in France was Louis Blériot. The survivor of many crashes, he was determined to win the prize of one thousand pounds offered by the London *Daily Mail* for the first person to fly across the English Channel. At 4:35 A.M. on July 25, 1909, hobbling on crutches from an earlier accident, Blériot set off in his monoplane, a cratelike machine called the X1. He headed out to sea and soon faced head-on squalls. He pressed forward, though he could not swim and had only a small supply of water. The plane responded and eventually he landed at Dover Castle. The crossing had taken just thirty-seven minutes. When British soldiers ran up to congratulate Blériot, he responded, "Be good enough to hand me my crutches."[26] An hour later he was joined by his wife, who had arrived by boat. Blériot received a hero's welcome on his return and was awarded the Légion d'honneur. His achievement was a source of pride to the French, who by 1911 had more than three times as many pilots as Germany and Britain combined.[27]

In conquering the air, humans violated an ancient law: the gravity that bound them to the earth. The world looked smaller from the air, easier to encompass. In the same way, the speed of automobiles gave people enormous new powers of mobility and independence. The telephone further compressed space and time. Some doubted these changes were for the better. The German writer Max Nordau feared that everyone would soon be required to "read a dozen square yards of newspaper daily . . . be constantly called to the telephone . . . think simultaneously of five continents of the earth," and "live half their time in a railroad carriage or in a flying machine."[28] But there was no stopping what people saw as "progress."

France's greatest philosopher of this era, Henri Bergson, rejected the mechanistic ordering of time by seconds and minutes, claiming instead that past and present were linked to the future by a free flow of moments, which he called "duration." Only by taking away mundane data, he wrote, could one reach the level of consciousness that permits highly creative people to assimilate impressions from childhood to adulthood in order to live a whole and fulfilling life. It was through intuition that duration could be grasped in all its complexity. Bergson's term for this creative and intense living in duration was élan vital, which became a catch phrase of the time.

Bergson gave free lectures each Friday at the Collège de France, open to the public. Society women and tourists as well as workers came to hear the man in his three-inch stiff collar "fashioning phrases like a sculptor with his slim white hands."[29]

Bergson believed that art played a special role in helping a person grasp "some secret chord which was only waiting to thrill."[30] At this time, the French were among the world's leaders in the brand-new motion picture industry, and the cinema was an ideal illustration of Bergson's ideas. A strip of motion picture film contains many individual frames. When these are run through a projector at a certain speed, the mind perceives them not as a series of stills but as a continuous flow—in other words, duration. (The impressionist artists, in their move away from a literal representation of reality in their works, were another example. So was the literary work of Marcel Proust, who is said to have been inspired by

Bergson in the conception of his six-volume novel, *Remembrance of Things Past*.)[31]

The first French movies, made by the Lumière brothers in 1895, were little more than filmed tableau and playlets. Soon, however, Georges Méliès, who had started his career as a magician, discovered how to work magic with a camera. He pioneered the use of trick photography, producing images that startled audiences of the time. His films showed ghosts produced by double exposures, made people abruptly appear and disappear, and transformed objects from one thing to another. Méliès's 1902 science fiction movie *A Trip to the Moon*, based on Jules Verne's novel, remains a classic. The young Picasso was fascinated by the movies; he saw his first in Barcelona in 1896. From the time of his arrival in Paris he was an avid moviegoer. A recent exhibition of his work in conjunction with Méliès's films showed the influence the Frenchman had on Picasso's depiction of reality.[32]

Movies were, of course, another way of transcending space and time, for they could preserve and reproduce the images of past events. The Parisian Charles Pathé pioneered the first newsreels, which permitted theatergoers to view events of the day as if they had been eyewitnesses. (Because cameras could not always get to scenes in time to film the actual events, Pathé and his imitators often reenacted them with actors.) By 1913, Pathé owned the largest cinema in Paris, which included the world's largest screen and a sixty-piece orchestra.

Léon Gaumont was one of the first filmmakers to discover that audiences would return on a regular basis if he divided his movie stories into installments, or serials. Crime stories, adventures, and even Wild West thrillers influenced by American novels drew enormous audiences to Paris's theaters. The month after the theft of the *Mona Lisa*, Parisians were flocking to see *Zigomar*, the first of a series that pitted an archcriminal against the Paris police—inevitably concluding with the triumph of the forces of evil.

Jean-Paul Sartre recalled going to the movies with his mother as a child in Paris:

> The show had begun. We would stumblingly follow the usherette. I would feel I was doing something clandestine. Above our heads, a shaft of light crossed the hall; one could see dust and vapor dancing in it. A piano whinnied away. Violet pears shone on the walls. . . . I would scrape my back against knees and take my place on a creaky seat. My mother would slide a folded blanket under my behind to raise me. Finally, I would look at the screen. I would see a fluorescent chalk and blinking landscapes streaked with showers; it always rained, even when the sun shone brightly, even in apartments. At times, an asteroid in flames would shoot across the drawing-room of a baroness without her seeming to be surprised. I liked that rain, that restless anxiety which played on the wall. The pianist would attack the overture to *Fingal's Cave* and everyone understood that the criminal was about to appear: the baroness would be frightened out of her wits. But her beautiful, sooty face would make way for a purple show-card: "End of Part I." I saw *Zigomar* and *Fantômas, The Exploits of Maciste, The Mysteries of New York* . . . As for me, I wanted to see the film *as close up as possible.* . . . I was utterly content, I had found the world in which I wanted to live, I touched the absolute. What an uneasy feeling when the lights went on: I had been wracked with love for the characters and they had disappeared, carrying their world with them. I had felt their victory in my bones; yet it was theirs and not mine. In the street I found myself superfluous.[33]

Time was altered not only by speed but also by the erasure of night. The electrification of the city transformed Paris, obliterating old patterns in great washes of illumination. The impressionists had often taken their canvases and paints into the countryside and worked in the midst of nature under sunlight. Picasso, on the other hand, liked to sleep during the day and paint at night by artificial light. He was far from alone in his after-midnight activities.

Though electricity could illuminate a city, it was itself invisible, one of a number of unseen forces scientists were now discovering. Radio waves could send a message across a continent; X-rays could expose the inside of the body; and radioactivity had other, not yet fully understood, powers. Picasso and his fellow artists were aware that these scientific discoveries were changing the world and that art would have to change with them. In 1840, the invention of photography by two Frenchmen had doomed the academic artists who sought to portray the world as it appeared to the eye: now any photographer could do that perfectly. There was a growing aware-ness that artists would have to uncover a deeper reality beneath the everyday appearances of things. Maurice Maeterlinck, a Bel-gian playwright living in Paris, wrote, "There lies a vast ocean of the Unconscious, the unknown source of all that is good, true and beautiful. All that I know, think, feel, see and will are but bubbles on the surface of this vast sea."[34] Paris was filled with people float-ing on that sea, searching.

V

For all its gaiety and progress, there were still dark shadows in the City of Light. The Third Republic, the current national govern-ment, had been born in the midst of the tragedy and humiliation of the Franco-Prussian War. When the Prussian army defeated the forces of Napoleon III at Sedan in northeastern France on September 2, 1870, it brought a crashing and ignominious end to France's Second Empire. In the span of less than a century, France had experienced eight different forms of government.[35] Now, a provisional leadership in Paris declared the establishment of a

Third Republic. Its prospects seemed bleak. As sporadic resistance continued in the countryside, the Prussian army surrounded the capital and laid siege to it. Starvation and bombardment took their toll, and the government had no choice but to agree to harsh terms for an armistice. Parisians had to endure the sight of German soldiers marching down the Champs-Élysées; the government agreed to pay a large indemnity and worst of all, to give up entirely the French provinces of Alsace and Lorraine. These were humiliations that the French never forgot.

The conditions of peace angered the populace, particularly in Paris. On March 18, 1871, as a precautionary measure, the head of the French government, Adolphe Thiers, sent troops to take back the cannons set on the heights of Montmartre. They met with resistance and two of the soldiers were killed. Workers in Paris, joining forces with some National Guard troops stationed in the city, set up a revolutionary municipal government called the Commune. Its goals were to carry on the war with Germany and to return to the revolutionary principles of 1793. Friction between the government in Versailles and the Commune in Paris broke into a bloody conflict marked by artrocities on both sides. The national army entered Paris on May 21, 1871, fighting its way through the city streets until the Communards made their last stand in the Père Lachaise Cemetery, in the center of working-class Belleville. The defenders were shot down among the tombs of French luminaries. Remembered as *la semaine sanglante* or Bloody Week, the urban battle caused death and destruction on a wide scale.

As the army tightened its hold on the city, the Communards killed the archbishop of Paris and wreaked vengeance on such landmarks as the Hôtel de Ville, Tuileries Palace, the Prefecture of Police, and expensive houses along the rue de Rivoli. The victorious army was far more ferocious, carrying out mass executions that made the Seine River run red with blood. The smell of burning bodies wafted through the city. Between twenty thousand and twenty-five thousand Communards were slaughtered and even more sent to penal colonies in Guiana and New Caledonia. The carnage on both sides and its legacy of hatred would haunt the Third Republic for decades.

The first goal of the government was to repair the material damage to the city. By the end of the decade, this was accomplished. Paris had sought to demonstrate its recovery by staging a World's Fair in 1878; a second, in 1889, added the Eiffel Tower to the city skyline. Ironically, its construction had been vehemently opposed by French intellectuals, who only relented on condition that the tower be demolished after a certain period. (Fortunately, it proved useful as a place from which radio transmissions could be sent overseas, so it was spared.) More controversial was the white-domed Basilica of Sacré-Coeur, which was built at the top of Montmartre as atonement for the violence of the Communards. Construction began in 1876 and did not end until just before World War I. Those who lived in Montmartre, most of whom were sympathetic to the memory of the Communards, resented the structure.

vi

More than most cities, Paris retained the memory of revolutions. In 1789, 1793, 1848, and 1871, Parisians had sacrificed their lives to overturn the established order—and, for a time, succeeded in doing so. The words "Liberté, égalité, fraternité" carved on buildings and monuments were a continual reminder of the ideals of the city's revolutionary past, and by the turn of the twentieth century, many still felt these were goals that had yet to be fully realized. At sidewalk cafés and in shadowy meeting halls, people engaged in heated debates about politics and philosophy. These were by no means theoretical discussions. Parisians understood that ideas could be turned into action.

Among the most ardent of the would-be revolutionaries were those who espoused anarchism. The idea that the state—government itself—is responsible for most of humankind's problems has deep roots in the French psyche. Jean-Jacques Rousseau, the Swiss-born philosopher whose ideas formed the underpinnings of the French Revolution, idealized the "natural man" who needed no government to enforce his proper conduct. (Rousseau, however, fell short of opposing government altogether.) The first French thinker to discuss what he termed "anarchism" was Pierre-Joseph Proudhon, in his 1840 work, *Qu'est-ce que la propriété? (What Is Property?*). His short answer: "Property is theft." Though Proudhon did not advocate the abolition of private property and did find a place for government in his ideal society (a national bank, for example, would finance workers' projects), his slogan appealed particularly to those who wanted a drastic leveling of social classes and an end to government that served to protect the wealthy.

The most prominent anarchist of the mid-nineteenth century was Mikhail Bakunin, a Russian émigré who had met Proudhon and tried to turn the Frenchman's ideas into action. Bakunin took part in the rebellions in Paris in 1848 and Dresden in 1849. Imprisoned, he escaped and joined other Russian agitators in London, where he initiated ambitious schemes for worldwide anarchist revolutions. (Interestingly, he bitterly quarreled with Karl Marx, because Bakunin believed Marxist revolutions would increase the power of governments over their people—a prediction that proved correct.) Bakunin's writings were not subtle or difficult to understand. He wrote: "The revolutionary is a man under vow. He ought to occupy himself entirely with one exclusive passion: the Revolution. . . . He has only one aim, one science: destruction. . . . Between him and society, there is war to the death, incessant, irreconcilable."[36] Bakunin died in 1876, but his ideas remained influential, and anarchism grew into a force that was widely feared by those who had an investment in the established order.

Anarchism exploded on the scene in the 1890s in Paris and in other European cities. Its adherents called bomb throwing the "propaganda of the deed." In Paris, a new reign of terror started in 1891, when workers protesting low pay marched under the black anarchist banner on May Day. This led to fighting between the police and anarchists in the Clichy section of Montmartre. Three marchers were arrested and one was sent to prison. In retaliation for the arrests, on March 11, 1892, bombs were set off at the house of the judge who had sentenced the protesters. A few days later another bomb went off at the house of the public prosecutor who had pressed the case. The chief culprit, a man named Ravachol, was captured largely through the efforts of Alphonse Bertillon, chief of the Service of Judicial Identity of the Paris police. Bertillon had developed a system of identifying suspects based on measurements of their faces and bodies and had introduced other scientific crime-fighting techniques. Ravachol's capture, however, made Bertillon a household name.

Even so, the violence continued when an anarchist named Auguste Vaillant struck inside the Chamber of Deputies in December 1893. Vaillant had gone to the Chamber with a bomb, intending to kill the premier of France and the president of the Chamber. But when he hurled his explosive device from the public gallery, a female spectator jostled his arm and the bomb hit a pillar, sending a shower of plaster and nails onto the floor, wounding many deputies and spectators.

Two months later, Émile Henry set off a bomb in a hotel café. It ripped through the crowd, killing one person and wounding twenty others. Running from the scene, Henry shot at a pursuing policeman but stumbled and was caught. Both Vaillant and Henry were convicted and guillotined. Nevertheless, Paris remained in a state of siege, with residents looking suspiciously at any package.

The greatest outrage of the anarchists was the assassination of French president Marie-François-Sadi Carnot in 1894. This time the culprit was an Italian named Sante Caserio, who had been booted from his homeland for distributing anarchist pamphlets. When he learned that Sadi Carnot was to go to Lyons to open the Colonial Exhibit, Caserio decided to assassinate him there. On June 24, as the president rode by in his carriage, Caserio pushed his way through the crowd, carrying a knife. While the noise of celebratory fireworks distracted the president's security guards, Caserio lunged inside the carriage and stabbed the president in the stomach. Shouting, "Vive l'Anarchie!" the assassin tried to run away, but spectators captured him and turned him over to the police. Caserio was unrepentant, declaring from his cell, "I am an anarchist and I have struck the Head of State. I've done it as I would have killed any king or emperor, of no matter what nationality."[37] Though his lawyers argued that he was insane and should not get the death penalty, he was guillotined on August 16.

Despite the violence and outrages, many artists and writers sympathized with anarchism, feeling that they shared the anarchists' aim of breaking down society's repressive rules. The cafés of Montmartre were particular hotbeds of support; entertainers there sometimes glorified the anarchists in song. Maxime Lisbonne, a former Communard who had returned from New Caledonia in 1880, ran a cabaret where the doors had bars, the tables were chained to the floor, and the waiters were dressed as galley slaves, dragging shackles behind them as they served customers. Lisbonne tried to take advantage of the anarchist outrages by advertising that his establishment was "the sole Concert sheltered from the Bombs."[38] This claim in fact brought to his establishment a slew of police informers who filed regular reports about the goings-on there.

Another cabaret associated with anarchism was Le Zut, owned by Frédéric "Frédé" Gérard and affiliated with the anarchist paper *Le Libertaire*. It was one of Picasso's favorite hangouts in his early years in Paris, and he decorated its walls with murals. After police shut down that establishment, Frédé went on to open a new place, which became famous as Le Lapin Agile. (Previously it had been called the Cabaret of Assassins because portraits of murderers were hung on the walls.) The new name came from a pun on the name of the sign painter André Gill, who painted over the entrance a rabbit hopping out of a stew pot (*le lapin à Gill*). Le Lapin Agile became a gathering place for anarchists and criminals as well as the artists and poets who patronized it for the cheap Burgundian food. Here, as late as 1910, informers were reporting on the anarchist clientele. In 1911, the owner's son was gunned down on the threshold of the café. His murderer was never found.

Anarchist newspapers continued to be published, and antigovernment sentiments remained active. In 1911, a Russian émigré named Victor Kibalchich, later known as Victor Serge, took over editorship of the newspaper *l'anarchie* and urged his comrades to resume the active struggle to overturn the state. His words caused a spark that would burst into flame when they reached Jules Bonnot, a onetime chauffeur. A series of disappointments in love and in his career had embittered him, and he had turned to stealing the cars of wealthy people. Now, embracing anarchism, he would make his own contribution to automotive history and become for a time the most feared criminal in France.

vii

Though Paris grew and prospered, the national government was perenially unstable. Unsure of how long the Third Republic would last, Parisians believed, in the words of one, that they were "dancing on a volcano."[39]

The execution of President Sadi Carnot's assassin was soon followed by the most severe internal crisis France faced during the Third Republic. The false accusation of a Jewish military officer for treason, known as the Dreyfus affair, divided the nation into bitterly opposed camps for years. It began in September 1894, when Major Hubert-Joseph Henry of the French intelligence service came into possession of a document that had been taken from a wastebasket at the German embassy. It was a note, afterward referred to as the *bordereau,* which indicated that someone in the French army apparently had provided the Germans with important information about French military plans. The type of information described in the *bordereau* implied that the traitorous informant had to be an artillery officer on the general staff of the army.

That brought Captain Alfred Dreyfus under suspicion, on no

grounds other than the fact that he fit that general description and that his handwriting was said to have resembled that on the *bordereau*. More importantly, Dreyfus was a Jew — a rarity at such an elevated rank — and his colleagues did not like him. France was experiencing an upsurge in anti-Semitism around this time. Despite the fact that there were only about 85,000 Jews in a French population of 39 million,[40] anti-Semites blamed them for many of the country's problems. The accusation against Dreyfus played directly into this metastasizing intolerance.

Military officials seeking to build a case against Dreyfus had asked Alfred Gobert, the handwriting expert of the Bank of France, to compare the handwriting on the incriminating *bordereau* with samples of Captain Dreyfus's writing. Gobert reported that although the two writing samples were "of the same graphic type," they "presented numerous and important disparities which had to be taken into account."[41] He concluded that the *bordereau* had been written by someone other than Dreyfus. This did not satisfy the military, which began to look for a second opinion. Prefect of Police Louis Lépine recommended Alphonse Bertillon, France's best-known expert on crime. Since he had identified and helped convict the anarchist Ravachol two years earlier, Bertillon's reputation had only increased. Police forces throughout Europe, the United States, and Latin America were keeping records of criminals and suspects according to Bertillon's identification system.

Unfortunately, Bertillon had no expertise as a handwriting expert, but at the urging of his chief, he acted as if he did — thus stepping into a morass from which his reputation never recovered. He pronounced his own judgment after a single day of examining the handwriting on the *bordereau:* "If the hypothesis of a document forged with the utmost care is eliminated, it appears clear to us that it was the same person who wrote the various items submitted and the incriminating document."[42]

In court, during Dreyfus's initial court-martial, Bertillon's testimony was far from compelling, for he tended to speak in a convoluted manner, complete with charts and diagrams that seemed dauntingly confusing. Moreover, the defense produced experts who contradicted his conclusion. By now, openly anti-Semitic publications, notably *La Parole Libre,* edited by the notorious bigot Édouard Drumont, had inflamed the public with their declarations that Dreyfus was a traitor. It was clear that if he were *not* convicted, the heads of those who accused him would roll. Desperate, Major Henry and others forged documents that added to the weight of "evidence" against the defendant. These were presented secretly to the judges, with the caution that "national security" would be compromised if they became public. Bertillon had no role in the forgery, but because he was the chief prop of the prosecution's case, he would eventually be tarred by the dishonorable conduct of those who sought to pillory Dreyfus.

The court, influenced by the forgeries, sentenced Dreyfus to a life term in the French penal colony at Devil's Island. But that was only the beginning of the Dreyfus affair. His brother and wife never ceased their efforts to clear his name, even while he sat in an isolated hut inside a walled compound off the coast of South America. In July 1895, Major Marie-Georges Picquart became chief of the Intelligence Bureau of the army and found that Germany was still receiving secret information, apparently from a French officer, Major Ferdinand Esterhazy. When Picquart reported this discovery to his superiors, he was reassigned to Africa to get him out of the way. Relentlessly, he continued to press the case against Esterhazy, who demanded a court-martial to prove himself innocent. He was, indeed, acquitted by the military judges, prompting the novelist and journalist Émile Zola to write "J'accuse," an open letter to the president of France, denouncing those who had conspired against Dreyfus. The minister of war successfully sued Zola, forcing him to leave the country.

By now, Esterhazy's handwriting had been compared to that on the *bordereau,* and the resemblance seemed compelling. France was divided into two warring camps: pro- and anti-Dreyfusard. Anti-Semitic mobs in the streets, urged on by demagogues, chanted

"Death to the Jews!" Even some of those who doubted Dreyfus's guilt worried that the French army's prestige would suffer an irreparable blow should his conviction be reversed. Some asked whether reviewing the conviction of one innocent man was worth weakening the nation's security at a time when many feared that a new war with Germany was imminent.

But Dreyfus's defenders were encouraged when Henry (by then promoted to lieutenant colonel) committed suicide after his forgeries were discovered; Esterhazy then fled the country. At last, in August 1899, the government yielded to public pressure and brought Dreyfus back from Devil's Island for another court-martial.

The military judges were determined to uphold the honor of the army; unfortunately, they saw honor only in clinging to what had clearly been discredited. Most onlookers were astonished by the verdict: once again, Dreyfus was found guilty, but this time with "extenuating circumstances," as if there could be extenuating circumstances for treason. The president of France offered him a full pardon, which Dreyfus accepted, while continuing the legal efforts to prove his innocence. A civilian court cleared Dreyfus of all charges in 1906, and by an act of the French Parliament, he was reinstated to the army and decorated with the Légion d'honneur.

The wounds of the Dreyfus affair were far from healed, however, and Bertillon in particular felt anguish, with good reason, that his own reputation had been damaged. He saw the theft of the *Mona Lisa* as a chance to show that he was still, as many believed, France's premier criminal investigator.

viii

Parisians were both fascinated and terrified by crime and criminals, *le prestige du mal.* Sensational accounts of the most lurid crimes thrilled readers of the mass-circulation newspapers. Supposedly true crime stories, called *faits divers,* and serialized novels, the *feuilletons,* were popular features of any newspaper wanting to attract readers. The historian Ann-Louise Shapiro has commented, "The culture seemed saturated with accounts of sensational crimes and infamous criminals. Mass-circulation newspapers entertained a wide popular audience with criminal stories, even as crime became the focus of scientific inquiry and the subject of articles that moved . . . out of professional journals into more popular formats and general social criticism. Medical and legal experts as well as professionalizing social scientists began to think of crime as a mirror held up to society, exposing the tendencies of the day writ large."[43] During the years 1906–8, the death penalty had been suspended for the first time in more than a hundred years, but the ban created such anxiety among the populace that it had to be reversed. Guillotinings, traditionally held in public, were so popular that even when officials held them at inconvenient times and without publicity, mobs of spectators still showed up.

The courtrooms were packed with spectators when the juicy trials of famous criminals were on the docket. People went to the morgue to look at corpses, sometimes to guess the identity of unknown victims. An underground railway carried groups of tourists through the city sewer system, which had been made famous by Victor Hugo in *Les misérables* and was in real life often used as a hiding place for criminals. Wealthy residents of Paris's fashionable Right Bank headed up the slope of Montmartre for a frisson, or thrill, as they rubbed shoulders with the dangerous criminal and lower classes. Cabaret singers sang of characters such as pimps, streetwalkers, and tramps. Sprinkled among the audience were real crooks, prostitutes, and pimps.

The French loved gossip and scandal, and Paris's numerous daily newspapers catered to their needs, though some tales were too hot even for the scandal sheets to repeat. Meg Japy, a twenty-one-year-old from the provinces, had married Adolphe Steinheil, an artist who was twenty years older. Steinheil was not an avant-garde artist like Picasso; each year he managed to have one of his canvases accepted for display in the Salon, the government-sponsored exhibition of art that had acquired a stamp of approval marking it as culturally stifling. Nor was Adolphe exciting in bed, but Meg, beautiful and vivacious, found it easy to attract other lovers. Her husband consoled himself by the fact that his wife's paramours were generally men of wealth and power, who graciously purchased some of his works, enabling the Steinheils to maintain a well-to-do lifestyle in Paris.

Meg eventually reached the pinnacle of her particular form of art: she became the mistress of Félix Faure, the president of France. At fifty-eight, Faure was twice her age, but as a connoisseur of feminine beauty, he remained a devotee of the *cinq à sept*—the traditional late afternoon tryst. And Meg, according to Maurice Paléologue, an official in the foreign office, "was expert at shaking men's loins."[44]

Late in the afternoon of February 16, 1899, Meg slipped through a side door of the Élysée Palace for a rendezvous with Faure in a room known as the Blue Salon. Sometime later, the president's male secretary heard cries that sounded more like signals of distress than of passion. He investigated to find Meg naked and Faure dead, with his fingers gripping her hair so tightly that she could not get free. Paris gossips later supplied the detail that she had been administering oral sex when the strain proved too much for Faure's heart. Servants were able to release Meg by cutting her hair and quickly spirited her away as a priest was brought in to belatedly administer the last rites.

Because Faure had been a determined anti-Dreyfusard, resolutely refusing all demands for a retrial of the imprisoned officer, his death was rumored to have been part of a conspiracy. By one account, he had been killed in a far more sinister and deliberate fashion; by another, his mistress had stolen some papers relating to the Dreyfus case from the president's office.

To those who knew the truth, none of this did anything to hurt Meg's reputation. She continued hosting her weekly salon at the four-story house on a cul-de-sac called the impasse Ronsin, where she and her husband lived. She might thus have continued for the rest of her life, taking occasional lovers and living off her reputation. But Meg was destined to burst into the headlines soon in her own right, as the defendant in a double murder trial that fully satisfied the public's appetite for scandal and intrigue.

A similar fate awaited the new bride of the man who was premier of France at the time the *Mona Lisa* was stolen. Henriette Rainouard Claretie had obtained a divorce from her first husband three years earlier, in 1908, after a fourteen-year marriage. After a decent interval, she expected to marry her lover, the rising politician Joseph Caillaux. Caillaux, however, found it difficult to obtain an amicable parting from the woman he was already married to (and who had also divorced a husband to marry him), and he did not press the issue until after he had attained the ultimate political prize, the post of premier of France, in June 1911. Four months later he made Henriette an honest woman—but unfortunately, not quite a respectable one.

It was unusual for French politicians to divorce and remarry. It was socially acceptable for them to take lovers, even long-term ones, but they were not supposed to elevate their mistresses' status to wife. Moreover, Caillaux's first wife, though agreeing to a divorce, had found and kept some incriminating letters that her husband and Henriette had exchanged during their illicit affair. When hints of these started to appear in a prominent newspaper, Henriette feared the correspondence itself would appear in print. She took drastic action and in so doing became the star of the era's most spectacular murder trial, in which politics played a major role and the murder victim was even accused of causing his own death.

ix

Parisians had a particular love-hate obsession with the apaches, or young gangsters, who made their headquarters in Belleville, on the Right Bank.[45] From that neighborhood, the apaches emerged to terrorize citizens on the central boulevards of the city. They specialized in violent tactics, using sudden kicks, sucker punches, and head butts as a prelude to robbing victims. (A crime reporter, Arthur Dupin of *Le Journal,* had coined the term *apache* in 1902 because the gangs' fierce tactics and violence resembled the French image of the Apache Indians in battle.) Soon the menace of *apachism* appeared to be the greatest threat to normal life in Paris.

A typical apache crime could start with a thug asking a potential victim for a light and tipping his hat. If the victim put his hand in his pocket, the apache would throw the hat in his face and head-butt him. Sometimes the attacker pulled the victim's jacket over his face to blind him. Some worked with a pretty female, a *gigolette,* serving as a foil. While she engaged the victim in conversation, the male would come up behind with a scarf and loop it around the victim's neck. Newspapers printed detailed accounts of the apaches' methods, increasing the public's fears of being accosted.

The apaches differed from ordinary street thugs by their lifestyle, which included distinctive clothing, argot, and even a dance. Similar to the tango and imitative of street fighting, the apache dance was sometimes dubbed the Dance of the Underworld. Because of its violent nature, in which the female partner is literally thrown around, it was popular as an exhibition dance. Upperclass Parisians enjoyed watching it performed in the cafés around Montparnasse and in dance halls called *musettes.* Adventurous tourists sometimes made a visit to a *musette* a part of their Paris experience. Bored upper-class women would pay an apache dance partner for a half hour's whirl around the floor — usually a toned-down version of the real thing.

Off the dance floor, entertainers sentimentalized the apaches' fatalism about life and love. Yvette Guilbert, the star of the Moulin Rouge, performed a popular song, "My Head," in which an apache defiantly contemplates his future, which must end on the guillotine in a perverse kind of triumph:

I'll have to wait, pale and dead beat,
For the supreme moment of the guillotine,

When one fine day they'll say to me:
It's going to be this morning, ready yourself;
I'll go out and the crowd will cheer
My head![46]

Parisians' appetite for entertainment that reflected their fascination with the underworld found its fullest satisfaction at the Théâtre du Grand-Guignol. Located at the end of Montmartre's rue Chaptal, the tiny theater presented a series of short, gruesome plays each night, alternating comedy and horror. The fare was not for the squeamish, for the creators of the Grand-Guignol brought incredible realism to grotesque special effects, regaling audiences with stabbings, ax murders, gouged-out eyes, torture, acid throwing, amputations, mutilation, and rape. Indeed, there was no outrage that the Grand-Guignol shrank from attempting to depict. Because of the theater's small size, the spectators were often sprayed with "blood" as well.

Oscar Méténier, a former secretary to the police commissioner of Paris, was the theater's founder and the author of some of its skits. Oscar knew what he was writing about because he often walked through the city's red-light areas and criminal dens searching for material. The other star was the playwright André de Lourde, called the Prince of Terror, whose works generally broke any boundaries of taste and decency. The son of a doctor, de Lourde had from an early age listened to the sounds of suffering from his father's patients. He had also developed a morbid fear of death, which his father tried unsuccessfully to cure by making him sit vigil over his dead grandmother's body the night before she was buried.

De Lourde used these childhood experiences to good effect by frightening others with his plays. His goal was to create something like a dream of Edgar Allan Poe, a man he admired, "to write a play so terrifying and unbearable that several minutes after the curtain rises, the entire audience would flee from the theatre en masse." De Lourde called his works "slices of death." [47]

The Grand-Guignol shared with the avant-garde artists a desire to break through barriers to express humankind's deepest fears and emotions. The size of the theater broke down the separation between the performers and the audience. All the tricks of the trade were used to heighten the horror for its own sake and induce a reaction from the audience—to shock people out of their conventional thinking. Success was measured by the number of audience members who fainted or threw up. The advertising for the show noted that there was always a doctor in attendance. Increasing the opportunity for stimulation, the bar at the theater served a special drink called Mariani wine, which contained, among other things, cocaine.

The theater's intention to shock the middle class, *épater les bourgeois,* made it popular with the intelligentsia, but it also attracted people from the working-class neighborhood in which it was located, slumming aristocrats, and tourists from all over the world. There were enough *guignolers,* regular customers, to guarantee that the performances were always sold out. They came not just expecting sex and violence, but also secure in the knowledge that the "good guys" would never win. Not all the sex was on the stage. Boxes in the back of the theater covered with latticework were trysting places, and janitors had to hose them out after performances. It was a place of taboo and transformation.

Agnes Peirron, an expert on this form of entertainment, has written, "What carried the Grand-Guignol to its highest level were the boundaries and thresholds it crossed: the states of consciousness altered by drugs or hypnosis. Loss of consciousness, loss of control, panic: themes with which the theater's audience could easily identify. When the Grand-Guignol playwrights expressed an interest in the guillotine, what fascinated them most were the last convulsions played out on the decapitated face. What if the head continued to think without the body? The passing from one state to another was the crux of the genre."[48]

In literature as well as in the theater, Parisians were fascinated with evil for its own sake. The French literary tradition is studded with celebrants of the dark side of humanity: François Villon, the Marquis de Sade, Arthur Rimbaud, Paul Verlaine, Charles Baudelaire. This preoccupation with evil also made itself felt in literature for mass consumption: in 1911 the most popular literary character in France was a criminal. Fantômas was the "hero" of a best-selling series of novels that sold as fast as their two authors could turn them out. Fantômas was no Robin Hood figure; he carried out ruthless crimes for his own pleasure, leaving the bodies of countless innocents behind. And in each book he outwitted the attempts of his nemesis, Inspector Juve of the Sûreté (France's equivalent of the FBI) to apprehend him. The criminal is always triumphant, and readers loved it. Adding to the appeal of the books were their full-color covers, which rivaled even the Grand-Guignol in their graphic detail. In the very first book in the series, the cover shows a masked man clad in evening dress and top hat towering over the landscape of Paris. A second glance reveals that the man is carrying a dagger in one hand and seems to be seeking a victim.

Apollinaire, Picasso's literary friend, author of experimental poetry and elegant pornography, embraced the Fantômas works as enthusiastically as if they had been high art. He called the first book an "extraordinary novel, full of life and imagination, lamely written but extremely vivid. . . . From the imaginative standpoint *Fantômas* is one of the richest works that exist."[49] Apollinaire founded a group of like-minded connoisseurs known as La Société des Amis de Fantômas; they included Max Jacob, the homosexual artist who at one time shared his apartment with Picasso. Other enthusiastic readers included Picasso himself, the writers Colette and Jean Cocteau, and the painter Blaise Cendrars, who called the series "the modern Aeneid." Apollinaire believed that though all social classes enjoyed the series, there were "only a few *bon esprits* who appreciated the series with the same good taste as himself."[50]

Fantômas's popularity may have been galling to the real-life members of the Sûreté. The truth was that in Paris, the forces of law were regarded with distrust. Since the time of Napoleon, one of the chief duties of the police had been to spy on the populace.

Through all of the changes in government that had taken place since then, the laws of the Napoleonic Code had not been repealed, and indeed a host of new criminal regulations had been passed. This left such a patchwork of a legal system that the police could find almost any reason to investigate or detain a person. Moreover, because the police files had been destroyed during the Commune, the authorities had rushed to build up new dossiers, compiling information on as many people as they could. Often the accusations in these hastily assembled files, gleaned from sources as diverse as professional informers or disgruntled neighbors, were utterly untrue.

Bertillon, despite his faults, was one of a number of people who were trying to bring a new spirit of scientific investigation to crime solving, a process that had been going on in France ever since the Sûreté had been founded nearly a century before. Joining him were social scientists and psychologists who investigated the roots and causes of crime, arguing whether people were innately criminal or not—and if not, what drove them to crime.

Bertillon's search for the *Mona Lisa* would bring him into the world of avant-garde artists in Montmartre, where Picasso was engaged in his own investigation of what was real and what was illusory. From the day he first arrived in Paris, the young artist knew the city, with its glitter and grit, its gaiety and gloom, was to be his inspiration. His canvases often portrayed people who existed in the demimonde between respectability and illegality, just as he experienced in the city around him. His most famous painting of this period shows five prostitutes whose expressions were as challenging in their way as the *Mona Lisa*'s famous smile. To create it, Picasso had to break the boundaries of his art, something only a genius could do. To solve the theft of the *Mona Lisa*, Bertillon would have to do that in his own field, and ultimately he would fail.

SEARCHING FOR A WOMAN

The disappearance of the *Mona Lisa* from the Louvre stunned Parisians, who had long dismissed any impossible task with the remark that doing so "would be like trying to steal the *Mona Lisa.*"[1] The theft was, however, a blessing for the city's newspapers and magazines, which had prospered during the Third Republic. As the government ended its censorship policies, the circulation of Paris's newspapers had nearly triple what it had been in 1880. Nothing sold papers as well as crime stories, and this one was unparalleled for its sensational qualities. For days, headline writers competed for the mot juste to describe the *Mona Lisa*'s theft, struggling for a word to adequately describe the shock: "INIMAGINABLE!" "INEXPLICABLE!" "INCROYABLE!" "EFFARANT!"[2] A newspaper printed a doctored photo of the Cathedral of Notre-Dame, with one tower missing. The caption read, "Couldn't this happen too?"[3] For Parisians, who loved both crime and art, it was an all-consuming event.

It was personal too. *Le Figaro*'s editor wrote, "Since it has disappeared, perhaps forever, one must speak of this familiar face, whose memory will pursue us, filling us with regret in the same way that we speak of a person who died in a stupid accident and for whom one must write an obituary."[4] Less seriously, the *Revue des Deux Mondes* wrote that the meaning of the famous smile was now clear: Mona Lisa had been thinking of the fuss her disappearance would create. Outside the Louvre, vendors sold postcards on this theme, with cartoon images of the woman in the painting "escaping" from the museum, often with a taunt at her "captors," the guards.

Someone who signed himself or herself as "Mona Lisa" expanded on this idea, writing a letter to *L'Autorité* that explained she had "divorced" the museum because she didn't like the way she was talked about: "They've bored me stiff with this 'famous smile!' . . . You do not know women or you do not know them well. If I smiled with an 'enigmatic' air it was certainly not for the ridiculous reasons attributed to me by the gentlemen of the literature. . . . This smile marked my lassitude, my scorn for all the skunks who paraded endlessly before me, and my infinite desire to carry out my abduction.

"I said to myself: what a face those officials will make when tomorrow the news will spread through all of Paris: *La Joconde*[5] has spent the night elsewhere!"[6]

i

Since there were few real developments in the case, reporters were free to print rumors and sheer speculation about who had perpetrated the crime. All that restrained them were the limits of their imaginations. Among the more creative guesses was that of the *Paris-Journal,* which reported that a professional clairvoyant, Mme. Albane de Siva, after "ascertaining at the Central Astronomical Office the position of the planets at the time of the theft," deduced that the picture was still hidden somewhere in the Louvre, and that the thief was "a young man with thick hair, a long neck and a hoarse voice, who had a passion for rejuvenating old things."[7]

Meanwhile, right-wing and monarchist publications alleged that the theft was only the latest manifestation of a crime wave that revealed "the extraordinary state of anarchy"[8] that characterized the government of the Third Republic, which, not by coincidence, was at that time led by Premier Joseph Caillaux, a member of the Radical-Socialist Party. The fact that Caillaux was currently negotiating with Germany over the two countries' rival claims in Morocco led to a darker accusation: that the Germans had taken the painting and were holding it hostage to secure favorable terms in the final settlement. On the other hand, there were also some who saw the theft as "a political plot to injure the prestige of the Republic and murmur that the [supporters of the monarchy] could say if they would, where the Joconde is."[9]

In the days immediately following the theft, anyone carrying a package received attention. Two German artists, suspicious apparently because they were German and possessed paints and brushes, were reported to the police and questioned. A man running for a train — the 7:47 express for Bordeaux — while carrying a package covered by a horse blanket, caused police to telephone the stationmaster at Bordeaux, asking him to search the train. When a shabbily dressed man approached an antiques dealer offering to sell a portrait of a "noblewoman," the dealer informed the police.

The investigation soon spread its net over a wider area. Checkpoints on roads leading out of the capital examined the contents of every wagon, automobile, and truck. Fearing that the thief must be trying to leave the country, customs inspectors opened and examined the baggage of everyone departing on ships or trains. Then, ships that had left during the day that had passed between the theft and its discovery were identified and searched when they reached overseas ports. In New York City, detectives swarmed aboard the German liner *Kaiser Wilhelm II* after it docked, and combed every stateroom and piece of luggage for the masterpiece.

Some thought the whole thing was a hoax, recalling that the satirical journal *Le Cri de Paris* had thrown the city into a panic the previous year by reporting that the *Mona Lisa* on view in the

Louvre was a copy, hung there to hide the fact that the original had been stolen. That had proved to be the editor's idea of a joke, but now people wondered if there had been some truth to the report, and whether this latest, actual disappearance would be covered up by the return of a "real" *Mona Lisa*. Not to be outdone, the editors of *Le Cri de Paris* now declared that the painting that had been stolen on August 21 was itself only a copy and that the genuine work was in the New York mansion of a millionaire identified as "J.K.W.W." [10]

"What audacious criminal, what mystifier, what maniac collector, what insane lover, has committed this abduction?" asked *L'Illustration*, which offered a reward of 40,000 francs[11] to anyone who would deliver the painting to its office, presumably so that it could gain the publicity of solving the case.[12] Soon the rival newspaper *Paris-Journal* offered 50,000 francs, and a bidding war was on, certain to attract dozens of people who wished only to collect the reward—or to attract attention to themselves. A waiter named Armand Gueneschan stepped forward, claiming to know where the painting was hidden. Supposedly it was in the hands of a rich nobleman who had financed the theft because he was obsessed with the image (not the last time this was suggested as a motive for the crime). Gueneschan offered to reveal the man's name for 200,000 francs. However, after the police questioned the waiter, they concluded that he was either a liar or deranged.

ii

Premier Caillaux, recognizing the importance of the theft to the nation, appointed a well-known jurist, Henri Drioux, as *juge d'instruction* (examining magistrate) to conduct an official inquiry. Louis Lépine, prefect of the Paris police, Octave Hamard, head of the Sûreté, and Alphonse Bertillon had already inspected the scene of the theft and turned up a few clues, finding the discarded case and frame in the stairwell. *Le Petit Parisien* sarcastically reported "Mona Lisa Stolen. . . . We still have the frame," [13] but on the glass of the protective case, Bertillon found a fingerprint. A few years earlier, he had been credited with being the first criminologist to solve a case by using fingerprint evidence, and some thought this latest discovery signaled the imminent arrest of the culprit. Unfortunately, Bertillon's files, comprising three-quarters of a million individual cards, were indexed under his own physical identification system and not according to fingerprint type. The only way to determine the owner of this incriminating fingerprint was to find the person who had left it there. Bertillon and his staff painstakingly began to collect the prints of every employee of the museum, 257 in all.

There was good reason to think that the theft was an inside job. That was certainly the personal view of France's undersecretary of state of beaux-arts, Étienne Dujardin-Beaumetz. He had just finished a months-long struggle with museum employees who wanted to unionize—a battle that the employees had lost. The undersecretary thought a malcontented employee had taken the picture as an act of "personal vengeance" and predicted that "one day they'll find the *Mona Lisa* hidden in some attic of the Louvre." [14]

Dujardin-Beaumetz was involved in another controversy that would for a time promise to throw light on the theft. The Department of Beaux-Arts had announced earlier in 1911 that it would allow a road to be built through the Saint-Cloud Park on the western outskirts of Paris, a move that people who lived around the park charged would destroy the natural beauty of the area. Protesters had demonstrated against the roadway throughout the summer of 1911. After the theft of the *Mona Lisa*, a handwritten note fell into the hands of the police. It declared that the painting was being held hostage to protect the park. It read, in part, "The *Mona Lisa* is well hidden in the house of the head stableman at the Parc de Saint-Cloud, where she was placed the very evening of her removal by the head gardener, who got it from one of the attendants of the museum. No use in looking elsewhere; she will be given back only if the park is left in its current state." [15]

The police searched the stableman's house, as well as other locations in the park. They even explored the possibility that the spokesperson for a preservationist group had written the phony ransom note to give publicity to the efforts to preserve the park. If so, he succeeded, for an investigation revealed that Dujardin-Beaumetz had lied about the amount of damage the road would cause to the trees in the park. Months later, the pressure became too much for Dujardin-Beaumetz to endure, and he resigned his post.

Besides losing a masterpiece, the Louvre itself had suffered a great loss of pride. *Paris-Journal* ran the text of a sign that its editors suggested should be posted in the museum:

**In the Interest of Art
And for the Safeguarding of the Precious Objects
THE PUBLIC
Is Requested to be Good Enough to
WAKE THE GUARDS
If they are found to be asleep.**[16]

The day after the theft was announced, an article by Guillaume Apollinaire appeared in the evening newspaper *L'Intransigeant*. The poet and critic, after assessing the painting's importance as art, criticized the museum's security:

> There is not even one guard per gallery; the small pictures in the Dutch rooms running along the Rubens gallery are literally abandoned to thieves.
> The pictures, even the smallest, are not padlocked to the wall, as they are in most museums abroad. Furthermore, it is a fact that the guards have never been drilled in how to rescue pictures in case of a fire.

> The situation is one of carelessness, negligence, indifference.
>
> The Louvre is less well protected than a Spanish museum.[17]

That last statement was a low blow indeed, although it would soon become clear to the authorities that Apollinaire knew far more about the Louvre's security arrangements than he let on.

There were numerous false trails and hoaxes in connection with the case. A fourteen-year-old prostitute, Germaine Terclavers, already in custody, startled the police by claiming that her pimp and his gang had stolen the painting and that it was stored in Belleville, the apaches' home base. She claimed that she had seen the painting herself and that the gang planned to ship it to the United States on an ocean liner.

Germaine had recently been arrested and sentenced by a judge to four years in a reform school, and she hoped to get a pardon by revealing what she knew. The police were able to find her nineteen-year-old boyfriend and pimp, named Georges. They placed him under arrest for carrying an illegal weapon—an all-purpose charge that the police routinely used to take into custody almost anyone they suspected of larger crimes. Georges turned out to be a feared gang leader, but whether he was skillful enough to carry off the *Mona Lisa*'s theft remained in doubt.

When questioned, Germaine provided more details, naming other gang members who she said had planned the crime for weeks. She had overheard them talking about a *gardien* (museum attendant), the Louvre, and *La Joconde*. According to her, she was even asked to serve as a lookout but turned the offer down. As she expanded her story, the police became more interested. She claimed that Georges had not come home the night before the Monday morning of the heist; when he returned late on Monday, he refused to say where he had been. Later, he bragged that he and his gang had committed a crime that had turned the city upside down.

"I remember," Germaine said of her boyfriend, "that each day he read *Le Journal,* anxiously following developments in the investigation and constantly telling me that the gang 'were going to get pinched.'"[18] Her denunciations were never corroborated, and the police could not tell whether Georges was simply trying to impress her or if there was some truth in the tale. In any event, Georges enlisted in the army to escape the charge of illegal gun possession, and Germaine was sent off to reform school, never again to receive as much attention as she had gained from her accusation.

Significantly, Germaine knew what buttons to push to gain credibility, for the theory that a rich American was the mastermind behind the theft was widespread. Countless letters poured into the Sûreté suggesting this scenario—often naming candidates for the "mastermind" behind the job. Since the earliest days of the Third Republic, Parisians had resented the increasing American population (sometimes called an invasion) in their city. Moneyed expatriates settled mainly in the eighth and ninth arrondissements, which became known as *la colonie américaine.* One 1905 visitor noticed that advertisements for American goods "hung everywhere."[19] Rumors spread that Americans were rapidly buying up buildings around the place de l'Opéra. Only half-jokingly, the story made the rounds that an American millionaire had offered to buy the Arc de Triomphe.

Responding to a tip, Prefect of Police Lépine authorized a plan to have a French police officer pose as an American millionaire to negotiate the purchase of the *Mona Lisa* from a ring of art thieves who claimed it was in their possession. The supposed thieves turned out to be poseurs who wanted the money but had no painting. Yet speculation about American involvement continued. The favorite candidate for the rich American mastermind was J. Pierpont Morgan, known for his avid, if not avaricious, collecting habits, which frequently took him through Europe on buying sprees. When Morgan arrived the following spring in the spa town of Aix-les-Bains for his annual visit and the *Mona Lisa* had still not been found, Paris newspapers reported that two mysterious men had come to offer to sell him the *Mona Lisa*. Morgan indignantly denied the account, and when a French reporter came to interview him, the American wore in his buttonhole the rosette that marked him as a commander of the Legion of Honor—France's highest decoration. He had recently been awarded it, causing some French newspapers to speculate that he had earned the decoration by offering "a million dollars and no questions asked" for the return of the *Mona Lisa* to the Louvre.[20]

Morgan's offer proved to be only rumor, and public sentiment turned against him, even in Italy. When Morgan and his sister prepared to leave Florence in April 1912, word spread that a painting was among the things they were taking with them. Hundreds of angry Florentines gathered at the railway station to block their departure. The financier had in fact purchased a painting while in Florence, but it was not the *Mona Lisa*. Even so, the crowd at the station had assumed that the stolen masterpiece had somehow returned to the place where Leonardo had begun to paint it (a suspicion that later proved prescient). Morgan had to strike about him with his heavy cane to fend off the mob and make a passage to board the train.

Though the best-known American collector, Morgan was far from the only one, and art-loving Europeans feared that American money would take many of their treasures overseas. (The fact that many of the works in European museums had been plundered from other countries in the first place was irrelevant.) Accusations of American involvement in the theft were so prevalent that the American railroad magnate H. R. Huntington felt compelled to issue a denial: "I have not seen the picture and have not been tempted," he told a reporter for the *Los Angeles Times*. "Besides, I don't believe that I would care to be in the position of dealing for stolen goods. I don't for the life of me see how they got away with it, assuming, of course, that it was really stolen."[21]

Was it really stolen? As time went by without a ransom demand, that question increasingly circulated through Paris. Suspicion began to fall on the photographers who were licensed to work in the museum. According to the magazine *Gil Blas,* those photographers had carte blanche to remove "any picture desired every Monday without any special authorization, and to remove it to the roof [where the sunlight was suitable for photographs] or any other suitable position for work." [22] According to this theory, a photographer had accidentally damaged the painting, and to cover up the careless way it had been handled, the museum had blamed its disappearance on thieves. Supposedly, a team of restorers was working to repair the painting, and when they finished, its "recovery" would be announced.

iii

After two weeks of investigation, the Louvre was once again opened to the public, and an even greater number of visitors than usual came to gape at the four hooks on the wall that marked the place where *La Joconde* used to hang. The crowds "didn't look at the other pictures," one reporter noted. "They contemplated at length the dusty space where the divine *Mona Lisa* had smiled. . . . And feverishly they took notes. It was even more interesting for them than if La Joconde had been in its place." [23] A tourist, the aspiring writer Franz Kafka, visiting the Louvre on a trip to Paris in late 1911, noted in his diary the "crowd in the Salon Carré, the excitement and the knots of people, as if the Mona Lisa had just been stolen." [24] People began to place bouquets of flowers on the floor at the spot where the painting had once hung.

Leonardo's masterpiece had been famous before among well-educated people, but the publicity surrounding its disappearance made it a subject of popular culture. Songwriters in the cabarets of Montmartre always made use of current topics, and the theft of a painting of a beautiful woman was a godsend. One song, "L'as-tu vue? la Joconde!!" ("Have you seen her? the Gioconda!!") had a stanza making fun of the guards ("It couldn't be stolen, we guard her all the time, except on Mondays") and had La Joconde herself complaining that she left because she didn't want to be constantly stared at.[25] Another cabaret revue was said to have featured a line of topless Joconde girls. The respected journal *La Comoedia Illustré* photographed twelve well-known actresses in the clothing and pose of Mona Lisa and published them under the heading *Les sourires qui nous restent!* ("The smiles that we still have").[26] One cabaret used a reproduction of *La Joconde* on a poster, with the caption, "I smiled at the Louvre. Now I am merry at the Moulin de la Chanson."[27] The Zig-Zag cigarette paper company proclaimed that Mona Lisa had left the Louvre because she was anxious to have a smoke. High Life Tailor ran an ad claiming that the undersecretary of state of beaux-arts, hoping to avoid public execution for his failure of duty, had implored the tailor company to send over a photograph of their suits to hang in the Salon Carré in place of the lost painting. Even a corset maker portrayed its newest garment on a figure of the Mona Lisa, who at last was revealed to have perfect hips.

Inevitably the French movie industry also began to capitalize on the furor over the theft. The Pathé company, which had filmed a series of adventures about the detective Nick Winter (a knockoff of the popular American fictional detective Nick Carter), released *Nick Winter et le vol de la Joconde* (*Nick Winter and the Theft of the Mona Lisa*) in the fall of 1911. Franz Kafka and his friend Max Brod were among those who went to see it at the grand Omnia Pathé theater. Brod summarized the plot of the five-minute film, which turned the event into slapstick:

> The picture opened with the presentation of M. Crou-
> molle (everyone knows that it means "Homolle"[28]
> and no one protests against the perfidious way they
> are going after the gray-haired Delphi scholar). Crou-
> molle is lying in bed, his stocking cap pulled down
> over his ears, and is startled out of sleep by a telegram:

"*Mona Lisa* Stolen." Croumolle—the Delphi scholar if you please, but I am not protesting, I was laughing so hard—dresses himself with clownlike agility, now he puts both feet into one leg of his pants; now one foot into two socks. In the end, he runs into the street with his suspenders trailing. . . . The [next part of] the story is set in the hall of the Louvre, everything excellently imitated, the paintings and, in the middle, the three nails[29] on which the *Mona Lisa* hung. Horror; summoning of a comical detective; a shoe button of Croumolle's as red herring; the detective as shoeshine boy; chase through the cafés of Paris; passers-by forced to have their shoes shined; arrest of the unfortunate Croumolle, for the button that was found at the scene of the crime naturally matches his shoe buttons. And now the final gag—while everyone is running through the hall at the Louvre and acting sensational, the thief sneaks in, the *Mona Lisa* under his arm, hangs her back where she belongs, and takes Velázquez's *Princess* instead. No one notices him. Suddenly someone sees the *Mona Lisa;* general astonishment, and a note in one corner of the rediscovered painting that says, "Pardon me, I am nearsighted. I actually wanted to have the painting next to it."[30]

iv

What everyone wanted to know—and speculated on endlessly—was where the thief could have gone with what was probably the most recognizable artwork in the world. Other than the fingerprint, the only clue was the doorknob, now recovered by the police from the gutter outside the museum. The plumber who had opened the stairway door for the man who dropped it there was set to work looking at hundreds of photographs of museum employees, past and present. Every sighting of the painting or rumor about its whereabouts had to be checked out—and they came in from places as distant as Italy, Germany, Britain, Poland, Russia, the United States, Argentina, Brazil, Peru, and Japan.[31]

As time went on without a solution to the case, many concluded that a gang of professional thieves had been at work. The only previous art theft comparable to this one had been the abduction of Gainsborough's *Duchess of Devonshire* from a London gallery in 1876. The man who carried out that heist was Adam Worth, a German-born American whose international career as a thief earned him the nickname the Napoleon of Crime. Said to have been the inspiration for Professor Moriarty, the archcriminal of the Sherlock Holmes stories, Worth had stolen the Gainsborough from a London gallery and had tried to obtain a ransom for its return. When that plan fell through, he took the work back to the United States, where it hung in Worth's Chicago house for the next quarter century. Some have suggested that Worth valued it as a trophy, even an object of desire, too much to accept any ransom for it. The Gainsborough did not surface until 1901, after further negotiations with the original owner through a friend of Worth's, a Chicago gambler named Pat Sheedy, who announced a year later that Worth had died and was buried under an alias in a London cemetery.

Despite Sheedy's claim, a popular historical novelist named Maurice Strauss published an article in one of France's largest newspapers, *Le Figaro,* declaring that Worth was still alive and had duplicated his most famous crime by stealing the *Mona Lisa.* Strauss, who claimed to have seen Worth in 1901, reported that on reading the description provided by the museum plumber of the *Mona Lisa*'s thief ("a man of fifty years, handsome in feature, figure, and carriage, height a little above the average, the eyes keen and cold"), he was certain it must be Worth. "There is only one man in the world who would have acted with such tranquil audacity and so much dexterity," Strauss wrote.[32] The public (and numerous journalists) embraced the idea; many believed that for such a great crime to seem plausible, an equally great criminal must have perpetrated it.

Worth was quoted as once having said, "All that I ever require is two minutes of opportunity. If I do not find those two minutes, I give up the job. Usually I find them, and 120 seconds, methodically employed, is enough for a man well-trained in his specialty to accomplish a great deal."[33] That was just the way most Parisians imagined the daring robbery had been carried out. Indeed, the criminologist Bertillon, well known for approaching every case from a scientific viewpoint, had placed a replica of the *Mona Lisa* on the wall of the Salon Carré and checked how long it would take to remove it from the wall and carry it away. Two men not accustomed to such work took more than five minutes to do it. However, a museum employee who knew how the hooks were placed was able to do it by himself in only six seconds, well within Worth's window of opportunity.[34]

Strauss himself was unusually specific about just how Worth had pulled off the heist: "It is he himself who carried off the 'Joconde,' and he did not have an accomplice. That is not his way. Nor did he take a train at the Quai d'Orsay terminus [closest stop to the Louvre]. After crossing the bridge, he turned to the left, with the picture under his arm, wrapped up in a piece of rep, traversed the Quai des Orfèvres, in front of the Prefecture of Police, and arrived at a friend's house in the Marais where he removed his workman's disguise. He hid his booty, the painted wooden panel, in the double bottom of his steamer trunk. Then, correctly clad as a gentleman traveler, he drove quickly in a taxicab to the Gare du Nord and got to London by way of Calais and Dover before Paris had sent its warnings to the English police."[35] Despite Strauss's seeming confidence, police investigations failed to turn up any trace of the legendary criminal Worth.

Contributing to the view that professional thieves must have been behind the disappearance of the *Mona Lisa* was a book, *Manuel de Police Scientifique*, published in 1911 by Rodolphe Reiss, a professor at the University of Lausanne. Reiss had for a time served as an assistant to Bertillon at the identification service of the Prefecture of Police, and his book was graced with an introduction by the prefecture's current head, Lépine, so journalists pored through it for indications as to what kind of man the police were searching for. Assuming the role of a criminal profiler, Reiss wrote:

> There are two classes [of *pègres*, or thieves], between which there is a profound distinction in their bearing, their manner of life, their habits, and the kinds of crime in which they engage. The upper *pègre* reserves itself for the audacious, difficult, profitable thefts or frauds, and leaves the brutal and bloody crimes to the lower *pègre*. It is notable, in fact, that the great robbers never kill; it is rarely, indeed, that they go armed. They work most carefully, with even a refinement of art . . . and they never indulge in those savage and useless acts — the breaking of furniture or the slashing of pictures, for example — whereby the lower *pègre* satisfies its barbarous love of destruction. Thus the nature of the crime, the aspect of the scene, afford to the police an immediate clue to the class of malefactor. Even cunning imitation . . . is not long successful. The touch is not the same. The robber cannot divest himself of his particular habit of doing things, which has fixed itself upon him more and more firmly during his long years of malfeasance.[36]

That clearly pointed to someone of the same "class" as Worth.

V

The theft continued to inspire newspaper stories for weeks; any report on the case, no matter how trivial, found its way into print, reflecting the fact that this was more than an ordinary crime. Among the newspapers' favorite topics was, What accounted for the fascination that this particular painting holds over people?

The Renaissance artist Giorgio Vasari (1511–74), who became better known for his biographical accounts of other artists, was the first to report that the portrait depicted Mona Lisa,[37] the young wife of Francesco del Giocondo, a citizen of Florence. According to Vasari, Leonardo worked on the painting for four years (today's researchers date the period to 1503–6), but it remained unfinished, like so much of Leonardo's other work. Leonardo took it with him when he traveled to France around 1517 at the invitation of King François I, an art lover and admirer. Leonardo died there two years later (a sentimental tradition has the king holding Leonardo in his arms at the artist's death), and the painting, along with Leonardo's other possessions, was left to Francesco Melzi, his friend and pupil. By the time Vasari wrote his book, around 1547, the painting had entered the collection of the French monarchy. (According to tradition, François I bought it from Melzi for four thousand gold florins. If the story is true, that was a considerable sum, for the king paid Leonardo about one-tenth that amount as an annual retainer.)

Vasari's description of the painting is secondhand, and there are some discrepancies between it and the portrait as it exists— leading some to question whether he was in fact describing the painting known as *Mona Lisa*. In any case, Vasari's description shows that the painting had already acquired the nearly legendary reputation it has had ever since.

> Anyone wishing to see the degree to which art can imitate nature can easily understand this from the head, for here Leonardo reproduced all the details that can be painted with subtlety. The eyes have the lustre and moisture always seen in living people, while around them are the lashes and all the reddish tones which cannot be produced without the greatest care. The eye-

brows[38] could not be more natural, for they represent the way the hair grows in the skin — thicker in some places and thinner in others, following the pores of the skin. The nose seems lifelike with its beautiful pink and tender nostrils. The mouth, with its opening joining the red of the lips to the flesh of the face, seemed to be real flesh rather than paint. Anyone who looked very attentively at the hollow of her throat would see her pulse beating: to tell the truth, it can be said that portrait was painted in a way that would cause every brave artist to tremble and fear, whoever he might be.[39]

The aura of mystery that gives the painting so much of its appeal arose from Leonardo's technical innovations. The varnish Leonardo made for the final protective coat has darkened severely over the centuries, dulling the once-bright colors of the original. Though most of his contemporaries still used tempera (in which egg yolk is a binder agent), Leonardo adopted the oil-based paint developed in northern Europe. Oil colors were more luminous and allowed for greater precision in the final work. They also required patience, for each coat had to dry before another could be laid down. Modern X-rays of the *Mona Lisa* show that Leonardo applied many coats of paint, using a brush so fine that the individual strokes are virtually invisible. Finally, Leonardo employed a technique called sfumato (meaning smoky), in which the transitions of light and shade are blended subtly, as Leonardo wrote, "without lines or borders, in the manner of smoke."[40] Sfumato gave depth to the landscape in the background of the portrait, and a lifelike expression to the face of the sitter. Anyone observing the painting closely will see that the corners of the eyes and mouth are blurred, giving them a lifelike softness.

There are numerous copies of the *Mona Lisa* in existence, some modern but others dating to the time when the original was painted. Some critics argue that Leonardo actually painted more than one version. (If so, perhaps he fulfilled his agreement with

Francesco del Giocondo and completed a portrait of his wife, but was so taken by his subject that he painted another that he continued to work on for years.) A *Gioconda* at the Hermitage in Saint Petersburg has an exposed breast and is thought to have been painted by Leonardo's pupil and heir, Francesco Melzi. It was not uncommon for pupils to imitate their masters' work in this way, nor would it have been unusual for one or more copies to be made, since there was no other way to increase the audience for a work of art. Donald Sassoon, a modern historian, has written, "We know that Leonardo was widely admired during his lifetime because of the number of copies made of his works. In an age when information about a painting could travel only through written comments and the production of copies, the activities of Leonardo's followers . . . functioned as an information system which contributed to the expansion of his fame."[41]

Vasari was also the first to note what has become the most commented-on feature of the painting: the smile. "Since Mona Lisa was very beautiful," he wrote, "Leonardo employed this technique while he was painting her portrait—he had musicians who played or sang and clowns who would always make her merry in order to drive away her melancholy, which painting often brings to portraits. And in this portrait by Leonardo, there is a smile so pleasing that it seems more divine than human, and it was considered a wondrous thing that it was as lively as the smile of the living original."[42]

Vasari never saw the actual painting. One contemporary who did was Antonio de Beatis, the secretary of an influential cardinal, who kept a journal of the cardinal's trip to France in August 1517. They visited François I in his castle at Rouen, where Leonardo lived in an adjoining residence connected by a tunnel. De Beatis wrote that Leonardo showed his visitors three paintings, one the portrait of a "Florentine lady." He describes them as "tucti perfectissimi" ("all of the greatest perfection").[43]

A century later, when the painting was at Fontainebleau, the royal château that François I had renovated and expanded, Cassiano del Pozzo, an Italian scholar, came to view it. He wrote of it afterward as "the best-known work of this painter, because she lacks only the power of speech."[44] More importantly, he called the painting *La Gioconda*, confirming the sitter's identity as Lisa Gherardini, who at the age of sixteen, in 1495, had married Francesco del Giocondo of Florence. The identification has been challenged over the years, but most authorities agree that the portrait is of this particular woman, who would have been in her midtwenties when she sat for Leonardo.

During the reign of Louis XIV (1643–1715), the painting occupied a place of honor in the king's personal gallery at the grand residence he built at Versailles. His successor, Louis XV (reigned 1715–74), however, preferred the more erotic, openly joyful works of such artists as Fragonard and Boucher and sent Leonardo's work to hang ignominiously in the office of the keeper of the royal buildings. In 1750, the king's courtiers selected the 110 best works of art in his collection for an exhibition. *La Joconde* was not included.

After the Revolution, the former royal palace known as the Louvre became a gallery open to all citizens, who could view the treasures formerly owned by kings and nobility. In 1797 the *Mona Lisa* was chosen to be one of the works displayed there. Ironically, Fragonard, once the court favorite, was now a lowly employee of the new regime's artistic policy makers and was assigned to transport the *Mona Lisa* from Versailles to the Louvre. It didn't remain there long, for when Napoleon Bonaparte took power, he ordered the painting to be hung in his bedroom. Later, after the Louvre was renamed the Musée Napoléon, he allowed the painting to be returned to public display. He was the last to enjoy such a personal relationship with the portrait until someone carried her off in August 1911.

vi

Tastes in art ebb and flow, and in the early part of the nineteenth century the *Mona Lisa* was not regarded with the same awe it enjoys today. Nor was Leonardo himself universally esteemed. William Hazlitt, an English critic, wrote in 1817 that Leonardo "vitiated his paintings with too much science."[45] At midcentury, a committee of experts was asked to give a monetary value to the Louvre's works. The *Mona Lisa* was valued highly, at 90,000 francs, but well below works by other masters. Two of Raphael's paintings, for example, were given price tags of 400,000 and 600,000 francs.[46]

The audience for fine art had previously been restricted exclusively to those who were able to travel to museums to view the works on display, and to the even fewer people who could afford to buy such works. But after about 1840, technological developments, such as photography and new printing techniques, made it possible to mass-produce reproductions of fine art. Critics who had previously confined themselves merely to describing and evaluating works of art expanded their role. For now that anyone could view fine art for themselves, critics needed to justify their superior position by taking on the role of popular interpreter.

Nevertheless, literary artists popularized *Mona Lisa* before the art critics did. The Irish poet Thomas Moore wrote of "Mona Lisa, on whose eyes / A painter for whole years might gaze."[47] The Goncourt brothers, Edmond and Jules, popular French novelists of the mid-nineteenth century, described a hero's mistress: "All women are enigmas, but she is the most mysterious of them all . . . and wears, like an enchanted mask, the smile full of night of the Gioconda."[48]

Théophile Gautier (1811–72), a prolific French author of novels, poems, travel books, and criticism, waxed ecstatic over the portrait of Mona Lisa. In a review of an 1855 play titled *La Joconde* (though the subject matter did not concern the real-life Mona Lisa), he began "*La Joconde!* This name makes me think immediately of this sphinx of beauty who smiles so mysteriously in Leonardo da Vinci's painting, and who seems to pose a yet unresolved riddle to the admiring centuries."[49] A dozen years later, writing a guide to the Louvre, he recalled those words and added, "I have seen her frequently, since then, this adorable Joconde. She is always there smiling with sensuality, mocking her numerous lovers. She has the serene countenance of a woman sure that she will remain beautiful for ever and certain to be greater than the ideal of poets and artists."[50]

Shortly afterward, in an essay published in November 1869, a thirty-year-old English critic, Walter Pater, offered his own paean to the *Mona Lisa*. "*La Gioconda* is, in the truest sense, Leonardo's masterpiece," Pater wrote. Expanding on Gautier's observations, he noted "the unfathomable smile, always with a touch of something sinister in it, which plays over all Leonardo's work. . . . From childhood we see this image defining itself on the fabric of his dreams; and but for express historical testimony, we might fancy that this was but his ideal lady embodied and beheld at last."[51] It was a thought later taken up by a certain Viennese physician.

vii

Only a year before the *Mona Lisa* was stolen, Sigmund Freud, one of the founders of the new science of psychology, wrote a small book titled *Leonardo da Vinci and a Memory of His Childhood*. In his notebooks, Leonardo had described a recurrent dream that he had, and dreams were to Freud significant indicators of the psyche. Like the scientists who were finding a new physical world — atoms, X-rays, quanta — previously hidden from view, so Freud sought to uncover secrets of the mind below the level of consciousness.

Leonardo had been born in Vinci, a small town near Florence, in 1452, the illegitimate son of a woman named Caterina; his father was Piero da Vinci, a notary who worked for the Signoria of Florence. Though Piero married another woman in the year of Leonardo's birth, he acknowledged the boy as his son and later brought him into his household. Leonardo's earliest years, however, were spent with Caterina.

Freud, like Pater, found the enigmatic smile not only in the *Mona Lisa* but in other paintings by Leonardo, notably *St. John the Baptist* and *Virgin and Child with St. Anne*. The smile, Freud wrote, "has produced the most powerful and confusing effect on whoever looks at it." [52] He felt that it held special meaning for the artist, because he used it several times, and surmised that when he first encountered it on the face of Lisa, the model for *Mona Lisa*, "it awoke something in him which had for long lain dormant in his mind—probably an old memory." It was, Freud concluded, "the smile of bliss and rapture which had once played on his mother's lips as she fondled him." [53] The recurring dream Leonardo described was of the tail of a bird striking his mouth over and over. That image, Freud suggested, may well have been caused by the memory of his mother kissing him.

Freud thought that Leonardo was a homosexual, though the only proof for this is that the artist never married and was once accused in court of practicing sodomy, a charge he was cleared of. Couching his argument in genteel terms, Freud said that at the time Leonardo encountered his mother's smile on the face of the real-life Mona Lisa, he

> had for long been under the dominance of an inhibition which forbade him ever again to desire such caresses from the lips of women. But he had become a painter, and therefore he strove to reproduce the smile with his brush, giving it to all his pictures. . . . The figures [in the pictures, including Leda, John the Baptist, and Bacchus, as well as Mona Lisa] . . . gaze in mysterious triumph, as if they knew of a great achievement of happiness, about which silence must be kept. The familiar smile of fascination leads one to guess that it is a secret of love. It is possible that in these figures Leonardo has denied the unhappiness of his erotic life[54] and has tri-

umphed over it in his art, by representing the wishes of the boy, infatuated with his mother, as fulfilled in this blissful union of the male and female natures.[55]

Perhaps following Freud's lead, others began to speculate that love must hold the secret behind the theft. Just as Napoleon had hung the painting in his bedroom, so perhaps now someone had felt such desire for the portrait that he had stolen it. Indeed, Leonardo himself had told the story of such a man, who conceived a carnal love for one of the artist's other works: "Such is the power of a painting over a man's mind that he may be enchanted and enraptured by a painting that does not represent any living woman," Leonardo wrote. "It previously happened to me that I made a picture representing a holy subject, which was bought by someone who loved it and who wished to remove the attributes of divinity in order that he might kiss it without guilt. But finally his conscience overcame his sighs and lust, and he was forced to banish it from his house."[56]

Contributing to the speculation along these lines was the fact that shortly before the theft, the Louvre had received a postcard addressed to the *Mona Lisa*. It was a "red-hot love declaration, peppered with 'I love you's' and 'I adore you's.' "[57] It raised the possibility that the theft had been the work of an erotomaniac, someone obsessed enough with the subject of the painting that he might steal it. The employees of the Louvre now recalled that a young man, blond with blue eyes, would come almost every day to stand enraptured in front of the *Mona Lisa* as if he could not drag himself away. Clearly, this person should be high on the list of suspects. But no one knew his name.

The editor of *Le Temps* found this idea appealing enough to ask Dr. Georges Dumas, professor of experimental psychology at the Sorbonne, to write about the psychology of the thief. Dumas eagerly responded to the suggestion. "As to the mentality of such a thief," he wrote, "one will find it described in medical works, where such lunatics are called fetishists, who tremble in the presence of beauty and become obsessed by it, often showing much ingenuity and energy in obtaining symbols of such beauty. Such a person would have carried *Mona Lisa* to his rooms trembling with joy, gloating over the possession like a miser, perhaps in frenzy injuring the picture. When at last his insane passion spends its force he may return the picture to the Louvre."[58] However, Dumas added ominously, there was the possibility that the thief would take pleasure in "mutilating, stabbing, and defiling" it.

Dumas, like Professor Reiss, was assuming the role of a criminal profiler, even though such an occupation did not exist at that time. He was making an educated guess, based on the new science of psychology. Fiction writers, who had employed psychology for a much longer time than psychologists, adopted his theory and elaborated on it.

"Le harem des images," a 1913 short story by the writer Jules Bois, has as its central character John Lewis. Like J. P. Morgan, Lewis is an American millionaire, but one who, unlike Morgan, steals his art treasures instead of purchasing them. (Perhaps, to French readers, stealing them was morally no different from buying them, as long as they ended up in the hands of uncivilized Americans.) In the story, Lewis has created a private museum in his Paris apartment, where he displays for his own enjoyment artistic treasures that he has stolen from European collections. The narrator of the tale lets the reader know that Lewis's motivation is that he suffers from a sexual compulsion when he is confronted by artistic renditions of female beauty. He has, in other words, created a "harem" of painted and sculpted women who are his sexual captives. Mona Lisa is only his latest, and greatest, possession. Eventually, when he tires of his captives, he returns them.

"Within a few years," the narrator of "Le harem des images" tells the reader, "Leonardo's marvel will be returned to the Louvre. Until then, may every Sherlock Holmes exhaust his imagination!"[59]

Sherlock Holmes, of course, was a fictional detective, but his combination of intuitive brilliance and scientific precision was indeed what was required, for the search for a solution to the *Mona Lisa*'s theft would involve science as much as art. To probe its secrets, the painting had earlier been photographed with magnifying lenses and even X-rayed, revealing that Leonardo had rearranged the position of the hands before settling on the final version. The pattern of *craquelure*—cracks that had appeared on the surface of the paint over time—had also been photographed. Since this pattern was impossible to duplicate, it was thought to be a guarantee against any copy's being used to replace the original.

But of course the theft raised issues that were uncanny and immeasurable. It was Pater who came closest to expressing the strange atmosphere that emanates from the figure in the painting:

> She is older than the rocks among which she sits;
> like the vampire, she has been dead many times, and
> learned the secrets of the grave; and has been a diver
> in deep seas, and keeps their fallen day about her; and
> trafficked for strange webs with Eastern merchants;
> and, as Leda, was the mother of Helen of Troy, and, as
> Saint Anne, the mother of Mary; and all this has been
> to her but as the sound of lyres and flutes, and lives only
> in the delicacy with which it has moulded the changing
> lineaments, and tinged the eyelids and the hands. The
> fancy of a perpetual life, sweeping together ten thou-
> sand experiences, is an old one. . . . Certainly Lady
> Lisa might stand as the embodiment of the old fancy,
> the symbol of the modern idea.[60]

Pater's essay made him famous and made the *Mona Lisa* seem more than merely a painting—it was a nearly living thing, eternal and bewitching, and now it was gone.

SYMPATHY FOR THE DEVIL

The headline of the newspaper *Paris-Journal* for Wednesday, August 23, 1911 (the day after the theft of the *Mona Lisa* was discovered), read

IS ARSÈNE LUPIN ALIVE?
MONA LISA GONE FROM THE LOUVRE![1]

Arsène Lupin was well known to the *Paris-Journal*'s readers, for he was as famous a fictional character in France as Sherlock Holmes was in England. Lupin, however, was a master thief. In Paris, where many people's sympathies were with the criminal, not with the police, imaginary heroes were often those on the wrong side of the law.

i

Crime in France had a long literary tradition, both in fiction and in fact—beginning with Vidocq, the real-life Frenchman who was the inspiration for countless crime stories (beginning with those written by the American Edgar Allan Poe). Vidocq had been a legendary criminal before he became a policeman—and some thought he continued to cross the line throughout his career.

He liked to suddenly reveal himself to people who had not seen through his current disguise, announcing, "I am Vidocq, and I arrest you."[2] Even today, his towering figure (contemporaries claimed he could appear tall or short, as suited his purposes) stands at the beginning of the history of modern criminology as well as the beginning of the detective story.

Much of what is known about Vidocq comes from his *Memoirs*, which were written with the assistance of Honoré de Balzac, one of France's great novelists, and even the *Memoirs* are apparently as much a product of imagination as of memory. Fact or fiction? Vidocq blurred the line.

François-Eugène Vidocq begins the story of his life in typically dramatic fashion:

> I was born at Arras, but as my constant disguise, the mobility of my features, and a singular aptness in make-up have caused some doubt about my age, it will not be superfluous to state that I came into the world on the twenty-third of July, 1775, in a house near where Robespierre had been born sixteen years earlier. It was during the night; rain poured down in torrents; thunder rumbled; as a result a relative, who combined the functions of midwife and sibyl, drew the conclusion that my career would be a stormy one. In those days there were still good people who believed in omens, while in these enlightened times men rely on the infallibility of fortune-tellers.[3]

Even as a young man, Vidocq stood out from the crowd. Very large and strong, he was the terror of his neighborhood and was continually in fights. "My father's house was on the Place d'Armes, the customary meeting-place for all the blackguards of the quarter, and here I early exercised my muscles in thrashing regularly my comrades. . . . All they heard at home were stories of injured ears, black eyes, and torn clothes. By the time I was eight I was the terror of all the dogs, cats, and children of the neighborhood."[4] He earned the name locally of Le Vautrin (the Wild Boar), a name that Balzac later gave to a recurring fictional character based upon Vidocq.

His criminal career began with stealing money from the till of his family's bakery. Later, after he pawned the family silver, his father insisted that the local authorities jail him—Vidocq's first experience behind bars. Released after two weeks, he stole his mother's savings and ran away from home. He had wanted to go to America and start a new life but lost his money to a con man along the way. Undaunted but wiser, he joined a traveling theater troupe and circus. He later recalled, "I went about the job, but I didn't like it. The grease disgusted me and I wasn't comfortable with the monkeys, which frightened by an unknown face, made unbelievable efforts to tear out my eyes."[5] Tiring of this adventure, he returned to Arras and begged his mother's forgiveness, something she could never resist giving him. He and his father were reconciled as well.

The uneventful life of a village soon bored him, and Vidocq joined the army. Here he fought fifteen duels in six months, according to his *Memoirs*. Vidocq saw much of Europe with the French army as it carried the Revolution into neighboring countries, but he learned that his chief loyalty must always be to himself. Frequently he was accused of crimes, ranging from assaulting an officer to forgery. Convicted, he usually managed to escape, mastering an ability to disguise himself—at least once in a nun's habit. Recapture brought him harsher sentences to the "galleys," which were prisons for hardened criminals, usually those convicted of capital crimes. But the galleys could not hold him either, and in the confusion of the times, Vidocq usually managed to enlist in another regiment—even serving with privateers and naval forces. It was simple enough to assume another name and hence another identity, for there were no records that could provide definite identification of criminals.

In addition to discarding identities, Vidocq left behind a trail of admiring women wherever he went. One of the conquests he describes in his *Memoirs*:

> At dark the evening of our departure, I met a woman
> from Brussels, named Elisa, with whom I had been intimate. She fell on my neck, took me to supper, and, overcoming weak resistance, kept me with her till the next
> morning. I pretended to Francine [another lover], who
> had sought me everywhere, that to throw the police off
> my tracks I had been forced to dash into a house, and
> I could not get out until daylight. At first she believed
> me; but chance led her to discover that I had passed
> the night with a woman. . . . In her excess of rage she
> swore that she would have me arrested. Having me put
> in prison was certainly the safest way to assure herself
> against my infidelities. As Francine was a woman to do
> what she said she would, I deemed it prudent to leave
> her until her anger had cooled.[6]

Vidocq's many stints in prison, as well as his frequent escapes, had earned him a reputation among criminals. This helped him to find refuge with lawless elements whenever he was out of prison, but it also meant that his only means of earning a living was through crime. Wishing to turn his life around, he managed to arrange a meeting with a man named Dubois, the *commissaire* of police in Lyons. Vidocq proposed to give him a list of criminals working in the area in return for his freedom. Dubois, who knew of Vidocq's reputation, was hesitant, fearing a trick. To prove his good faith, Vidocq said he would give the slip to the two gendarmes who were waiting to take him to prison, and voluntarily return to Dubois' office. Dubois agreed. Not long after Vidocq left, the door opened and he stood there again — without the guards.

Thus began Vidocq's double career: as criminal and police informer. He was forced to leave Lyons to save his skin when the criminals who were being rounded up suspected he had betrayed them. He returned to Arras, where his mother still lived, but was unable to convince the police there that he had gone straight. His good intentions rebuffed, he returned to crime again and wound up in Paris, where he developed a relationship with a woman named Annette, whom he later married.

Paris in the early nineteenth century was not the City of Light it would later become. It was a city of narrow, maze-like streets that were dark and dangerous, twisted alleys and dead ends where bodies were dumped. There were no spacious boulevards or parks with gas lighting. The metropolis was a hotbed of vice and disease. Hordes of people lived in ramshackle ancient buildings; epidemics of cholera periodically swept the city. In this world, the poor were forced to steal for their bread, and street urchins needed sharp wits to survive.

In 1809, during Napoleon's rule, Vidocq decided once again to make a break with his criminal past. He sent a letter to "Papa" Henry, divisional chief of the Police Prefecture of Paris, offering his services as a spy in the underworld. Henry could see the value such a man would have, and referred the letter to Baron de Pasquier, the prefect of police, who agreed to give him a chance. In his *Memoirs,* Vidocq referred to the two men as "my liberators."[7] For the next two decades, he would employ his talents on the right side of the law.

At first he served as an informant in La Force Prison in Paris. The authorities had spread rumors that Vidocq had committed a particularly heinous crime. This earned him the respect of the other inmates, who "whispered and even said aloud in talking about me, 'He's a murderer,' and as in that place a murderer ordinarily inspires great confidence, I was careful not to refute an error so useful to my projects."[8] Some inmates also recognized Vidocq from having served with him in other prisons and knew that he had escaped, adding to his criminal reputation. Finally, after twenty months, he feared that his cover was blown and he "escaped" once again, this time with the connivance of his jailers.

He returned to Paris, where he lived with his wife in the Marais section. At night he frequented the gaming dens, saloons, and brothels in the most dangerous sections of the city. He listened to the schemes and plots being hatched—sometimes being invited to take part in them—and then reported them to his superiors at the prefecture. "The rogues and thieves whom I daily met there firmly believed me to be one of themselves," he wrote.[9] He did not see himself as a traitor, because he did not believe that he was a criminal—only a person who had taken up crime out of necessity. He further claimed that he never turned in anyone for stealing bread to feed himself or his family.

All the while, Vidocq's ability to disguise himself continued to improve. His biographer Joseph Geringer wrote, "He played pirates with black-patched eyes, runaway convicts under a month's chin growth, aged thieves behind gray side whiskers, pickpockets with a limp and a cane and a ragged frock, even persons displaced from their homeland—a scar-faced German swordsman wanted by the Berlin police for killing two men in a duel, the dark Sicilian Gypsy who had killed a wife in Castelvetrano, the British barrister, complete with spectacles, wanted for cutting the throat of a rival attorney in London. With dialect and colloquialism to accompany each caricature, Vidocq carried every animation with aplomb."[10] He was so adept at disguise that he was once approached to make a hit on himself.

In real life, changing one's looks and name to alter one's history, even when practiced by lesser men than Vidocq, was a perennial problem for police forces. In France, galley "slaves"—those who had been sentenced to forced labor—were branded to prevent them from escaping,[11] a practice that was banned in 1832. Afterward, the police had no real way of knowing whether a suspect was a recidivist, or career criminal, because it was nearly impossible to determine if he had ever been arrested before. Vidocq himself, adept at shifting personae, began to tackle that problem.

ii

The population of Paris grew to more than one million people between 1800 and 1850, making it the largest city on the mainland of Europe. Vidocq recognized that the sheer size of the metropolis caused difficulty for the police, who were poorly organized. At the time, the Prefecture of Paris, still led by the Baron de Pasquier, was composed of the First Division, or Administrative Branch, and the Second Division, or Special Investigative Branch, under "Papa" Henry. The city was divided into several geographic sectors, each under the jurisdiction of a *commissaire* with a small staff. The *commissaires* worked only within their own domains, so criminals who ranged freely over the whole city were hard to track down. Vidocq recognized in this confusion a possible job for himself. He suggested that a small group of crime fighters be formed to operate throughout Paris, to keep the criminal and ex-convict population under surveillance. His group could stop crimes before they occurred, a novel idea for the time.

Henry and de Pasquier had been impressed by Vidocq's earlier services and agreed to give him four assistants; his staff would grow over time to twenty-eight. They were paid from secret funds and not publicly acknowledged. In the autumn of 1812, Vidocq and his men were formalized as the plainclothes bureau. Thus began the Sûreté, or security police, which was eventually to become the official investigative branch of the French judiciary.

Vidocq chose ex-criminals and ex-cons for his agents, believing they were the only ones with the street smarts and toughness to do the job he had in mind. Even at this time, Vidocq had it in his mind that, like him, these ex-offenders could become useful members of society. He proudly recalled: "I preferred men whose record had given them a little celebrity. Well! I often gave these men the most delicate missions. They had considerable sums to deliver to the police or the prison offices; they took part in operations in which they could have easily laid hands on large amounts [of money], and not one of them, not a single one, betrayed my trust." [12]

The men of Vidocq's force received no salary; instead they were paid a fee and expenses for each arrest. As a result, regular police officers, who disliked the idea of these irregular forces, spread rumors that his men were solving crimes that they themselves had organized. Vidocq denied this, though he readily acknowledged that he and his men mingled with the criminals of Paris: "I did not hesitate to risk myself in this herd of wretches. I associated with them; I fraternized with them; and I soon had the advantage of being considered one of them. It was while I was drinking with these gentlemen that I learned about the crimes they had committed or premeditated. . . . So I obtained from them all the information I needed. When I gave the signal for an arrest, it was almost certain that the individuals would be taken in the very act, or with the stolen goods, which would justify their sentence."[13] In case of a shootout, Vidocq would often pretend to be hit and have himself carried away as dead under a quilt.

Having served in prisons himself, Vidocq knew that they were training grounds for criminals; upon their release, many prisoners promptly returned to a life of crime. So he often visited Bicêtre Prison on the outskirts of Paris and had the warden line up the worst prisoners in the exercise yard. He would walk up and down the line, studying their faces and looking for distinguishing characteristics such as moles, tattoos, and scars, so that he would recognize them when they returned to Paris. Vidocq proved to have a keen memory for faces, perhaps because he himself was so adept at disguise. Among those he arrested was a man who was passing himself off as nobility; Vidocq recognized him as having been in prison for stealing bank notes.

Vidocq's superiors approved of his work, and the number of his assistants grew. In 1817, his organization was credited with more than eight hundred arrests. Over time, Vidocq professionalized his department, becoming the first to formalize the process of criminal investigation. He compiled a card-indexing system identifying every criminal he knew of in Paris. He created plaster of paris casts to make molds of footprints. He held patents on indelible ink and unalterable bond paper. (Some of his judgments were less professional. He believed, for instance, that being bowlegged was a symptom of criminality.)

In 1827, the Police Prefecture's new head, the Chevalier Duplessis, forced Vidocq to resign for political reasons, although the plainclothes department continued to operate under one of Vidocq's own ex-criminal agents, Coco Lacour. After the July Revolution of 1830 brought Louis-Philippe, the Citizen King, to power, another prefect of police rehired Vidocq, giving him for the first time the title Chef de la Brigade de Sûreté (Head of the Security Brigade).

During his brief retirement, Vidocq had written his *Memoirs,* which became a best seller on both sides of the English Channel. He had completed it with the aid of professional writers and admitted that parts might not be completely true; still, he claimed, "the facts are there."[14]

Vidocq lost his job for good, however, in 1832. Gisquet, the prefect of police responsible for rehiring and then firing him, wrote in his memoirs: "Vidocq's methods were so definitely provocative that I decided to dismiss him as well as all the suspect characters of whom he made use. Up to that time it had been very generally thought that a thief must be set to catch a thief. I proposed to use honest men as detectives, and the results proved that I was right. . . . I ordered the immediate dismissal of all ex-convict employés and decided that in future all members of the regular police should be men with a clean record."[15] But Vidocq was not finished.

iii

On January 3, 1834, Vidocq opened the world's first private detective agency, which he called his own "private police" business.[16] He offered clients a way of dealing with crime without encountering the bureaucracy of the regular police. His shingle read "Le Bureau de Renseignements," or Office of Intelligence. He advertised in the newspapers and flooded the streets with flyers passed out by well-dressed young men at the entrances to banks and brokerages.

The most influential politician of the reign of Louis-Philippe was François Guizot, who expressed the spirit of the times when he famously proclaimed, "Enrich yourself." Parisians responded enthusiastically. Bankers, merchants, and manufacturers were making fortunes, and in turn confidence men, swindlers, and forgers sought to siphon off some of this new money. Vidocq specialized in cases of financial irregularities. Still believing that it took a thief to catch a thief, he hired investigators who had committed the same crimes they would now solve. Vidocq offered his clients plaques saying they were under the protection of "Vidocq's Information Bureau." The small fee it cost was well worth it, for no criminal in France wanted to rob a place protected by Vidocq.

Like the modern private eye, Vidocq also handled domestic problems. Husbands and wives who suspected their spouses of infidelity hired the agency to find out whether such suspicions were accurate. If a spouse or an employee had disappeared, Vidocq's men would try to find the individual or determine if he or she had met with foul play. His new offices included a laboratory as well as Vidocq's extensive files, which were open to only a few trusted employees.

Vidocq still faced difficulties with the uniformed police, many of whom were jealous of him. His further successes in solving crime only infuriated them more, and they went so far as to plant compromising objects and letters in his office before raiding it. But Vidocq was always able to foil these schemes and divert false accusations. In answer to the charge that his agents robbed people in the street, for example, he ordered his men to wear suede gloves on duty to show that it was impossible for them to pick pockets.

At the end of November 1839, the police raided the Office of Intelligence and carried off its files. The newspapers reported that more than half were secret documents of the Sûreté that should not have been in private hands. Vidocq promptly filed a lawsuit against the prefect of police, Paul Delessert, a man new to the job, with little experience in law enforcement. The head of the Sûreté responded by arresting Vidocq on December 23. He spent that Christmas in a Paris jail, although Mme. Vidocq was allowed to bring a roasted goose with trimmings and have dinner with him. In February, Vidocq was acquitted of all charges and was commended by the court as a man of honor.

The police were further embarrassed when Prefect Delessert's brother, Maurice, a wealthy banker, was robbed of seventy-five thousand francs. When the police could not find the thief, Maurice, using a pseudonym, turned to Vidocq for help. Vidocq, who was not deceived about his new client's identity, took personal charge of the case. Through his underworld informants, he found out where the loot was located and made his own deal with the robbers: in return for the money, he would not expose their identities. Seventy-two hours after he got the case, Vidocq returned the money to Maurice Delessert, grandly refusing to take a fee. He sent a letter explaining the matter to Prefect Delessert. The letter "leaked" and appeared in a newspaper, letting all Paris know who was the city's greatest detective.

In the last two decades of his life, Vidocq took up a new career, writing novels based—with considerable exaggeration, if not outright invention—on his experiences as an investigator. He published the first of them, *Les voleurs* (*The Thieves*), in 1836. He seems to have undertaken the book partly to make money and also to publicize his agency. Its success made Vidocq a trailblazer in another field: the first author of best-selling crime fiction.

Les voleurs was a virtual how-to of crime. Vidocq showed how thieves broke into houses and offices using short swords of the finest steel, explained how pickpockets filed their fingers to increase their sensitivity of touch, and warned brothel patrons that many of the rooms had hidden peepholes so that when they were engaged in lovemaking, someone could enter the room and rifle their wallets. He described the nearly invisible dots that sharpers used to mark playing cards. He also cautioned people about beginning a correspondence with strangers who were in fact forgers hoping to get a sample of their handwriting.

Age eventually slowed even Vidocq. At age seventy-five, in 1847, he closed his detective agency, though he still took on cases for favorite clients. Seven years later, he suffered a paralytic stroke. He dictated his will and then died on May 11, 1854, just a month short of his eighty-second birthday. His epitaph could have been his speech to French lawmakers in which he idealized himself: "I have the consolation of having remained an honest man amid the darkness of perversion and the atmosphere of crime. I have fought for the defense of order, in the name of justice as soldiers fight for the defense of their country, beneath the flag of their regiment. I had no epaulettes, but I ran as many risks as they, and I exposed my life every day as they do." [17] Before his body was even removed from his home, the Paris police arrived to confiscate his files and records.

iv

It can be argued that all detective fiction owes something to Vidocq. Certainly his outsize persona intrigued some of France's greatest and most popular writers, among them Honoré de Balzac, Alexandre Dumas, Victor Hugo, and Eugène Sue. Balzac used the character Vautrin, modeled after Vidocq, in several books of his massive sequence of novels, *La comédie humaine*. At one point, Vautrin explains crime and the world:

> It is a strange mud pit. . . . If you get that dirt on you while you're driving around in a carriage, you're a very respectable fellow, but if it spatters all over you while you slog along on foot, then you're a good-for-nothing rogue. Make the mistake of grabbing anything out of the mud, no matter how insignificant, and they'll pillory you in the courts of law. But steal millions, and

they'll point you out as a hero, in the very best houses. That's an ethical system you pay the cops and the judges thirty million a year to keep in good working order. It's just great![18] Vautrin also offers Balzac's famous observation on wealth: "The secret of all great fortunes . . . is always some forgotten crime—forgotten, mind you, because it's been properly handled."[19]

Victor Hugo, author of what has proved to be the most durable of nineteenth-century French novels, *Les misérables,* also knew Vidocq personally and is said to have modeled both of the main characters of his great book after Vidocq: Inspector Javert, the relentless policeman, and his quarry the ex-convict Jean Valjean represented the two sides of Vidocq's nature and career.

The works of these authors were best sellers among a new class of reader that had developed along with the growth of literacy in nineteenth-century France. As the reading public grew, mass-circulation newspapers and journals sprang up to fulfill the demand for news, commentary, and popular literature. Newspapers printed sensational stories of crime and scandal, called *faits divers;* to improve their tales, authors of *faits divers* wrote in a style more usual for fiction than for journalism. Henry de Roure, a journalist of the Belle Époque, wrote that the reader sitting down to read a *fait divers* "licks his chops. Believes himself to experience one by one—and with what transports of joy!—the emotions of an unfortunate woman attacked at night and cut into pieces with successive blows of a sword; then, in trying to enter into the character of the assassin, he tastes the incomparable psychological pleasures which [the reader], as a practical man, has never experienced directly."[20]

Seeing the popularity of such lively journalism, the newspaper publisher Émile de Girardin decided to publish fiction outright and developed the *feuilleton,* or serial. In 1836, the first issue of his *La Presse* contained the premier installment of an exciting novel with the promise of additional chapters to come. The French public took to the *feuilletons* with such enthusiasm that they became virtually obligatory for any newspaper trying to increase its circulation. Major authors' works often appeared first in this format and were afterward released in book form. Perhaps the most popular of the *romans feuilletons,* or serial novels, was Eugène Sue's *Les mystères de Paris,* which tripled the circulation of *Le Journal des Débats,* where it appeared between 1842 and 1843. The author received an offer of 100,000 francs for his next serial even before a word was written, a fantastic figure for the day, making Sue one of the highest-paid authors in France.

Fait divers and *feuilletons* were new only in format, for people had written stories about crimes since ancient times. The truly innovative literary genre of the nineteenth century was the detective story, in which the crime is only a prelude. Detective stories appealed to a more sophisticated public by presenting a puzzle that the reader seeks to solve before, or at least along with, the detective-hero.

The first modern detective story, in which the central character's importance lies in his ability to detect, was written by an American, Edgar Allan Poe. He was inspired by Vidocq's *Memoirs* to create the sleuth C. Auguste Dupin, who first appeared in the story "The Murders in the Rue Morgue" in 1841.[21] Poe set the tale in Paris and even included a reference to Vidocq. The character Dupin, portrayed as a man of culture and scientific learning, remarks, "Vidocq was a good guesser and a persevering man. But without educated thought, he erred continually."[22]

Poe's detective stories were written before many American cities had any kind of organized police force and before London's Scotland Yard had been established. Indeed, the very word *detective* did not appear until two years after the publication of "The Murders in the Rue Morgue," when Sir James Graham, the British home secretary, formed a special group of officers called the Detective Police. Poe himself called his stories "tales of ratiocination."[23]

Poe had scientific interests as well as literary ones. Indeed, the very same issue of the magazine that published "The Murders in the Rue Morgue" also contained an article by Poe on photography, which had just been invented by two Frenchmen, Nicéphore Niepce and Louis Daguerre. And Poe's detective was a particularly modern hero, one who used his mental faculties to resolve the crisis—the mystery—he faced. He might carry a weapon, but his true power came from his intellect and a rigorous scientific mind-set.

That was not the only precedent set by Poe. As the critic Julian Symons notes about him: "He . . . established the convention by which the brilliant intelligence of the detective is made to shine more brightly through the comparative obtuseness of his friend who tells the stories." [24] This obtuse friend—not an outright bumbler, but someone unable to come close to the detective in terms of deductive brilliance—became another standard of the genre, most notably, of course, with Dr. John Watson, the foil to Sherlock Holmes. Holmes's creator, Sir Arthur Conan Doyle, acknowledged his debt to Poe, slyly having Watson remark to Holmes, "You remind me of Edgar Allan Poe's Dupin." And Conan Doyle would write frankly in *Through the Magic Door:* "Poe is to my mind, the supreme, the original short-story writer of all time." [25]

Though Poe's stories were set in a Paris that didn't exist, they were soon translated into French. In November 1845, the *Revue Britannique* published a translation of "The Gold Bug," but it was not until the following year, when the Parisian newspaper *La Quotidienne* published a loose three-part translation of "The Murders in the Rue Morgue," that the French public discovered Poe. The translator changed the name of the street to the rue de l'Ouest (because there is no rue Morgue) and ramped up the gory details for audiences that were accustomed to *feuilletons*. The story—in which two women are brutally murdered by an escaped orangutan—caused a stir, and essays on Poe began to appear in respected publications such as the *Revue des Deux Mondes*. More translated stories of his followed.

The great French poet Charles Baudelaire was amazed by Poe, saying that he "experienced a strange commotion" on first reading him.[26] Searching through American magazines for more, and finding stories that he himself had "thought vaguely and confusedly" of writing,[27] Baudelaire became a devotee of the American author. In 1852, he published translations of Poe's tales along with commentaries that increased Poe's literary reputation in France, where he became better known than in his native land. The French particularly responded to Poe's Gothic elements, the dark side of the psyche that Poe would write of as "the blackness of darkness."[28] Baudelaire, learning of Poe's mysterious death in Baltimore in 1849, investigated the circumstances and declared, "This death was almost a suicide — a suicide prepared for a long time."[29]

France's fascination with Poe did not stop in the 1850s. Pioneers of modernism — among them the symbolist poets Stéphane Mallarmé, Paul Verlaine, and Arthur Rimbaud — found inspiration in Poe's works. So did the composer Claude Debussy, who was working on an opera based on Poe's "The Fall of the House of Usher" when he died. Debussy wrote to a friend, "I have recently been living in the House of Usher which is not exactly the place where one can look after one's nerves — just the opposite. One develops the curious habit of listening to the stones as if they were in conversation with each other and expecting houses to crumble to pieces as if this were not only natural but inevitable. . . . I have no confidence in the normal, well-balanced type of persons."[30]

V

It was not long before Poe inspired French imitators. The first great French fictional detective (not counting Vidocq's inventions) was Monsieur Lecoq, who initially appeared in 1865, the creation of Émile Gaboriau. In his name, personal vanity, and frightening reputation, Lecoq echoed Vidocq. Moreover, Lecoq had also been a crook before becoming a detective. His methods, however, came from Dupin: the young Gaboriau had read Baudelaire's translation of Poe.

Gaboriau was the son of a public official in the provinces who wished for his son to become a lawyer. Rebellious, the young man joined the army and then came to Paris to be a writer. He began as a ghost writer for Paul Féval, a newspaper editor, dramatist, and author of criminal romances for *feuilletons*. To do research, Gaboriau attended trials, visited prisons, and even roamed the morgues. He was fascinated by the details of police work, the operations of the Sûréte, and the duties of *juges d'instruction* (investigating judges) — ironically finding a certain fulfillment in the profession his father had urged him to follow.

Gaboriau had a large collection of police memoirs and literature on police work. As a result, his detectives, including Lecoq, are very realistically portrayed; for this reason, Gaboriau is regarded as the father of the modern police procedural and, for some, as the inventor of the modern detective novel (for Poe wrote no novels, only short stories). Like Poe, Gaboriau used the science of his time — the chemistry of poisons, photography, and the telegraph. Equally influential was his stress on the importance of logic, the "calculus of possibilities," [31] in solving the crime.

Lecoq first appeared in a *feuilleton,* which was published the following year in book form under the title *L'affaire Lerouge.* Lecoq is initially described as a former criminal, now a young member of the Sûreté, whose mentor, a bedridden old man nicknamed Tirauclair ("bringer of light") helps him solve a case. In this first book, Lecoq has already become a master of disguise. Though handsome, with thick black hair and "bold piercing eyes," [32] he passes himself off as an official by donning a stiff cravat, gold spectacles, and a wig. Like Dupin, Lecoq is an educated man, who earlier in life had been employed by Baron Moser, an astronomer. (In his spare time he solved complicated astronomical problems.) The baron warned the young Lecoq: "When one has your disposition, and is poor, one will either become a famous thief or a great detective. Choose." [33]

L'affaire Lerouge sold well, and Gaboriau produced three more novels in 1867, all with Lecoq as the central character. (In the later works, the author no longer referred to him as a former criminal.) Before Sherlock Holmes appeared, Lecoq was already a master of deduction. In *Le crime d'Orcival* he states, "The inquest of a crime is nothing more nor less than the solution of a problem. Given the crime . . . you commence by seeking out all the circumstances, whether serious or superficial; the details and the particulars. When these have been carefully gathered, you classify them, and put them in their order and date. You thus know the victim, the crime and the circumstances; it remains to find the third term of the problem, that is X, the unknown quantity—the guilty party. The task is a difficult one, but not so difficult as is first imagined." [34] This effort to classify and hypothesize revealed the scientific mind-set that characterized the new detective. Gaboriau's description of Lecoq's quarters made this intellectual bent unmistakable: "On the other side of the room was a bookcase full of scientific works, especially of medicines and chemistry." [35]

Unlike Dupin, Lecoq is not just an armchair detective. He actively pursues clues and personally confronts suspects and villains. Gaboriau's novels include interesting descriptions of Parisian life, as his detective tracks criminals to their locales, revealing their social and family life, sexuality, and politics. Many of his villains are aristocrats gone wrong, frequently big-time financial swindlers, who are particularly frightening because their self-confidence, knowledge, and connections make them more difficult to catch. The police, on the other hand, are sometimes unscrupulous in their methods—as they were in real life. Reflecting Gaboriau's (and Parisians') cynicism about the police, he portrays plain-clothes detectives provoking fights with criminals whom they cannot arrest on legal grounds in order to charge them with assault and hold them in jail while they look for evidence of more serious charges.

Gaboriau's fiction looked toward the later achievements of Bertillon. He described the difficulty of identifying criminals, a problem that the real-life criminologist was later to solve. In *Monsieur Lecoq* (1869), Gaboriau wrote:

Railroads, photography, and telegraphic communication have multiplied the means of identification in vain. Every day it happens that malefactors succeed in deceiving the judge in regard to their true personality, and thus escape the consequences of their former crimes.

This is so frequently the case that a witty attorney-general once laughingly remarked — and, perhaps, he was only half in jest: "This uncertainty in regard to identity will cease only on the day when the law prescribes that a number shall be branded upon the shoulder of every child whose birth is reported to the mayor."[36]

This sort of interplay between fiction and reality was characteristic of much of detective fiction. The fiction writers were inspired by the latest in crime techniques, while real criminologists got ideas from fiction, as one of Bertillon's contemporaries, Edmond Locard, was to admit.

It was also common for one fictional detective to compare or contrast himself with another. In *A Study in Scarlet* (1887), Dr. Watson asks Sherlock Holmes, "Have you read Gaboriau's works? Does Lecoq come up to your idea of a detective?"

Holmes "sniffed sardonically" at the idea. "Lecoq was a miserable bungler," he says angrily. "He had only one thing to recommend him, and that was his energy. That book made me positively ill. The question was how to identify an unknown prisoner. I could have done it in twenty-four hours. Lecoq took six months or so. It might be made a text-book for detectives to teach them what to avoid."[37]

That was rather uncharitable of Holmes, for many commentators feel that the progression of Vidocq to Lecoq to Sherlock indicated the literary debt incurred by Holmes's creator, Sir Arthur Conan Doyle. Conan Doyle, like Poe, wanted to portray his fictional sleuth as a scientific detective. An ophthalmologist, Conan

Doyle had criticized Edgar Allan Poe for using what Conan Doyle termed the "illusion" of the scientific method, and he believed that he could succeed where Poe had failed. By the 1880s and 1890s, when Conan Doyle wrote his classic Holmes stories, real-life detectives were beginning to use technologies and practices borrowed from their peers in the fields of chemistry, biology, and physics. As Sherlock Holmes tells Watson: "Detection is, or ought to be, an exact science, and should be treated in the same cold and unemotional manner. To tinge it with romanticism produces much of the same effect as if you worked a love-story or an elopement into the fifth proposition of Euclid." [38]

Watson, the narrator of Conan Doyle's stories, provides a convenient foil to whom Holmes can explain his reasoning, since the reader, unassisted, can no longer be expected to follow the detective in solving the case. That was true of science as well. By the end of the nineteenth century, science was sufficiently complex to be well beyond the knowledge of the ordinary educated person. The inner workings of the world, it turned out, were their own encoded mystery. The critic J. K. Van Dover observed, "The detective, who claims to speak the language of the thinking scientist yet who acts morally in the sphere of the common man, offers an imaginative bridge between the two worlds of the scientist and the layman." [39]

vi

"O Paris! O Paris! You are the true Babylon, the battlefield of the spirits, the temple where evil welcomes its worshippers and disciples, and I believe that you feel the eternal breath of the archangel of darkness upon you, as the high seas tremble upon the winds of the storm." [40]

So wrote Pierre Alexis Ponson du Terrail in 1857 in his novel *L'héritage mystérieux* (*The Mysterious Inheritance*), the first of a series featuring a new type of fictional character. Ponson, who had written Gothic novels in which horror was the chief attraction, sought to duplicate the success of Sue's *The Mysteries of Paris*. Indeed, the major characters in *L'héritage Mystérieux* closely parallel those in Sue's book. However, the work took on a life of its own as readers responded favorably to a character named Rocambole, who initially appears as a fourteen-year-old orphan but by the story's end is a strapping sixteen-year-old who helps the main character expose the villain. So popular was Rocambole that the following year he appeared as the twenty-one-year-old hero of another novel and continued to star in what became an eight-book series, published from 1857 to 1870, in which the action carries over from one volume to the next.

Rocambole is very much like Vidocq, except that Ponson's fictional creation stays far more on the criminal side of the line. He is what modern critics would call an antihero, but to the French he was an irresistible rogue. Motivated by sheer greed, Rocambole becomes a cynical and ruthless murderer. Among his victims are his adopted mother (strangled by Rocambole's own hands) and his mentor in crime, the Irish lord Sir Williams. Ponson apparently felt his villain-hero must be punished, so at the end of the second book, Rocambole, his face horribly scarred with acid, is imprisoned at the hard-labor camp of Toulon. His beloved stepsister does not even recognize him when she sees him.

Readers demanded more, however, and in his further adventures, Rocambole acquired colorful criminal allies and combated equally fantastic evildoers, such as a gang of Thugees who have come to France from India to kidnap virgins for their goddess, Kali. (In literary circles, the word *rocambolesque* came to refer to any fantastic adventure.) Like his predecessors, Rocambole was a master of disguise and used modern science to achieve his goals.

Rocambole's adventures were ended by the outbreak of the Franco-Prussian War in 1870. Ponson du Terrail fled Paris to his country estate near Orléans, where he gathered friends to wage a guerrilla war against the Germans, just as his fictional character might have done. One of his friends exclaimed before dying, "Ah, if only Rocambole was here to save us!"[41] There was no savior, however; the Germans burned down Ponson de Terrail's mansion and executed many of his friends and even his dogs. Ponson du Terrail managed to escape but died soon afterward.

The Rocambole series marked the beginning of a type of crime novel that the French made particularly their own. It reflected the ambivalent attitude of Parisians toward the forces of law and order. Whereas Jean Valjean in Victor Hugo's *Les misérables* is an escaped convict, he is not really a criminal, but Rocambole is truly a malefactor, and not one who occasionally aids the police or helps damsels in distress. French readers liked him for his cleverness and resourcefulness and elaborate adventures—and also because he lived outside the law. This sympathy for the devil had deep roots in French literature, starting with François Villon, the great poet and criminal of medieval Paris, whose works celebrate the pleasures of life—wine and women—at the same time that they lament illness, poverty, old age, and death. It was in this spirit that other Belle Époque writers developed further the idea of criminal as hero.

Maurice Leblanc (1864–1941) had wanted to be a serious writer but was forced to work as a journalist; as a police reporter he learned about the procedures of the courts and the methods of those who were brought before the judges. In 1905, the editor of a magazine, *Je Sais Tout*, asked him to write a crime story, and the result was the first tale featuring Arsène Lupin, *gentleman-cambrioleur* ("gentleman burglar"). Leblanc met with immediate acclaim and would write twenty-one more stories with the character.

Lupin, in the French tradition, is completely amoral. He steals for himself, not for the poor. (Leblanc is said to have modeled him after the anarchist Marius Jacob, whose trial had made headlines only a year earlier.) Lupin is young, handsome, and daring—a dandy, frequently portrayed in high silk hat and evening dress, sporting a monocle. Fastidious, he sends his shirts to be laundered and starched in London. He enjoys the company of beautiful women, who are fashionably attired in the latest in French couture. He finds crime amusing and fun—staging some of his exploits just to show that he can, which was why newspapers in 1911 half-jokingly suggested that he was the only man who could have stolen the *Mona Lisa*.

Lupin does stop short of murder and has moments of remorse. Occasionally he uses his knowledge of the underworld to solve crimes committed by less savory outlaws. Lupin likes to masquerade as different characters and for four years, posing as Lenormand, the head of the Sûreté, actually directs operations against himself. But nothing inspires him to permanently reform as Vidocq did.

Above all, Lupin takes pleasure in outsmarting the authorities, which was one of the qualities that most endeared him to readers. When he solves crimes, he often chooses those that have stumped others, so that he can show off his quick mind and vast knowledge of the criminal world. Leblanc felt so confident of Lupin's abilities that he even pitted him against Sherlock Holmes, who appears in several of the stories as Herlock Sholmes. In one, Lupin captures Sholmes and ships him back to England on a ferry. Sholmes tricks the captain and confronts Lupin, turning him over to the police. Lupin returns the favor, escaping just in time to bid farewell to Sholmes. He was one French detective that Conan Doyle did not allow his creation to comment on.

vii

At the time the *Mona Lisa* was stolen, Paris was fascinated by a new fictional criminal, whose exploits had been appearing monthly since February 1911. For the previous six months, Fantômas, an aristocratic villain with seemingly supernatural powers, had been thrilling and delighting readers. More terrorist than criminal, Fantômas is a ruthless killer who decapitates people, blows up ocean liners, spreads plague germs through Paris, fills perfume bottles with acid in a department store, and hijacks a Métro train—all with no apparent reason.

Fantômas is virtually impossible to capture or stop. His strength lies in his very elusiveness. As one of his chief adversaries says, "I am frightened, because Fantômas is a being against whom it is idle to use ordinary weapons; because he has been able to conceal his identity and elude all pursuit for years; because his daring is boundless and his power immeasurable; because he is everywhere and nowhere at once and . . . I am not even sure that he is not listening to me now."[42]

Fantômas's crimes often seem to be committed out of a desire for sheer anarchy and on a scale far beyond that of any previous character in crime fiction. His spectral infamy—and the fear it inspired—were clear from the very first lines of the series:

> "Fantômas."
> "What did you say?"
> "I said: Fantômas."
> "And what does that mean?"
> "Nothing. . . . Everything!"
> "But what is it?"
> "Nobody. . . . And yet, yes, it is somebody!"
> "And what does the somebody do?"
> "Spreads terror!"[43]

The Fantômas novels were published by Arthème Fayard, who specialized in low-priced books intended to attract a large number of readers. In 1905, Fayard started a line of books with sensational full-color covers, called Le Livre Populaire. Most of them were reprints of novels that had been *feuilletons,* including works by Gaboriau and Ponson du Terrail. But in 1910, Fayard approached Marcel Allain and Pierre Souvestre, both of whom wrote for magazines intended for automobile and sports fans, to see if they could write an original four-hundred-page novel a month. Souvestre, the elder by ten years, had met Allain when looking for an assistant.

The younger man amazed his boss by being able to churn out in two hours a seventeen-page article on a new truck about which he knew nothing. Thus began their collaboration.

The title for the series had come to the two men while riding on the Métro to meet Fayard. Souvestre had suggested the title *Fantô-mus,* a mock latinization of the French word *fantôme,* or phantom. Fayard, hearing it in his office, wrote it down incorrectly. Fayard's other contribution was to suggest the cover art, based on an advertisement that showed a masked, elegantly dressed man. An Italian illustrator, Gino Starace, put a dagger in the man's hand as he brooded over Paris. Starace continued to provide lurid and imaginative cover illustrations that did much to ensure the series' popularity.

The decision to make the hero evil was inspired by the success of fictional antiheroes such as Arsène Lupin and the master criminal Zigomar, created by Léon Sazie. Zigomar, who wore a hood and always escaped from the police, had first appeared in a *feuille-ton* in 1909, but now was the lead character in a Pathé movie studio series that was packing in audiences. Fayard was hoping to capitalize on Zigomar's popularity, not guessing that Fantômas would surpass it.

The two writers followed a grueling publication schedule, which led them to produce twelve thousand pages of fiction in a little under three years. They used all the modern methods, dictating to secretaries and even recording their words on wax rolls. Usually they started with a basic plot outline and divided the chapters between themselves. During the final week of each month, they exchanged chapters and wrote transitional paragraphs. Fantastic plot twists and developments were often more imaginative than realistic—or even coherent. Fantômas performs superhuman acts and switches identities at will, going well beyond the bounds of physics in the process. Yet the readers, carried along by the spirit of the books, did not mind. It was an age in which anything seemed possible. Fact or fiction? With Fantômas, there was no division between them.

A recent critic, Robin Walz, summed up the improbability of the series: "One of the fundamental characteristics of the *Fantômas* series is the ability to swerve the story through space and time. Narrative coherence depends upon the title character's ability to be anyone and anywhere, at any time, in order to sustain the action. It is a further condition that the reader set aside the question of what happens to one or another of his identities when Fantômas is yet someone else. . . . To enjoy the story, the reader has to accept these fundamental incoherences of time, space, and character."[44]

And readers did. The books were an immediate hit, their popularity cutting across all classes. Bourgeois shopkeepers, countesses, bohemians, and poets devoured the Fantômas stories as soon as they were published. The masked man in evening clothes who towered over Paris appeared on kiosks and billboards and the walls of the Métro. The image was everywhere, like Fantômas himself, showing that no one was safe. The two authors ultimately produced thirty-two novels before Souvestre's death in 1914; Allain then did eleven more on his own, marrying his ex-partner's widow as well.

The reader always knows that the criminal will be Fantômas. The puzzle is in seeing through his disguises and finding him among the other characters. He could be in the guise of a nun hiding a weapon under her habit or posing as a physician arriving at a patient's bedside not to heal but to poison. Sometimes he is the lover of a beautiful woman; at other times, a doddering old man or a professor.

Fantômas's many guises reflected a particular concern of the French police: to establish with certainty the identity of those people who were arrested. Bertillon had in the 1880s worked out a scientific method of enabling law enforcement officials to penetrate disguises. With Fantômas, there seemed to be no real person underneath: he had taken the power of disguise that Vidocq possessed, and extended it to his essential nature. Part of the appeal of the series, especially to Apollinaire and other avant-garde thinkers who embraced it, was that it asked readers to search beneath the surface to find the nature of things—a common theme of modernism in both art and science. Just as Fantômas disregards the conventions of morality, so too does he defy ordinary logic. He has entered that elusive fourth dimension that mathematicians, scientists, and artists were then trying to discover.

It was, of course, easier for fictional characters to break old patterns and shatter rules, but Paris's real-life crime fighters were taking note of what their make-believe counterparts (and make-believe villains) were doing. They too were pushing forward, creating new tools and methods. For better or for worse, they would soon have plenty of opportunities to experiment with these innovative techniques.

SCIENCE VS. CRIME

Vidocq, the first head of the Sûreté, had begun the practice of taking a scientific approach to the detection of crime, even though his primary tools were his phenomenal memory and his psychological insight into the criminal mentality. As the nineteenth century advanced, however, the police increasingly used new scientific discoveries in their work. Chemistry and physics, as well as statistics, physiology, biology, psychology, and the new social sciences of anthropology and sociology all made contributions to crime fighting. Developments in technology, such as the microscope and the camera, gave detectives even greater power. Over time, a science of criminology was born and the modern detective came into being.

i

Émile Zola's description of a naturalistic novelist's work could be used equally well as a pattern for the criminologist: "The novelist starts out in search of a truth . . . he starts from known facts; then he makes his experiment, and exposes [the character] to a series of trials, placing him amid certain surroundings in order to exhibit how the complicated machinery of his person works. . . . The problem is to know what such passion acting in such a surrounding and under such circumstances would produce from the point of view of an individual and of society . . . Finally you possess knowledge of the man, scientific knowledge of him, in both his individual and his social relations."[1] It was just such knowledge that enabled one relentless detective to bring to justice the most celebrated criminal of his time.

"To kill without remorse is the highest of pleasures," wrote Pierre-François Lacenaire. "It is impossible to destroy my hatred of mankind. This hatred is the product of a lifetime, the outcome of my every thought. I never pitied any one who suffered, and I don't want to be pitied myself."[2] These were the words—written as he faced the guillotine—of the most notorious criminal to appear in the decade after Vidocq's retirement from the Sûreté in 1827. At heart a dandy with literary pretensions, Lacenaire sought to project himself as the greatest criminal of his generation. Though most of his crimes were petty ones, his self-promotion invited others to attempt to use him as a doorway into the criminal mind.

Born Pierre-François Gaillard, the son of a wealthy iron merchant in Francheville, he grew up with a profound sense of resentment. In his memoirs he recalled that his older brother was the favored son in the family. When Pierre was sixteen, he and his father had passed through the town square with the guillotine looming over it. "Look," his father had said, "that is how you will finish up if you don't change your ways."[3] Lacenaire saw this moment as a turning point in his life. "From that moment," he wrote, "an invisible bond existed between me and the frightful machine."[4]

As a young man, he went to Paris to study law; it was at this time that he adopted the name Lacenaire. Because the money his father sent him was not enough to survive on, he worked at many jobs, never achieving the success that he believed he deserved. Inspired by the Greek war for independence, Lacenaire went off to join the rebel forces. When he returned to France in 1829, he found that his father was bankrupt. Lacenaire had to fend for himself.

According to his memoirs, around this time Lacenaire fought a duel with the nephew of Benjamin Constant, a politician and writer. Lacenaire was the victor, and though the duel was not fatal, he claimed that the experience made him see how he could kill a person without remorse.

It was also in 1829 that Lacenaire served his first jail term, having been convicted in a swindling scheme. He was soon on the street again, and for the next three years he wrote lyric poems, songs, and essays. As no one would pay much for his literary creations, he continued his career of petty fraud, which brought him a second short prison sentence. After his release, the editor of *Bon Sens*, a radical political journal, asked Lacenaire to write an exposé of French prison life. This gave him a chance to express his contempt for authority and brought him some fame as well. "In this atmosphere . . . the wretched youth finds himself blushing at the last remnant of innocence and decency which he had still preserved when he entered the prison; he begins to feel ashamed that he is less of a scoundrel than those about him, he dreads their mockery and their contempt; for, make no mistake, there are such things as respect and contempt even in the galleys, a fact that explains why certain convicts are better off in jail than in a society which has nothing for them but contempt."[5]

Working for *Bon Sens* brought Lacenaire a forum but little money. Few others shared his delusions about his artistic talent, so in 1834 he embarked on the path of crime yet again. As a career choice, it was a mistake, for he was often inept in carrying out his criminal plans. At the time, banks sent messengers to their customers' homes and offices to collect deposits. Since the messengers often carried large sums of money, Lacenaire thought they would make fine victims.

He took on a partner, Pierre Victor Avril, a former carpenter. "I was the intelligence, Avril the arm," Lacenaire wrote later.[6] He requested a bank to send a messenger to a certain address, giving a false name. When the messenger arrived, however, the porter of the building told him that no one of that name lived there. On Lacenaire's second attempt, no messenger showed up.

Coming up with a new plan, Lacenaire remembered a former friend from prison, a man named Chardon, who now lived with his bedridden mother. Unwisely, he had once told Lacenaire that she had saved a hoard of money. One December morning, Lacenaire and Avril knocked at Chardon's door. Chardon, too trusting, allowed his former prison mate inside. Without a word, Lacenaire stabbed him with a dagger and Avril used a hatchet to deliver a deathblow.

A low moaning in the next room attracted Lacenaire's attention. It was the bedridden mother, and the two thieves showed her no more mercy than they had the son. Looking for hidden valuables, they overturned the mattress on which she was lying, suffocating her. They ransacked the house, taking everything that looked valuable. Despite what Chardon had said, the loot was worth no more than seven hundred francs—far less than they had expected. But the killers celebrated what they considered a "perfect crime" by washing off the evidence of their crime at a Turkish bath, followed by a dinner at a fancy café.

Emboldened by this success, Lacenaire struck again two weeks later, trying the messenger scam again. Posing as a M. Mahossier, he appeared at a bank and arranged to cash a forced check. The teller told an eighteen-year-old messenger named Genevay to take three thousand francs to the address Lacenaire had given. Because Avril was not available, Lacenaire's accomplice this time was a man named François, also known as Red Whiskers. After the messenger put the bank notes on the table and turned to leave, François attacked him from behind with a file. He was as inept as his partner, failing to kill Genevay, whose screams brought neighbors to the scene. Both of the would-be robbers fled.

Genevay survived and gave the police a description of his attackers. He noted that Mahossier had a copy of Rousseau's *Social Contract* hanging out of his pocket. Vidocq's successor at the head of the Sûreté, M. Allard, assigned his chief inspector, Paul-Louis-Alponse Canler, to the case.[7] Canler had won a reputation as the Sûreté's best detective because of his uncanny ability to read the minds of criminals and because he was incredibly persistent. He was a shoe-leather detective at heart — which he had to be: a social scientist named Honoré-Antoine Frégier had published a lengthy work in 1840 in which he claimed some sixty-three thousand criminals were living in Paris — nearly 10 percent of the population.[8]

Canler assumed that Mahossier was not the real name of the man he was after, but he also knew that criminals often used the same alias many times. So he began to visit lodging houses, looking through registers for the name. After a tedious search, he found a seedy place with the name Mahossier in the register. The concierge's description of him sounded like the man who had stabbed the bank messenger — a distinguished-looking man with a high forehead, silky mustache, and smooth manner. She also remembered that he had stayed there once before under the name Bâton.

Canler interviewed five hundred people before he found a thief named Bâton and arrested him, even though he did not match the description of Mahossier. The inspector clung to his theory that following the trail of names would lead him to the culprit. Bâton, given plenty of brandy during questioning, revealed that he knew someone who fit the description of the man Canler was looking for — a nattily dressed man with a high forehead. Bâton knew him as Gaillard, Lacenaire's real name.

Canler went back to checking the registers of flophouses. When he found a Gaillard, the innkeeper remembered that the man in question had left some papers behind. These included some republican songs and poems — a link with Canler's only other clue: the copy of Rousseau that the perpetrator had carried.

The detective was sure he had identified his man, but he still had to find him. He got a break when Avril, Lacenaire's accomplice in the double murder, was arrested on another charge. Hoping for leniency, he offered to help Canler. He told him that the man known as Gaillard had a rich aunt who lived in the rue Bar-du-Bec. When Canler went to see her, she admitted she had a disreputable nephew whom she feared. Indeed, she had put a grill on her door because she feared that he would murder her some day. The aunt gave Canler his quarry's current name: Lacenaire.

Canler issued a general alert throughout France with Lacenaire's description. On February 2, 1836, the police arrested a man at Beaune. It was Lacenaire, trying a new scam: selling forged bonds. He was brought back to the Paris Prefecture, where he greeted Canler politely. He admitted that he had robbed the bank messenger but at first refused to give the name of his accomplice. When told that his cohort in the double murder had cooperated in his capture, he confessed to that as well, revenging himself on Avril and Red Whiskers for good measure with further incriminating testimony. When Canler pointed out, "You realize, of course, that it will finish you," Lacenaire replied, "I know that. It doesn't matter so long as it finishes them too."[9] His sense of grievance had overcome self-preservation.

The trial of the three criminals—Lacenaire, Avril, and Red Whiskers—began in the Cour d'Assises[10] of the Seine on November 12, 1836. The highlight of the trial was Lacenaire's speech to the court. Dressed in a stylish blue coat, he reached heights of self-dramatization, portraying himself as an alienated genius at war with society. He mesmerized those present in the courtroom, and reporters wrote everything down for the next day's newspapers. Since Lacenaire had already declared that he was eager to meet his fiancée, the guillotine, the death sentence for him and Avril was almost anticlimactic.

Lacenaire became a celebrity, and while he awaited execution, visitors flocked to his prison cell, where he presided over a virtual salon for writers, doctors, scientists, and journalists. He gave visitors calling cards bearing the inscription "Pierre-François Lacenaire, fiancé of the guillotine."[11] Gifts of fine food and wine as well as messages of goodwill flooded into the prison from ladies of the highest society. One man offered Lacenaire an expensive coat, which he refused on the grounds that he would not be able to give it much wear. The literary world fawned on him; both Victor Hugo and Théophile Gautier came to visit and listen to him recite his poetry.

Lacenaire also found time to write his memoirs, certainly the most notorious such document up to that time. With them, he finally achieved his longed-for literary success, interspersing his poetry with the account of his life. While he claimed that he had modeled the memoirs on those of Vidocq, Lacenaire's are marked by self-pity, with few descriptions of crimes and many more romantic explanations of why he became a criminal. His rationalizations further reveal him as a highly intelligent man who used the injustices—real and perceived—of society to excuse his behavior. This view led him to see himself as a victim and any crime as defensible.[12]

Scientists came to his cell to examine and measure him, trying to find the essence of what made him a criminal. Adherents of the pseudoscience of phrenology claimed to be able to determine a person's personality from examination of his skull, and right before the execution, a phrenologist came to make a model of Lacenaire's head.

Lacenaire was concerned that his execution be handled just right. He wrote, "I make no secret of it—it would have been very disagreeable to me to have been dispatched by a provincial executioner."[13] Thus he was displeased to learn that he would meet his fate at seven in the morning, when he would have preferred noon to attract a larger audience.

On January 9, 1836, a cold and foggy day, Lacenaire and Avril were led to the guillotine at the Saint-Jacques barrier on the south side of Paris. Though the authorities had tried to keep the time and place of execution secret and had hastily erected the guillotine at night, a crowd of five hundred people appeared—as happened at almost every execution.

Avril went first, and the execution proceeded without incident. Then Lacenaire looked at the executioner and said: "Nothing simpler. I am not afraid."[14] But when he placed his head on the block, the blade made it only halfway down before becoming stuck in one of the grooved sides. The executioner hauled it up again, and as he did, Lacenaire looked up at the triangular blade. It was the last thing he saw.

Lacenaire had one last contribution to offer. On the eve of his death, he had spoken to a Dr. Lelut of the Bicêtre Prison. One of the scientific questions of the time was whether consciousness continued after the head was severed from the body. Did decapitation instantly end consciousness? This was just the sort of thing that interested Lacenaire, and he had promised that he would give a signal by winking—specifically, closing his left eye and leaving the right one open. Dr. Lelut stood over the basket that caught the severed head of the criminal, but could see no movement of the eyelids at all.

ii

People have used poisons to dispatch their enemies from ancient times. Through experience or experiment, several reliably fatal substances were identified, including mercury, antimony, hemlock, and henbane. But over the centuries the most popular poison has been arsenic. From ancient Greece to Renaissance Italy, arsenic murders were common. In seventeenth- and eighteenth-century France, white arsenic (the powder form) was even called *poudre de succession*, or "the inheritance powder," because of its common use.

The advantage of arsenic as a poison was that it was tasteless and colorless, so that it would be undetectable when mixed with food or drink. Also, the symptoms of the poison could be confused with cholera, a very prevalent disease at the time. Thus police and judges had no way to ascertain whether a victim had died of poison or something else. The only way to convict someone was to catch him or her in the act of administering the poison.

That began to change at the end of the eighteenth century. In 1787, the German chemist Johann Daniel Metzger discovered that when substances with arsenic content were heated over charcoal and a copper platter was held above the vapors, the platter became covered with a white material that was arsenous oxide.[15]

It was now possible for investigators to test for arsenic, though their methods didn't work well under certain conditions. It was found, for example, that traces of arsenic occur naturally in the human body. One man in particular was to help solve these problems: Mathieu Joseph Bonaventure Orfila, today remembered as the "father of toxicology." Born in Minorca in 1787, the young man developed a passion for chemistry and medicine. In 1811, he went to Paris, where he became a doctor of medicine and set up his own laboratory to study poisons. Two years later he published a two-volume work on toxicology that was highly regarded throughout Europe.

In his lab, Orfila experimented on animals to try to understand the chemistry of poisons, particularly arsenic. He showed how the poison passed through the stomach and intestine to other organs such as the liver, spleen, and kidney and finally permeated the nerves themselves,[16] demonstrating that even when no poison remained in the stomach, it would show up in other parts of the body. He further discovered that the arsenic was easier to detect when the animal tissue was charred.

Orfila still faced the problem posed by trace elements such as iron, zinc, and iodine, which occur naturally in the body and may conceal the presence of arsenic. The solution was found by James Marsh of the Royal British Arsenal, who developed the Marsh tube. Marsh's discovery was based on the principle that when either sulfuric acid or hydrochloric acid is mixed with any liquid containing arsenic and brought together with zinc, a chemical reaction results, producing the gas arsine. Marsh's device was a U-shaped glass tube in which the elements could be combined and a scientist could check for the presence of arsine.

Marsh published a paper on his device in 1836, and Orfila saw its potential immediately. Meanwhile, Orfila had improved on his earlier method of charring the sample with nitric acid to remove "animal matter." He also showed that traces of natural arsenic appeared only in the bones and therefore did not interfere with testing of body organs. In addition he realized that the ground where a body was buried might contain arsenic, which should be taken into account in cases of exhumation in determining whether arsenic poisoning had been the cause of death.

Orfila's work earned him enormous respect, and he was named dean of the Medical School of Paris in 1831. (One of his colleagues there was Marie-Guillaume-Alphonse Devergie, the first man to use a microscope in practical forensic pathology.) For his part, Orfila would make history as the first expert to use the science of toxicology to convict a person of murder.

Marie Lafarge developed delusions of grandeur at an early age. Born Marie Capelle in 1816, she was the daughter of one of Napoleon's favorite officers. Her maternal grandmother was a natural daughter of Philippe-Égalité, duc d'Orléans, whose legitimate son Philippe, the so-called Citizen King, had ruled France when Marie was a teenager. Though she could claim a noble lineage, Marie never became securely established in the aristocratic society that she aspired to. After the deaths of her parents when she was a teenager, she was shuffled between two aunts.

Still, Marie was educated in fine schools in Paris, where she learned the proper etiquette and made friends of high social standing. She grew to be a striking young woman, tall and slender, with a porcelain complexion and jet black hair. Despite her intelligence, Marie lived in a fantasy world of ideal love, turning down one proposal of marriage by saying it was impossible for her to marry a "commoner."

When Marie was twenty-four, one of her aunts decided it was time to marry her off and placed her name with the De Foy Matrimonial Agency in Paris, which specialized in pairing well-born men and women. She got a response. The man, Charles Joseph

Pouch Lafarge, claimed to be a wealthy ironmaster with a huge estate, Le Glandier, in Corrèze in southwestern France. Drawings showed a beautiful château that looked out over a splendid landscape. Marie fantasized herself as the mistress of her own private realm.

When she met Lafarge, reality began to set in. He was a large, crude twenty-eight-year-old man with little education and no culture. What Marie did not know was that he was a bit of a fraud as well. He had misrepresented his wealth, hoping for a woman with a large dowry to invest in his iron business, and Marie's dowry of 100,000 francs looked very good to him.

Marie tried to back out of the arrangement, but her aunt insisted. In August 1839, within two weeks of their first meeting, the two were married. Marie set out for Le Glandier with her new husband and her servant Clémentine. On the trip to the estate, Joseph's manners offended Marie. He ate noisily with his hands, ignoring napkins and licking his fingers. When she tried to engage him in conversation, he exclaimed, "For God's sake, stop talking!"[17]

As Marie reached the château, she experienced another shock. Le Glandier was a seedy, dilapidated wreck. Inside, conditions were even worse. Rats scampered over the floor, and the smell of decay and animal excrement attacked Marie's refined nose. She was so horrified that she locked herself in her room with Clémentine and refused to see anyone. She sent her maid with a letter to Charles, begging him to let her leave, promising he could keep the dowry and her possessions and even agreeing to take the blame for the failure of the marriage. She also threatened to poison herself with arsenic if he would not release her — a threat that would later take on sinister significance.

Charles's mother persuaded her son to make concessions. He agreed to allow Marie to renovate the estate and begin a round of social activities. Her piano was sent from home and she received a subscription to the Paris newspapers. Finally, her husband would not claim his "marital privileges."[18] For a short time she was mollified. But she soon found out that there was no money to clean up the estate, and no opportunities for her to have a social life in this place. Marie began to plot another way to escape from her husband: murder.

She proceeded with caution and hid her embittered state. In letters to her aunts in Paris, she described a happy life. "All my new family are delightful and kind to me. I am admired. I am adored," she wrote.[19]

In December, learning that her husband was taking a trip to Paris, she persuaded him that they should both make out wills, naming each other as beneficiaries. He agreed, and Marie gave Charles part of her dowry for expenses and wrote letters of introduction to powerful friends who might invest in his business. But unknown to Marie, Charles was a cheat as well as a boor—he secretly made out another will leaving all his possessions to his mother.

Right after Charles set out on his journey, Marie ordered some arsenic by mail from a druggist named Eyssartier in a neighboring town. She claimed that she needed it to use against the rats that infested the château. Then Marie asked her mother-in-law to make some cakes to send Charles for his Christmas holiday in Paris. Marie personally wrapped the package, including a small portrait of herself with an affectionate letter.

When Charles received the present on December 18, he found a single large cake, instead of the six small ones that his mother had baked. Not suspecting anything, he had a piece of it. Within a short time he began vomiting and suffered from violent cramps. Servants found him writhing with pain on the floor of his hotel room. A doctor was called, but he could not stop the vomiting. The diagnosis was extreme dysentery. Charles slowly recovered but could not travel until January 3, when he telegraphed his family that he was coming home.

The day before Charles arrived, Marie ordered more arsenic from Eyssartier, telling him there were many rats. When the family physician, a Dr. Bardon, came to examine Charles, she asked him for arsenic as well. Though Marie personally tended to him,

Charles did not improve and even seemed to get worse. As his condition declined, members of the Lafarge household became suspicious of Marie. Some claimed to have seen her put white powder in his food. When she was confronted with the accusation that she was trying to murder her husband, she called a groom named Alfred, who claimed that he had personally beaten all the arsenic Marie had ordered into a paste, which he had stuffed into the nooks and crannies of the château to kill the rats.

On January 13, a new doctor, named Lespinasse, was called to the estate to look at the now desperately ill patient. He was told that many in the household believed that M. Lafarge was being poisoned by his wife. After examining him, the doctor concurred. In his opinion, Charles Lafarge "is indeed being poisoned to death — all the symptoms show it. But it is too late to save him. He is a dying man."[20] The diagnosis was correct: Charles died the next day.

Marie's mother-in-law called her to the bedside of the corpse and accused her of killing Charles. Marie remained calm, answering the accusations only with a stony stare before retiring to her room. A few hours later, Mme. Lafarge called the police to the château. The local magistrate, named Moran, arrived on the fifteenth and listened to the accusations. He took evidence that members of the household had collected — the remains of food that Charles had eaten, including eggnog, soup, and sugar water. So suspicious had the servants been that they had even preserved some of Charles's vomit for examination.

The doctors who had attended Charles in his last days were called in to do an autopsy. They removed the stomach, tying the ends together so that its contents were saved for examination, before the rest of the body was buried. After testing, the doctors declared that they had found arsenic in the stomach of the deceased, as well as in all the foods that Charles had ingested. The only substance that did not show arsenic was the rat paste that Alfred the groom had turned over to them. Magistrate Moran thought that he had enough evidence to charge Marie with murder. On

January 25, she was arrested and taken to the jail at the town of Brives.

The crime became a cause célèbre. Marie declared that she was being persecuted by antiroyalists because of her links to the royal family. Throughout the country, people took up sides for or against her. Some saw her as a saint, a political martyr because of her royal blood. Other people saw her as a liar who had killed her husband to avoid having sex with him. Not until the Dreyfus case of the 1890s would a trial so divide the country.

Marie received more than six thousand letters in prison, most of them showing support. Some of them, often heavily cologned, were proposals of marriage. Others promised support in her legal defense. Money poured in, as well as such lavish gifts as perfumes, wines, lingerie, and expensive foodstuffs. Marie clearly enjoyed her celebrity, fantasizing that she was the Marie Antoinette of her time. Writing her memoirs in prison, she portrayed herself as "the poor reviled one."[21]

Her trial began on September 3, 1840, in the town of Tulle in the Dordogne region. Though it was a hot day, gendarmes had to be stationed to keep back the crowds. All the inns in the vicinity were filled with journalists and curiosity seekers who had arrived from all over Europe. The prosecutor opened what he saw as a very strong case. He described Marie's unhappiness with the marriage and read to the jury the letter she had written Charles on her arrival at Le Glandier, emphasizing her reference to arsenic. He linked her purchases of arsenic to Charles's bouts of illness: Her first purchase came only a few days before she had sent her cake to Charles in Paris. Her second was one day before he returned home, where he steadily grew worse after eating food that she fed him. One of the most damning pieces of evidence seemed to be the chemical analysis of the so-called rat paste, which turned out to be bicarbonate of soda. The prosecutor drew the conclusion that Marie had substituted bicarbonate for the arsenic when she gave the material to the groom and used the real arsenic to poison her husband. When Marie was asked why the "arsenic" she had given to the groom was harmless, she cheerfully answered, "Now I understand why the rats continued coming. Bicarbonate would never stop them."[22]

But Marie's high-powered Paris lawyer, Maître Paillet, was ready to refute the prosecution. In Paris, he had shown Orfila copies of the autopsy and chemical reports, and Orfila picked holes in them. The local doctors in Brives were using outdated methods and were inept to boot. During one of their analyses, the test tube had exploded. Paillet grilled the doctors about their knowledge of the newest developments in toxicology, exposing them as woefully behind the times. He asked the doctors if they had ever heard of the Marsh apparatus, developed just four years earlier; they had not.

Paillet called his own experts—three noted chemists from Limoges. They were asked to use Marsh's method of measuring the amount of arsenic in Charles's stomach. The chemists reported the results of their tests on February 5, dealing a severe blow to the prosecution's case. The conclusion was that "in the materials presented to us no trace of arsenic is contained."[23] The court record noted, "These final remarks produced an indescribable commotion in the court . . . Madame Lefarge, clasping her hands, raised her eyes to heaven."[24] Paillet "wept tears of triumph."[25] Couriers rushed to the nearest telegraph in Bordeaux to spread the word throughout France. The news elated Marie's supporters everywhere.

The prosecutor was not ready to give up. He pointed out that Paillet had referred to Orfila as France's leading expert on poisons, but Orfila had not personally examined the evidence in the case. The counsel for the defense had often said that chemists could make errors. Did this not also apply to the chemists from Limoges? The prosecutor had learned that Orfila had stated that in case of arsenic poisoning, arsenic is not always found in the stomach, but in other organs, such as the liver. Had the Limoges experts tested anything but the stomach? As it turned out, they had not. The prosecutor insisted that Orfila himself should be called on to testify. Perhaps this move was one of desperation, for he could not have known what Orfila would say.

The defense attorney had little choice but to assent. Orfila was asked to come to Tulle, and he agreed. Lafarge's body was exhumed and samples of other organs were taken from it. (The stomach was found in the drawer of a court clerk, where it had decayed considerably.) Nonetheless, Orfila set up the Marsh apparatus and set to work under the eyes of several of the other experts who had testified. He continued through the night of September 13 and appeared the next morning before a hushed court to give his opinion. Orfila declared that there "is arsenic in the body of Lafarge." [26] Anticipating objections, he said that the poison did not come from the reagents with which he tested the material, nor from the earth around the coffin, which he had also tested. He further testified that the arsenic he found was not the arsenic compound that was naturally found in the human body. Only the bones, the scientist explained, have minute amounts of arsenic. The presiding judge asked the key question: "Do you consider the amount of arsenic obtained by you to be sufficient to indicate murder by poisoning?" [27]

Orfila went further than that. He declared that considering the victim's symptoms, there was no doubt he died from the administration of arsenic. The jury found Marie guilty on the toxicological evidence. She collapsed and had to be carried to her cell, where she sobbed for two days.

Unswayed by Marie's noble lineage, the judge sentenced her to hard labor for life and public exposure in the pillory at Tulle. Marie's appeal was rejected, but King Louis-Philippe reduced his cousin's sentence to life imprisonment.

Sent to Montpelier Prison, Marie corresponded with Alexandre Dumas and wrote her memoirs, along with a tragedy, *The Lost Woman*. In 1852, after she contracted tuberculosis, Napoleon III released her from jail. She died six months later in a spa in the Pyrenees, without ever having confessed to the murder. Her memoirs merely added to the legend—which many still believed at her death—that she was a martyr.

The Lafarge case was a milestone in criminological history, establishing the standard for expert scientific testimony. Chemists would subsequently develop tests for other kinds of poisons, and trial attorneys for both sides would continue to call dueling experts, as they do to this day.

iii

During the Christmas season of 1869, human remains began turning up all over Paris. Body parts wrapped in packages appeared in different parts of the city—a human thigh bone was discovered in the rue Jacob, and a thigh with flesh still attached, wrapped in a sweater, was pulled out of the Seine. These gruesome discoveries were taken to the Paris mortuary, where it was concluded that they came from the same person. But there was no clue to the identity of the victim of such a hideous crime.

On December 19, the proprietor of a riverside laundry near the Quai Valmy told the police that he had seen a short, stout man with a mustache taking pieces of meat from a large hamper and scattering them in the Seine. On being asked what he was doing, the man claimed that he was "baiting the river" so that he could catch fish on the following day. The laundryman recalled only that the man was short and wore a long coat and tall hat.

In January, the owner of Lampon's Eating House, a small restaurant in the rue Princesse a few blocks south of the Seine, noticed a bad odor coming from his well. Customers started to complain that the water tasted foul. On investigation, the owner fished up a smelly package wrapped in cloth. When he cut it open, he was horrified to find the lower portion of a human leg.

He went to the local police to report his discovery and found a friend, Sergeant Ringué, who came to the restaurant to view the latest ghastly find. The discovery reminded Ringué of a man that he had stopped and questioned late on the evening of December 22. The man had been carrying a large hamper and a package that he said contained some hams. He told Ringué that he had just arrived from Nantes and was carrying his luggage to his room on the rue Princesse. Ringué had let the man go on his way but now regretted that he had not looked inside the package. He further recalled that the man was short and wore a tall hat.

The young policeman went to his superior, Gustave Macé, the police *commissaire* of the district. Then unknown, Macé was on a career path that would, ten years later, bring him to the top of the Sûreté. Now he was an eager young man, fascinated with his work and very ambitious. Macé went to the restaurant and discovered another parcel in the well, which he fished out with difficulty. Like the first, the package was wrapped in black calico, sewn shut. Within lay a second severed lower leg, encased in a drab cotton stocking on which was stitched in red thread the initial *B* with a small cross on each side of it. This was Macé's first clue. He noticed that the sewing was very fine, probably done by a professional.

The first pathologist to do a medical examination on the legs concluded that they were those of a woman and that the killer had not been very adept in the dismembering. He estimated that the legs had been in the well for about a month. The well was emptied, but no further body parts were found. Next, Macé, like Canler trying to trace Lacenaire, started the tedious work of going through a list of eighty-four females reported missing in the previous six months. Unfortunately, he found none who could be connected to the embroidered stocking.

Then Dr. Auguste Tardieu took a look at the evidence. A former student of Orfila's, he was now the foremost forensic physician in France. After a thorough examination, he declared that Macé was wasting his time looking for a woman. "These remains," he said, "are those of a man advanced in years. . . . The feet are larger than those of a woman. The dismemberment has been done skillfully by a cleaver or chopper. The cuts were made soon after death. There has been a considerable effusion of blood. I observe also that there is a clearly marked scar on one leg, only recently healed. But without the head it will not be easy to establish the identity, and the murderer appears to have taken good care to conceal that most important piece of evidence." [28]

This information put Macé on the right track. He was now convinced that the other human parts recently discovered in Paris were part of the same victim whose legs were in the well at Lampon's. He believed that the murderer must live near the rue Princesse; the man questioned by Ringué must have been frightened into dumping his incriminating burden into the well instead of taking it to the Seine, and he had to have been sufficiently familiar with the area to do so. The concierge of the building where Lampon's was located, an old woman, told Macé that an outsider could get to the well only if he knew about a small button on the outer door that worked a string latch.

Macé was still looking for someone who was skilled at sewing. When he asked if any tailor had ever lived in the building, the concierge told him about a Mlle. Dard, a seamstress who had lived there but was now singing at café concerts. She had done piecework for a tailor who visited often. When Macé located Dard, a pretty young woman, she gave him the name of her tailor friend, Pierre Voirbo. He used to live nearby in the rue Mazarine, but very recently he had married and moved away. Her description of him matched that given by Sergeant Ringué and the witness who had seen someone scattering meat into the Seine. Dard suggested that Mme. Bodasse, the aunt of one of Voirbo's friends, might know were Voirbo was.

Inspector Macé noted the matching initial *B* and had Mme. Bodasse brought for questioning. She said she had last seen Voirbo when he had gone to a concert with her nephew, Désiré Bodasse, who lived in the rue Dauphine. That was on December 13, a month earlier, and she hadn't seen Désiré since, but that did not worry her, for he was eccentric and sometimes disappeared for periods of time. Macé asked her to describe Voirbo. "He was short," she said, "and generally wore a long overcoat and a tall hat." [29]

On a hunch, Macé took Mme. Bodasse to the morgue to show her the stocking with the initial *B*. Shocked, she said it had belonged to her nephew. She herself had sewn the *B* and the two crosses on the stocking. She identified her nephew's leg by a scar which had come from a fall on the jagged edge of a bottle. Macé was now sure he knew the name of the victim, and he had a good idea who his killer was.

Macé went to Bodasse's apartment at 50, rue Dauphine. No one answered his knock, but the concierge claimed that he had seen light in the room each night. Indeed, after gaining entrance to the rooms, Macé found a candle still flickering, making him think that someone had tried to make it seem as though Bodasse was still living there. There was another notable absence: Mme. Bodasse had told Macé that her nephew had a strongbox containing valuables hidden in a secret compartment of his old bureau. It was gone. Further search turned up a slip of paper hidden in the case of a silver watch; it contained a list of numbers of Italian securities. These could easily be negotiated, for they were payable to the bearer.

Macé assigned two policemen to keep watch over Bodasse's rooms while he proceeded to Voirbo's old apartment on the rue Mazarine. The concierge of the building confirmed that Voirbo and Bodasse were very good friends, though she did think it strange that Bodasse had not been at Voirbo's wedding. She did recall that the two men had argued about Bodasse's stinginess. Voirbo had been angry when his friend had refused to lend him ten thousand francs for the wedding. Most interesting of all was the story told by Voirbo's former maid. When she had arrived to clean his apartment on the seventeenth of December, she found that it had already been scrubbed down—some of the floor tiles were still wet. She was surprised, for Voirbo had not been very tidy and never cleaned his own room. When she asked him why he had done so this time, he claimed that he had spilled some kerosene on the floor accidentally. Even more incriminating was the fact that when he was about to move to a new place, he paid his remaining rent with an Italian stock certificate. Macé was able to determine that it bore one of the serial numbers from the list found in Bodasse's watchcase.

The police on duty at Bodasse's apartment reported that nothing unusual had happened except that Voirbo had dropped by to see his friend. It turned out that Voirbo was a police spy who pretended to be an anarchist and attended meetings of radicals to report on their activities. The policemen, not knowing that he was in fact a suspect in the murder, accepted him as one of their own and told him what they were doing in Bodasse's place.

Annoyed that Voirbo must now know that he was a suspect, Macé decided to call him in and confront him. He saw before him a short, stout man with a high hat and long coat. Voirbo was very calm and confident and answered questions precisely. He explained that he had been worried about his old friend and that as a member of the secret political police, he had used his contacts to investigate his disappearance. His chief suspect, he told Macé, was a butcher named Rifer. Rifer was a gambler and heavy drinker who hung out in low-class dives. Macé was not deceived, but he agreed that Voirbo should keep up his surveillance of Rifer. In fact, Voirbo was pushing the hapless Rifer to heavier drinking; the butcher soon suffered a bout of delerium tremens and was taken to an asylum, where he died the same night.

As soon as Voirbo learned of the butcher's death, he hurried to Macé to report. He was astonished when Macé placed him under arrest. A search of Voirbo's pockets revealed that Macé was just in time. Voirbo had a false passport and a ticket for steamship passage to the United States on the following day. He was to have left for the port of Le Havre that very afternoon.

Taken before the *juge d'instruction,* Voirbo was defiant. He refused to be photographed, making faces so that capturing an image was difficult. Macé knew that he was dealing with a clever man and went looking for more proof. He visited Voirbo's young wife, Adélia, who had brought a dowry of fifteen thousand francs to her marriage. Pale and delicate, she struck Macé as naive. Before meeting Voirbo, she had planned to enter a convent and become a nun. Expressing shock that her husband had been arrested, she told Macé that the dowry and some Italian stocks belonging to Voirbo were kept in a strongbox. But when Macé asked her to open it, she discovered that it was empty. Searching the premises, the detective found in Voirbo's workshop items that seemed strange for a tailor: huge sharpened shears, heavy flatirons, a metal mallet, and a large butcher's cleaver. There was also an old iron spoon that had been used for melting lead. Finally, Macé found some cord very much like that which had been used to tie the bundles found in Lampon's well.

Voirbo's cellar yielded more. The detective noticed that the bung on one of the two casks of wine was higher than on the other. He removed it and discovered a string attached. He drew up from the barrel a tin cylinder. When he broke it open, he found the Italian securities for which Bodasse had been killed. There was only one missing—the one Voirbo had used to make his final rent payment on his former room.

Macé had a fair idea of where and how Bodasse had been murdered; now he set out to re-create the scene of the crime to prove his hunch. Scouring the crime scene as a source of clues was one of Vidocq's ideas. Later, Bertillon would take extensive photographs of crime scenes and measure them as carefully as he measured suspect's faces. But Macé's experiment produced its own spectacular result, one that made such examinations a regular part of the investigation of violent crimes. Collecting Voirbo and several officers from the station, he took them to Voirbo's former room in the rue Mazarine. With the help of the concierge, Macé arranged it exactly as it had been when Voirbo lived there. Given the small space, he realized that Voirbo would have had to dismember the body on the table in the middle of the room. He noticed that the tiled floor had a sharp slope that ended under the bed.

With a theatrical flourish, Macé picked up a carafe of water. "I notice a slope in the floor. Now, if a body had been cut up on a table here in the center of the room, the effusion of blood would have been great, and the fluid must have followed this slope. Any other fluid thrown down here must follow the same direction. I will empty this jug on the floor and see what happens!" [30] With that, he poured out the water on the tiles. Everyone present watched it gather in a pool beneath the bed. Voirbo remained tight-lipped as Macé ordered that the tiles there be removed. As each tile came up, dried bloodstains could clearly be seen on the sides and underneath.

Realizing that the game was up, Voirbo broke down and confessed. He had needed money to show his fiancée in order to prove that he would be an equal partner in the marriage. Bodasse was a miser who hoarded his money, and he refused to lend it to Voirbo. On December 13, 1868, Voirbo had lured Bodasse to his apartment, battered him unconscious with a flatiron, and then slit his throat. Afterward, dressed only in his underwear, Voirbo had chopped up the body. Later he wrapped it and threw pieces into the Seine from the Pont de la Concorde. Though he thought that he had cleaned up the mess thoroughly, he had failed to notice the recess beneath the bed. After sewing the legs in calico bags, he had indeed dropped them in the well on rue Princesse. To make sure the head would sink in the water, he had melted some lead and poured it into the mouth. Afterward, he had moved to the rue Lamartine and in January 1869 had married Adélia.

Ultimately, Voirbo cheated the guillotine: while he was in jail awaiting trial, he cut his throat with a razor that had been hidden in a loaf of bread. No one knew where he got it. Perhaps some of his friends in the secret police had given it to him as a hint.

It was the detective, not the criminal, who emerged as a celebrity from this case. Macé wrote an autobiography in which he told how he walked alone at night in the most dangerous parts of the city, satisfying his "desire to see all and know all."[31] Macé even established his own *musée criminal,* or museum of criminality, where he displayed artifacts from actual crimes, including murder weapons.

He first reached fame with his brilliant solution to the Voirbo case and indeed devoted an entire book, *Mon premier crime,* to it, continuing in the tradition established by Vidocq. Macé's writing shows the clear influence of Edgar Allan Poe, indicating that the Paris police were well aware of detective fiction. Macé makes

Voirbo sound particularly like one of Poe's characters in describing what happened after he hit Bodasse with a flatiron:

> Not a sound escaped him. His head sank on to the
> table, his arms hung down inert. I was astonished, and
> satisfied with my strength and skill.
>
> Then, blowing out the light, I opened the window
> and pulled the shutters to. In silence and darkness
> I listened to discover if he stirred. But I heard nothing,
> except his blood which fell on the floor, drop by drop!
> This monotonous drop, drop, drop, made my flesh
> creep. Still I kept on listening, listening. All of a sudden
> I heard a deep sigh, and something like a creaking of
> the chair. Désiré was moving, he was not dead! Sup-
> pose he were to cry out. This thought restored all my
> presence of mind to me. Lighting a small lamp, I saw
> the body had moved sideways, he was then still liv-
> ing. He was certainly no longer in a condition to make
> himself heard, to call for help, but his death-agony
> might be spun out and I did not want to see him suf-
> fer a long while. I therefore took a razor, approached
> him from behind and placed my hand under the chin
> of my ex-friend. Yielding to my pressure, the head rose
> up and then fell backwards. The lamp was shining full
> on his blood-smeared face. His round eyes were not
> yet lifeless—for a moment they fastened on the blade
> of the razor I was holding above him, and suddenly as-
> sumed such an expression of terror, that my heart beat
> violently. It was necessary to put an end to it. The same
> way a barber does when about to shave a customer,
> I pressed the blade just below the Adam's apple, where
> the beard commences, and with a vigorous sweep
> I drew the blade from left to right. It entirely disap-
> peared in the flesh, the head fell lifeless on the back
> of the chair.[32]

iv

L'Affaire Gouffé started as a missing persons case. On Saturday, July 27, 1889, a man reported that his brother-in law, Toussaint-Augustin Gouffé, a Parisian court bailiff, had disappeared. Gouffé, a middle-aged widower with three daughters, had last been seen on the twenty-sixth. The inspector on duty did not think the matter was terribly serious. Gouffé was a known philanderer and might just have been on some amorous adventure. But when he was still missing on the thirtieth, the case was referred to Marie-François Goron, the chief of the Sûreté.

Goron was a small, fair, asthmatic Breton with a waxed mustache and pince-nez. He could be brusque in manner, but he was passionate about hunting criminals. Like Vidocq, he commanded a troop of "beaters" who posed as ex-convicts while roaming the dens of the Paris underworld. Goron had also developed new techniques for questioning criminals. He subjected suspects to alternating light and dark cells, and alternated bread and water with sumptuous meals. (His interrogation rooms were called "Monsieur Goron's cookshop.")[33] He went so far as to promise suspects women if they talked. These techniques proved successful, and Goron took full credit, for he was a genius at garnering publicity; newspapers frequently ran flattering stories about him.

Goron would later write memoirs that he described as "social photographs that, without retouching, by their unadorned simplicity and horror, conveyed the truth."[34] Contrary to his assertion, his accounts came close to crossing the line of voyeurism, confusing the literary and popular with the real. Perhaps that was not too surprising, given his claim that his memoirs were an attempt to "raise the roofs of the houses of the capital" in order to see the "human perversity" found there.[35]

Taking over the case of the missing bailiff, Goron visited Gouffé's office on the rue Montmartre. He discovered burned matches in front of the safe, which had not been broken into. A sum of fourteen thousand francs was found hidden behind some papers. The hall porter told Goron that a man had gone upstairs on the twenty-sixth, the night of Gouffé's disappearance. Though the man opened the door with a key and stayed there for a while, he was a stranger whom the porter had never seen.

Looking into the missing man's background, Goron found that he had a prodigious sex life—he visited many women regularly and was known to have a taste for kinky sex. Thus the suspect list included husbands who might have had a motive for murdering him. Paris newspapers regaled readers with stories of Gouffé's escapades.

The bailiff's finances were in order, so it seemed unlikely he had run away—particularly leaving fourteen thousand francs behind. Suicide also seemed unlikely in a person with such a lust for life. Goron sent descriptions of Gouffé to all the police stations in France in the hope that someone had seen him. He was a slim man, five feet nine inches tall, with chestnut hair and a carefully cropped beard. Goron also asked his assistants to look through out-of-town newspapers for stories about missing bodies. His curiosity was aroused when he read that on August 13, a road mender in Millery, a small town near Lyons, had followed a bad smell to a canvas sack hidden in some bushes. He almost fainted from the stench when he opened it and found the body of a dark-bearded man. Goron sent a query to Lyons but was told that the dead man's physical characteristics were different from Gouffé's. The Lyons police made it clear that they did not want any help from the capital.

On August 14, the Lyons coroner, Dr. Paul Bernard, conducted an autopsy. The advanced stage of decomposition of the body made it difficult to study, but Bernard came to the conclusion that the victim had died from strangulation. He estimated that the age of the man had been between thirty-five and forty and that his hair and beard were black.

A few days later, a traveler's trunk was found on the banks of the river. The odor inside marked it as the container in which the body had been transported. Two labels indicated that the trunk had been shipped from Paris to Lyons-Perrache on July 27, with the year indistinct but thought to be 1888.

Goron, not trusting Dr. Bernard's findings, sent Gouffé's brother-in-law, named Landry, to Lyons with a Sûreté officer to take a look at the corpse. The Lyons morgue was on a barge anchored in the Rhône River, and a hideous stench arose from it. Landry, taken aboard, held a handkerchief to his nose and took only a quick glance. He said that the corpse was not Gouffé, for it had black hair, much darker than his brother-in-law's had been.

Goron was not to be deterred. He continued his investigation in Paris. In September an informer told him that on July 25, Gouffé had been seen with a lowlife named Michel Eyraud and Eyraud's mistress, Gabrielle Bompard. The couple had vanished from Paris on July 27, the same day the bailiff had disappeared. Goron assigned men to look for the pair, but without success.

Goron further investigated the labels that were on the trunk in Lyons, checking the baggage shipment registry for July 27 in both 1888 and 1889. In the latter year, a trunk weighing 105 kilograms had left Paris, bound for Lyons. He was certain that the Millery corpse had been transported from Paris in the trunk, but he still had to establish that it was Gouffé.

Goron himself arrived at Lyons and talked to Dr. Bernard, the local coroner, who showed him a strand of the dead man's hair. It was indeed black, but after Goron dipped it in distilled water and washed away the blood and grime, it came out chestnut. Goron demanded that the corpse be exhumed from the cemetery and sent to Jean Alexandre Eugène Lacassagne, professor of forensic medicine at the University of Lyons.

When Lacassagne was called in on this case, he was forty-six years old and had already made several contributions to the field of forensic medicine. He was in fact to become known as the "father of forensic science." As a young man he had served as an army physician in North Africa, which gave him a chance to study bullet wounds. He also noted the importance of tattoos in identifying bodies.

Lacassagne combined the scientific skills of a physician with the curiosity of a policeman. He was to use both throughout his career. In 1880 he founded the Department of Forensic Science at Lyons University, where he liked to remind his students, "One must know how to doubt."[36]

Doubt was distinct from ignorance. Lacassagne had started his career when morgues and sometimes even cemeteries had bell-pulls for supposedly dead people to yank in case they were still alive and had only been in a coma when death was pronounced. The normal test for life was to place a mirror or feather in front of the mouth of the body, to see if the mirror would steam or the feather move, but these methods were by no means infallible.

Lacassagne studied the significance of blotches on the body that appeared after death, deducing that blood collects at the lowest points of the body after circulation stops. If the body was moved within a certain time after death, the blood was still motile and the blotches could move, but after about twenty hours, the discoloration was permanent. He also noted that the body did not always cool at a given rate; earlier observers had generalized that the body temperature dropped one degree centigrade per hour during the first hours after death, but Lacassagne found that there were variations depending on the temperature of the environment. He also studied the onset and duration of rigor mortis, the stiffening and then relaxation of the body after life ceased. Such information was helpful in ascertaining the time of death.

Lacassagne was also the first forensic scientist to show that a bullet could be matched to a particular gun. A few months before being called in on the Gouffé case, he had studied under a microscope a bullet that had been removed from the body of a murder victim named Echallier. Lacassagne noticed that the bullet had seven longitudinal lines, or striae, and theorized that they were the result of rifling—the grooves that were made inside gun barrels to cause the bullet to spin and thus move in a more accurate path. In the Echallier case, when the suspect's gun was fired, it produced the same seven lines as were found on the test bullet. On that basis the suspect was convicted of murder. The science of ballistics was born.

Nevertheless, when the exhumed body found at Millery was delivered to Lacassagne's laboratory at Lyons University, he could not have been optimistic. Not only was it in a state of advanced decay, but as he told his students, "A bungled autopsy cannot be revised."[37] Though Dr. Bernard had been a student of Lacassagne's, he certainly had botched his attempt. Lacassagne decided to concentrate his examination on the bones and the hair. The work was gruesome, for the pathologist did not have the advantages of refrigeration or latex gloves. He plunged his hands into the putrid, maggoty flesh, cutting and scraping it away until the bones were exposed. The skeleton told him a lot. He found a deformation on the right knee that would have caused the man to walk with a limp. He discovered that the victim's right ankle had been injured as well. Family members confirmed that Gouffé had walked with a limp owing to a childhood accident.

Lacassagne agreed with the earlier pathologist's conclusion that the cause of death had been strangulation, because there was clear damage to the thyroid cartilage. He thought, however, that it might have been manual strangulation, rather than strangulation by ligature or rope. He also disagreed with Dr. Bernard's estimate of the victim's age. Bernard had believed that the man was no older than forty, but Lacassagne put his age closer to fifty, which matched the forty-nine-year-old Gouffé. Lacassagne had based his estimate on the corpse's teeth. Dental forensics were in as primitive a state as dentistry, and Lacassagne's achievement here was another breakthrough: he judged the wear of the dentin in the teeth, the amount of tartar at the roots, and the thinness of the roots themselves to produce his estimate.

Lacassagne clinched the identification with a hair from one of Gouffé's hairbrushes. He compared it under the microscope with a hair from the corpse, checking for hair-dye residue, which came up negative. Then he measured the thickness of the hairs and found them identical. Certain in his conclusion, Lacassagne dramatically addressed Inspector Goron: "I present you with Monsieur Gouffé!"[38]

"The Corpse Has Been Identified," trumpeted the Paris newspaper *L'Intransigeant* on its front page the following day, November 22. The newspaper ran two illustrations side by side—one showing the decomposed head of the corpse and the other the face of Gouffé in life. "It Is He," the headline crowed. Other newspapers treated their readers to the gory details and stressed the glory of French forensic medicine. *Le Petit Journal* paid tribute to Dr. Lacassagne's skills, concluding, "The solving of the mystery of Millery demonstrates that French medicine can show criminology the way to great progress in the future. Identification of the Millery corpse is a milestone in history."[39]

Goron was content for now to let the spotlight shine on someone else and to take up the next stage in the case: finding who killed Gouffé. The brother-in-law was now shown police photos of several known criminals. Goron was pleased when he identified pictures of Michel Eyraud and Gabrielle Bompard as the pair previously seen with Gouffé. On his return to Paris, Goron had found yet another witness who linked the lovers to the murdered man. But Eyraud and Bompard seemed to have dropped out of sight.

Goron was creative in his search. He hired a carpenter to make an exact copy of the rotten trunk that had been used to take the body to Lyons. Put on display at the Paris morgue, the trunk attracted some thirty-five thousand curious viewers in the first three days. Photographs of it were sent around the world. The Gouffé family offered a reward for information, and letters poured in from all over France. Soon Goron heard from a man in London who claimed that a Frenchman and his daughter, later identified as Eyraud and Bompard, had lived in his lodgings and before departing had bought a trunk like the one shown in the newspapers.

A police spy in Paris gave Goron more important details. Michel Eyraud was an army deserter and a small-time crook and, though married, had taken up with a prostitute, Gabrielle Bompard. The two of them operated the traditional badger scheme: Bompard would take a client to her apartment, and after a suitable amount of time, Eyraud would burst in, pretending to be her husband. He would threaten the john, who was usually ready to pay to get out of the situation.

The con worked well, but Eyraud was a greedy man. One of Bompard's clients was Toussaint-Augustin Gouffé, who had foolishly let her know that he kept large sums of money in his office. Eyraud, Goron's spy reported, had decided to kill Gouffé and take the money.

Despite massive newspaper coverage and the fact that photos of the pair were sent to police throughout Europe and North America, they managed to keep one step ahead of the law. They reached San Francisco, where Bompard met another man who fell for her charms. She ran off with the American after telling him that Eyraud planned to kill her. Jealous, Eyraud followed the pair, tracking them from city to city.

It was not until January 1890 that Goron firmly connected with the culprits—not through detective skills, but by sheer luck. A resentful Eyraud sent him a letter, protesting his innocence and putting all the blame on "that serpent Gabrielle," whom he accused of the murder. "The great trouble with her," he wrote, "is that she is such a liar and also has a dozen lovers after her." [40]

Even more astonishingly, a few days later, Gabrielle Bompard herself appeared in Goron's office. Small, delicate, and well-dressed, she was accompanied by her new lover, who believed that she had been victimized by Eyraud. She told a racy story of greed, sex, and murder. Gouffé had been killed during an assignation at a room on the rue Tronson du Coudray south of the boulevard Haussmann. Bompard admitted that she had lured him there, but claimed that she had not been directly involved in the murder and did not know that Eyraud planned to kill the bailiff. Nevertheless, she was placed under arrest.

After Bertillon took her facial and body measurements for identification purposes, Bompard was subjected to "Monsieur Goron's cookshop" treatment—being kept hungry and questioned day and night. Female police spies were placed in her cell to win her confidence. Eventually, she was taken to the crime scene, where the concierge immediately recognized her, causing Bompard to confess.

Bompard explained that she had brought Gouffé to her room on July 26, 1889. While she was getting him ready for a lovemaking session, she playfully tied the cord of her dressing gown around his neck. Eyraud, hiding behind a curtain, sprang into action. Using a series of pulleys he had set up earlier, he yanked the hapless victim into the air, but when the cord broke, Eyraud finished him off, strangling Gouffé with his hands.

Eyraud searched the victim's pockets for the key to his office and stuffed the dead body into the trunk. He then coolly returned home to his wife, leaving Bompard to spend the night with the corpse. Goron, curious, asked her what the experience had been like. Her response was chilling. "You'd never guess what a funny idea came into my head! You see it was not very pleasant for me being thus *tête-à-tête* with a corpse, I couldn't sleep. So I thought what fun it would be to go into the street and pick up some respectable gentleman from the provinces. I'd bring him up to the room, and just as he was beginning to enjoy himself say, 'Would you like to see a bailiff?' open the trunk suddenly and, before he could recover from his horror, run out into the street and fetch the police. Just think what a fool the respectable gentleman would have looked when the officers came!"[41]

The next morning, Eyraud had gone off to the bailiff's office, which he searched frantically. Even though the police had no trouble finding the money later, Eyraud was unsuccessful. When he heard the footsteps of a guard in the hall, he fled through a window. He returned to Bompard's room, where the two made passionate love on the floor next to the trunk that held the corpse. In confessing to this, Bompard insisted that Eyraud had forced her to do it.

The next day the pair rented a carriage and set off for Millery, where they dumped the body in the woods and left the trunk on the banks of the Rhône River. From there they fled to Marseilles and then to England, where they took a ship to New York.

Bompard's spectacular confession set off a feeding frenzy in the Paris press. Parisians rushed to the rue Tronson du Coudray, where the landlady charged admission to view the murder scene. When Bompard was taken back to Lyons to reenact the dumping of the body, the crowds trying to watch were so large that cavalry troops had to be called to keep order. Some people even threw flowers at the murderer, whose celebrity overcame her deeds.

Goron still had to find her accomplice. Two French detectives were sent to North America, where they followed Eyraud's trail from New York to San Francisco and into Canada. But Eyraud managed to elude them. Meanwhile, he sent a letter to the newspaper *L'Intransigeant,* placing all the blame for the murder on Gabrielle and an unknown man.

Eyraud's flight from justice could not last forever: his photograph was in every police station in North America, and on May 20, 1890, Cuban police arrested him while he was leaving a brothel. The French detectives arrived to take him back to Paris. When their ship landed at Saint-Nazaire on June 30, a huge mob was waiting. Someone in the crowd had a parrot that had been trained to call the name Eyraud over and over. Enterprising reporters clung to the sides of the train taking the killer to Paris.

The trial opened in the Paris Cour d'Assises on December 16, 1890, and it was everything the journalists could have hoped for. Each of the accused pointed a finger at the other. Few codefendants had shown such hatred and acrimony against each other, and the demand for seats in the courtroom was so great that the chief judge personally distributed the tickets of admission to friends and influential people.

Gabrielle Bompard portrayed herself as a victim, claiming that Eyraud threatened her life if she did not cooperate with him. She had a brilliant defense lawyer, Henri Robert, who caused a stir when he claimed that his client had been raped as a child while under hypnosis and as a result was very sensitive to hypnotic suggestion. Eyraud, he claimed, had made her his slave by hypnotizing her. The burgeoning science of neurology grappled with the question of whether hypnosis was powerful enough to compel someone to commit a crime, but Robert made this a main point of Bompard's defense.

The prosecution countered with a Dr. Brouardel, a respected medical jurist, who said that there were no known cases of crimes committed by a perpetrator under the influence of hypnosis. Three doctors appointed by the examining magistrate came to the conclusion that though Bompard might be susceptible to hypnotic suggestion, her main problem was that she was morally deficient. Robert asked that his client be put under hypnosis on the witness stand to give the truest possible account of the crime. It would have been a dramatic scene, but the judges turned down the request, since there was no precedent for it.

The outcome of the trial was never in doubt, for the evidence against the defendants was overwhelming: only the severity of the sentence was open to question. At the end of five days, the jury found both Bompard and Eyraud guilty. French courts had traditionally been lenient toward female criminals, especially attractive ones. As a result, Bompard received a twenty-year sentence at hard labor. Released early after having served only thirteen years, she published her memoirs, which sold quite well. Despite her criminal past, she retained her celebrity status and was often seen at fashionable restaurants. Alberto Santos-Dumont, the pioneer Brazilian aviator, escorted her regularly.

Things went worse for Eyraud. Although the jury members recommended that he be spared from execution, the justices ignored them in passing the death sentence, and the president of France, Sadi Carnot, turned down Eyraud's plea for mercy. On February 3, 1891, Eyraud was led to the guillotine. He considered his sentence unfair, telling newsmen earlier, "It was *her* idea, not mine. Why should I forfeit my life alone? Why not the woman, too?"[42] On the streets of Paris, vendors were selling miniature replicas of the trunk with a little corpse inside. The souvenirs were inscribed "L'Affaire Gouffé."[43]

V

Dr. Lacassagne would have a long and influential career as a pathologist. A true intellectual who had interests in the social sciences and philosophy as well as biology, Lacassagne worked to make medicine an integral part of psychology and forensics, cutting-edge fields of the time.

He also took a strong stand against the widely accepted theories of Cesare Lombroso. Lombroso was a pioneer Italian criminologist and the inventor of the first polygraph. In 1876, his book *Criminal Man* presented his theory of the "atavistic" or born criminal. Lombroso held that criminal deviance arose because of biological traits that made criminals less fully evolved than other members of society. These throwbacks could be identified by outward physical traits that Lombroso called stigmata. Such traits included a low forehead, bushy eyebrows, and long arms that gave the individual an apelike appearance. Other indicators of criminal tendencies were excessively large or small hands, too large jaws or cheekbones, oversize lips, and ears of unusual size. Another bad sign, though not a biological trait, was tattooing, which signified primitive instincts.

To reach these conclusions, Lombroso had studied more than five thousand skulls of criminals and felons. He concluded that there were two different kinds of criminals. The first was the born criminal, which he believed made up about 40 percent of the criminal population. Such people were hopeless cases, biologically inferior and thus doomed to degeneracy. The physical characteristics of the second group, which Lombroso termed "criminaloids," were not so easily distinguishable from those of noncriminals. Criminaloids were more strongly influenced by external factors in choosing to commit crime. Crimes of passion, for example, were examples of criminaloid actions.

Many drew the conclusion from Lombroso's work that if criminals could be identified by physical traits, then they should be detected and restrained before they committed crimes. (In fairness to Lombroso, he advocated more humane treatment for prisoners and believed that the death penalty should be greatly limited.) But Lacassagne would stress the important role society played in fostering criminal behavior. Injustices and the pressures of life, he felt, were more important than inbred traits in creating a criminal. Lacassagne expressed this principle in his motto: *"Les sociétés ont les criminels qu'elles méritent"* ("Societies have the criminals that they deserve"). His ideas were put to the test when Lacassagne dealt with the notorious case of a serial killer, Joseph Vacher, who earned the nickname the French Ripper. In fact the nickname was an understatement: Vacher killed more people than his London counterpart did.

Joseph Vacher was the fifteenth son of an illiterate farmer. As a young man, he joined the army and rose to the level of noncommissioned officer. While serving in the military, he fell in love with a young woman who failed to return his affections. When his army service was over in 1893, he begged her to marry him. She refused in a manner that made him think she was mocking him. Enraged, Vacher shot her four times in the face, but although she was badly injured, she survived.

Vacher then tried to kill himself, firing two shots into his skull. He failed at this too, although one of the bullets remained permanently lodged in his head. Vacher was left with brain damage that paralyzed the muscles on the right side of his face and damaged his eye, which often leaked pus and gave him a grotesque appearance.

Following a year in a mental institution in Dole, near the Jura Mountains in eastern France, Vacher was released after doctors declared him "completely cured." They were wrong.

At age twenty-five, Vacher became a drifter who worked as a

day laborer and begged for food. He committed at least eleven homicides over the three-year period from 1894 to 1897. (There may have been more that he did not confess to.) His victims included a number of teenage girls and boys—shepherds who were tending their flocks in isolated fields—most stabbed repeatedly and sometimes disemboweled, raped, or sodomized.

In August 1897, Vacher assaulted a young woman in a field in Tournon. Her screams brought her brother and father rushing to her aid. They subdued Vacher and brought him to the local police. Called before a judge, Vacher made the shocking admission that he had slaughtered numerous people. In October, Vacher wrote a full confession for the judge, Émile Forquet, describing himself as suffering from urges he could not control. Vacher claimed that these urges came from a childhood bite by a rabid dog, which he said had poisoned his blood. A quack doctor's treatment had made the condition worse. Vacher admitted that as his victims were dying, he drank blood from their necks.[44] Vacher argued that he was not culpable because his motive was neither theft nor vengeance.

The case became a national obsession. The scarred face of Vacher, wearing the white rabbit-fur hat he had made himself, holding the accordion he carried with him in his murderous travels, appeared in every newspaper in France for a year. The French people were already fearful of the many homeless, out-of-work vagabonds who roamed the land; Vacher gave that fear a terrifying face. Nursery rhymes were written about him to frighten children.

Excited by his growing fame, Vacher began to think of himself as a great man. He boasted that he was a scourge sent by God to punish humanity. "I am an anarchist, and am opposed to society, no matter what the form of government may be," he declared.[45]

His sense of publicity caused him to ask to be tried separately for each murder in the territory where it was committed. He would agree to discuss his crimes only if the interviewer published his words in one of the leading French newspapers.

The full story of his crime spree will never be known. He began to boast of more murders as he recalled them. When investigators checked his new stories, they found corroboration—and bodies. Corpses were discovered in the midst of thickets and in abandoned wells. Vacher was quoted as saying, "My victims never suffered for, while I throttled them with one hand, I simply took their lives with a sharp instrument in the other." [46] In fact, it appeared that after Vacher attacked and stunned his victims, he often experienced a frenzy in which he brutally slashed and mutilated them.

These seemingly insane rages were followed by cunning attempts to elude capture. In one case, he killed a shepherd boy and walked away. Soon he was overtaken by a gendarme on a bicycle, who asked him for identification papers. Vacher showed his discharge papers as a noncommissioned officer of a regiment of the Zouaves. "Why, that is my old regiment," exclaimed the gendarme. "I am hunting for a man who has just cut a boy's throat. Have you seen any suspicious characters?"

"Oh, yes," answered Vacher. "I saw a man running across the fields to the north about a mile back from here." [47]

In January 1898, Vacher showed he was still capable of murderous rages. The warden of his prison unwisely allowed himself to be alone with Vacher, who nearly beat him to death with a chair. The warden's screams brought other guards to his rescue.

Judge Forquet retained jurisdiction in the case and assigned a team of doctors, led by Alexandre Lacassagne, to examine the defendant. The panel was asked to decide whether Vacher was sane enough to stand trial. A strong case could be made against that, because of his earlier stay in an insane asylum. Lacassagne had been interested in the Jack the Ripper murders of the 1880s in England and had written a monograph on what the photographs of those crime scenes revealed. Now, studying Vacher allowed him to apply modern theories of the human psyche to a serial killer.

Lacassagne and his panel spent five months examining the defendant's behavior, interviewing him and those who had known him. Vacher had a history of "confused talk," spells of delerium, and persecution mania. He was openly delusional at times and even went into mad rages when seen by the panel. Neighbors recalled him torturing and mutilating animals as a child. During his military service, some officers claimed, he had demonstrated a violent temper.

In the end, the medical experts concluded that Vacher's crimes reflected an extremely sadistic personality that, while very rare, was not a manifestation of insanity. The panel of doctors arrived at this judgment primarily because Vacher had been able to clearly state and remember his crimes and appeared to be sufficiently aware to be fit to stand trial. Lacassagne wrote, "Vacher is not an epileptic nor is he an *impulsif*. He is a violent, immoral man who was temporarily overcome by delerious melancholy with his ideas of persecution and sucide . . . Vacher, cured, was responsible when he left the Wiant-Rokebert asylum. His crimes are those of an anti-social, a bloody sadist, who believed in his invincibility. . . . At the present time, Vacher is not insane: he fakes madness. Vacher is therefore a criminal and he could be considered responsible, this responsibility being scarcely attenuated by his previous psychological problems."[48]

Vacher, now twenty-nine, was put on trial for eleven murders. He entered the courtroom shouting, "Glory to Jesus! Glory to Joan of Arc! To the greatest martyr of all time! And glory to the Great Savior!"[49] The defense lawyers, as expected, tried to convince the jurors that Vacher was insane and not responsible for his actions. But the opinion of Lacassagne and his experts doomed Vacher. He was found guilty and sentenced to death on October 28, 1898.

On the last day of 1898, Vacher was executed at Bourg-en-Bresse, capital of the department of the Ain in eastern France. Magistrate Forquet reported his last words as he was being prepared for the guillotine: "You think to expiate the faults of France in having me die; that will not be enough; you are committing another crime; I am the great victim, *fin de siècle*."[50] Louis Deibler, the national executioner, was performing his last execution, and a huge crowd had turned out. Vacher refused to walk and had to be half dragged, half carried to the guillotine. He protested his innocence and pretended to be insane right up to the end. Deibler,

wearing a top hat and frock coat with his trademark umbrella, released the blade to the singing and wild applause of the crowd.

Afterward, the medical experts studied the serial killer's skull.
Vacher's brain was cut up and sections were sent to interested
criminologists. One of the recipients was the Italian clinic of Cesare Lombroso, who claimed to find indications of criminality in
its sample.

vi

When the *Mona Lisa* was stolen, the chief of the Paris police was
M. Louis Lépine. A legendary figure, Lépine was a small man with
a white beard who always wore a bowler hat and an old-fashioned
morning coat as he walked the boulevards of Paris. He liked to see
with his own eyes how his police were performing, and his men
knew that he could turn up at any time in unexpected places. He
demanded high performance and was unsympathetic to anyone
who didn't deliver it.

Jean Belin, who joined the police in 1911, remembered his
boss:

> Lépine was a remarkable character: a man of un-
> doubted if unpredictable ability, with idiosyncrasies
> and prejudices no one could overcome. He had ruled
> that no man more than five feet seven could be admit-
> ted to the detective force. At the same time, no uni-
> formed constable was allowed on the streets unless he
> was five feet nine. And I came in between. Lépine con-
> tended that an ordinary uniformed cop ought to be im-
> pressive by reason of his height and physical fitness. On
> the other hand, a detective should be unobtrusive in ap-
> pearance. In these respects he was inflexible. He went
> even further. He insisted on personally inspecting every
> recruit. If an applicant for the plain-clothes branch had

red hair, or a pot belly, or other marked distinguishing feature, he had no chance. In every circumstance
he must appear just plain ordinary. A mole on the face
or a scar on the hand was sufficient disqualification no
matter how able the man might be. . . . I have come
to the conclusion that in the long run he was probably
right. In real life a man with the distinctive appearance
of a Sherlock Holmes or the beard of a Hercule Poirot
would never get near his quarry.[51]

Lépine had to deal with several high-profile cases during his ten-
ure, including the *Mona Lisa* theft and the notorious Bonnot Gang
of bank robbers. But it was an ongoing threat that probably caused
him the most anxiety: the growth of the apaches, the young street
criminals who had been glamorized by fashionable Parisians.

Women apaches, known as *gigolettes,* were important members
of the gangs. When police raided dance halls looking for weapons, the young women would conceal their companions' knives,
guns, and blackjacks under their clothing. A woman known as La
Grande Marcelle was a sort of apache queen whose followers carried out her orders without question. Several murders of women
concierges, killed for the rent money that they collected, were attributed to Marcelle's gang. Her companion was Jacques Liabeuf,
regarded as one of the most vicious of the apaches. He became famous for the special outfits that made him a fearsome adversary:
Liabeuf wore a bulletproof waistcoat and a suit with brass sleeves
and wristbands bristling with sharp points that inflicted grave
damage on anyone trying to grab him. He carried a pistol but preferred an enormous knife for fighting.

In early January 1910, a policeman named Deray was killed,
allegedly while attempting to arrest Liabeuf. Prefect of Police
Lépine stood at the grave of the murdered policeman, in a section
of Montparnasse Cemetery reserved for those killed in the line of
duty, and promised that Deray's killer would be brought to justice.
He issued instructions that his men "must not hesitate to use weap-

ons in cases where they were in danger of serious bodily injury." Paris, he said, was "the refuge for too many bandits and justice treated them too tenderly."[52]

Many Parisians, particularly in the working classes, felt differently. Another view of the killing of the policeman came from the pen of M. Hervé, editor of *La Guerre Sociale,* the most extreme socialist newspaper in Paris. "Do you know," he wrote, "this Apache who has just killed Deray is not lacking in a certain beauty, a certain greatness, not often found in this century of feeble wills and beastlike submission. He has given a fine lesson of energy, perseverance, and courage to us revolutionists. He has set a fine example to the honest workmen who are every day victims of police brutality. Did you ever hear that one of them avenged themselves?"[53] The radical journalist was sentenced to four years in jail for publishing these words.

The police finally caught Liabeuf during a raid on a house in Montmartre. It seemed surprising that he was taken alive, but he soon remedied that. While in jail, he overpowered a guard who was bringing him food and made his way to the roof. A standoff resulted, and his lawyers were called to persuade him to come down. Despite their pleas, Liabeuf remained on the roof until a brigade of firemen arrived to retrieve him. Crying out, "To hell with the police and long live anarchy!" he threw himself to his death.[54]

vii

Among those who attempted to discover the roots of the apaches' criminal behavior and rage was Edmond Locard, the greatest of French criminologists, born in 1877. After studying medicine and law, he became Lacassagne's assistant before setting up his own crime lab at Lyons in 1910. Locard was a forensic pioneer in many fields. He became particularly adept at handwriting analysis, forgery detection, and dental comparisons.

In studying the apaches, Locard was influenced by Lacassagne's views that urban crime was different from rural crime. He further sought to understand the apaches through their art, which he collected. Examples often depicted such scenes as murders and guillotinings.

Locard felt that fiction could be a source of real-world inspiration. He wrote:

> I hold that a police expert, or an examining magistrate, would not find it a waste of his time to read [Arthur Conan] Doyle's novels. For, in the adventures of Sherlock Holmes, the detective is repeatedly asked to diagnose the origin of a speck of mud, which is nothing but moist dust. The presence of a spot on a shoe or pair of trousers immediately made known to Holmes the particular quarter of London from which his visitor had come, or the road he had traveled in the suburbs. A spot of clay and chalk originated in Horsham; a particular reddish bit of mud could be found nowhere but at the entrance to the post office in Wigmore Street. . . . Holmes also insists upon the interest or fascination to be found in collecting tobacco ashes, on which he says he has "written a little monograph concerning one hundred and forty varieties." I must confess that if, in the police laboratory at Lyons, we are interested in any unusual way in the problem of dust, it is because of having absorbed the ideas found in Gross[55] and Conan Doyle.[56]

One of Locard's cases showed that Locard had read Poe as well as Conan Doyle. Police were mystified by a series of jewel thefts in wealthy homes. Each of the thefts took place in broad daylight, and there were no signs of forced entry. The intruder came in through an upper-story window and each time took just one piece of jewelry, even though there might be many pieces in the room. Suspicions fell on young boys, but there was no proof.

Locard came on the case. He had adopted the use of finger-prints while others still clung to outmoded systems of identification. Now he asked to see photographs of the window ledges where the intruder had apparently entered. Checking the fingerprints carefully, he became convinced that the prints were not those of a human. The great detective came to the conclusion that the thief was a monkey. The next step was to find it. Locard ordered the city's organ grinders, who ordinarily used monkeys, to come to the police station in three days. When they arrived, all the monkeys were fingerprinted, and Locard compared their prints with the ones from the crime scenes. The guilty monkey was retired to a zoo, and its owner was arrested.

The most important of Locard's many contributions to criminology was Locard's Exchange Principle, which remains the basis of modern forensic science. It states that a criminal will always take something away from the scene of the crime and will in turn leave something behind. In essence, Locard declared that every contact leaves a trace of the victim and of the perpetrator.

> Wherever he steps, whatever he touches, whatever he leaves, even unconsciously, will serve as a silent witness against him. Not only his fingerprints or his footprints, but his hair, the fibers from his clothes, the glass he breaks, the tool marks he leaves, the paint he scratches, the blood or semen he deposits or collects. All of these and more, bear mute witness against him. This is evidence that does not forget. It is not confused by the excitement of the moment. It is not absent because human witnesses are. It is factual evidence. Physical evidence cannot be wrong, it cannot perjure itself, it cannot be wholly absent. Only human failure to find it, study and understand it, can diminish its value.[57]

Though technology has made great advances since Locard's

day, his principle is still the starting point for all crime scene investigations.

Locard himself certainly made good use of it in 1912 when the body of a young woman, Marie Latelle, was found strangled. Investigators found that she had a boyfriend, Émile Gourbin, who was very jealous. Marie apparently liked to flirt with other men to tease Gourbin. Was it possible that she had gone too far?

Gourbin, however, seemed to have a perfect alibi. Tests on Marie's body indicated that she had died around midnight. Gourbin had been playing cards with friends when the clock struck twelve. While Locard questioned him, he took fingerprints and also scrapings of the material under Gourbin's nails. Examining the scrapings under a microscope, Locard found pink dust. Further testing showed that the dust was face powder from a woman's makeup kit. Police searching Marie's lodgings found the same kind of makeup. Gourbin had absorbed the powder while strangling his victim and taken it from the crime scene.

Confronted with this evidence, Gourbin confessed. He told Locard that he had established his alibi by changing the time on the wall clock where he had been playing cards. Thus, when the game ended at what the other players thought was midnight, it was in reality half an hour earlier.

Locard, whose career continued till his death in 1966, acknowledged the debt he owed to two *maîtres*. One was Lacassagne; the other was Alphonse Bertillon, who was regarded even by Sherlock Holmes's creator as the highest expert on crime in Europe. Bertillon was the scion of a brilliant family, whose members were so devoted to intellectual pursuits that they donated their bodies to be dissected and examined after death for the advancement of science. If anyone could have used the most recent technological advances to find the *Mona Lisa*, it was this tortured and flawed individual.

THE MAN WHO
MEASURED PEOPLE

É mile Forquet, the judge who received Joseph Vacher's confession, had done a bit of detecting himself to bring the serial killer to justice. Forquet liked to collect and review the files of unsolved cases. He then arranged them according to the categories of crimes and types of injuries, along with reports of people seen in the vicinity. Noticing a pattern, he realized that witnesses' reports seemed to point to a single person. Forquet circulated copies of a card that used a system of identification known as bertillonage to describe the ears, nose, scars, and eyes of this man. The responses he received helped him to identify Vacher, and when the man was finally in front of him, Forquet pressed him to confess.

Alphonse Bertillon's method of identification, which he had named anthropometry, or "man measurement," was by 1900 in general use by police departments all over Europe and the United States. So great was Bertillon's fame that Sir Arthur Conan Doyle even mentioned him as a rival to Sherlock Holmes. In *The Hound of the Baskervilles,* a prospective client arrived to consult Holmes. As his friend Watson recalled the scene, the client said:

"I am suddenly confronted with a most serious and extraordinary problem. Recognizing, as I do, that you are the second highest expert in Europe—"

"Indeed sir! May I inquire who has the honor to be the first?" asked Holmes, with some asperity.

"To the man of precisely scientific mind the work of Monsieur Bertillon must always appeal strongly."

"Then had you not better consult him?"

"I said, sir, to the precisely scientific mind. But as a practical man of affairs it is acknowledged that you stand alone. I trust, sir, that I have not inadvertently—"

"Just a little," said Holmes.[1]

i

Bertillon came from a family renowned for intellectual achievement. His maternal grandfather, Achille Guillard, was a doctor and statistician who coined the term *demography* in 1855 and had written one of the first books on the subject. In the early years of the Second Empire, a time of such political repression that it was illegal for citizens to assemble in groups larger than three, Guillard ran afoul of the authorities and was tossed into prison. There he shared a cell with a young doctor named Louis-Adolphe Bertillon, who had been arrested for tending the wounded on both sides of the street fighting. They were not in jail long, and on their release, Guillard introduced Dr. Bertillon to his daughter, Zoe. The two were soon married. Zoe Bertillon was a brilliant woman who argued the merits of the philosophical systems of Comte and Spinoza with Jules Michelet, a family friend and France's foremost historian of the time. Lean and graceful, taller than her husband, she kept her home in simple republican good taste. In 1862, Zoe and a friend started a school called the Free Society for the Professional Instruction of Young Women, which emphasized intellectual subjects.

Her husband, Louis-Adolphe, was one of the first members of the Anthropology Society of Paris, founded by his brilliant friend the surgeon Paul Broca. Broca wished to create "a scientific society where one would have the right to draw all the philosophical consequences from one's observations."[2] When Louis-Adolphe was asked to join, he expressed concern that he was not knowledgeable in this field. "I wouldn't be able to render it any service," he said, "as I don't know a word of anthropology." Broca was unfazed. "Neither do I," he responded. "All the more reason to learn it or, rather to create it, because in truth, it doesn't exist!"[3]

Though the founders of the society had little knowledge of their subject, they would become the pioneers of the field in France. They saw anthropology as a way to express their progressive ideas about humanity and identify "all that is still present of the savage and barbaric in our modern civilizations."[4] Among the things they wanted to do away with were the priesthood, militarism, the cult of authority, and the subjugation of women.

Louis-Adolphe was also a founder of the Society of Mutual Autopsy, whose members agreed to donate and dissect one another's brains after death to promote the advancement of science. Fifteen years earlier, in 1861, Paul Broca had demonstrated through a postmortem that the left frontal lobe of the brain controlled speech. When it was damaged, speech was impaired in a symptom called "Broca's aphasia."[5] Broca further developed several instruments to measure and classify skulls,[6] the highest classification being "brachycephalic." Conan Doyle used Broca's terminology in his writing. Like Holmes, the archvillain Professor Moriarty is brachycephalic, and at their first meeting, he greets Holmes with the comment: "You have less frontal development than I should have expected."[7] (Despite Broca's proclaimed progressivism, women and people from non-European cultures were believed to have smaller and therefore inferior brains.)

It was into this intellectual community that Alphonse Bertillon was born on April 24, 1853. Not surprisingly, anthropometric techniques and measurements were part of Alphonse's life almost from birth. When Alphonse was very young, his father had a biologist friend feel the heads of his two sons. The doctor proclaimed that both had "methodical and precise" minds and would be capable of scholarly work. When Alphonse was three, he and his brother imitated their elders by measuring with ribbons everything that they could get their hands on.

Both the Guillard and Bertillon families were experts in the new study of statistics, particularly as it related to human affairs. Louis-Adolphe was pleased when his elder son, Jacques, followed the family tradition and became a renowned statistician himself. Alphonse too seemed likely to head in that direction. He was particularly fond of quoting a sentence from his father's works about the purpose of science being to find order within what seems to be chaos.

Unfortunately, Alphonse found that schools were not to his liking. At six, he was kicked out of his first one for lack of discipline. His home tutor also found Alphonse a problem, for the boy hid in a cupboard at lesson time, took the teacher's glasses, and teased him so dreadfully that the tutor quit. Sent to the Rossat Institute in Charleville, a school for problem children, Alphonse was expelled from there as well, when he was eleven. In his teens he attended the lycée at Versailles and there he accidentally set fire to his desk while using a spirit lamp to make hot chocolate. When the teacher investigated the source of the smoke, Alphonse clamped down the lid of the desk, refusing to let the teacher open it, and for good measure hit him over the head with a Greek dictionary. He was sent home once more.

After France suffered its ignominious defeat at the hands of Prussia in 1870, eighteen-year-old Alphonse was called up for his required army service, possibly to the relief of his long-suffering father. The young man stood five feet ten inches tall — well above the average for his day — and his physical presence won him the respect of his fellow conscripts and the officers. He attained the rank of corporal, probably the first distinction he had ever achieved in life. Even so, a military career was not for him; he suffered from many tics and ailments, including migraine headaches and nosebleeds. He was so unmusical that the only way he could distinguish bugle signals for reveille and roll call was to count the notes. After his discharge he contracted typhoid fever. Perhaps these physical hardships were a reason for his lifelong sour disposition, which manifested itself in sarcasm and unsociability as well as habitual suspicion of others' motives.

Two years later, however, after studying on his own, he passed the national examination, the *baccalauréat,* in science and literature. Clearly, Bertillon had a fine mind, but he wanted no more of formal schooling. Nonetheless, he failed to demonstrate the qualities required to hold a job—first as a bank clerk and then as a French teacher in an English school. He was sarcastic with co-workers and had a bad temper; it appears that in order to keep control of his emotions, he needed to keep everything slow and steady. Around 1879, however, he met an upper-class Swedish woman and fell madly in love. For unknown reasons, marriage was impossible, but they exchanged letters and pictures. It appears to have been an obsession that lasted a lifetime. Bertillon never revealed her name to family or friends, but he kept her photograph and letters until his death. Young Alphonse dedicated himself to her memory and used it as a goad to find some kind of success in the world. He began that search by asking his father for help in finding a job.

ii

There seemed no chance that Alphonse could follow an academic career like his father and brother. But his father had done statistical work for the Municipality of Paris and used his influence to obtain for his errant son a position as a junior clerk in the Prefecture of Police. Alphonse began work in March 1879, just short of his twenty-sixth birthday, in the corner of a storage cellar that was steaming hot in the summer and so cold in the winter that his gloved fingers could barely hold a quill pen. Making a pittance, Bertillon plunged into the tiresome task of copying the identification forms that were required to be filled out for each prisoner.

Ever since the branding of convicted criminals with a hot iron had been outlawed in 1832, there had been no sure way of knowing whether a person accused of a crime had been in police custody before.[8] A clever person could even get a new birth certificate if he knew the date and place of birth of someone whose identity he wanted to steal. In Bertillon's time, it was still up to the police to determine on sight if they had seen a prisoner before. Officers of the law were, in fact, offered a reward of five francs for each individual they could identify (a practice that, according to one authority, resulted in police offering to share the five francs with prisoners who would admit to having been arrested before—whether they had been or not). And, of course, identifications produced merely by someone's memory were always subject to challenge.

Vidocq had prided himself on his prodigious memory for faces and names to catch criminals by whatever name they were going under. He had started the first documentary records with descriptions of criminals in words and drawings. After his retirement, the records continued to expand. In theory these forms should have proved useful by being compared to other records to find a match. But because newly arrested suspects frequently gave false names, and since the descriptions given by arresting officers were hopelessly vague ("tall, dark-haired, average build"), the forms were in practice totally useless. In the 1860s, police had started using photographs of known criminals. But these were often taken from family or friends of the suspect and could be in any pose. Moreover, they had to be searched through one by one. This was the big problem with the identification records: the larger the collection grew, the more unwieldy it became.

In 1871, the Communards, as one of their last acts, had destroyed many of the police records and pictures. The Paris police subsequently had to rebuild their photographic records from scratch. By the end of the decade, the prefecture had about sixty thousand images in its possession. The quality of these varied with the skill of the photographer, and there was no way of classifying records by the image on them, so only by chance—and then without certainty—would two cards made at different times be matched with each other.

Thus Bertillon soon realized that, in addition to the strain of ten daily hours of rote copying, every minute of his time was wasted on an activity that was of no use whatsoever. The schoolboy who refused to spend time on subjects that he didn't like now reasserted himself. Except for his father's disapproving gaze (and the fact that it was at last necessary for the son to do something to earn a living), Bertillon might simply have quit. Instead, he drew on his knowledge of statistics, the field in which his grandfather, father, and brother excelled.

About 1840, a Belgian named Lambert Adolphe Jacques Quetelet, who is often called the father of modern statistics, stated that no two human beings in the world have exactly the same physical dimensions. Other statisticians accepted this as a given, and Bertillon began to develop a series of measurements of the human body that could be used for identification purposes. He got permission from the head of the local jail to measure the prisoners, and by August 1879, he believed that creating such a system was possible. He sent a report to the prefect of police, Louis Andrieux, who did not reply. When Bertillon was advanced to assistant clerk in October of that year, he sent a second letter to the prefect. He explained that the system he proposed was based on the Quetelet study of French crime statistics in *A Treatise on Man*, which included measurements of the human physique.

Andrieux had little patience for this young upstart who was trying to bring about an upheaval in the department's methods—even though he knew from personal experience that much of the information in the records was incorrect: when appointed prefect, Andrieux had taken a look at his own dossier and found it riddled with false information and groundless accusations, the kind of material the police typically gleaned from informants and spies.

Nevertheless, Andrieux sent Bertillon's proposal to the chief of the Sûreté, Gustave Macé, who likewise was unimpressed. Macé had considerable experience with police work and had by now attained fame by solving the Voirbo case. But he was a man who had worked his way up from street cop to the head of the Sûreté and along the way had become convinced that gut feelings and practical skills were superior to scientific methods. The detective's "nose" and his memory (à la Vidocq) were the most important tools to him. It did not help that Bertillon, by even the most sympathetic accounts, was an unprepossessing person. Regarded by some as a pompous pedant, he tended to lecture others, even his superiors, in a manner that aroused resentment. This was certainly true in the case of Andrieux, who, after getting a negative reaction from Macé, not only rejected Bertillon's proposal but wrote a letter to the young man's father, suggesting that Alphonse might be mentally disturbed and that if he continued to make bizarre suggestions, his job would be at risk.

No doubt Andrieux was well aware that Dr. Bertillon had pulled strings to obtain the police clerk position for his ne'er-do-well son, and there may have been a certain amount of resentment behind the letter. Sadly, Louis-Adolphe showed Andrieux's missive to his son, who responded with his only defense—the "evidence" of his derangement, the report he had prepared for Andrieux.

To Dr. Bertillon's credit, he read the document with an open mind and found it impressive; he even admitted that his son might well be onto something. But Louis-Adolphe also knew that politics played a greater role in changing the way governmental agencies worked than did brilliant ideas. It would be better, he told his son, to wait. The tenures of police prefects tended to be short; Andrieux would one day retire or move to another government post. Alphonse should prepare for that day by developing his identification system more thoroughly—perfecting it.

So Bertillon did so, selecting body parts to measure that he felt were least likely to change as a person aged. In the final version of what he called anthropometry, but became better known as bertillonage, eleven measurements are used. These fall into three categories:

1. Body: height, width of outstretched arms, and sitting height.
2. Head: length of head, breadth of head, bizygomatical diameter, and length of the right ear.
3. Limbs: length of left foot, length of left middle finger and left little finger, and length of the left arm from the elbow to the tip of the outstretched middle finger. Bertillon favored making measurements on the left side because that side was least likely to be affected by work.

Bertillon calculated that the chances against all eleven points being found in any two individuals was 268,435,456 to 1. For him, that was not quite certain enough, and so he added three more points — descriptive, instead of those, like the first eleven, that could be obtained by scientific instruments. These were the color of the eyes, the hair, and the pigmentation of the skin.

Around this time, Bertillon met an attractive woman who asked for his help crossing the street. There comes a moment in most men's lives when they manage, if only momentarily, to shed their natural awkwardness and social ineptitude. This was Bertillon's. He commented on the woman's accent and learned that she had been born in Austria. She said she had only recently arrived in Paris and was earning a living by giving German lessons. Bertillon replied that he had long wanted to learn German. And so . . .

The young woman's name was Amélie Notar. During the course of his German lessons, Alphonse noticed that her handwriting was unusually small and neat. Bertillon's own reflected his physical awkwardness, making his task of filling out cards at the department even more onerous. When Amélie learned of Bertillon's hope to one day introduce his system to the police files, she offered her assistance. Her clearly written cards made possible the next step of bertillonage—finding a way to classify the descriptive cards so that they could be easily referenced. Bertillon's niece, who wrote a biography of him, commented on their collaboration: "For him the thought; for her the action."[9]

Now he was able to solve the problem of classification. Random filing of the cards would, of course, produce no benefits once the number of cards grew, so Bertillon had to come up with a cascading system of options. He began with the length of the head. The resulting measurements (like those of all eleven physical dimensions in Bertillon's method) were divided into three groups: small, medium, and large. The process was then repeated with the breadth of the head, producing nine groups (three squared)—and so on through seven of the eleven measurements. The cards were further divided by seven gradations of eye color, defined by Bertillon. These may seem like a lot, but in practice it was actually a fairly rapid process, once a subject's measurements were taken, to find the file in which his card would be found, presuming that he had been measured once before. "A criminal could be measured, looked up and identified in a matter of minutes," according to one modern authority.[10]

Increasingly impatient, Bertillon occupied his spare time taking prisoners' measurements and recording them, preparing for the day when he would be allowed to show what he could do for the police. He began to enhance the value of the cards he was still making (using the tried-and-true descriptive method) by affixing to them photographs of the prisoners. This had been done on an irregular basis before, but Bertillon saw the need to standardize the poses; he originated the front- and side-view mug shots, which were eventually adopted by police photographers everywhere. Dissatisfied with the shoddy work of others, he learned to take photographs himself, carefully lighting the subjects so that a clear and precise image could be made.

Finally, a new prefect of police took Andrieux's place, and Bertillon's father once more used his connections to introduce his son's plan. The prefect, a man named Jean Camecasse, listened to Alphonse's explanation. Unfortunately, Bertillon could not refrain from explaining the relationship between demography and etymological classifications and its importance in identifying recidivists. In his customary fashion, the discourse grew long and complex.

Camecasse shrugged. The young man's father had connections, so it would be best to humor him. "We must be practical here," Camecasse reminded Alphonse. "We are not scientists, who can afford the luxury of experimenting without result." [11] Bertillon must have bitten his tongue. Still, Camecasse gave Bertillon three months to prove that his system could in fact identify a prisoner who had previously been arrested. Camecasse did not want to appear unreasonable; he assigned two clerks to assist Bertillon in taking the measurements and recording them on the new cards. (Apparently, he also looked the other way when Bertillon added an irregular volunteer to his small force: Amélie.)

Three months was not a long time. To prove the value of his system, Bertillon had to hope that some malefactor would be arrested not only once but twice during that ninety-day span. Amélie urged him not to lose heart; she was confident he would succeed.

Still, his mood was gloomy late one afternoon in February 1883. Two months had passed, more than a thousand men and women had been measured after having been taken into custody, but as far as Bertillon could determine, no one had appeared on his cards twice. As if to mock him, seven of the men arrested that day had given their name as Dupont—for some reason an alias that was in vogue in Paris at that time. After measuring the seventh man, however, Bertillon's memory clicked: the prisoner seemed familiar. Of course, he might have seen the man anywhere, but even his measurements rang a bell in Bertillon's mind. *Length of head 187 millimeters, width 156 millimeters. . . .* He went to the card file and began to trace his way through the system, finally reaching a drawer with some fifty cards in it, all with the same approximate measurements as Dupont no. 7. Bertillon began to flip through them until he reached one with exactly the same measurements.

On the original card the prisoner had given his name as Martin, but he was undeniably the same as the Dupont now in custody.

Confronted, Dupont at first denied that he had been arrested before. (The reason that Dupont was now on the street again was that his previous offense was so trivial that he had received no jail time: he had been caught stealing empty bottles.) He hoped to evade jail once again, as first-time offenders often did. Bertillon pointed out that his measurements were identical to those of the man arrested for stealing bottles. Dupont said it was a coincidence, so Bertillon showed him the photograph on the earlier card. There was no denying *that* similarity, and Dupont/Martin confessed.

It was the success Bertillon had hoped for. He could hardly wait to tell those few who had believed in him: Amélie and his father, who was now living in the countryside at Neuilly. When Bertillon visited him, he found that his father's health was rapidly failing. Louis-Adolphe rallied a bit on hearing that his wayward son had at last accomplished something, but a full recovery was beyond him, and Bertillon and his brother, Jacques, were at the old man's bedside when he died. Before passing, Louis-Adolphe told his sons, "I have always been in search of truth. You, my dear boys, must do the same." [12]

At the prefecture in Paris, skeptics still argued that the success Bertillon had proclaimed might have been merely a fluke. When Camecasse extended the time of the system's trial, however, more recidivists began to appear. By the end of 1883, Bertillon was uncovering one every three days, and there was no doubt that bertillonage was here to stay. Amélie, who had written out 7,336 cards during that year, received her reward by becoming Mme. Bertillon; it was a marriage that continued to double as a partnership.

iii

Despite the success, many in the police department resented the new system, just as they had earlier bridled at Vidocq's methods.

Whenever possible, they tried to discomfit Bertillon by making him come to the morgue and identify mangled bodies, a task he hated. Though such trips made him almost sick, he did finally gain the respect of his critics. One day a detective who faced the problem of identifying a decaying body with a very large head mentioned it to Bertillon. The circumstances—the corpse had been fished from the Marne—created some suspicion that the dead man had a criminal background, so Bertillon came to measure him. Although the body's condition made it impossible to take all eleven critical measurements, there were enough to make an identification: Bertillon's files showed that the man had been accused of assault a year before. That brought the police to question those involved and to discover that the victim had been murdered in revenge for the earlier incident. After that, identification of unknown corpses became a regular duty for Bertillon and his assistants.

The press, as always, was fascinated by crime stories, and the ensuing publicity helped Bertillon's program. In November 1887, *L'Illustration* sent a reporter to Bertillon's lab. The journalist wrote of men on pedestals, leaning over calibrated iron tables and seated on bolted-down chairs as they used calipers, meter sticks, and cameras. The technology of precise measurements, the reporter made clear, was supplementing and replacing the system of relying solely on policemen's memories.

Gradually, Bertillon's superiors realized how valuable his work was. On February 1, 1888, six years after his first success, he was made chief of the newly established Service of Judicial Identity. He set up shop on the top floor of the Palais de Justice. Perhaps it was to Bertillon's liking that the office had to be reached via a long and steep staircase, discouraging casual visitors and those who didn't have something important to report. By this time, his system had become well enough known that other police forces in Europe and America were beginning to adopt it. As it became widespread, some complained that taking the eleven measurements was too difficult for an ordinary underpaid police clerk and that not everyone was able to produce measurements as precise as those Bertillon himself made. The founder of the system brushed aside such objections, saying that "anyone who was not an imbecile could learn to measure in five minutes and never forget the process."[13] In Paris alone, by the end of the first decade of its use, Bertillon's measurement system led to the capture and identification of thirty-five hundred criminals.[14]

Bertillon was continually searching for new ways to employ scientific methods in crime solving. At one point, he added to his reputation by making duplicate copies of identity photographs and cutting them into pieces. He divided the pieces into groups according to facial parts—noses, ears, eyes, and so forth—and compiled charts to show illustrations of the various types of each. By doing so, he was trying to find a way to assist policemen in making more precise descriptions of the suspects they brought into custody. Bertillon proved in a series of experiments that detectives who had failed to identify a suspect based on a regular photograph could often identify their target if just one feature was isolated. It was the skill of the detective "to analyze each of these traits separately and, consequently, to compare each isolated trait with the corresponding trait of another face."[15] Bertillon put special emphasis on the ears of criminals for making an identification, for he believed ears were both difficult to disguise and easy to remember. Eventually, his efforts produced what was called a *portrait parlé,* or spoken portrait. Lecture courses trained policemen in the technique of observing and memorizing the formation of ears, noses, and other characteristics according to a gradated scale.

As the historian Matt Matsuda has written, "The nose, for example, was divided into three distinct features, its height, width and projection, each part precisely designated and numbered. . . . Bertillon maintained that as long as a particular anatomical feature had not received 'a name permitting the form and descriptive value to be stored in the memory,' it would remain 'unperceived,' as if it 'did not exist.' Seeing a face was a fine thing, but such memories were easily tricked. Better to concentrate the identifications of memory in language. As Bertillon put it, 'it has been said for a long time: we only think that which we are able to express in words.' "[16]

Similarly, modern artists and scientists, using their own methods, were finding fresh vocabularies, visual and verbal, for new concepts of the world. Artists in particular shared with Bertillon the requirement that viewers must put together the pieces themselves, forming an image from discrete elements. One can see the process in movies, cubism, impressionism, and statistics, the very science that underlies Bertillon's method. His philosophy, which could easily have been adopted by Picasso, was written in large black letters on the wall of the room where he trained recruits: "The eye sees in each thing only what it is looking for, and it looks for what is already an idea in the mind." [17]

Just as the basis of anthropometry was the idea of providing precise measurements of the human body, so Bertillon hoped to develop other measuring tools to assist in crime detection. After having honed his photographic skills to produce mug shots, Bertillon started to bring a camera along to crime scenes. Police officers became used to his instructing them to touch nothing until he could make a photographic record, often from several angles, of a body or a burglary. Bertillon pasted his photographs onto cards that showed the precise scale of measurements on the border. Today's crime scene investigators may use Polaroids or digital cameras to get instant images, but they are following the same procedure Bertillon pioneered more than a century ago.

Another innovation was the Bertillon Box, a sort of portable forensics unit that was small enough to slip into a coat pocket. Someone else had already used plaster of paris to make impressions of footprints; Bertillon went a step further in making metallic copies that were more durable and easily displayed to juries.

Bertillon also discovered that pure rubber, similar to that used by dentists, was a valuable crime scene tool. For example, if Bertillon wanted to copy the marks on a doorjamb or window frame made by a crowbar or "jimmy," he would place softened rubber over the surface. When the rubber was pressed down, it would penetrate all the grooves. After the material had hardened, it would be removed carefully to show all the grains and indentations of the wood. Employing this as a negative mold, Bertillon would then make a positive one with plaster of paris. He could use this to identify the specific jimmy that had been used.

The instrument he was proudest of, however, was the dynamometer, which was designed to measure the force used by a house burglar to break locks on doors or windows. It was not, as even Bertillon's biographer admits, a particularly useful instrument—merely one that satisfied the urge to quantify every aspect of a crime scene. It was a hit at the time, however, even being mentioned in a Fantômas story.

iv

Bertillon could not have achieved the fame he did had his system not produced tangible results. One of his greatest successes came in March 1892, after a bomb exploded on the boulevard Saint-Germain outside the home of a judge who had presided over a trial of a group of anarchists the previous year.

To find out who had planted the bomb, police at first employed their tried-and-true method of using informants. A woman identified in police files as X2S1 pointed the finger at Chaumartin, a teacher at a technical school in the suburb of Saint-Denis. The informant had learned from Chaumartin's gossipy wife that he had planned the bombing, although the act was carried out by a man named Léon Léger. Taken into custody, Chaumartin confessed his role in showing Léger how to build the bomb but said the other man had stolen the dynamite and hatched the plot. He told the police where Léger was staying and described him as a man about five feet four inches in height, with a dark beard and a sallow complexion. Chaumartin also informed them that Léger's real name was Ravachol. That too was only an alias, though it was the name by which he became best known.

Ravachol had fled by the time police reached his quarters, but all over Paris and the surrounding area, short men with dark beards were stopped and questioned—to no avail. The newspapers were screaming for results in solving the outrage. "France is in the hands of impotent men who do not know what to do about the barbarians in our society," complained a writer for *Le Gaulois*.[18] The new prefect of police, Henri Lozet, called Bertillon in and presented him with the only lead that had turned up: police in the town of Saint-Étienne recalled having arrested a man calling himself Ravachol on suspicion of theft. Ravachol was apparently a career criminal; smuggling, burglary, murder, and even grave robbing were among the offenses he had been suspected of committing. Fortunately, the police in Saint-Étienne had taken his measurements and description according to Bertillon's method. On March 24, Bertillon received the data from the filing card in Saint-Étienne: "Claudius François Koenigstein, alias Ravachol; height: 1.663; spread of arms: 1.780; chest: .877; length of head: .186; breadth of head: .162; length of left foot: .279; left middle finger: .122; left ear: .098; color of left iris: yellowish verging upon green."[19] Bertillon was certain that this precise data, circulated through the arrondissements of Paris, would eventually bring Ravachol to justice.

Before Ravachol could be apprehended, however, he struck again. Two weeks after the first bomb, a second exploded in the basement of a house, 35, rue de Clichy, home of the state prosecutor who had conducted the case against the anarchists. There seemed to be no doubt that this was the work of the same man who had planted the first device.

Anarchists weren't shy about declaring their allegiances, and several anarchist newspapers proclaimed the bomber as a new hero of the movement. The police responded by rounding up all known anarchists, but none had physical measurements that matched those of the elusive Ravachol. Someone, however, disclosed an ad-

The *Mona Lisa*, one of the world's most recognizable images. The French call her *La Joconde* and the Italians, *La Gioconda*, since the woman in the painting is considered to be Lisa Gherardini, who in 1495 married Francesco del Giocondo of Florence. Leonardo da Vinci began work on the portrait around 1503, when Lisa was twenty-four.

The sensational French newspapers of the day reflected the feelings of Parisians that the theft of the painting was an unimaginable crime. Headline writers struggled to describe its enormity. (*Paris Préfecture de Police museum*)

Next door to each other in Montmartre, the two cabarets of Le Ciel (Heaven) and L'Enfer (Hell) were elaborate theme restaurants where the waiters dressed as angels or devils and the irreverent entertainment poked fun at religious (or irreligious) practices. *(Bibliothèque nationale de France)*

A journalist dubbed the young criminals who terrorized Paris in the early 1900s "Apaches." Edmond Locard, a criminologist, collected examples of their art, such as this clay depiction of a criminal about to face the guillotine. *(From the authors' collection)*

A newspaper artist depicted the police arresting the anarchist bomber Ravachol in 1892. A restaurant owner had recognized him from the description of Ravachol circulated by Alphonse Bertillon, who pioneered the science of criminal identification. On the way to jail, Ravachol struggled to break free, shouting to others in the street for help: "Follow me, brothers! *Vive l'anarchie! Vive la dynamite!*" *(Paris Préfecture de Police museum)*

François-Eugène Vidocq was truly a larger-than-life figure. In real life a criminal imprisoned many times, he changed course to become the first head of the Sûreté, France's equivalent of the FBI, and later set himself up as a private detective. He was the model for countless fictional criminals and detectives as well. *(From the authors' collection)*

Pierre Ponson du Terrail was among the first to write novels that featured a criminal as the hero. Gino Starace, the cover artist for this later reprint of one of Ponson's books, captured the ghoulish spirit that Parisians loved. *(From the authors' collection)*

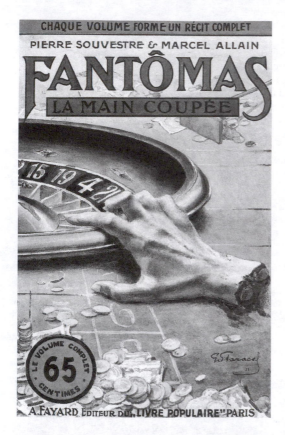

The ultimate French criminal "hero" was Fantômas, the creation of Marcel Allain and Pierre Souvestre, who turned out a 400-page novel every month for nearly three years. Able to change his appearance almost at will, Fantômas committed countless acts of cruelty and violence, evading his hapless nemesis Inspector Juve in every one of the books, delighting readers. *(From the authors' collection)*

Pierre-François Lacenaire, depicted here smothering an old woman in her bed while his accomplice finishes off her son in the next room, became as famous for his literary work as for his crimes. "To kill without remorse is the highest of pleasures," he wrote. "It is impossible to destroy my hatred of mankind. This hatred is the product of a lifetime, the outcome of my every thought." *(Paris Préfecture de Police museum)*

Marie Lafarge was another criminal whose self-portrayal earned her notoriety; to many, she was a saint who had been unjustly accused. Despite Marie's protestations of innocence, however, scientist Mathieu Orfila demonstrated conclusively that she had poisoned her husband. It was the first time that the science of toxicology had been used to convict a person of murder. *(From the authors' collection)*

Joseph Vacher was nicknamed "the French Ripper," but in fact his victims far outnumbered those of the English serial killer. Alexandre Lacassagne, one of the founders of French scientific criminology, convinced a jury that Vacher's claims of insanity were unfounded. *(From the authors' collection)*

The trunk in which the body of Toussaint-Augustin Gouffé was transported from Paris to Lyons. Lacassagne performed an autopsy on the remains that conclusively identified them and led to the apprehension of his murderers. At their trial, miniatures of the trunk were sold by vendors outside the courthouse. *(Paris Préfecture de Police museum)*

The Parisian Apaches acquired a romantic aura because of their distinctive dances and styles of dress. Nevertheless, newspapers portrayed them as ruthless thugs, as in this drawing of an Apache strangling a victim while the Apache's girlfriend watches without emotion. *(From the authors' collection)*

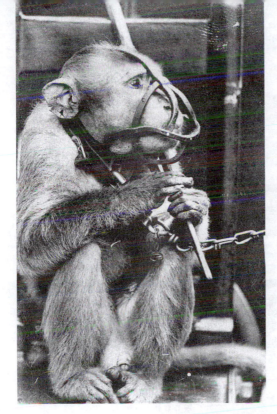

Edmond Locard took fingerprints of monkeys throughout
Paris to find this particular
animal, whose owner was using
him as a thief. The case echoed
Edgar Allan Poe's classic detective story "The Murders in the
Rue Morgue." Locard acknowledged that real-life detectives
often followed the lead of their
fictional counterparts. *(From
the authors' collection)*

Alphonse Bertillon, the
complicated and conflicted
individual who developed
the first effective system of
identifying criminals. *(From
the authors' collection)*

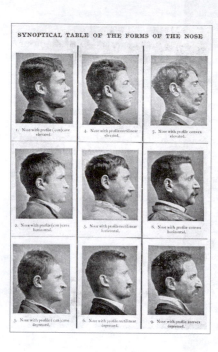

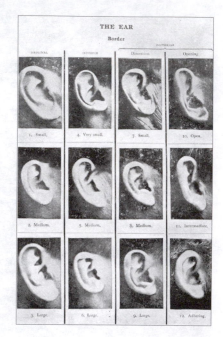

Three of the charts Bertillon prepared to categorize parts of the face: types of noses, ears, and eyes. Bertillon felt that giving names to different forms of body parts would enable police to create a *portrait parlé*, or "spoken portrait," of suspects. *(From the authors' collection)*

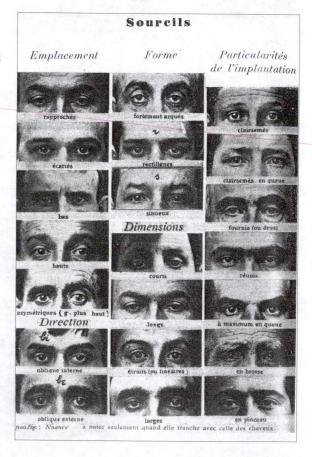

Bertillon was the first to make detailed photographs of crime scenes as references for police investigating crimes. *(From the authors' collection)*

As criminals realized that their photographs could be used to associate them with other crimes they may have committed, they began to resist sitting for the camera. Since exposure times were longer then, it was sometimes necessary to strap the prisoner in place to obtain a sharp image. *(From the authors' collection)*

Guillaume Apollinaire was himself a noted poet, but his contributions to art went well beyond that. His enthusiasm, generosity with praise, and openness to all forms of new art made him what one historian called a "ringmaster of the arts." *(From the authors' collection)*

Pablo Picasso and his mistress Fernande Olivier with their two dogs. Picasso always had a variety of animals around him, including a pet mouse he kept in a drawer. *(© RMN / Droits réservés)*

A survey taken in 2008 indicated that Picasso's *Les demoiselles d'Avignon* was the most frequently illustrated work in art history texts. Yet when he first showed it to friends and colleagues, their reaction led him to roll up the painting and keep it hidden for several years. *(Digital Image (c) The Museum of Modern Art/Licensed by SCALA/Art Resource, NY; © 2008 Estate of Pablo Picasso/Artists Rights Society (ARS), New York)*

Les transformations de

Si Garnier et Valet réussirent si bien à échapper à la surveillance de la ...
les filait avenue de Saint-Ouen ...

GARNIER SANS BARBE   GARNIER AVEC BARBE

Two views of Octave Garnier, one of the three principal members of the Bonnot gang. The change in appearance that he accomplished indicates how important Bertillon's methods of identification were to the police. *(Paris Préfecture de Police museum)*

Raymond Callemin, known to his friends as "Raymond-la-Science" because he inevitably found scientific backing for his beliefs. At the commune of anarchists, he introduced a "scientific" diet of brown rice, raw vegetables, porridge, and pasta with cheese. Salt, pepper, and vinegar were banned as being "unscientific," although herbs were acceptable. *(Paris Préfecture de Police museum)*

Jules Bonnot, the ostensible leader of the Bonnot Gang, the man the press dubbed "the Demon Chauffeur" for his reckless feats at the wheel of the world's first "getaway car." Some allege that Bonnot was earlier a driver for Sir Arthur Conan Doyle, creator of Sherlock Holmes. *(Paris Préfecture de Police museum)*

The Delaunay-Belleville that Bonnot and his cohorts used to escape from the scene of their first crime. This French marque was widely regarded as the finest automobile in the world. Purchasers had to supply their own "coach," or upper body, so the cars were identifiable only by the distinctive circular radiator. *(Paris Préfecture de Police museum)*

André Soudy, posed by a police photographer reconstructing the scene of the bank robbery at Chantilly. Though Soudy never killed anyone, he was later guillotined for his involvement with the Bonnot Gang. Several others, either peripherally involved or outright innocent, received harsh prison terms. *(Paris Préfecture de Police museum)*

There were several Paris newspapers that illustrated the
news with drawings of crime
scenes. This one depicts one of
the Bonnot Gang's most spectacular crimes: the shooting of
Louis Jouin, the head of the
police force assigned to apprehend the gang. Cornered in his
hiding place, Bonnot himself
shot and killed Jouin before
jumping from an upstairs window and escaping. *(From the
authors' collection)*

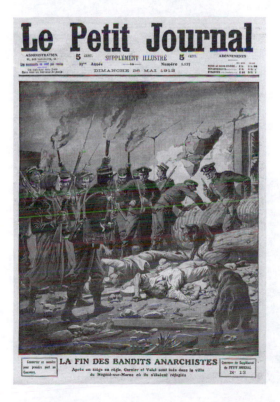

A newspaper artist's render-
ing of the last stand of Octave Garnier and René Valet,
the last two members of the
Bonnot Gang at large. The
two men had held at bay a
force of over 700 police and
soldiers for an entire day
before dynamite blasts destroyed their refuge. *(From
the authors' collection)*

FIN D'UNE TERREUR — LA TRAGÉDIE DE CHOISY-LE-ROI
La Fusillade

Postcards like this one depicted the seige at Choisy-le-Roi, where Bonnot single-handedly resisted a force of at least a hundred men. Newsreel cameras recorded the scene, and when it was shown in theaters, audiences cheered whenever Bonnot appeared on a balcony to fire his rifle. *(Paris Préfecture de Police museum)*

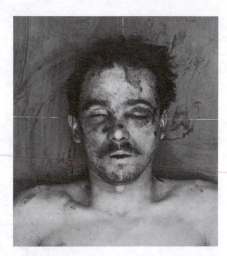

Bonnot in the morgue. He had recognized that he had become famous and wrote a testament justifying his crimes and exonerating those who were unjustly accused. *(Paris Préfecture de Police museum)*

Vincenzo Perugia, the man who confessed to stealing the *Mona Lisa*. Had he acted alone? That was a mystery whose answer took another two decades to solve. *(Paris Préfecture de Police museum)*

L'HISTOIRE D'UN CHEF-D'ŒUVRE
L'achat de la Joconde par François Ier. — Le Rapt. — Le Retour.

When the *Mona Lisa* returned to the Louvre, *Le Petit Journal,* Paris's most popular pictorial newspaper, devoted its front page to a history of the painting from Leonardo's presentation of it to King François I to its theft from the museum. *(From the authors' collection)*

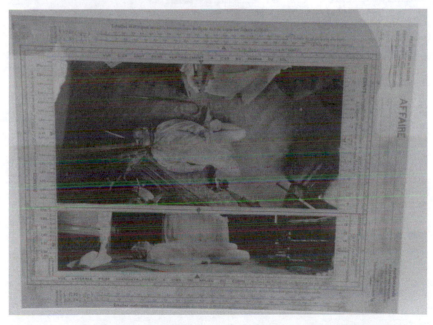

Alphonse Bertillon's crime scene photographs, overhead and from the side, of the body of Adolphe Steinheil. Nearly two decades older than his beautiful wife, Meg, he had looked the other way while she engaged in a series of sexual liaisons, including one that reputedly killed Félix Faure, the president of France. *(Paris Préfecture de Police museum)*

LA FIN D'UN PROCÈS SENSATIONNEL
Mme Steinheil écoutant la lecture du verdict

Meg Steinheil in the dock at her trial for murder. Her performance under questioning was so affecting that journalists dubbed her the "Sarah Bernhardt of the Assizes," after the most famous actress of the day. *(From the authors' collection)*

GASTON CALMETTE.
Editor of the Paris *Figaro*, killed by Madame Caillaux.

MADAME CAILLAUX.
Seemingly in some such mood as when she faced her husband's foe.

JOSEPH CAILLAUX.
French Minister of Finance, who resigned after his wife's crime.

CENTRAL FIGURES IN THE FRENCH TRAGEDY.

At left, Gaston Calmette, who was shot to death in his office on March 16, 1914, by Henriette Caillaux, center. At right is her husband, Joseph, at that time the finance minister of France, who had been the object of constant attacks by the newspaper Calmette edited. Henriette explained her action by saying, "There is no justice in France. There is only the revolver." *(From the authors' collection)* ditional physical detail about the wanted man: he had a scar on his left hand. A few days later, once this description had been circulated, the owner of a restaurant on the boulevard Magenta noticed a customer with such a scar and immediately notified the police. When uniformed officers arrived, the man drew a pistol; fortunately he was not able to fire it, and after a struggle, the police cuffed him and led him away. On the way to the local police station, he tried to break free, shouting to others in the street for help: "Follow me, brothers! *Vive l'anarchie! Vive la dynamite!*"[20]

Later that day, the suspect was brought to the headquarters of the Sûreté, where Bertillon prepared to photograph and measure him. The man again resisted, pointing out that his face was bruised and bleeding; in his struggle to escape, the police had beaten him. Bertillon courteously agreed to put off the photography session if the man would allow his measurements to be taken. Impressed, he agreed. To Bertillon, the photograph was secondary to his beloved system of measurements, which never changed once a subject reached adulthood, and when the suspect's measurements proved to be the same as those taken by the police in Saint-Étienne, Bertillon knew he had Ravachol in custody.

However, the evidence against Ravachol in the two Paris bombings was flimsy; he denied everything that Chaumartin said, and Chaumartin was himself the only person to have confessed to a role in the bombing. Furthermore, another bomb was set off while Ravachol was in jail—at the very restaurant where he had been arrested, killing the owner who had turned him in.

Nervously, the judges sent Ravachol to Saint-Étienne, where the pending charges against him seemed to offer a stronger case. Here, in fact, faced with the evidence, Ravachol gave up trying to deny his crimes and proclaimed himself the anarchist bomber. He defended himself by claiming that his violence was aimed at ending the suffering of the weak. "My object," he declared, "was to terrorize so as to force society to look attentively at those who suffer."[21]

Sentenced to the guillotine, he was brought back to Paris for the execution on July 10, 1892. He sang as he was paraded through the streets of Paris: "If you want to be happy, hang your masters and cut the priests to pieces." His final words, "You pigs, long live the Revolution!" were cut off when the blade of the guillotine severed his neck.[22]

Bertillon was hailed as the savior of Paris. The capture of Ravachol earned him the Legion of Honor and a new position as head of the Bureau of Identification, which he would hold till his death. The general feeling was that his key identification had provided the only link between the criminal in Saint-Étienne and the Paris bomber and that without that identification, Ravachol might have continued his deadly career. The publicity did much to encourage police departments in other countries to adopt anthropometric identification systems.

V

After the Ravachol case, Bertillon's reputation was secure, and the use of his system became as routine a procedure as fingerprinting is today. One notable case was solved personally by Marie-François Goron, the head of the Sûreté and one of Bertillon's admirers. Goron, who had already gained fame for solving the Gouffé case, was asked by the Belgian government to try to find a swindler, Karslake, who was reputed to be in Paris. Goron immediately sought to question people who were rumored to have had dealings with Karslake. One in particular, Charles Vernet, struck him as being familiar — something in his attitude and manner awakened suspicion. But Vernet was a wealthy gentleman who had made a fortune on the Paris Bourse. His manner with Goron was open and indicated that he was willing to assist the police. Still, Goron could not shake his suspicions.

Goron began to search through police records from the time he had first joined the force. Finally he found what he was looking for. When he had been the police commissary of the Pantin Quarter in northern Paris, some twelve years earlier, a young clerk named Moulin had been stabbed to death after a fierce struggle in his home. The sounds of a fight had awakened a lodger on the floor below, who opened his door in time to see a man running down the stairs. The next day the police arrested a man named Simon, who was identified by the neighbor. Because the evidence was slight, he evaded the guillotine but was sentenced to twenty years at the French penal settlement at Cayenne in French Guiana.

Goron felt certain that Vernet, the wealthy stock trader, was that very man, but Simon should still have been serving his term on the blistering hot island prison. Checking further, Goron found that Simon had attempted to escape from Cayenne, accompanied by a fellow convict named Aymard. The pair had tried to make their way to the South American mainland, but pursuers found the body of Simon. Aymard had disappeared, but was presumed dead as well. Reading further, Goron found that the dead man's face was battered beyond recognition; he had been identified only by his jacket, which bore the number assigned to Simon when he arrived at Cayenne.

Goron was not convinced. He was certain that if the Bertillon method was used, it would show Simon to be alive and prospering in Paris under the alias Vernet. The escaped prisoner could easily have switched jackets with Aymard after beating the man's face so that it was unrecognizable. However, Vernet's wealth and influential friends made him powerful enough that Goron could not simply march him into Bertillon's laboratory and have him measured—one of the flaws in the method. Moreover, since Simon was legally dead, Goron would face the inertia of the police bureaucracy in trying to prove Simon was alive and still active. Goron had little to go on except his own intuition.

Vernet frequently appeared at society functions, cementing his reputation as a cultivated gentleman. Goron himself was a man of artistic and literary tastes and felt comfortable traveling in upper-crust society. Through a friend, Goron arranged for Vernet to be invited to a reception given by a distinguished woman sculptor at which some of the latest scientific achievements would be demonstrated. Goron and a "nephew"—actually a young detective—would also attend. When they arrived, Goron was carrying a parcel, which he put aside. Vernet, in formal evening dress, bowed graciously to the detective. The lights were turned down as the guests observed a demonstration of the then-new cinematograph, an early form of motion picture. When that was over, a scientist showed some of the uses of an electrometer, which measured electrical charges. This was at a time when electricity was still a strange and powerful force whose many uses were yet to be discovered, and the audience was fascinated. Then the hostess called on Goron to present his part of the evening's entertainment.

The detective chief stood and made a little speech about the evolution of criminal investigation.

> Years ago, the man whose duty it is to fight the enemies of society had only his own powers to rely upon. Between him and the criminal it was skill against skill, art against art. Then came the modern inventions— railways, steamers, the telegraph, the telephone—and matters grew worse for the detective. Alas! it was the murderers, the forgers, who had the advantage, inasmuch as they could steal a long march upon Nemesis, and get their accomplices to use the telegraph and the telephone for their benefit.
>
> The question, therefore, was to discover a system by which society and not its foes would reap the advantages. Ladies and gentlemen, this system has been found, and the man to whom we owe it, and whose name will go down to posterity, is M. Bertillon.[23]

Goron's nephew handed him the package, which he opened. Here, Goron explained, were the instruments used in the new science of bertillonage, "for the identification of those who, having previously fallen into the hands of the police, expect to escape detection by changing their names or altering, as they think, their appearance."[24]

The name Bertillon sent a thrill of excitement through the room. When Goron asked for individuals willing to be measured, several young women were the first to volunteer. Alphonse Daudet, a well-known writer, offered his own physiognomy for the measurements. While Goron was at work, he noticed Vernet moving to the door.

"Ah, there's M. Vernet," he cried. "Don't go away. Come and be measured."

The financier shook his head with a smile. "No, thank you," he responded. "I have seen the thing done before."

Seemingly joking, Goron appealed to two American girls who were standing by the door. "Catch him, ladies. Don't let him escape."

By this time, all eyes were on Vernet, and he was unable to get away without causing a scene. "This is a bad joke," he told Goron.

"Oh, it's part of the fun," returned the detective.

Vernet was compelled to put the best face on things. He shrugged and permitted Goron to take his measurements. Goron recorded them on a blank Bertillon card and handed it to his nephew, who had in his pocket another card with the measurements of the supposedly dead convict Simon. After a brief comparison, he nodded to Goron, who took Vernet by the arm and led him to another room.

"I advise you not to make a scene," Goron said. "I know you to be Simon, an escaped convict, and the suspected murderer of Aymard. You will have to come with me. My 'nephew' over there is a detective, and I have three others within call. Say good-bye to your hostess and follow me."

Vernet's nerve had taken him from Cayenne to Paris, and he tried to bluff his way through this setback as well. Drawing himself up, he told Goron coolly, "This is a mistake, which I will make you regret."[25]

After Bertillon himself had confirmed Goron's measurements, however, Vernet confessed. He was sent to prison to await transport back to Cayenne. It was a fate he could not endure. He hanged himself in his cell.

vi

Harry Ashton-Wolfe, a British citizen who worked for several years with Bertillon, later wrote several books about his experiences. Ashton-Wolfe was a friend of Sir Arthur Conan Doyle, and he portrayed Bertillon as very much in the mold of the world's most famous literary detective.[26] In "The Clue of the Blind Beetles," Ashton-Wolfe described how a package containing the body of a man was found in the Bois de Boulogne, on the western edge of Paris. Indications were that the victim had been struck on the head from behind by a club or hammer. He wore only a shirt and trousers, but other items of clothing had been enclosed in the package with him.

Even though the ground was soft from recent rains, there were no traces of footprints or wheels. The wrapped package was heavy and unwieldy, and if it had been left there by one man, he must have been enormously strong. Bertillon took a stroll toward the Seine, which loops around the Bois, and found markings of a boat on the riverbank. Leading away from it were shapeless impressions, made, Bertillon deduced, by a man who had tied a thick cloth over his boots to conceal his tracks. Since the paper of the package was dry, it had to have been left there after midnight, when the rain had stopped.

Using a cable attached to the battery in his automobile, Bertillon activated a new device he had recently devised. "A short arc, enormously magnified by complex lenses and reflectors, produced a concentrated beam of dazzling brilliancy, which could be focused to any angle," Ashton-Wolfe wrote. While he held the lamp, Bertillon attached a mask containing magnifying lenses to his face and examined the body. Spotting something on the victim's shirt, he called for a collodium slide, which was a sticky glass plate used to pick up tiny bits of evidence — in this case, what appeared to be insects. The body was then sent for an autopsy while the clothes went to Bertillon's laboratory.

Ashton-Wolfe described the results: "In the hair, which, although still dark at the roots, was grey at the points, were fragments of coal, sand, and sawdust. The microscope proved the coal to be anthracite; the sand, silicate, ferruginous silicate, and quartz; and the sawdust, when split with a microtome, turned out to be composed of pine and oak. The stains on the shirt were also coal, intermingled with traces of mildew. When I carried my report to my chief, I found him at work on the collodium slide."[27] Bertillon reported that "the two tiny insects we found on the shirt are *Anophthalmi,* a species of blind beetle. Moreover, they are quite colorless — absolutely devoid of pigment. They've bred for generations in the dark. Taken together with the coal and sand, I should say that it proves the body was hidden for a time in a cellar or a vault. It only remains to find it."[28]

Ashton-Wolfe commented that if they had to search all the cellars in Paris, it would be a long process. Bertillon frowned and told him, "I see you forget the formulae that apply to every premeditated murder: *Who profits by the crime?* and *Seek the woman.* One or the other will lead us to that cellar."[29]

Chemical analysis of the dead man's clothing provided another clue. The coat and vest were covered with *Saccharomyces cerevisiae,* which were the bacteria used in fermenting alcohol. Bertillon surmised that the cellar they were looking for might well be in a café. Because a boat was used to transport the body, the café must be near the Seine. The oak and pine sawdust indicated that the same cellar must be used for sawing firewood.

Bertillon's darkroom technicians produced a reconstructed photograph of the victim's face, and detectives began to show it around the city's cafés. Bertillon instructed Ashton-Wolfe how to proceed. "Say that you are searching for a relative. . . . Take care not to let it appear that you fear something has happened to him." [30] Bertillon believed the man was an accountant or a clerk. His boots and hands showed no signs of manual labor, and his right sleeve was fresher-looking than the left. This indicated that, like many people in clerical jobs, the victim wore a protective lustrine sleeve on the end of the arm he used to write with. A typist, on the other hand, wore lustrine sleeves on both arms. [31]

Bertillon's assumptions were soon proved correct, as someone recognized the man in the photograph: he was a forty-year-old bookkeeper named Charles Tellier. Tellier had disappeared ten days earlier but had told his landlady he was going on vacation, so she had not reported him missing. Neighbors said Tellier was quite a ladies' man and sometimes got into trouble when the ladies were married to someone else. He was also known to patronize illegal bookmakers. A search of his room turned up numerous betting slips, and some love letters that were signed "Marcelle."

The landlady reported that Tellier ate his meals at a tavern in the Latin Quarter called La Cloche de Bois. Dressed as an art student ("peg-topped trousers and velveteen jacket, with the wide-brimmed hat and flowing tie" [32]), Ashton-Wolfe went to investigate the place. He found that the proprietor, "red-faced, jovial, and generous," was a burly man named Jacques Cabassou. Less congenial was Cabassou's wife, who served as bartender and cashier and kept Cabassou from buying too many drinks and meals for the needy students who frequented the place. Ashton-Wolfe became more interested when he learned that her name was Marcelle, and he filched one of the meal bills she had written. He compared it with the handwriting on the love letters from Tellier's room. They matched.

Before Ashton-Wolfe could look further into La Cloche de Bois, another detective, named Rousseau, came up with a new lead. One of Tellier's co-workers, a man named Guillaume, had taken a leave from work at the same time that Tellier disappeared. Guillaume was known to have owed Cabassou a sizable debt from gambling losses. Rousseau followed Guillaume's trail to Antwerp, where he had sold some diamonds. Tellier's landlady had said that her tenant often wore rings and tiepins set with diamonds. The conclusion Rousseau had drawn was that Guillaume killed Tellier for his diamonds to pay for his gambling losses.

Bertillon expressed doubts but sent Ashton-Wolfe and Rousseau to arrest Guillaume, now back at work. The detectives took Guillaume back to his apartment and searched it. They found two rings and a tiepin from which the stones had been taken. Guillaume paled when they showed him the evidence, and said that someone must have planted it there. The detectives had heard that excuse before and took him before the *juge d'instruction*.

Guillaume's story was that he had lost all his money gambling, and Cabassou gave him a chance to make it back. He gave him a letter of introduction to a man who needed a courier to take some diamonds to the market in Antwerp and sell them there. In return, Cabassou asked a favor: proof that Tellier and his wife were lovers. "As Cabassou said this," Guillaume recalled, "he changed from the smiling, jovial fellow I had always known, until his face was that of a fiend." [33] Now it was clear that Cabassou had a motive for killing Tellier, though Guillaume insisted that he had not found the evidence of infidelity Cabassou had demanded.

Ashton-Wolfe and Rousseau went back to La Cloche de Bois, still disguised as mildly drunken students. They were reluctant to arrest Cabassou without further proof. So, pretending to be interested in better wine than they were served, they persuaded the tavern keeper to take them to his cellar. There, Ashton-Wolfe found what appeared to be bloodstains. The two men arrested Cabassou and called in Bertillon to examine the scene.

Bertillon pointed out all the signs he had expected except for the blind insects. "See, there is the sand, the sawdust, the coal; and in a place filled with barrels and bottles of wine, you will have an abundance of the bacilli of alcohol fermentation." Bertillon insisted that there must be another cellar, and a further search revealed "a tiny, pitch-dark recess, gained by a door under the stairs. Bertillon's theory was vindicated: at last we stood in the place where the murder had been committed. Blood had splashed on the floor and walls, and the roof was alive with the *Anophthalmi* [the blind beetles]."[34] After killing Tellier, Cabassou had removed his diamonds and sent Guillaume to sell them, hoping to throw suspicion onto him. If it had not been for Bertillon's scientific methods and acute observation, Guillaume might well have been convicted. With a note of triumph, Bertillon pointed out to Ashton-Wolfe that jealousy had been at the heart of the case. *Cherchez la femme,* as he had predicted, had been the key to solving it.

vii

Accounts like this one, and some whose details are as fantastic as any in fiction, made Bertillon a legend in Paris — even throughout Europe and the Americas. Though he ostensibly shunned publicity, this kind of adulation would turn almost anyone's head, and at the height of his career, Bertillon made a blunder in the most controversial investigation of his lifetime. It would stain his reputation ever after.

Bertillon was unwise, or unfortunate, enough to enter the Dreyfus case at the very beginning. Once he had given his opinion about the handwriting on the incriminating *bordereau*—that Captain Dreyfus was the author—he found it impossible to retract it.

Some writers have called Bertillon a "notorious anti-Semite" and suggested that it was bigotry that led him to that rash—and ultimately false—judgment. But there are no other instances in Bertillon's life where he seems to have demonstrated anti-Semitism, and his brother, Jacques, was married to a Jewish woman.[35] Moreover, at the time Bertillon pronounced his judgment on the handwriting, he may not even have known the name of the person who was alleged to have written the *bordereau,* or that the suspect was Jewish. All he did know was that high-ranking military officers strongly believed that the writer was guilty. But though Bertillon probably did not act in the beginning out of anti-Semitism, he refused to change his mind as facts emerged to challenge his findings, and he came to speak of "the Jews" as being part of an attempt to undermine French military and governmental authority.[36] As a result, the Dreyfus affair divided the Bertillons, an egalitarian, anticlerical family, with Jacques becoming a passionate Dreyfusard who did not speak to his brother for several years.

What Bertillon was certainly guilty of—and this was quite characteristic of him throughout his career—was obstinately refusing to admit, once he had passed judgment, that he might be wrong. Through several courts-martial and trials over the next five years, Bertillon would be called on to testify. Offered a chance to change his mind by expanding on his earlier warning that a forgery might have been attempted, Bertillon decided that the forger was—Dreyfus himself! His rationale for this startling conclusion became increasingly convoluted. Bertillon posited that Dreyfus had adopted the formation of certain letters from the handwriting of his brother and wife in an attempt to disguise his own script. In support of his convoluted claim, Bertillon produced a schematic chart that made no sense to anyone who saw it. General Auguste Mercier, the minister of war who had staked his reputation on convicting Dreyfus, brought Bertillon to the president of the republic, Jean Casimir-Périer, to explain his reasoning. Casimir-Périer told a confidant that Bertillon was "given to an extraordinary and cabalistic madness. . . . I thought I had an escapee from La Salpetrière or Villejuif [asylums] before me." The word the French president used to describe the detective was "madman."[37]

The officers who were pressing for Dreyfus's conviction, however, portrayed Bertillon's judgment as a scientific certainty. Bertillon himself, swept along by the flattery, declared, "The proof is there and is irrefutable. From the very first day, you knew my opinion. It is now absolute, complete, and admitting of no reservation."[38] He was never to soften that self-confident assertion, despite later evidence that overwhelmingly contradicted it.

Several more highly publicized trials marked the course of the affair, Bertillon testifying at all of them. At each, he violated the very principle that he tried to instill in those who adopted his system: to see as truly and objectively as possible. Abandoning that only subjected him to more ridicule. At the 1898 trial at which Émile Zola was tried for libel after he accused the minister of war of framing Dreyfus, Bertillon's performance had drawn hoots of laughter from Zola's supporters. There too, he brought as part of his evidence diagrams and charts and enlarged photographs to defend his system, but they only confused everyone who saw them.

An observer at the trial, an official of the Ministry of Foreign Affairs, wrote in his journal his impressions of the participants: "I nearly forgot the *handwriting experts,* absurd creatures incapable of agreeing on the most elementary deductions, flinging their extraordinary theories in one another's faces and running down and abusing one another like Molière's doctors. But one of them deserves special mention—Bertillon, who is a madman, a maniac, armed with the crafty, obstinate, and powerful dialectic that is the characteristic of interpretative psychosis."[39] Zola's defense lawyers mocked Bertillon so cruelly that he became tongue-tied. The judge rescued him by declaring, "Let us say that the witness does not want to speak."[40]

At Dreyfus's second court-martial, Bertillon once again stunned objective observers with his labyrinthine presentations. When the defense attorney cross-examined him, he punctured Bertillon's self-assurance, drawing laughter from the spectators. An English reporter described the scene: "Now and again M. Bertillon's voice rose in hateful shrieks. There were interludes when he clenched his fist and struck the bar, swearing that Dreyfus was the traitor. The voice rang out with passion and excitement. You beheld in him the man vain unto madness with confidence in his atrocious phantasies. He was at last taking his revenge for all the insults of those who had called him a fit subject for an asylum of the insane."[41]

In April 1904, at the Cour de Cassation, three of France's most eminent scientists reviewed Bertillon's work. Using the cutting-edge scientific instruments of the time, the trio took a fresh look at the *bordereau.* They tested Bertillon's argument that the writing had to have come from a person using the type of grid used in drawing military maps and utilized a *macro-micromètre*, developed for astronomy and the mapping of the skies, to check the handwriting and measure the distances between and within the letters. Their instruments were far more exact and technologically advanced than those of Bertillon, and in a sense, he was outmeasured. Stating their conclusions based on statistical probability, they demolished Bertillon's argument and concluded that Bertillon's work was devoid of all scientific value.

The scientists' testimony was crucial in clearing Dreyfus of all charges. Perhaps it was surprising, then, that Bertillon was not correspondingly disgraced and discredited, like some of the military officers who had concocted false evidence against Dreyfus. In fact, Bertillon kept his job, and his prestige does not seem to have declined appreciably.

viii

As impressive as the Bertillon identification system was, it had two flaws. First, it had little use at the crime scene itself: criminals did not leave their measurements behind. Second, its effectiveness was tied to accuracy and diligence. The system's detractors proved correct when they asserted that police officers required very careful training to make measurements that were precise enough to be effective. Those two deficits were addressed in a new system that began to be developed shortly after Bertillon's: fingerprinting.

Perhaps it was the humiliation he suffered when he ventured beyond strictly scientific matters that led to Bertillon's other great failure—his refusal to recognize the importance of fingerprinting. It was particularly poignant, for had he reacted differently, he could have turned this failure into his greatest success.

From antiquity, it has been known that the patterns on the tips of fingers could be used as identification; ancient Chinese documents were sometimes signed with thumbprints. Mark Twain mentions thumbprint identification of a criminal in *Life on the Mississippi,* written in 1883. But the modern use of fingerprints is said to date from a letter written by Henry Faulds, an English physician working in Japan, to the journal *Nature* in October 1880. Faulds based his observations on his examination of Japanese pottery, where the makers had left fingerprints in the clay. He suggested that the prints never changed throughout a person's life, and he also took the first step toward the classification of fingerprints by describing the three categories of whorls, loops, and arches. This suggestion prompted a response from Sir William Herschel, a British official in India, who since 1858 had been using fingerprints affixed to paper as a means of identification for the residents of Bengal, the territory where he served. Sir Francis Galton, a British anthropologist, took notice of Herschel's work and began to investigate further; his books and articles, published in the early 1890s, popularized the subject of fingerprint identification. Galton—an adherent of bertillonage—realized that fingerprints could be important as an identification tool, but he failed to grasp their real significance: that they could connect a criminal to the scene of the crime.

The first country in which fingerprints would be used to solve a crime was Argentina, owing to the influence of Juan Vucetich. Born in Croatia, Vucetich had immigrated to Argentina in 1881. He went to work at the Central Police Department in La Plata, where he impressed his superiors with his intelligence and hard work. Two years later he became head of the Statistical Bureau and was given the responsibility of organizing the Department of Identity. The country had been using the anthropometric system since 1889, so Vucetich had to apply bertillonage to the prisoners and suspects. When Vucetich read about fingerprinting, he immediately saw that it would revolutionize police work. Fingerprints, he realized, were easier to obtain and more accurate than Bertillon measurements—but his superior told him to stick to anthropometry.

Pursuing a dual track, Vucetich developed his own system of fingerprint classification while he was filling out anthropometry cards. He identified four common fingerprint traits: arches, prints with a triangle pattern on the right side, prints with a triangle pattern on the left side, and prints with triangles on both sides. Vucetich represented these patterns with the first four letters of the alphabet. He called the system dactiloscopia.[42]

In 1892, a sordid murder case gave Vucetich the opportunity to show the worth of his system. In Necochea, a coastal town two hundred and fifty miles south of La Plata, Francisca Rojas informed the police that a man named Valásquez had killed her two children in a frenzy of jealousy. Taken into custody, Valásquez admitted that he loved Francisca, even that he had threatened her, but denied that he had killed her children. Even when police tried to beat a confession out of him, he did not change his story. The local authorities had Valásquez tied up and laid next to the bodies of the dead children overnight in the hope that guilt would make him confess. But the next morning the suspect still claimed he was innocent.

An informant told the police that Rojas, the children's mother, was involved with a young lover who said he would marry her if not for her children. Focusing now on Rojas, the local police spent a night outside her house rattling windows and making ghostlike sounds, supposed to mimic an avenging angel. (Such was the advanced state of police investigation in Argentina at the time.) That had no effect either. The police now looked for help from the regional headquarters of La Plata. Vucetich sent Carlos Álvarez, one of his most trusted men, to try to solve the case.

Inspector Álvarez examined the crime scene and saw a stain on the bedroom door illuminated by the evening sun. A closer look showed it to be a bloody thumbprint. He cut it out with a saw and took the wooden piece to the station house. He called Rojas in and rolled her right thumb on an ink pad, then pressed the print on a piece of paper. Studying the two with a magnifying glass, he saw that the prints were the same. When he questioned Rojas again, she broke down and confessed. She was tried for murder and convicted.

Vucetich had followed the case and felt it proved his argument for the superiority of fingerprints. He wrote a friend, "I hardly dare to believe it, but my theory has proved its worth. . . . I hold one trump card now, and I hope I shall soon have more."[43] He did, and within a few years, Argentina became the first country to change from bertillonage to fingerprints. With this success, Vucetich's prestige—and his method—spread thoughout South America.

A skeptical Bertillon saw fingerprints as a threat to his own system, which, among other things, had brought him the respect he craved. In 1893 he wrote in his *Textbook of Anthropometry,* "Skin markings have insufficiently distinct gradations to serve as a basis for archives."[44] But starting the following year, he began to include some fingerprints on his file cards, taking the prints of the thumb and three largest fingers of the right hand, though the cards were still filed according to the anthropometric system.

Two failures made it clear that fingerprints were needed. In 1901, it was found that twin brothers curiously named Albert Ebenezer and Ebenezer Albert Fox—English criminals who provided alibis for each other—could only be differentiated by fingerprints, not by bertillonage. (Identical twins do not have the same fingerprints.) Two years later in the United States, another case showed the limitations of bertillonage. Two convicts at the U.S. Penitentiary at Leavenworth, Kansas, turned out to have identical measurements. Though unrelated, the men looked amazingly alike and even had the same name, Will West. The only way to tell them apart was through fingerprints.

Ironically, however, Bertillon is often credited as being the first European detective to apprehend a criminal based on fingerprint evidence alone. On October 17, 1902, he went to the rue du Faubourg Saint-Honoré to photograph a murder scene. Joseph Reibel, the servant of a dentist named Alaux, had been murdered in the dentist's office. A desk and a cupboard with glass panes had been broken open, but so little had actually been stolen that Bertillon immediately guessed that the killing had not been the product of a robbery. While photographing the scene, Bertillon found a pane of glass with fingerprints. He took it to his lab to see if it would be possible to photograph the prints. Sure enough, by placing the glass against a dark background and using an arc lamp, he obtained an excellent reproduction.

Then, because he had some fingerprints on file, having collected them for eight years by that time, he started his assistants checking to see if any matches would turn up. Of course, this was a laborious process because Bertillon's files were still arranged by physical measurements, and in the search for fingerprint identification, each card had to be examined. Remarkably, a card was found with the same prints (luckily, the killer of Reibel had used his right hand on the pane of glass; Bertillon at this time did not take prints from the left hand)—those of an ex-convict named Henri-Léon Scheffer, who soon turned up in Marseilles. He confessed and was sent to prison for life. Bertillon's surmise that the crime was not motivated by robbery proved correct. Reibel and Scheffer had been homosexual lovers, and when Reibel was no longer interested, Scheffer had killed him in a moment of passion.

This latest feat of deduction brought Bertillon new acclaim. A caricature even appeared in *L'Assiette au Beurre,* a Paris newspaper, showing Bertillon peering through a magnifying glass at some prints left on the grimy wall of a public toilet. But in this instance, Bertillon was annoyed by the publicity. He failed to see that the case illustrated perfectly the value of fingerprints: left at the scene of a crime, they could identify the perpetrator as certainly as if he had left a calling card. Even so, as a result of the case, a legend (frequently repeated) grew that Bertillon had actually invented fingerprint identification.

For Bertillon, this case was a mere episode. He would not listen to his French colleagues, such as Lacassagne and Locard, who by now recognized the importance of fingerprinting. Indeed, Locard had been fascinated from the beginning by the new method and performed painful experiments on himself—burning his fingers with cold and hot irons—to see if his fingerprints would change, finding that they did not. But Bertillon treated the new discovery as a minor supplement to anthropometry. He never repudiated his statement, "My measurements are surer than any fingerprint pattern,"[45] and by 1910, France was the only country in Europe that was not using fingerprinting as its primary identification system.

ix

With or without fingerprints, Bertillon was still successful in solving many crimes, and his accomplishments were recognized throughout Europe and the United States. Among his commendations was a medal from Queen Victoria for helping to identify bodies from the wreck of the ship *Drummond Castle* in 1896; though there were few comparative materials for Bertillon to work with, his ability to take precise measurements allowed some relatives to claim their dead.

The American muckraking writer Ida Tarbell came to interview Bertillon in 1894. "The prisoner who passes through his hands," an admiring Tarbell wrote, "is subjected to measurements and descriptions that leave him forever 'spotted.' He may efface his tattooing, compress his chest, dye his hair, extract his teeth, scar his body, dissimulate his height. It is useless. The record against him is unfailing. He cannot pass the Bertillon archives without recognition; and, if he is at large, the relentless record may be made to follow him into every corner of the globe where there is a printing press, and every man who reads may become a detective furnished with information which will establish his identity. He is never again safe."[46] Tarbell said that the Parisian apaches had invented a new phrase in their street argot: being arrested was referred to as *un sourire pour le studio Bertillon,* or "a smile for the Bertillon studio."[47]

In the same interview, Tarbell asked Bertillon whether his measuring system proved or disproved the theories of Cesare Lombroso and many other criminologists, who believed that certain physical characteristics were signs of criminality. He dismissed these theories, many of which were based on sheer racism. "No, I do not feel convinced that it is the lack of symmetry in the visage, or the size of the orbit, or the shape of the jaw, which make a man an evil-doer," he answered.

> A certain characteristic may incapacitate him for fulfilling his duties, thus thrusting him down in the struggle for life, and he becomes a criminal because he is down. Lombroso, for example, might say that since there is a spot on the eye of the majority of criminals, therefore the spot on the eye indicates a tendency to crime; not at all. The spot is a sign of defective vision, and the man who does not see well is a poorer workman than he who has a strong, keen eyesight. He falls behind in his trade, loses heart, takes to bad ways, and turns up in the criminal ranks. It was not the spot on his eye which made him a criminal; it only prevented his having an equal chance with his comrades. The same thing is true of other so-called criminal signs. One needs to exercise great discretion in making anthropological deductions.[48]

Anthropometry led to a significant change in the way nations viewed their populations. A French law passed in July 1912 required "nomads and itinerants"—people such as traveling peddlers and the like—to carry "anthropometric identity cards."[49] These cards, which included the bearer's name, date and place of birth, parents' names, a photograph, and fingerprints, were the forerunners of the national identity card.

Significantly, it became a crime *not* to carry evidence of who one was. Neither criminals nor law-abiding citizens could disappear into a crowd or find anonymity by moving from place to place. As the requirements to provide proof of identity grew stronger, one would always be connected with one's past through records.

Of course, in some places, people resisted encroachments on their privacy, mourned their right to be anonymous. This may explain the popularity of fictional criminals, particularly those—like Fantômas—who were able to change their appearance and identity easily.

In 1911, a short time after the theft of the *Mona Lisa,* the reporter Katherine Blackford interviewed Bertillon about his system. He demonstrated several kinds of measuring and photographic equipment. At the end of their talk, she wrote, "we went up to the roof of the Palais de Justice [where he worked] whence we could see the Panthéon, the towers of and spire of Notre Dame, and Sainte-Chapelle. Only a few days before, on account of the theft of 'la Joconde' from the Louvre, he had photographed this view."[50]

Bertillon was now fifty-eight years old, with a worldwide reputation. Robert Heindl, commissioner of police in Dresden, said of Bertillon's long term of service, "Paris became the Mecca of the police, and Bertillon their prophet."[51] Solving the theft of the masterpiece would be the capstone of his career, if he could accomplish it. In a promising development, two suspects were soon brought into custody. However, they would lead Bertillon and the Sûreté on a false trail into the world of art, which was in the midst of its own identity crisis: struggling to define reality and to rediscover how to portray it.

THE SUSPECTS

The fifty-thousand-franc reward that the *Paris-Journal* had offered for information leading to the return of the *Mona Lisa* naturally brought numerous replies that proved to be hoaxes or false alarms. One response, however, led to the arrest of two suspects whose names were well known to the avant-garde art community of Paris: Pablo Picasso and Guillaume Apollinaire.

The letter that set off this train of events appeared in the *Paris-Journal* on August 29, 1911, addressed to the editor, who reprinted it on his paper's front page with the precise sum and time omitted:

> *Monsieur,*
> *On the 7th of May, 1911, I stole a Phoenician statuette from one of the galleries of the Louvre. I am holding this at your disposition, in return for the sum of _____ francs. Trusting that you will respect my confidence, I shall be glad to meet you at [such and such a place] between _____ and _____ o'clock.*[1]

As the editor commented, although the newspaper had offered a reward for the *Mona Lisa,* it "has never undertaken to ransom *all* the works of art stolen from the Louvre." Nonetheless, this "was an opportunity to check a detail that would be interesting if proven genuine," so one of the paper's reporters went to meet "a young man, aged somewhere between twenty and twenty-five, very well-mannered . . . whose face and look and behavior bespoke at once a kind heart and a certain lack of scruple."[2]

This was indeed the thief, and he showed the reporter what he had taken from the Louvre. The reporter described it as "a rather crude bust, an example of the somewhat rudimentary art of the Phoenicians."[3] When a curator of the museum examined it, he confirmed from markings that it was from the Louvre's collection (no one had even noticed it was missing) but said it was not a Phoenician but an Iberian sculpture, recently excavated from diggings at Cerro de los Santos near Osuna, Spain. Such details didn't interest the *Paris-Journal,* which gleefully exhibited the object in its window and paid the young thief, who happened to be a writer, to tell its readers how he had obtained it:

> It was in March, 1907 that I entered the Louvre for the first time—a young man with time to kill and no money to spend. . . . [Other newspapers had insisted that the *Mona Lisa*'s theft was the result of allowing the public into the museum free of charge. This letter seemed to confirm that, and the practice was soon stopped.]
>
> It was about one o'clock. I found myself in the gallery of Asian antiquities. A single guard was sitting motionless. I was about to climb the stairs leading to the floor above when I noticed a half-open door on my left. I had only to push it, and found myself in a room filled with hieroglyphs and Egyptian statues . . . in any case the place impressed me profoundly because of the deep silence and the absence of any human being. I walked through several adjoining rooms, stopping now and

again in a dim corner to caress an ample neck or a well-turned cheek.

It was at that moment that I suddenly realized how easy it would be to pick up and take away almost any object of moderate size. . . . I was just then in a small room, about two meters by two in the "Gallery of Phoenician Antiquities."

Being absolutely alone, and hearing no sounds whatever, I took the time to examine about fifty heads that were there, and I chose one of a woman, with, as I recall, twisted, conical forms on each side. I put the statue under my arm, pulled up the collar of my overcoat with my left hand, and calmly walked out, asking my way of the guard, who was still completely motionless.

I sold the statue to a Parisian painter friend of mine. He gave me a little money—fifty francs, I think, which I lost the same night in a billiard parlor.

"What of it?" I said to myself. "All Phoenicia is there for the taking."[4]

The thief went on to describe how he stole and sold several other pieces before leaving the city. He had returned in May 1911 and resumed his career of looting objects from the Louvre. He noticed that the collection in the Phoenician room, his favorite hunting ground, was much diminished, and blamed that on "imitators of mine."[5]

Unfortunately, the thief wrote, what promised to be a steady source of income was now ruined because of "this hullabaloo in the paintings department [the *Mona Lisa*'s theft]. I regret this exceedingly, for there is a strange, an almost voluptuous charm about stealing works of art, and I shall probably have to wait several years before resuming my activities."[6]

i

Naturally enough, the article caused a sensation. *Paris-Journal* encouraged its readers to think that the unnamed thief might well be the culprit in the *Mona Lisa* case as well. France's undersecretary of state of beaux-arts, Étienne Dujardin-Beaumetz, under pressure because he was ultimately the person responsible for the Louvre, filed a complaint with the public prosecutor against a "person or persons unknown," in an attempt to get the newspaper to reveal the name of the person who stole the "Phoenician" heads.

But nowhere was the consternation greater than at 11, boulevard de Clichy, in Montmartre, the artists' quarter on the Right Bank of the Seine. This was the residence and studio of Pablo Picasso and his mistress Fernande Olivier — and Picasso was the artist who had bought the "Phoenician" statuettes from the Louvre thief. The apartment was a comfortable one, very different from the "starving artist" garret of myth. Picasso had finished with that phase of his career two years earlier when he moved out of his previous apartment, where the only heat had come from a rusty iron stove and there was no gas or electricity. There, Picasso had to hold a candle next to the canvas when he worked at night, his favorite time for painting. Now, he was selling paintings regularly to admirers like Gertrude Stein and her brother Leo, wealthy Americans who had settled in Paris. Picasso also had a dealer, Daniel-Henry Kahnweiler, who relieved the young Spanish artist of the need to struggle to find gallery space or, even worse, submit his paintings to a jury for the annual Salon des Indépendants. The Picassos (as Fernande liked to call the couple, mistaking Pablo's affection for a permanent attachment) even had a maid now, the hallmark of the Parisian bourgeoisie. The maid liked her job, for the Picassos often slept late, relieving her from early morning duties.

On his first visit to Paris in 1900, just before his nineteenth birthday, Picasso and his friend the poet Carles Casagemas found rooms in Montmartre, where the atmosphere was startingly free compared to that in Barcelona, their hometown. Pablo discovered that young, beautiful women were willing to pose nude for him (and sleep with him), and he and Carles often stayed out all night at cafés where art and literature and sex and politics were discussed far into the night. They took girlfriends dancing at the Moulin de la Galette, a gaslit dance hall next to one of the few working windmills left on Montmartre. Picasso was inspired to paint the scene, brilliantly capturing its garish, underworldly quality. He and Carles visited the Louvre, no doubt standing like any other tourists in front of the *Mona Lisa,* and the Museé du Luxembourg, where the works of then-modern artists like the impressionists were on display. When he left Paris, keeping a promise to his parents to be home by Christmas, Pablo told himself that he would return.

Early in 1901, Picasso started an avant-garde art magazine in Madrid while Carles returned to Paris, trying to rekindle his relationship with a woman he had fallen in love with. When she spurned him, Carles shot himself (after trying to kill her first and missing). The news shocked Picasso, and he threw himself into the creation of art. This was the beginning of his Blue Period, named not only for the predominant color in his canvases, but for the melancholy quality he gave his human subjects. Later that year he moved into the apartment Carles had occupied in Paris and found backers for a well-received exhibition of his own work. He also met a neighbor named Max Jacob, a homosexual poet and would-be painter who would become one of Picasso's closest friends. (Picasso, seeing Jacob's paintings, advised him to stick to poetry.[7])

After a return to Barcelona, Picasso settled in Paris for good in April 1904, renting a run-down apartment in an oddly shaped building on the hill of Montmartre at 13, rue Ravignan. Max Jacob called it the Bateau-Lavoir because it resembled one of the laundry barges moored in the Seine. The place was a haven for artists and other bohemians, and arguments, singing, weeping, and cries of passion could be heard through the thin walls at all hours. Picasso, who loved animals, kept two dogs and, in a drawer, a small white mouse. In August, during a thunderstorm, he found a sodden kitten on the street and picked it up. After he reached the Bateau-Lavoir, he encountered a young woman who had gone inside to seek shelter from the storm. He offered her the kitten, and when she laughed, he invited her to see his studio.

Her name was Fernande Olivier (the last name was her own invention) and although she was only a few months older than Picasso, she had already been married and given birth to a son. To him, she was a woman of the world, the first he had ever known other than prostitutes. Asking her to move into his apartment, as he did a few months later, was a rite of passage for him.

As for his appeal to her, "There was nothing especially attractive about him at first sight," she was to recall. After all, he was five feet three inches tall, with stiff, unkempt hair and a gnome-like face. "But his radiance, an inner fire one sensed in him, gave him a sort of magnetism which I was unable to resist." [8] That volcanic energy made itself felt through his penetrating dark eyes, which shine out from every photograph made of Picasso, regarding the camera with defiance.

Picasso was possessive of Fernande, preventing her even from going shopping alone, lest some man see her and carry her off. He forbade her to do housework, for he liked chaos where he worked (even later, when they had a housekeeper, the woman was instructed not to touch his studio), and Fernande was perfectly content to serve as his sexual companion. She showed up increasingly in his paintings, which now took on a rosy hue. It must have increased Fernande's sense of security that he sometimes painted her with a husband and child.

Now with her on his arm, he circulated through the cabarets and bars of Montmartre, meeting others who aspired, as he did, to become artists of one kind or another. The most important of these to his career would be Guillaume Apollinaire, two years older than Picasso but very much a man of the world who had learned the invaluable skill of appearing to know far more than he did.

The story of how Apollinaire and Picasso met has many versions. Not even the year is certain, and the two principals themselves recalled it differently. Nevertheless, it was a signal moment in the history of art. Apollinaire would serve as Picasso's herald and publicist; doing so would enhance Apollinaire's reputation as well. Picasso was inarticulate on the subject of his art, and Apollinaire was articulate on everything. They were like two elements that, when combined, created an explosion.

Max Jacob offered one version of the first meeting between the two, at a bar on the rue Amsterdam:

> Apollinaire was smoking a short-stemmed pipe and expiating on Petronius and Nero to some rather vulgar-looking people. . . . He was wearing a stained light-colored suit, and a tiny straw hat was perched atop his famous pear-shaped head. He had hazel eyes, terrible and gleaming, a bit of curly blond hair fell over his forehead, his mouth looked like a little pimento, he had strong limbs, a broad chest looped across by a platinum watch-chain, and a ruby on his finger. The poor boy was always being taken for a rich man because his mother—an adventuress, to put it politely—clothed him from head to toe [Apollinaire was living in a suburb of Paris with his mother]. . . . Without interrupting his talk he stretched out a hand that was like a tiger's paw over the marble-topped table. He stayed in his seat until he was finished. Then the three of us went out, and we began that life of three-cornered friendship which lasted almost until the war, never leaving one another whether for work, meals, or fun.[9]

It was not long before Apollinaire visited Picasso's studio, and he later recalled that it was "cluttered with canvases representing mystical harlequins and drawings on which people walked and which everyone was allowed to carry off."[10] Viewing the Blue Period work, Apollinaire recognized the younger man's genius and promptly took it upon himself to interpret and publicize it.

Picasso's paintings had previously been of interest to a limited circle, but now Apollinaire began to give life in print to the somber figures in Picasso's canvases: "These children, who have no one to caress them, understand everything. These women, whom no one loves now, are remembering. They shrink back into the shadows as if into some ancient church. They disappear at daybreak, having attained consolation through silence. Old men stand about, wrapped in icy fog. These old men have the right to beg without humility."[11] Descriptions such as these made others curious about Picasso's art and led them to the Bateau-Lavoir to see it.

And because Picasso habitually worked late at night and slept mornings, the studio became a meeting place for many of the artists and writers who lived in the building or nearby. Picasso, encouraging them, painted a slogan on his door: "Au rendezvous des poètes" ("Meeting place of poets").[12] Apollinaire frequently brought people who had new ideas that he thought Picasso should know about. Roger Shattuck, in his influential book *The Banquet Years,* called him "a ringmaster of the arts."[13]

ii

One of Apollinaire's great gifts was the ability to rapidly absorb the intellectual currents that swarmed around him. Paris at the turn of the twentieth century was a ferment of ideas and theories—not merely artistic, but scientific, and often the two worlds overlapped. Shattuck called Montmartre at this time a "central laboratory,"[14] where collaboration gave birth to radically new kinds of art. Experimentation was the order of the day, part of a shift in thinking that heralded the true beginning of the twentieth century. The dominant intellectual spirit of the nineteenth century had been positivism, the philosophy that posited that the only knowable reality was what could be observed. Yet even before the old century wound to a close, an increasing number of people were rebelling against that notion. The poet Paul Claudel wrote, "At last we are leaving that hideous world . . . of the nineteenth century, that prison camp, that hideous mechanism governed by laws that were completely inflexible and, worst of all, knowable and teachable."[15]

In science the new trend manifested itself through the work of such men as Max Planck, who in 1900 formulated the quantum theory, and Albert Einstein, who in 1905 extended Planck's insight in a series of groundbreaking papers, one of which (his doctoral thesis) offered a proof for the reality of atoms and molecules.[16] These and other discoveries revolutionized the science of physics, establishing the fact that there was a whole world of unseen particles beneath the level of ordinary vision. Awareness of such theories was not confined to a narrow circle. Henri Poincaré, France's leading scientist, gave public lectures and wrote pamphlets that were intended to make high-level mathematics and science accessible to the average person. These ideas, even if not fully understood, made their way to the cafés where Picasso and his friends met. Poincaré wrote, "A scientist worthy of the name, above all a mathematician, experiences in his work the same impression as an artist; his pleasure is as great and of the same nature."[17]

That held true in reverse for many of the avant-garde artists living in Paris at the beginning of the twentieth century. The great achievement of Renaissance art had been the discovery of perspective, which allowed artists to portray three-dimensional scenes and objects realistically. However, the invention of photography by two Frenchmen, Nicéphore Niépce and Louis Daguerre, around 1840, made it possible for anyone to accomplish that perfectly. Though academic artists continued to work in the old tradition, others began the quest for a new kind of art that would reveal more than photography could. Manuel "Manolo" Hugué, a sculptor and fellow Spaniard who had known Picasso for years, said, "Picasso used to talk a lot then about the fourth dimension and he carried around the mathematics books of Henri Poincaré."[18] (These were not textbooks, but books that Poincaré had written at a popular level for ordinary people to read.)

Picasso was not alone in his fascination with the fourth dimension. Inventions such as the telephone, wireless communication, and the airplane had revolutionized people's experience of time and space. One could be there without being there. (In Paris, people with telephones sometimes connected them to a line that allowed them to listen to performances at the opera without leaving home.) Now, people speculated on the possibility of traveling through time as easily as one moved through space. If time was merely a dimension, as some scientists were already claiming, then it could be traveled. The publication of H. G. Wells's popular novel *The Time Machine* in 1895 further brought the idea into the public consciousness.

As originally proposed, the fourth dimension was not merely identified with time; it was part of a new, non-Euclidean geometry and actually occupied some higher, unseen realm of space. Poincaré, among others, argued that "the characteristic property of space, that of having three dimensions, is only a property of our table of distribution, an internal property of human intelligence, so to speak. It would suffice to destroy certain of these connections, that is to say of the association of ideas, to give a different table of distribution, and that might be enough for space to acquire a fourth dimension." [19]

It was this more technical meaning of the term *fourth dimension* that most interested writers such as Apollinaire, who sought to find literary forms to express it. He began to abandon the traditional method of printing poems on the page in horizontal lines — instead creating arrangements of words that were intended to express as much as the words themselves. One of these so-called *calligrammes* was about time, and the words formed the shape of a pocket watch. Another formed the shape of the Eiffel Tower, which had a radio antenna at the top to transmit messages.

In some of Apollinaire's prose works, he invented characters who moved across time and space simultaneously (a concept later termed *simultanism*). Apollinaire advised others to read the Fantômas novels as rapidly as possible, to heighten the impression of simultanism. In Apollinaire's story "Le roi-lune" ("The Moon-King"), the hero wears a belt that enables him to make love to all the women of all times. A story in another work, *L'hérésiarque et Cie.*, has as its central character the Baron d'Ormesan, whose *toucher à distance* enables him to appear simultaneously in many places around the world.[20] Not by coincidence, the baron was a movie director, for Apollinaire, like Picasso, was a great admirer of this new art form. (Apollinaire once wrote that typography itself was "brilliantly finishing its career, at the dawn of an age of new modes to reproduction, which are the cinema and the phonograph."[21] French filmmakers had already discovered special effects, and Paris audiences had seen time speeded up and people disappear from one place only to reappear in another an instant later, exactly as Apollinaire's characters did. One reason Apollinaire admired the Fantômas detective novels was that the antihero was able to create endless new identities for himself, changing with his surroundings.

Playing the role of "ringmaster of the arts," Apollinaire introduced Picasso to Alfred Jarry, the playwright who had shocked and enraged Paris in 1896 with his play *Ubu roi*—not so much for its scatalogical dialogue as for its ferocious ridicule of bourgeois life and values. Jarry was known for his personal eccentricities—even in Montmartre, a milieu where eccentricity was commonplace. He would sometimes sit in a café and in a monotone utter endless strings of nonsensical phrases. He liked to carry two pistols, displaying them openly and occasionally firing them into the air. People enjoyed recalling the occasion when a stranger asked Jarry for a light, and he fired his pistol at the end of the man's cigarette.

Jarry's personal style as well as his artistic vision was rooted in his passionate anarchism. He saw society as corrupt and took every opportunity to mock it. Picasso too had been associated with anarchists in both Spain and France, and in fact the French police kept an eye on him, probably for this reason. (The police dossier on him is sealed until the year 2033.) The poet André Salmon, another member of what people called La Bande à Picasso ("the Pi-

casso Gang"), traveled in anarchist circles and had even met Jules
Bonnot, who was to achieve fame as the head of a gang that carried
out spectacular crimes in the name of anarchy. When Picasso and
Salmon first met, Picasso had recommended a book of anarchist
poetry, which included calls to violence such as

> *But our mission is big.*
> *If we kill, if we die,*
> *It's for the wealthy pig*
> *Asleep in his money-sty!*[22]

Apollinaire embraced anarchy too, but his was of a more literary
type, best expressed in poetry and essays. He promoted Picasso
and other avant-garde painters partly because they attacked the
established order, which—as an outsider himself—he opposed. It
was, he believed, necessary to break down not merely the political
order but the artistic establishment as well. A friend recalled that
Apollinaire "took . . . me to the Louvre, to the gallery of antiquities. He spoke with great verve against the *Antinoüs;* it wasn't that
he was trying to destroy classical sculpture but rather that, in his
love for a new art, for the need to surpass all that was known in art,
he was attacking the foundations, impeccable in themselves, but
the consequences of which lead to the academic style."[23]

Jarry, seeing Picasso as a kindred spirit, gave him a Browning
automatic pistol (the same kind that the Bonnot Gang later used).
Max Jacob saw this gift as the transference of a sacred symbol to
encourage Picasso to break through to new artistic territory, the
recognition by one anarchist of his successor. (Picasso is said to
have fired the pistol whenever someone asked him to answer a
question about what the meaning of his paintings was.)

Jarry also helped point Picasso in the direction that the new art
might take. Numerous European countries were still using their
military might to colonize and control nations in Africa and Asia.
In the case of France, this was justified as a "civilizing mission."
Jarry satirized this by telling the story of a Negro who had left a

Paris bar without paying. Actually, Jarry said, he was an explorer from Africa investigating the culture of France and had simply neglected to provide himself with "native" currency.[24]

iii

In the summer of 1905, Clovis Sagot, a former circus clown, opened an art gallery at 46, rue Laffitte, in the ninth arrondissement, and Picasso provided some works to put on the walls. While visiting Sagot's establishment, Picasso was struck by the appearance of a woman who had come to view the art. His mistress Fernande later described the visitor as "masculine, in her voice, in all her walk. Fat, short, massive, beautiful head, strong, with noble features, accentuated regular, intelligent eyes."[25] It was a thirty-two-year-old expatriate from the United States named Gertrude Stein. She and her brother Leo lived off an inheritance and collected art in their apartment at 27, rue de Fleurus. As it happened, Leo liked one of Picasso's paintings, *Young Girl with a Basket of Flowers*, but Gertrude did not. It was the girl's feet that she detested, to the point where she asked if they could be cut out of the painting. Her more amenable brother purchased it for 150 francs — feet intact.

Picasso painted his address on the work he was doing, and the Steins came to visit his studio. In turn, they invited Picasso and Fernande to come to the soirées at their apartment. At one of these, Picasso met Henri Matisse, who was outgoing and charming in contrast to Picasso's customary demeanor of moody silence (which may have been due to the fact that French was not his native language). Matisse was the leading figure of a group of painters who were called fauves ("wild beasts") because of their extravagant use of color — again in contrast to Picasso's almost monochromatic styles. That spring of 1906, Matisse displayed at the Steins' apartment a large canvas titled *Le bonheur de vivre* (*The Joy of Life*), which represented a step forward not only in his own artistic development but in solving the problem modern artists were preoccupied with: of finding a new way to represent reality on canvas. Matisse had actually begun to discard perspective, the great achievement of Renaissance art, instead utilizing color and form to suggest the movement of human figures. Picasso, whose ambition was boundless, certainly saw the painting as a challenge—and Matisse as a rival. (Picasso's friend Salmon loyally wrote on the walls of Montmartre slogans like "Matisse is mad!" "Matisse is more dangerous than alcohol!" and "Matisse has done worse than war." These annoyed Matisse, who in spite of his revolutionary art sought respectability in his private life.)

Among the first of those searching for an artistic style that would reveal more than photographs were the impressionists, beginning around 1880. Much of their work is concerned with light especially in landscapes, creating effects that earlier artists would have regarded as distortions. One of the impressionists' artistic successors was Paul Cézanne. (He originally exhibited with them.) Not well known until later in his life, his work received major exhibitions in Paris from 1905 through 1907, the year after his death. Cézanne believed that all objects could be expressed as spheres, cubes, or cylinders, and this can be seen in his later work, though the objects are still represented in a recognizable way. Cézanne also took the first steps toward painting objects from different perspectives in the same picture. All of these techniques made their impression on Picasso, who was still searching for a new path of his own.

Picasso offered, or was asked, to paint the portraits of Leo and Gertrude Stein. The one of Leo was quickly completed, but Gertrude's seemed more of a problem. She must have been unusually patient, for after she had come to his studio for eighty sittings, he still pronounced it unfinished. Usually a fast worker, he painted the head out entirely, leaving a blank space. "I can't see you any longer when I look," he told Gertrude.[26]

Perhaps feeling for the first time that Paris did not provide enough inspiration, perhaps unhappy that Matisse seemed more successful, Picasso thought about going away. Apollinaire suddenly came to the rescue, bringing the prominent art dealer Ambroise Vollard to the Bateau-Lavoir studio. Vollard had previously rejected one of Picasso's works when Max Jacob tried to sell it to him, and had even called Picasso mad. Now, however, he seemed eager to purchase almost everything he saw. He went off in a taxi with thirty paintings stuffed into the backseat, for which he gave Picasso two thousand francs. Though this was actually one of the great art bargains of all time, it was a windfall to Picasso, who had been scraping by on far less than one thousand francs a year.

To celebrate, Picasso took Fernande to Barcelona to meet his parents, showing off not only the beautiful woman he had acquired but some of his sudden wealth as well. He decided to spend the summer in Gósol, a tiny village in the Pyrenees that could be reached only on the back of a mule. It was a wild place, nestled between Spain and France, yet seeming to belong to neither. Fernande recalled, "In that vast, empty, magnificent countryside . . . he no longer seemed, as he did in Paris, to be outside society."[27]

There, that summer, he found the inspiration he had been seeking: the Iberian heads he recalled from the Louvre came to life in this desolate, ageless locale. When he returned to Paris, Picasso took out the unfinished portrait of Gertrude Stein and painted in a masklike face with almond-shaped eyes and a stern mouth. With the hands of the sitter in the foreground the only other visible parts of the body, it is Picasso's *Mona Lisa*. When he showed the painting to Gertrude, she was delighted and put it on her wall. When others complained that she didn't look like that, Picasso replied calmly, "She will."[28]

Later that same year, he made a self-portrait with a face clearly inspired by the same source. "I did not use models again after Gosol," he explained. "Because just then I was working apart from any model. What I was looking for was something else."[29]

Picasso became interested not just in the Iberian heads that had inspired Gertrude Stein's portrait, but in African art as well, particularly angular masks. The Bande à Picasso, perhaps inspired by their leader, began to look for and even purchase examples of "primitive" masks and statuettes in small shops. André Derain, a painter who frequently visited the Bateau-Lavoir studio, recalled, "On the rue de Rennes, I often passed the shop of Père Sauvage. There were Negro statuettes in his window. I was struck by their character, their purity of line. . . . So I bought one and showed it to Gertrude Stein, whom I was visiting that day. And then Picasso arrived. He took to it immediately." [30]

Years later, on one of the few occasions Picasso talked about his influences, he recalled those days. He had gone to the Trocadéro Palace, where an exhibition of African masks was on view. "I understood that it was very important: something was happening to me, right? The masks weren't just like any other pieces of sculpture. Not at all. They were magic things. . . . The Negro pieces were *intercesseurs,* mediators; ever since then I've known the word in French. They were against everything—against unknown, threatening spirits. . . . I understood; I too am against everything. I too believe that everything is unknown, that everything is an enemy! Everything! . . . I understood what the Negroes used their sculpture for. . . . They were weapons. To help people avoid coming under the influence of spirits again, to help them become independent. . . . If we give spirits a form, we become independent. . . . I understood why I was a painter." [31]

iv

At the beginning of 1907, Apollinaire met a young Belgian named Géry Pieret; they were working as writers for a magazine that offered advice to investors. (Evidently, the advice was not entirely objective, for the police appeared one day and shut down the publication.) The year before, Apollinaire had moved into his own apartment on the rue Henner, near the base of Montmartre. Picasso had introduced him to Marie Laurencin, a young woman who aspired to be a painter, and she had moved in with him. Marie recalled that they would make love in an armchair because Apollinaire did not like to muss the bed.

Pieret needed a place to stay, and Apollinaire unwisely let him use the couch to sleep on. Marie Laurencin recalled that he tried to make himself useful. One day, Pieret said to her, "Marie, this afternoon I am going to the Louvre: can I bring you anything you need?" [32] She assumed he meant the Magasins du Louvre, a department store. Instead he returned with the stone statuette that four years later, in his letter to the *Paris-Journal*, he admitted stealing from the "real" Louvre, the museum. The person he sold it to was Picasso, who purchased a second when Pieret pilfered that from the museum the following day. The theft of those two statuettes was to have a greater impact on the history of art than the disappearance of the *Mona Lisa* itself.

The previous winter, Picasso had ordered a large canvas stretched and mounted. He was preparing to paint a major work with several figures, something that would rival Matisse's *Le bonheur de vivre* and even Cézanne's unfinished painting *Baigneuses*. Both of these works had depicted nudes in a landscape. Picasso almost never worked outdoors, so he chose a setting for his nudes that would, by itself, guarantee to shock: a brothel.

Picasso had patronized brothels in the prostitute's quarter in Barcelona before he reached his fifteenth birthday,[33] and he painted this picture entirely from memory. His first sketches for the planned painting showed four prostitutes with two customers, a sailor and another man carrying a skull. Eventually Picasso dropped the crude symbolism of the skull and then eliminated the men altogether, adding a fifth prostitute. The viewers of the painting would now be the "customers."

Picasso continued to draw studies for the work, experimenting, trying new forms. No one is sure how long it took him, but finally he applied paint to his huge canvas, finishing the work, by some accounts, in May 1907. There are five figures in it, all apparently nude women covered only by a few scraps of white cloth. The faces of the three on the left reflect the Iberian sculpture that had already contributed to the portrait of Gertrude Stein and to Picasso's 1906 self-portrait. The faces of the two figures on the right are more out of the ordinary—grotesque, some would call them. What they most resemble are bronze masks from the French Congo, like those then on display in the ethnological museum at the Trocadéro Palace. The Congolese masks were often covered with striations and incised lines, but Picasso had distorted even those characteristics, twisting and shaping them to his own design so that they are ultimately his own, not African.

The faces were not the only stunningly different element of the painting. Picasso had abandoned perspective altogether, flattening the images and showing the women in contorted poses. One, squatting at the far right, lets the viewer see her back, front, and sides at the same time. These are not the soft, fleshy nudes of earlier painters; they are all jagged edges and triangles, lines and plane surfaces. The only other recognizable object in the painting is a haphazard collection of fruit at the bottom of the painting, as if Picasso were thumbing his nose at all the formal still lifes and lovingly painted bowls of fruit of previous artists. Much later, Picasso was to remark, "When the cubist painter thought, 'I'm going to paint a fruit bowl,' he set to work knowing that a fruit bowl in art and a fruit bowl in life had nothing in common.' "[34]

As a work by a serious artist, the painting was a departure of shattering proportions. It was as if Picasso had taken the pistol Jarry[35] had given him and fired it at all previous painting. He had committed what anarchists called the "propaganda of the deed"—he had put the ideology into action. Though the figures are static, the overall impact was violent.

No one except Fernande had seen the painting while it was in progress. Now, Picasso allowed those closest to him, those he most respected, to view it. No one understood it. Max Jacob thought that the best thing a friend could do was to remain silent. André Derain worried that "one day we shall find Pablo has hanged himself behind his great canvas."[36] Apollinaire, Picasso's herald and promoter, muttered, "Révolution," but could not bring himself to express anything at all about this painting in print. Later, writing about the theft of the two statuettes, Apollinaire said that he had tried to persuade Picasso "to give the statues back to the Louvre, but he was absorbed in his esthetic studies, and indeed from them Cubism was born. He told me that he had damaged the statues in an attempt to discover certain secrets of the classic yet barbaric art to which they belonged."[37] But it was not cubism that the statuettes inspired: it was this strange painting, which as yet had no name, so friends dubbed it *The Philosophical Brothel*. Not till later would it be given the title by which it is known today: *Les demoiselles d'Avignon* (*The Young Ladies of Avignon*).

Some viewers were more outspoken. Matisse interpreted it as an attack on modern art, a mockery, and vowed revenge.[38] Leo Stein laughed when he saw it, thinking the painting a joke, but came closest of anyone to understanding it when he said, "You've been trying to paint the fourth dimension. How amusing!"[39] It was indeed a new dimension that Picasso had discovered, blazing a trail that other painters would follow. Just as non-Euclidean geometry posited a realm unfamiliar to those who saw only with their eyes, and quantum physicists dealt with things that could not be seen, so did Picasso, who once said, "I paint objects as I think them, not as I see them."[40]

At first, few were able to see his accomplishment clearly. The dealer Vollard, who had so recently bought up virtually every canvas Picasso had to offer, now pronounced a virtual death sentence on the young Spaniard, saying he had no future as a painter.[41] However, at the very moment Vollard was leaving Picasso's studio, in walked Daniel-Henry Kahnweiler, a German who had become a banker in London before deciding that his true calling in life was to own an art gallery in Paris. That day at the Bateau-Lavoir, he purchased most of the studies that Picasso had done for the startling new work—a windfall for Picasso because he usually let visitors carry such things away for nothing—and asked to purchase the painting as well. But Picasso must have realized from the reaction of others that it was not yet time for his vision to be displayed, and he refused to sell it. A year later, he removed it from its stretcher, rolled it up, and put it away. Kahnweiler, however, would remain Picasso's dealer for the rest of his life.

V

One of those who had seen the painting and been awed by it was Georges Braque, a former housepainter from Normandy who had come to Paris and studied art in night classes. His first paintings were in the fauve style, of which Matisse was the master. Matisse, who may have been having second thoughts about *Les demoiselles,* brought him to Picasso's studio to see it. Timidly, Braque pointed out that the noses were wrong. Picasso insisted, "Noses are like that." Braque protested that Picasso was asking the viewer to accept something too difficult: "It's as if you wanted us to . . . drink kerosene in order to spit fire." [42]

However, Braque turned out to be the first to imbibe. That winter he painted a large nude that had the striated features characteristic of the two African-inspired figures in *Les demoiselles.* He spent the following summer, 1908, at L'Estaque, a fishing village in Provence, where Cézanne had worked in his later years. The landscapes and village scenes Braque painted took another step toward simple geometric forms. At the same time, Picasso was working at La Rue des Bois, near Paris. *Les demoiselles* had exhausted him, and now—having actually discovered the body of another painter in the Bateau-Lavoir hanging from a beam, the victim of drugs and despair—he fled the city, searching for inspiration as he had once done in Gósol. He too began to turn everything he saw into geometric forms—not as spectacularly as the nudes of Avignon, but more severely and rigorously. Taking the most radical of the five nudes, the one on the far right, he further developed the ideas that had led him to paint it as if trying to see all sides at once.

When Picasso and Braque next met, they compared their summer work and discovered that they were going in the same direction. They decided to work together, in what became a unique artistic partnership that Braque described as two mountain climbers roped together. They stripped their palettes of all but a few colors—brown, white, gray, black—for what was important now was form alone. This new style was still (often just barely) representational: if the viewer looks hard enough, he can discern the subject of the painting. But perspective and three-dimensionality were gone completely. What Picasso and Braque did was to break down their subjects into plane surfaces that reflected all angles of view and then rearranged them on the canvas, where they fought for the viewer's attention. If they were to be put together, it was the viewer who would do it.

Supposedly, when Braque submitted his work for an exhibition, Matisse, one of the jury members, scornfully said the canvases were full of "petits cubes."[43] A reviewer, Louis Vauxcelles, is credited with coining the term *cubism* to describe the work. He didn't expect cubism to last, but it proved to be one of the most influential artistic movements of the century.

Later critics pronounced cubism to be another reflection of the scientific currents of the time. William R. Everdell, in his book *The First Moderns*, says, "In effect, Picasso had done for art in 1907 almost exactly what Einstein had done for physics in his 'Electrodynamics' paper of 1905."[44] Einstein had said that it was impossible for any single observer, standing at a fixed spot, to observe reality. Now, Picasso and Braque were trying to capture reality by depicting an object from many points of view at the same time.

Though it is doubtful that Picasso or Braque ever read Einstein's work, ideas like his were part of the intellectual atmosphere that made Paris such a stimulating place. Anybody could attend, for free, Henri Poincaré's lectures at the University of Paris or Bergson's at the Collège de France. Anarchists, socialists, and other groups sponsored free educational programs for their adherents. And of course, anyone dropping into a café in Montmartre might hear people like Apollinaire expounding on such topics. The cubists (there were soon more of them) sought, as scientists were doing, to find a deeper reality underneath the surface reality that anyone could see. It took an artist, like a detective, to find that hidden reality.

Kahnweiler displayed some of the cubist paintings in his gallery, where they attracted attention both among patrons and other artists. Some, like Juan Gris, enthusiastically took up the new style, contributing their own visions to it, and showing to what degree the concepts behind cubism were a part of the intellectual atmosphere of Paris. Albert Gleizes and Jean Metzinger, who exhibited their work at the Salon des Indépendants, even claimed to have been cubists *before* Picasso and Braque, who responded by calling them *les horribles serre-files* (the awful stragglers).[45]

Kahnweiler was successful in promoting and selling cubist art, and Picasso profited accordingly. In 1909, he left the Bateau-Lavoir and took an apartment on the boulevard de Clichy. This was a real home, with a living room, dining room, bedroom, and pantry, as well as a studio. By contrast, the furniture Picasso and Fernande brought with them was so shabby that the movers thought the young couple must have won the lottery to be able to live there.

It was certainly a more fashionable neighborhood. Paul Poiret, a dress designer who made clothes for the dancer Isadora Duncan and the actresses Eleanore Duse and Sarah Bernhardt, lived nearby, as did Frank Haviland, a porcelain manufacturer who was an admirer of African sculpture. Poiret was famous for the parties he threw for his customers, and he carefully chose art that would reflect his refined sense of taste. He visited Picasso's studio, praised the paintings, but did not purchase any.

Picasso received numerous invitations from people like Poiret and Haviland and often accepted, but he was uneasy in their company. Fernande later explained, "Artists hate growing old. When they leave poverty behind them they are also bidding farewell to a purity and a dedication which they will try in vain to find again."[46] Even going to the regular Saturday evening parties at the Stein's apartment lost some of its appeal. According to Fernande, people would ask Picasso to explain his paintings, and he found it difficult to reply, partly because his French was poor, but also because he felt the work needed no explanation. He "would remain morose and dejected for the greater part of the time."[47] To his old friends, he admitted experiencing moments of self-doubt, as if he had run up against a wall in his exploration of how far painting could take him.

vi

As he had done before when his spirits ebbed, Picasso left Paris for a simpler environment. He spent the summer of 1911 in Céret, a little village in the western Pyrenees. Fernande, who evidently liked the comforts of the city more than he did, came down to join him after he rented a house. So did Braque. In the bucolic atmosphere, with Kahnweiler in Paris able to sell his paintings and provide him with an income, all seemed well.

Then a copy of the *Paris-Journal* arrived, carrying the story written by the thief who had stolen two stone heads from the Louvre in 1907. Picasso knew just where those statuettes were: in his apartment on the boulevard de Clichy. He rushed back to Paris, where he found Apollinaire in a panic. The news of the *Mona Lisa* theft had meant more to him than it had to Picasso. Apollinaire knew that Pieret had returned to Paris — had in fact been living in Apollinaire's apartment. "He came to see me," Apollinaire later wrote, ". . . his pockets full of money which he proceeded to lose at the races. Penniless, he stole another statue. I had to help him — he was down and out — so I took him into my flat and tried to get him to return the statue; he refused, so I had to put him out, along with the statue. A few days later the *Mona Lisa* was stolen. I thought, as the police later thought, that he was the thief."[48]

Things had only gotten worse when the *Paris-Journal* editors announced that a thief had brought them a statue he had stolen from the Louvre. André Salmon was now the art critic for the *Paris-Journal*. If he learned Pieret was the anonymous thief, he would certainly make the connection between him and Apollinaire. Salmon and Apollinaire were currently on bad terms, not having spoken since quarreling three months earlier, so Apollinaire could not appeal to him. When Pieret turned up again, Apollinaire took him to the railroad station, bought him a ticket to Marseilles, and gave him 160 francs. The police would later regard these actions as incriminating.

Neither Picasso nor Apollinaire was a French citizen, and thus they could expect harsh treatment from the authorities. Fernande wrote, "I can see them both now, a pair of contrite children, terrified and thinking of fleeing abroad. It was thanks to me that they did not give in to their panic; they decided to stay in Paris and get rid of the compromising sculptures as quickly as possible. But how? Finally they decided to put the statues in a suitcase and throw it into the Seine at night." [49]

Fernande thought that much of this was playacting. The pair ate dinner and then sat around nervously, not wanting to venture out with the statuettes until the streets were deserted. They whiled away the time by playing cards, but "neither of them knew the first thing about cards," [50] Fernande wrote. They just thought it was something gangsters would do, so they did it to build up their courage.

Finally, at midnight, they left, carrying the statuettes in a suitcase. But walking through the silent streets, their nerve began to fail. They feared that they were being followed, "and their imagination conjured up a thousand possibilities, each more fantastic than the last." [51] If they were seen throwing the statuettes into the river, the penalty would be harsher than if they simply tried to return them. Finally they decided that turning the statuettes in would be the best course after all. And so they went back to the apartment at two in the morning, exhausted and still carrying the suitcase.

Apollinaire spent the night at Picasso's apartment and in the morning took the statuettes to the *Paris-Journal,* which by now seemed the proper place to turn in such stolen objects. The news of this latest recovery ran under the headline

WHILE AWAITING MONA LISA
THE LOUVRE RECOVERS ITS TREASURES

That was just the sort of publicity Apollinaire and Picasso did not want, but at least the newspaper did not mention their names. In fact, the "mysterious visitor" who returned these stone objects was described as "an amateur artist, fairly well-to-do, [whose] greatest pleasure is in collecting works of art."[52] That, they felt, was surely enough to keep the police off their trail. Moreover, a curator at the Louvre had examined the statuettes, which were described as the heads of a man and a woman, and pronounced them genuine. If Picasso had damaged them in his investigations, it was not noticed. He and Apollinaire hoped the entire affair would now blow over, particularly since Pieret had left Paris—though not before sending a mocking farewell letter to the *Paris-Journal*, writing, "I hope with all my heart that the *Mona Lisa* will be returned to you. I am not counting very heavily on such an event. However, let us hope that if its present possessor allows himself to be seduced by the thought of lucre, he will confide in your newspaper, whose staff has displayed toward me such a praiseworthy degree of discretion and honor. I can only urge the person at present holding Vinci's masterpiece to place himself entirely in your hands."[33]

Unfortunately, Pieret's comments only made it appear more likely than ever that he knew something about the *Mona Lisa* theft, and the police intensified their search for those who had purchased his previous stolen goods. No one ever learned how they identified Apollinaire, but on the evening of September 7, two detectives from the Sûreté appeared at his door. A search of his apartment turned up some letters from Géry Pieret, which apparently mentioned the theft of the statuettes. The police took Apollinaire into custody and brought him to Henri Drioux, the examining magistrate in charge of the *Mona Lisa* case. Drioux told him that the prosecutor's office had received "anonymous denunciations . . . stating that he had been in contact with the thief of the Phoenician statuettes, and also that he was a receiver of stolen goods."[54] He ordered Apollinaire to be imprisoned pending the results of an investigation.

Two days later, on September 9, *Le Matin* reported the sensational news:

> It was not without emotion and surprise that Paris learned last night of the arrest made by the Sûreté in connection with the recent restitution of Phoenician statuettes stolen from the Louvre in 1907.
>
> The mere name of the person arrested is enough to account for this reaction. He is M. Guillaume Kostrowky [sic], known in literature and art as Guillaume Apollinaire . . .
>
> What exactly are the charges against him? Both the Public Prosecutor and the police are making a considerable mystery of the affair.[55]

Mystery or no, the police intimated that it was far more than a case of a few missing statuettes. According to *Le Matin*'s editors, they were told, "We are on the trail of a gang of international thieves who came to France for the purpose of despoiling our museums. M. Guillaume Apollinaire committed the error of giving shelter to one of these criminals. Was he aware of what he was doing? That is what we are to determine. In any case, we feel sure that we shall shortly be in possession of all the secrets of the international gang."[56]

Apollinaire had been held in jail for twenty-four hours even before the police announced his arrest. Later, he wrote an account of his imprisonment: "As soon as the heavy door of the Santé closed behind me, I had an impression of death. However, it was a bright night and I could see that the walls of the courtyard in which I found myself were covered with climbing plants. Then I went through a second door; and when that closed I knew that the zone of vegetation was behind me, and I felt that I was now in some place beyond the bounds of the earth, where I would be utterly lost." [57]

Under further questioning, Apollinaire admitted that the person who had stolen the statuettes was Pieret, only confirming what the police already knew. The investigators wanted the name of the person Pieret sold the statuettes to, but Apollinaire would not reveal that. Back to the Santé he went, and surveyed his bleak cell with the eye of a literary man: "As reading matter they gave me a French translation of *The Quadroon,* by Captain Mayne Reid, whose adventure novels I remember reading as a schoolboy. During my confinement I read *The Quadroon* twice, and despite certain shocking improbabilities I found it a book not to be dismissed contemptuously." [58]

Géry Pieret, safely out of Paris, sent a wry note to the *Paris-Journal,* lamenting Apollinaire's imprisonment and calling him "kindly, honest, and scrupulous." Pieret signed himself "Baron Ignace d'Ormesan," a reference to the main character in Apollinaire's novel, who has the power to appear in many places at the same time. Artists and writers signed petitions to protest Apollinaire's arrest, but the police still wanted to know who was the third man in the case. Finally, Apollinaire gave up Picasso's name. "I did not describe his actual part in the affair, I merely said that he had been taken advantage of, and that he had never known that the antiquities he bought came from the Louvre." [59]

Early the next day, September 12, Fernande answered the doorbell at Picasso's apartment to find a detective there. Trembling, Picasso dressed hastily. "I had to help him," wrote Fernande, "as he was almost out of his mind with fear." Picasso was taken to the office of the investigating magistrate and "saw Apollinaire—pale, dishevelled and unshaven, with his collar torn, his shirt unbuttoned, no tie, and looking gaunt and insubstantial: a lamentable scarecrow." [60]

There are differing accounts of what happened next. Fernande, writing long after she and Picasso had separated, declared:

Picasso became completely desperate: his heart failed him. . . . He too could only say what the magistrate asked him to say. Besides Guillaume had admitted so many things, true as well as false, that he had totally compromised Picasso. . . .

It has been said that Picasso denied his friend and pretended not to know him. That is quite untrue. Far from betraying him, that moment brought out the true strength of his friendship with Apollinaire.[61]

Fernande, however, knew the story only as she had heard it from Picasso.

It seems significant that after the hearing, Magistrate Drioux allowed Picasso to go home and sent Apollinaire back to the Santé. Rumors spread that Picasso had denied everything, making Apollinaire out to be a liar. Nearly half a century later, Picasso told a journalist a version of the affair:

> [Apollinaire] got himself arrested. Naturally, they confronted us. I can see him there now, with his handcuffs and his look of a big placid boy. He smiled at me as I came in, but I made no sign.
>
> When the judge asked me: "Do you know this gentleman?" I was suddenly terribly frightened, and without knowing what I was saying, I answered: "I have never seen this man."
>
> I saw Guillaume's expression change. The blood ebbed from his face. I am still ashamed. . . .[62]

vii

After another night in jail, during which he consoled himself by composing poetry, Apollinaire was taken to the court once again.

Although this time he would have a lawyer present, he feared that Magistrate Drioux might find him guilty of complicity in the theft. He was held in the Mousetrap, a nickname for the "narrow, stinking cells" where prisoners awaited trial. Then a guard led him, handcuffed, down the corridor to the courtroom. The reporters and photographers pounced. "What a surprise to find myself suddenly stared at like a strange beast! All at once fifty cameras were aimed at me; the magnesium flashes gave a dramatic aspect to this scene in which I was playing a role. I soon recognized a few friends and acquaintances. . . . I think that I must have laughed and wept at the same time." [63] It was humiliating for him, nonetheless, to be led through the crowd in handcuffs—and without a tie.

The prosecutors had raised the stakes: Apollinaire was now accused of being not merely an accomplice but the chief of the international gang of criminals who had come to Paris to loot its museums. Magistrate Drioux, however, seemed skeptical and questioned Apollinaire at length about his relationship with Pieret, whom Apollinaire was now calling his "secretary." Apollinaire admitted allowing Pieret to stay with him in 1911, even though he knew he had stolen before, in 1907, and was even now resuming his career of crime. The judge expressed surprise at this "degree of indulgence."

"Here is part of my reason," Apollinaire said. "Pieret is a little bit my creation. He is very queer, very strange, and after studying him I made him the hero of one of the last stories in my *L'hérésiarque et Cie*. So it would have been a kind of literary ingratitude to let him starve." [64]

Apollinaire's friends in the courtroom must have held their breaths, for no one knew if Magistrate Drioux had a sense of humor or if Apollinaire's sally might offend him. Opening the dossier that the Sûreté had prepared, Drioux started to read the accusations. Apparently there were some anonymous messages that he found absurd.

"You bought, very recently, it has been alleged," Drioux said, "a castle in the *département* of the Drôme?"

Apollinaire could not resist another humorous reply. "You must be referring to a castle in Spain," he told the magistrate. "I have seen many of those evaporate."

"I have a letter here," Drioux continued, apparently falling into the spirit of Apollinaire's testimony, "from someone who says you borrowed two books from him, and that one of them . . . you never returned."

"I imagine his reason for lending them to me was that I might read them," said Apollinaire. "I haven't read them yet. I will return them to him as soon as I can." [65]

Magistrate Drioux finally announced that he was granting the petition of Apollinaire's lawyer for the release of his client.

Ironically, the incident gave Apollinaire the fame that his writings had never brought him. Because the story of his arrest was so entangled with the theft of the *Mona Lisa,* it was reported worldwide. The *New York Times* called him "a well-known Russian[66] literary man living in Paris [who] underwent a searching examination on the charge of having shielded Pieret from the law." [67] Publicity of whatever kind proved beneficial to his career: afterward, Apollinaire's writings reached a wider audience.

Moreover, imprisonment provided inspiration for what may be his most enduring work, a book of poetry titled *Alcools (Spirits),* published two years later. One of the poems is "À la Santé":

I
Before I enter my cell
I am required to strip naked
And then a sinister voice cries
Guillaume what have you become

I am a Lazarus entering the tomb
Not leaving it as he did
Farewell farewell the rounds are singing
To my years To the young girls

. . . .

V

How slowly the hours pass
Like a funeral procession

You will mourn the hour that you wept
Which will pass too quickly
As every hour passes

VI

I listen to the clamor of the city
A prisoner without a view
I see nothing but a hostile sky
And the naked walls of my prison

The daylight draws within itself
Yet here a lamp still burns
We are alone in my cell
Beautiful clarity Beloved reason

While Apollinaire looked for solace from clarity and reason in his cell, elsewhere in the city were many who sought to create chaos and disorder. Very soon, a few of those avowed anarchists—and not ones who merely fired pistols into the air, like Picasso—would tear the city's attention away from the missing *Mona Lisa*. Real criminals were plotting a modernist crime.

THE MOTOR BANDITS

On the night of the thirteenth of December, 1911, three men traveled by train to the fashionable Paris suburb of Boulogne-sur-Seine. They had purchased one-way tickets, for they planned to return by automobile. Not just any automobile either. They had scouted the area in daylight, looking at the shiny new cars parked outside the grand houses, before selecting one that belonged to a family named Normand. It was a Delaunay-Belleville, which many people regarded as the finest automobile in the world. The company, through its showroom on the Champs-Élysées, sold only the chassis, complete with six-cylinder engine and tires. Each purchaser then had to arrange for the construction of his own distinctive body, or coach, with companies that catered to this trade. However, every Delaunay-Belleville was still easily recognized by its distinctive circular radiator, which reflected the company's origins as a boiler manufacturer.

A Delaunay-Belleville was not a casual purchase. The chassis alone cost fifteen thousand francs, the equivalent of five years' wages for the skilled workmen who built it. It was a favorite of Nicholas II, the czar of Russia (he is said to have owned twenty), and—to make a point about the superiority of the French auto industry—virtually the required form of transportation for the president of France.

The three men waited until all the lights inside the house were extinguished, and allowed time for everyone inside to fall asleep. Then they forced a side door to the garage, not a difficult task, for all of them were familiar with burglars' tools. Once inside, they used flashlights to examine the car. One of the men, Jules Bonnot, was an experienced mechanic and professional driver.

The men opened the large door of the garage and pushed the car outside. Starting it would be a noisy process, but one of the men stood in front of the radiator and turned the crank that rotated the driveshaft while Bonnot sat in the driver's seat and worked the ignition lever.

Nothing happened. A light went on in an upstairs room of the house, and the three men huddled. Deciding that they could not abandon their plan now, they pushed the automobile into the street and managed to roll it around a corner. Bonnot examined the controls with his flashlight and discovered what he had been doing wrong. On a second attempt, the engine roared into life. Bonnot, who would become notorious as "the Demon Chauffeur," felt a thrill of pleasure as he opened the throttle and felt the power at his fingertips. He had grand plans for this car. He would use it for something that had never been done with an automobile before.

i

What the newspapers came to call the Bonnot Gang began well before Bonnot himself arrived on the scene. In August 1909, nineteen-year-old Victor-Napoleon Lvovich Kibalchich, who later became known as Victor Serge, arrived in Paris. His father had fled Russia some years earlier, wanted for revolutionary activities there, and settled in Belgium. The family was poor, and one of Victor's brothers is said to have died of starvation because his father could not afford to buy enough food. The home was decorated with portraits of executed revolutionaries, and on many nights, as young Victor listened, would-be revolutionaries met there to discuss ideas and plans. While still in his teens, he began to write articles for an anarchist newspaper named *Le Révolté,* signing them with the pseudonym Le Rétif ("the Restless One").

Anarchists were by no means united on the course of action they should pursue to attain their goals. One of the points of dispute centered around the practice of *reprise individuelle* ("taking back by individuals," which a bourgeois might call stealing). In theory, *reprise individuelle* was intended to adjust the inequality between rich and poor. A more radical idea was *illégalisme,* which, although it might appear at first glance to be the same thing, justified *any* action that anarchists might use to support themselves or the cause of anarchism.

Victor was among the extremists. When two anarchist Latvian sailors stole the payroll from a factory in North London, they shot twenty-two people, killing three, including a ten-year-old boy, in their attempt to escape. Finally the two sailors, cornered, committed suicide. The event was widely commented on. In *Le Révolté,* Victor praised the bandits for having shown that "anarchists don't surrender." What about the innocent people they shot? "Enemies!" Victor declared. "For us the enemy is whoever impedes us from living. We are the ones under attack, and we defend ourselves."[1]

Though Serge was never to take part in any of the robberies carried out by the Bonnot Gang, his ideas provided the intellectual underpinnings and motivation for its members. When he reached Paris, he began to write for a newspaper named *L'Anarchie.* Despite its name, the newspaper espoused a variety of views, not all political; it crusaded against smoking, drinking, and the consumption of meat. Its writers stood firmly in opposition to work, marriage, religion, military service, and voting. The editor, twenty-five-year-old André Roulot, who wrote under the name Lorulot, welcomed Serge as a colleague. Victor also reacquainted himself with Henriette "Rirette" Maîtrejean, a young woman anarchist he had met in Belgium. Two or three years older than Victor, she still looked like a teenager even though she had two children, by a husband she had married because he was an anarchist. Soon Rirette and her children moved in with Victor, and she too became a member of the staff of *L'Anarchie*.

Victor's inflammatory articles were popular and caused the circulation of *L'Anarchie* to rise, but they also created problems for Lorulot, who wasn't willing to embrace illegalism. Anarchist activity in Paris had stepped up lately, inspiring a police crackdown. A young worker had been sent to jail on the charge of being a pimp, even though the woman in the case was his lover and he had hoped to rescue her from prostitution. After serving his term, the worker obtained a revolver and shot four policemen. At the demand of the prefect of police, Lépine, he was sentenced to death. On the date of his scheduled execution, a mob gathered at La Santé Prison, determined to halt it. Rioting broke out and lasted through the night, and cavalry had to be assembled as the guillotine was set up. Victor and Rirette were among the protestors. "At dawn," Victor later recalled, "exhaustion quietened the crowd, and at the instant when the blade fell . . . a baffled frenzy gripped the twenty or thirty thousand demonstrators, and found its outlet in a long-drawn cry: '*Murderers!*' "[2]

Publications like *L'Anarchie* had to be careful not to be seen as inciting such violence, for they could be closed or raided by the police. The newspaper also faced attacks by others within the anarchist movement. Its windows were smashed by members of a rival paper, which felt that Victor's illegalism discredited the movement. Quarrels even broke out among *L'Anarchie*'s staff: one night, Lorulot caught a former editor trying to steal the printing equipment from the building in Montmartre where the newspaper had its offices. Someone actually summoned the police, who arrived only to find that both sides in the dispute insisted the others be arrested. Afterward, Lorulot received a bomb threat, which caused the landlord to demand that the newspaper's staff vacate the premises.

Lorulot decided to move the entire operation away from Paris, to a northeastern suburb called Romainville. Here he rented a house with a large garden where fruit trees and lilacs grew. A train station put Paris within easy reach, and the bucolic atmosphere soon attracted others to what became a commune. It was also the seedbed for the Bonnot Gang.

One of the first to move into the house at Romainville was Raymond Callemin, an old friend of Victor Serge's. The two had known each other since boyhood (as teens, they had lived in a commune south of Brussels) and followed the path to anarchism together. Raymond's father was a disillusioned socialist who repaired shoes to eke out a meager living. Both Raymond and Victor avoided school, teaching themselves by reading radical books such as Émile Zola's *Paris* and Louis Blanc's *History of the French Revolution*. They began as socialists, but as Victor later recalled, "Anarchism swept us away completely because it both demanded everything of us and offered everything to us."[3]

Raymond would not have fit Lombroso's physical description of a criminal type. He was nearsighted, handsome, and a strict vegetarian, and he liked to sprinkle his conversation with the phrase "La science dit . . ." ("Science tells us . . ."), which earned him the nickname "Raymond-la-Science." After leaving Belgium, he had drifted through France and Switzerland. Like Victor, he contributed articles to socialist and anarchist newspapers and was often in trouble with the police, both for his writings (publishing antimilitarist articles was a crime in France) and for taking part in demonstrations, where he tended to get into fights with policemen.

Raymond-la-Science seems to have set the tone for the commune at Romainville, at least in its early days. Those who stayed there were served a "scientific" diet—brown rice, raw vegetables, porridge, and pasta with cheese. Salt, pepper, and vinegar were banned as being "unscientific," although herbs were acceptable. Tobacco, alcohol, and coffee were banned. The members were encouraged to keep fit by taking part in Swedish exercises. Many would bicycle to the nearby Marne River and rent a boat for an afternoon of rowing.

The outwardly idyllic lifestyle, however, concealed darker activities, for there were characters in the group more sinister than Raymond-la-Science. Octave Garnier, also in his early twenties, admitted that he had been a rebel against authority from his earliest years, without even knowing why. At thirteen, he began to make his own way in the world, and his ideas crystallized: "I began to understand what life and social injustice was all about; I saw bad individuals and said to myself: 'I must search for a way of getting out of this filthy mess of bosses, workers, bourgeois, judges, police and others.' I loathed all these people, some because they put up with and took part in all this crap."[4]

He began to shoplift, was caught, and spent three months in jail. Subsequently it was difficult for him to find a job because he needed certificates of good behavior. Garnier learned to forge those, but the work he did in a bakery for sixteen to eighteen hours a day paid barely enough to live on. Garnier knew he needed an education, "to know more about things, and develop my mind and body."[5] He attended labor meetings and added his body to demonstrations and strikes, but felt that the union leaders were too prone to give in to employers.

Then, at the age of eighteen, he discovered anarchism. "Within this milieu," he later wrote, "I met individuals of integrity who were trying as much as possible to rid themselves of the prejudices that have made this world ignorant and barbaric. They were men with whom I found discussion a pleasure, for they showed me not utopias but things which one could see and touch."[6] One of those things was *reprise individuelle,* and Garnier set out to put it into practice. Caught during one of his attempts at theft, he went back to jail. That was the pattern he followed for nearly two years. As he approached his twentieth birthday, when (despite his criminal record) he would face required military service, Garnier kept a job long enough to save travel money and left France for Belgium. There he took up with Marie Vuillemin, a young woman who had been married for only a month and already wanted to escape her husband.

Belgium was a haven for French political refugees and draft dodgers; by one estimate, some seventy thousand young Frenchmen had left the country to avoid military service, and most of them headed for Belgium. Naturally enough, Garnier gravitated toward anarchist meetings, where he met Raymond Callemin. The man of thought and the man of action thus united.

In addition, Garnier added to his criminal education by falling in with Édouard Carouy, a professional housebreaker who sympathized with the anarchist cause. A year later, probably at the invitation of Callemin, both Garnier and Carouy, along with Garnier's lover, Marie, returned to Paris and moved into the house at Romainville. They were welcomed because they contributed funds to the commune by foraying out to commit burglaries from time to time. Garnier and Carouy, now carrying 9-millimeter Browning automatics, which were readily available in Belgium, disturbed the pastoral atmosphere by conducting target practice in the commune's garden.

With the newcomers' presence, the nightly discussions of illegalism became more than theoretical. Serge, recalling those days much later, wrote that "they were already, or were becoming, outlaws, primarily through the influence of Octave Garnier, a handsome, swarthy, silent lad whose dark eyes were astoundingly hard and feverish. Small, working-class by origin, Octave had undergone a vicious beating on a building site in the course of a strike. He scorned all discussion with 'intellectuals.' 'Talk, talk!' he would remark softly, and off he would go on the arm of a blonde Rubensesque Flemish girl, to prepare some dangerous nocturnal task or other."[7] Lorulot, who was never enthusiastic about illegalism, disliked being the nominal head of a group that actually practiced it. He decided to leave Romainville and start a new publication in Paris. That promoted Victor to the editorship of *L'Anarchie,* although his lover, Rirette, was listed on the masthead as the actual editor. Perhaps this was a concession to feminism, or possibly a way to divert police attention away from Victor.

Communes can be delicate things, held together by relationships that can break apart for seemingly trivial reasons. In this case, it seems that Victor and Rirette craved coffee and were tired of bland food. Now that they were the group's leaders, they began to eat by themselves, choosing a "nonscientific" diet, and then violated the free-spirited editorial policy of the newspaper by refusing to print an article Garnier had written, titled "Salt Is Poison." Toward the end of August 1911, everyone except Victor, Rirette, and her children left the commune. This departure may have partly been due to the fact that the police were now closing in on Carouy for one of the burglaries he had recently committed. Carouy rented a new place farther down the Marne, giving his name as "Leblanc," the name of the author of the Arsène Lupin series. Anarchists thought Lupin had been modeled after one of their own, Marius Jacob.

The others drifted back to Paris. Garnier and his mistress moved into his mother's house in Vincennes, one of the capital's eastern suburbs. During the next three months, he continued his career as a burglar, more successfully now (if for no other reason than he was never caught). But since he gave much of the proceeds of his crimes to comrades in need, he was hardly prosperous. He kept in touch with the others from the commune, including Raymond, who took him to Chopin concerts to broaden his horizons. In their discussions, they agreed that they should be more focused in their efforts, but they struggled to formulate a coherent plan. Raymond, as usual, insisted that the way forward would be found in science. He was dazzled by the fast cars he saw on the streets of Paris, but unfortunately neither Raymond nor Garnier could drive. And then Bonnot entered their lives.

ii

Jules Bonnot was at least ten years older than most of those who would join him. He was not an idealistic young man in his early twenties, seeking to find himself; he had a more mature outlook on the world but was at the same time angrier and more reckless than the others. Born in 1876 in a small village in the Jura Mountains, he had grown up in the same region as Proudhon, the founder of French anarchism, and absorbed the rebellious spirit that still thrived there. His family life was anarchic as well. Bonnot's mother died when he was five, and his father was an alcoholic. When Bonnot's older brother was fifteen, he threw himself off a bridge because a girl had stood him up. Police records show that young Jules was often arrested for fighting and twice served jail terms of three months.

In 1897 he was called up for his required military service and fortuitously assigned to a company of engineers that had just received motorized trucks. Bonnot showed a knack for repairing them and soon learned to drive as well. He thrived in the army, never getting into trouble. Shooting a rifle came naturally to him, and he was the champion marksman of his company for his entire three-year career. And the army even brought him a wife, for when he was billeted in a farmhouse, he and the eighteen-year-old daughter of the family, Sophie-Louise Burdet, fell in love. When he was discharged, he returned to ask for her hand, and they were married in August 1901. He found a factory job in Bellegarde, and soon Sophie discovered she was pregnant. Bonnot's future seemed rosy, or at least conventionally bourgeois.

But his old attitude toward authority figures flared up again, and Bonnot lost his job for being a troublemaker. Branded as such, he had difficulty finding work, so the young couple had to move in with Sophie's mother, certainly a humiliation for Bonnot. It turned into tragedy when Sophie gave birth to a baby daughter who lived only four days.

For the next few years, Bonnot moved through Switzerland and France with Sophie, finding work and then losing it. Sophie again became pregnant and gave birth to a son in February 1904. At her suggestion, Bonnot went to see Besson, the secretary of a mechanics' union. He found Bonnot a job, and the little family settled down in the city of Lyons. Luck was not with Bonnot, however, for he had to enter a sanitarium because he had contracted tuberculosis. While there, he received the news that Sophie had run off with the friendly union leader, Besson. Discharged from the hospital, Bonnot tried to gain custody of his son, but failed.

Bonnot found work as a mechanic in the Berliet automobile factory in Lyons. There he met anarchists who introduced him to the idea of *reprise individuelle*. One of them was an Italian named Platano, who also educated Bonnot in the techniques of burglary. Since Bonnot knew how to repair and drive automobiles, the two of them began to specialize in car theft. They did so well that they opened a garage where they could secretly strip or hide their plunder.

Prosperous for the first time, Bonnot showed a taste for fine clothing and fastidious grooming. His friends laughingly called him Le Bourgeois. He found a new girlfriend, a married woman named Judith Thollon. Her husband was a cemetery keeper, and at night Bonnot and Judith would lie among the graves and make love.

Taking a risk, Bonnot and Platano went for a big payday and burgled the house of a wealthy lawyer. Bonnot was able to open the man's safe, and the two came away with thirty-six thousand francs. After splitting the haul, they left Lyons for a time to avoid pursuit. Bonnot left most of his share with Judith, promising to come back and take her with him.

In late 1910, he went to England, which is where he is said to have worked as a chauffeur for Sir Arthur Conan Doyle. Evidence for this is slight; Conan Doyle's friend Harry Ashton-Wolfe, who often worked with Alphonse Bertillon at the Sûreté, supposedly recognized Bonnot when he became a famous criminal. In one of Ashton-Wolfe's books, he claimed that Bonnot was *his* chauffeur, not Conan Doyle's.

At any rate, when Bonnot thought the heat was off from the earlier burglary, he returned to Lyons and again opened a garage where he could hide the cars he stole. Selling hot cars, especially the luxury models that Bonnot favored, was difficult because there were comparatively few of them and they could be identified easily. On one occasion, Bonnot drove his latest prize to a garage kept by an anarchist named Jean Dubois in Choisy-le-Roi, just outside Paris. Bonnot and Dubois liked each other on sight, and Bonnot stayed with him for a while, stealing cars for Dubois to sell. Later, when Bonnot was the most wanted man in France, he would return to Choisy-le-Roi seeking refuge.

Not long after Bonnot returned to Lyons, the police raided his garage. Fortunately for Bonnot, he wasn't there, and hearing the news, he took a car from another location and fled to Paris. There he met his old accomplice Platano, who was flush with cash, which he said came from an inheritance. They spent their evenings in the bars of Montmartre, where Platano introduced Bonnot to Octave Garnier.

Bonnot kept in touch with Judith by letter and decided to go back to Lyons to visit her. Platano accompanied him for some reason; he may possibly have stood guard while Judith and Bonnot made love in the cemetery for the last time.[8] It was late November and they may not have tarried long.

On the way back to Paris, an incident happened that remains murky. The outcome, however, was clear: Platano's body was found on the road with two bullet holes in the skull. Not far from there, near a train station, the car Bonnot had stolen was found abandoned and out of gas. Hearing the story, one of Platano's Italian friends in Lyons went to the police and reported that Platano had been riding with Bonnot. The police began a search for Bonnot, which took them to the house of his mistress, Judith Thollon. There they uncovered Bonnot's cash hoard and stolen property, along with some books, among them *Revolutionary Manual for the Manufacture of Bombs*. Judith and her hapless husband were taken into custody and a warrant was issued for Bonnot on a charge of murder.

Bonnot was in Paris, safe from the Lyons police. However, Platano's anarchist friends in the capital learned about his mysterious death and demanded an explanation. Bonnot appeared before a meeting of anarchists, who had gathered to judge him. His story was that when they stopped to repair a flat tire, Platano started to show off his new Browning automatic. It went off accidentally and Platano fell, mortally wounded. Fearing that someone would come along, Bonnot administered a coup de grâce to put him out of his misery. He forcefully denied taking what remained of Platano's inheritance, pointing out that the police had now seized his own funds from the house of his mistress.

Not a very convincing explanation, it would seem, but Garnier was present and was impressed enough to approach Bonnot with an attractive proposal. Along with Raymond-la-Science Callemin, they began to plan their big job.

Their first step was to steal the Delaunay-Belleville, which they drove through the dark streets of Paris and out to Bobigny, a suburb to the northeast, where their friend Édouard Carouy was currently staying with a family named Dettweiler. Georges Dettweiler was an anarchist sympathizer, but a small businessman as well; he had opened a garage, and that night, much to his later regret, he allowed the car thieves to hide their prize inside. The first step in Bonnot's plan had been carried out.

A week went by, during which the conspirators scouted for a target. They found one at the branch of the Société Générale bank on the rue Ordener in Montmartre, virtually the home territory of Paris's anarchists. Every weekday morning, punctually at nine o'clock, a messenger arrived on foot from the main office of the bank, carrying cash and securities to be deposited in the local branch. Since it was the midst of the Christmas season, his leather carrying case was likely to be as full as Père Noël's. Easy to identify because he wore a uniform, the messenger seemed not even to be armed. A bodyguard came from the bank to meet him at the street-car stop, and of course anyone desperate enough to rob him would immediately be seized by pedestrians on what was one of the most crowded streets of the eighteenth arrondissement.

It seems almost impossible now, since everyone has seen car chases on film countless times, but no one had yet conceived the idea of escaping a robbery via automobile.

So it was that on the morning of December 21, Bonnot, Garnier, and Callemin sat on the rue Ordener in their stolen Delaunay-Belleville, engine idling, waiting for the messenger. Passersby may have paused to admire the car, but a cold rain was falling, and no one tarried long. Nor had anyone, it seems, read or remembered an advertisement that appeared in that morning's *L'Auto*, a newspaper dedicated to car enthusiasts. It offered a reward of five hundred francs to anyone finding the green and black Delaunay-Belleville limousine, model 1910, motor no. 2679V, that had been stolen from M. Normand a week before. (The experienced Bonnot had already switched the license plates.)

The thieves were prepared for any kind of interference. "We were fearfully armed," Garnier wrote later.[9] He carried six revolvers, each of his companions had three more, and among them they had four hundred rounds of ammunition.

As nine o'clock drew near, a butcher across the street noticed that the magnificent automobile had been parked in the same spot since 8:00 A.M. He stepped outside to stare at it, and the chauffeur, dressed in a gray cap and coat, wearing driving goggles, put the car in gear and moved slowly forward, only to stop again a few doors down. The butcher recalled later that the curtains in the rear compartment had been drawn, making it impossible to see if there were any passengers.

The messenger that day was a man named Caby. As he emerged from the streetcar, his escort-bodyguard stepped up and shook his hand. They headed down the street toward the bank—walking right into the hands of the thieves. Garnier and Callemin stepped out of the car, hands in their pockets. As they reached their quarry, they pulled out their 9-millimeter automatics and ordered Caby to hand over his case. Apparently unprepared for any show of force, the bodyguard put his hands over his face, turned, and ran. Caby was less cooperative, either from fear or from misplaced bravery. He refused to release his hold on the case, even after Callemin dragged him down the sidewalk with it. Garnier, ever impatient, shot Caby twice in the chest, leaving him bleeding on the pavement.

Bonnot had moved the car up alongside them, and his two companions jumped inside. Some horrified passersby made tentative attempts to stop them, but a blast of gunshots drove them back. Bonnot, displaying the daring skill that was to win him the nickname the Demon Chauffeur, immediately made a hairpin turn that took him down the rue des Cloys, where it seemed for a moment that he would collide head-on with an approaching motor bus. He swerved, narrowly dodging a taxi in the process. Garnier and Callemin continued to fire out the windows, spreading panic through the streets.

The wide, straight boulevards created by Baron Haussmann seemed designed specifically for a driver like Bonnot, who pressed the accelerator to the floor and never let up. Fulfilling the fantasies of countless future drivers, he avoided obstacles by jumping the curb and roaring down the sidewalk, as frantic pedestrians leaped out of his way. Anyone who might have wanted to pursue the bandits was soon left behind.

Another sharp turn and the Delaunay-Belleville was barreling down the rue Vauvenargues, headed north toward the city gate at Clichy. A few minutes later, customs officials halting traffic there were scattered by gunshots fired from the speeding vehicle as it roared through the gate. The getaway car (a term nobody had ever used before) was soon lost from sight, heading north in the rain.

iii

The Paris newspapers had a field day with the latest sensational crime, and—as *La Presse* called them—*les bandits en auto* ("the motorcar bandits"). Though there were twenty thousand police in Paris, a city with a population of three million, journalists suggested that the force was undermanned in light of this new development. Most fascinating, of course, was the thieves' method of escape; the police used motor vehicles only for transporting high officials and thus were considered powerless against this new form of crime. Moviemakers saw the dramatic potential immediately. One studio reenacted the robbery as soon as the news became public, and by the next day the film debuted at theaters throughout Paris. Though popular, it also attracted protesters, who felt that it glorified crime.

The hunt for the thieves soon spread across national borders. The following day, the Delaunay-Belleville limousine was found abandoned in a street in the town of Dieppe, a port city on the north coast. It was assumed that the criminals had taken a boat for England, and Scotland Yard was asked to trace any passengers arriving at Southampton.

In fact, by that time Bonnot and his friends were back in Paris, having deliberately reversed course at Dieppe and taken a train to the capital, where they were sure no one would expect to find them. The three were not ready to celebrate, however, for they were a bit disgruntled with their gains. The bank messenger's case had contained mostly bonds and checks that would be difficult to cash, and the bills and gold coins came to a value of only about fifty-five hundred francs. Bonnot knew a man in Amsterdam who might be willing to accept the bonds at a discount, so, undaunted, they stole another car and were soon on the road to Holland. That trip proved to be unproductive, for Bonnot's friend told him that the serial numbers of the stolen securities were being circulated to every bank in Europe. They were too hot to try to move.

Meanwhile, having found the stolen Delaunay-Belleville and located its owner, the police tried to find where it had been kept between the time it first disappeared and the day of the robbery. As it happened, some of Georges Dettweiler's neighbors in Bobigny had complained about the noise coming from his garage at late hours, and one of them thought he had seen the now-famous car inside. Like so many Frenchmen, the neighbor was suspicious of the Sûreté and merely told a town official about it. The official then sought to make himself a quick franc or two by selling the story to a tabloid newspaper, *Le Petit Parisien*. After its publication, the chief of the Sûreté himself, Octave Hamard, led a raid on the garage, arresting

Dettweiler, his wife, and a girlfriend of Carouy's. Carouy himself escaped, but Bertillon found his face, along with several aliases, in his voluminous card file, along with the notation that the missing man was an anarchist.

The newspaper editors couldn't have asked for a greater gift than being able to add the feared word "ANARCHISTS!" to their headlines. Even better, when Carouy's photograph was shown to the bank messenger in his hospital bed, Caby mistakenly declared that it was the man who had shot him. Carouy was immediately named by the Sûreté as the head of the "motor bandit" gang and the mastermind behind the rue Ordener outrage.

Carouy himself, seeing his mug shot on the front page of every newspaper in Paris, felt a little aggrieved, for he had earlier turned down Bonnot's offer to join in the caper, feeling that it would be too dangerous. Now he needed money to leave the country, and he had no way of getting it from the three actual thieves.

Carouy may have declined to participate in the bank heist, but his reflex was that of a habitual criminal: if he needed money, he would steal it. Along with a friend named Marius Medge, who had carried out robberies with him before, Carouy plotted what appeared to be an easy job. In the southern suburb of Thiais, Medge knew an elderly man who lived off rents from properties and reputedly kept large amounts of cash at home. His only companion was a seventy-two-year-old housekeeper. On the night of January 2, 1912, Medge and Carouy broke into the house, but things did not go as easily as they had expected. The old man unwisely resisted, and the crooks beat him to death with a hammer. To eliminate any witnesses, the burglars strangled his housekeeper as well.

Bertillon's lab later found fingerprints at the scene that identified Carouy as one of the perpetrators of the crime. That meant — to both editors and the Sûreté — that the anarchist gang were no longer merely thieves but brutal murderers engaged in a crime spree.

Nevertheless, Carouy continued to elude capture. According to Ashton-Wolfe, Carouy had gone to extreme lengths to change his appearance: his "eyes were peculiarly small and round, and every police officer had been informed of this. Carouy sent a friend to buy a lancet, some cocaine, and a hypodermic syringe. When his skin was sufficiently numbed by an injection of the drug, the outer and inner corners of the eyes were slit and held apart by sticking-plaster until the slit skin was healed. The effect was extraordinary. His round eyes now appeared to be long and narrow." [10]

Meanwhile, the newspapers called for action and got it: ten days after the Thiais murders, Hamard was given another post. Replacing him as head of the Sûreté was Xavier Guichard, widely known as a tough and uncompromising police officer. (Many also thought him crude, partly because he had never advanced beyond elementary school.) Guichard ordered a series of raids on locations where anarchists were known to congregate, including newspaper offices and social clubs. Little useful information was turned up, but Guichard could point to "successes" such as a raid on a dance in Belleville: of the fifty people in the hall, twenty-nine were arrested on charges of illegally carrying firearms. None, however, could be tied to the robberies and murders.

Guichard got a break when he forced the still-hospitalized messenger Caby to look at photographs of some of the many known anarchists in Bertillon's files. When the investigator turned up a picture of Garnier, Caby nearly fainted. This, he cried, was him—the man who had shot him. Hadn't he already identified Carouy as the man? Yes, said Caby, but he was mistaken.

Luckily for Guichard, Garnier's girlfriend, Marie Vuillemin, had been arrested in a raid on the offices of the new anarchist magazine Lorulot had founded, *L'Idée Libre*. Her apartment was searched, turning up signs that Garnier had lived there, but Garnier himself was nowhere to be found. Along with Bonnot and Callemin, he had gone to Belgium, where they stole another car, driving it to Amsterdam and selling it for eight thousand francs. So far, car theft was bringing in more money than bank robberies. But they were not discouraged.

Returning to Paris, where Bonnot checked into a hotel under the name Lecoq (in homage to the fictional detective and crook made famous by Émile Gaboriau), the three men saw Garnier's photograph on wanted posters everywhere. Instead of fleeing the city, however, he moved in with a friend named René Valet in a sixth-floor walk-up on, of all places, the rue Ordener, near the scene of the original crime, as if thumbing his nose at the police. Valet was also a friend of Serge's, who recalled that they used to meet in little bars along the boulevard Saint-Michel and discuss literature and poetry. "I can see him there now," Serge recalled thirty years later, "standing up like a young Siegfried . . . his fine, square-set ginger head, his powerful chin, his green eyes, his strong hands, his athlete's bearing."[11] Valet owned a locksmith's shop but had an anarchist's spirit. Inexorably he would be drawn into the gang's orbit by Garnier, and he would die for it.

iv

Bonnot meanwhile retained fond memories of his mistress Judith Thollon, who was still in jail, and even drove to Lyons with his share of the car-theft loot to see if he could hire a lawyer to bail her out. The lawyer told him that the charges against her were serious (possession of stolen property) and also let him knew that the Sûreté—having apparently been tipped off by a friend of Platano, Bonnot's "mercy killing" victim—now suspected Bonnot of being one of the auto bandits. If Judith were released from jail, it would only be because the police hoped she would lead them to him.

Instead of lying low, however, Bonnot continued to travel around stealing cars with Garnier. Once, when a chauffeur refused to give up his automobile, Garnier clubbed the man with a log, killing him. They also shot a watchman, who survived and was later able to identify them from photographs. The newspapers didn't shy from letting their readers know that the police continued to prove as helpless against the anarchists as their fictional counter-part, Inspector Juve, was against Fantômas in book after book.

If that weren't bad enough, Victor Serge decided to show where his sympathies lay and demonstrate his credentials as an advocate of illegalism. His childhood friend Raymond-la-Science had paid him a visit just before Christmas, so Serge knew exactly who had carried off the robbery in the rue Ordener. At the beginning of the New Year, he published, under his pen name, Le Rétif, an article in *L'Anarchie* that began:

> To shoot, in full daylight, a miserable bank clerk proved that some men have at least understood the virtues of audacity.
>
> I am not afraid to own up to it: I am with the bandits. I find their role a fine one; I see the Men in them. . . . I like those who accept the risk of a great struggle. It is manly.[12]

Publishing sentiments like that only made Serge and the newspaper a prime target of police attention. At the end of January, the Sûreté staged a raid on *L'Anarchie*'s office, arrested all eleven people in-side, and seized two Browning automatics that had been stolen in an armory robbery. Rirette claimed that she had bought them from a comrade for personal protection, but the police regarded these as important evidence, since the auto bandits were the prime suspects in the theft of the cache of weapons.

Serge was questioned by Louis Jouin, deputy chief of the Sûreté and the nominal head of the force tracking the auto bandits. Jouin struck Serge as "a thin gentleman with a long, gloomy face, polite and almost likeable."[13] He told Serge that he identified with his cause, for he too was a man of the people. He even quoted Sébas-tien Faure, an anarchist writer. Though Jouin claimed to admire the ideals of many anarchists, he pointed out that the brutal ac-tions of the auto bandits were discrediting their comrades. What about the old man and his housekeeper in Thiais, slaughtered in their beds? Was that something that made anarchists proud? Jouin promised that if Serge gave him information about the bandits, no one need ever know. In his memoirs, Serge claimed to have been "embarrassed" by the offer. He was sent back to a cell in La Santé Prison to think things over. He would remain there for fifteen months before a trial began.

The motor bandits, meanwhile, were planning further crimes. Raymond-la-Science obtained some silver nitrate, which the thieves used to lighten their hair. Bonnot and Garnier shaved off their mustaches, and Bonnot went on a shopping spree to buy them all new suits, complete with bowler hats, that would make them seem respectable. A fellow anarchist, Élie Monier, who used the alias Simentoff, proposed that they join him in a payroll robbery in the city of Nîmes, in the south of France. On February 26, the three bandits stole another Delaunay-Belleville (evidently Bonnot favored them). The owner had planned to drive it in the upcoming Tour de France, and in the passenger compartment, the trio found an added bonus: a fox-fur-lined cloak, an overcoat with an astrakhan collar, stopwatches, and maps.[14] With these additions to their own new wardrobes, the criminals now truly resembled the wealthy, fashionable people they despised—not unlike Fantômas himself.

Unfortunately, on their way south, the car required repairs that took several hours. It was not so easy in those days to find a place to stay on the road, and Bonnot feared that someone would notice the stolen car if they parked and slept in it, so he turned around and headed back to Paris. Once more disregarding a customs barrier, this time at the Porte d'Italie, he crossed the Île de la Cité, virtually within sight of police headquarters, turned left onto the rue de Rivoli, passing the Louvre and the Tuileries, and then headed north into the eighth arondissement. Bonnot picked up speed as the street ran downhill, and he nearly hit a bus that was backing out of a bay at the Gare Saint-Lazare.

Bonnot avoided the collision, but the car jumped the curb, ran onto the sidewalk, and stalled. Garnier had gotten out to turn the crank that would restart the engine when a traffic policeman walked up to chide the driver for his reckless speed. By the accounts of witnesses, Bonnot never looked up at the man, staring ahead stone-faced, waiting for the engine to roar into life. As soon as it did, he put the car in gear, and Garnier had to rush to get back inside. The policeman, naturally incensed at this blatant disregard for his authority, stepped onto the running board and grabbed the steering wheel. Garnier didn't hesitate: he leaned across Bonnot and fired three shots into the policeman, who fell, dying, onto the pavement as Bonnot hit the gas and roared off.

Now the car was hotter than ever, but the bandits, reluctant to abandon it, somehow hid it long enough to use for another attempted heist two days later. At midnight, they entered the town of Pontoise, northwest of Paris, somehow having learned the location of the home of a wealthy lawyer. They broke in through a side door and found a safe. Their efforts to try to move it—they apparently hoped to make off with it in the car—woke the lawyer and his wife. The lawyer looked out of an upstairs window and, as luck would have it, saw a baker going by on his way to work. He asked the baker to check to see if the door was locked. As he approached, Callemin and Garnier ran out, fired their guns into the air, and headed for the car, where Bonnot sat waiting for them. The lawyer had his own pistol and returned fire as they drove out of sight. Disgusted, the three men who had terrified all of Paris abandoned their magnificent automobile after setting fire to it.

What had been for the bandits a comedy of errors was portrayed in the newspapers as the triumph of lawlessness over order. The anarchist gang, which was now thought to number in the dozens, had shot down a police officer in cold blood in the heart of Paris and driven off unmolested. Politicians were not immune to criticism, and the minister of the interior instructed Guichard's boss, Louis Lépine, the prefect of police, that he wanted results *tout de suite*. Anyone who had ever been suspected of anarchist leanings found themselves in jeopardy. The important thing was that arrests had to be made.

Perhaps predictably, the crackdown only heightened Parisians' fears that a large, organized gang was roaming the streets, liable to attack anyone at any time. One right-wing newspaper declared that there were two hundred thousand criminals in the city, a horde of lawless individuals against whom the police were powerless. Such comments were echoed at the funeral of the policeman who had been shot by Garnier, where the perfect of police warned that "the criminals of Paris are numbered in their thousands." [15]

Even though Lorulot had tried to distance himself from the crime wave by adding the equivocal slogan "Neither for illegalism, nor for honesty" to the masthead of his new magazine, the police kept his offices under close surveillance. They also arrested a couple of the employees on weapons charges, including a man named Eugène Dieudonné, destined to play an unfortunate role in the case.

Still trying to turn the bonds they had stolen into cash, the auto bandits got in touch with two counterfeiters Bonnot had known earlier. They in turn found a shady stockbroker who offered them 5 percent of the face value of the bonds. Bonnot reluctantly agreed and sent the counterfeiters to Amsterdam, where the gang had earlier hidden the bonds. Returning to Paris, they temporarily deposited the haul in a luggage locker at the Gare du Nord. An informer tipped off the police, and when the two men returned to the locker, they were arrested. One of them, Alphonse Rodriguez, agreed to tell all that he knew about the gang in exchange for clemency. Shrewdly determining who the police wanted him to implicate, he identified Eugène Dieudonné, one of those rounded up at Lorulot's magazine office, as one of the men who had taken part in the rue Ordener burglary.

Elated, the police decided to check his statement by bringing in the bank messenger, Caby, now released from the hospital. They showed him Dieudonné, handcuffed and sitting alone in an interview room. Caby promptly declared that *this* was the man who had shot him—a statement that should have embarrassed the police,

since this was now the third suspect that Caby had positively identified as his assailant. But of course it also meant that at last the
police had one of the robbers in custody, so the next day's papers
duly trumpeted the Sûreté's announcement that one of the gang
members was under lock and key.

If the three actual robbers had really been nothing but unscrupulous killers, they would have been delighted by this latest development. They were not. Garnier and Bonnot had made a collection
of newspaper clippings about their exploits and were annoyed that
anyone else should receive credit for what they had done. Garnier
sent the newspaper *Le Matin* an open letter addressed to the head
of the Sûreté, Guichard. In a missive both solemn and ominously
prescient, he declared:

> *Your inability for the noble offices you exercise is so*
> *obvious that a few days ago I had a mind to present*
> *myself at your offices in order to give you some fuller*
> *information and correct a few of your errors, whether*
> *intentional or not.*
>
> *I declare Dieudonné to be innocent of the crime that*
> *you know full well I committed. I refute Rodriguez' al-*
> *legations; I alone am guilty. . . .*
>
> *I know there will be an end to this struggle which*
> *has begun between me and the formidable arsenal at*
> *Society's disposal. I know that I will be beaten; I am the*
> *weakest. But I sincerely hope to make you pay dearly*
> *for your victory.*
>
> *Awaiting the pleasure of meeting you.*
>
> *Garnier*[16]

Just to prove the letter was no hoax, Garnier enclosed a sheet onto
which he had carefully placed his fingerprints, along with an inscription taunting Bertillon to put on his glasses and "watch out."
Bertillon duly checked the prints and reported that they were indeed Garnier's.

As if that were not bold enough, Bonnot personally marched into the offices of a major newspaper, *Le Petit Parisien,* to complain about mistakes in one of the stories it had printed about the gang. At first no one recognized him—blond, without facial hair—until he sat down with a reporter named Charles Sauerwein and placed a 9-millimeter Browning automatic on the desk in front of him. Bonnot declared, "We'll burn off our last round against the cops, and if they don't care to come, we'll certainly know how to find them." [17] (The Demon Chauffeur intended to deliver on his promise. He had obtained four Winchester repeating rifles, accurate and deadly. By contrast, the French police were armed only with cavalry revolvers.)

Just as calmly, Bonnot strode out of the building without interference. Sauerwein claimed journalistic ethics prevented him from notifying the police, or perhaps he hoped he would get another such sensational scoop sometime. Sauerwein and *Le Petit Parisien* showed their gratitude by henceforth calling the criminals La Bande à Bonnot, which somehow stuck, probably to Garnier's annoyance.

Other events must have convinced the gang that their dream of overturning the government was drawing nearer. Paris's taxi drivers had been waging a strike for more than four months. The cab companies had brought in scab drivers from Corsica (who, unsurprisingly, were unable to comprehend the Paris street system), and the strikers began to bomb taxis. A striker leaving a union meeting was shot by one of the scabs, further raising tensions in a city already apprehensive about anarchist murderers who could apparently carry out their crimes with impunity.

Though the newspapers reported that the Bonnot Gang had scores of members, in reality it was quite small. For its next crime, however, it would be augmented by René Valet, Élie Monier, and a shy, tubercular eighteen-year-old named André Soudy, who had decided he was soon to die anyway because he could not afford treatment for his illness, so why not go out with a bang? Soudy defiantly flaunted his nickname, Pas de Chance ("Out of Luck"). Though publicity about the gang's exploits had frightened Parisians, it also made it increasingly difficult to find unguarded automobiles waiting to be stolen outside the houses of wealthy citizens. The gang still wanted to accomplish their original goal of robbing a bank, so they developed yet another tactic: carjacking. Now six in all, they camped out all night in the Forest of Sénart, on the road between Paris and Lyons. By 7:00 A.M. on March 25 they were awake and waiting for their prey, another luxury car: a blue and yellow De Dion-Bouton limousine, just purchased from a showroom on the Champs-Élysées. A De Dion employee was chauffeuring it to the Côte d'Azur, where its new owner, the comte de Rouge, was vacationing. The only passenger was the comte's male secretary, who had come to Paris to make the eighteen-thousand-franc purchase. The De Dion company was known for the high quality of its engines; if Bonnot had somehow gotten wind of the delivery and chosen this car on purpose, it may have been because of his dissatisfaction with the way the previous Delaunay-Belleville had broken down.

The gang had earlier stopped two horse-drawn carts at gunpoint and forced their drivers to block the road. As the De Dion-Bouton approached, Garnier waved his arms, indicating to the driver that there had been some kind of accident. When the car stopped, Garnier, Bonnot, and Callemin walked toward it, each of them carrying automatic pistols. Shouting, "It's only the car we want," Garnier raised his weapon to indicate that the driver should surrender. The driver, prepared for such a situation, drew a pistol of his own, but before he could use it, Bonnot shot him. The secretary, unarmed, raised his hands in surrender, but Garnier fired at him anyway. The bandits rolled both men into the ditch along the road; the secretary, unknown to them, was only wounded and later was able to identify pictures of the men.

After turning the car around, the bandits were soon heading back toward Paris. Elated at the feeling of power driving always gave him, Bonnot began to sing "Le temps des cerises" ("Cherry

Blossom Time"), and the others, recognizing the words, joined in. It had been an anthem of the Communards, a song of eerie poignancy, since it implied that good times were always as short-lived as the spring blossoming of cherry trees—followed by death.

Bonnot skirted the capital city and took the main road north. By ten o'clock that morning they reached Chantilly, a rather sleepy town famous for its lace making. The bandits were not there to purchase cloth; what interested them was that it was the location of another branch of the Société Générale bank. The car stopped in the town's main square, and Garnier, Callemin, Valet, and Monier went inside the bank. Outside, Soudy stood on the sidewalk with one of the Winchester rifles and Bonnot sat chain-smoking in the driver's seat.

The bank clerks looked up in surprise as the four armed men appeared. Callemin shouted, "Messieurs, not a word," but one of the clerks dropped to the floor, and Garnier, nervous and trigger-happy, fired six shots into a cashier. Callemin shot a third employee; Valet followed his lead but proved a poor shot, merely hitting a fourth clerk once in the shoulder. Monier remained at the door. Garnier leaped over the counter and ran for the safe. This time, he had said, they would take only cash and leave the worthless bonds alone.

The bank manager, as it happened, had gone across the street for a coffee. Hearing shots, he started back, and Soudy fired several times at him, missing his target but certainly alerting everyone near the square that something was going on. People from shops and restaurants began to gather outside, keeping at a safe distance, all eyes on the idling automobile and the preternaturally calm man at the wheel.

Maurice Leblanc, creator of the fictional thief Arsène Lupin, wrote a dispatch for an American newspaper describing the scene:

> But where is Bonnot? At the steering wheel. All the
> danger centers on him, isolated in the middle of the
> street, the center of a gathering crowd. . . . He does not

move an inch. My informants have told me he was terrible to look upon. His whole body was contracted under the fearful strain of his muscles, rendered rigid by the anxiety of the moment. His face was distorted, almost disfigured. . . . His sense of hearing and of sight were concentrated to the last degree. And there he stood, huddled up behind the wheel, his foot on the clutch pedal, his right hand on the gear lever, every tendon straining, ready to spring—the tiger bandit![18]

The four bandits emerged from the bank with bags filled with money and piled into the car. Soudy, who must have felt even more tension than Bonnot on this, his first job, collapsed on the pavement, and his comrades had to lift him inside before Bonnot could drive off, starting with one of those signature tire-squealing U-turns that astonished everyone who watched.

Bonnot headed south, once more with guns blazing from the seat behind him to scatter anyone who tried to block the car's path. Someone in Chantilly used a telephone to alert the police in the next town south, but since their only transportation was a bicycle and a horse, they were unable to stop the powerful De Dion-Bouton as it roared through. The automobile was finally found abandoned in the town of Asnières, northeast of Paris. Because it was near a railway station, the police who discovered it assumed the gang had boarded a train. The Sûreté, on receiving this report, sent agents to the Gare du Nord, hoping to meet the bandits as they arrived in Paris. Unfortunately for them, the robbers had stayed on foot. Casually, they walked into the suburb of Lavallois-Perret, which was swarming with police because it was the site of the taxi drivers' union headquarters. The bandits soon disappeared in the crowds of demonstrators, richer by some fifty thousand francs, the largest haul they had ever made.

V

That was the high point of the auto bandits' career. Their exploits had thrown the government into turmoil and the population into panic. Prime Minister Raymond Poincaré (a cousin of the mathematician) called an emergency meeting of his cabinet to discuss how to deal with the situation. After conferring with President Fallières, Poincaré announced that the police would be given additional powers and better equipment. For the first time, they would have a motorized unit, consisting of eight automobiles and armed with automatic pistols and repeating rifles. Two hundred men were added to the Sûreté and six hundred to the Parisian police force—all assigned to hunt down what was in reality half a dozen men. Equipped with lists of the addresses of known anarchists, even the most peaceful ones, police swooped down on working-class neighborhoods, rounding up suspects. The Société Générale offered a 100,000-franc reward for information leading to the gang's capture. Hundreds of reports flowed into the Sûreté from all over Paris and the countryside. Faced with the necessity of checking them out, the police were continually chasing phantoms. As in the *Mona Lisa* case, they had too many potential suspects.

Aware of the intense manhunt, the gang had split up. Each of the members found hiding places, sometimes changing them every night. Despite the huge reward on their heads, they found no lack of sympathizers and comrades who would shelter them. But of course the more people who knew of their whereabouts, the greater the likelihood that someone would betray them.

André Soudy, who had taken part in only one of the gang's robberies, fled to the coastal town of Berck. There he found a haven in an isolated cottage, home of Bartholémy Baraille, an elderly man who had lost his job on the railway when he joined a strike in 1910. Baraille was well known to the local community for his anarchist sympathies—he subscribed to *L'Anarchie*—and apparently someone informed the Sûreté of his visitor. (Soudy's description, given by those who had seen him with a rifle in Chantilly's main square, had been widely circulated.) Inspector Jouin and some of his associates arrived from Paris and staked out the cottage. When Soudy emerged, they followed him to the railway station. After he purchased a ticket, they placed him under arrest. He surrendered meekly, even though the police found on him a loaded Browning automatic and a vial of potassium cyanide, along with a thousand francs, presumably from the Chantilly heist. But Soudy refused, or was unable, to give the police any information on the whereabouts of the other gang members.

Meanwhile, Raymond Callemin found a hiding place in a small apartment occupied by two friends in the nineteenth arrondissement. Having turned twenty-two the day after the gang's most recent theft, Raymond-la-Science bought himself a birthday present with his share of the loot: a new bicycle, specially built for racing, and a cycling outfit that suited his taste in elegant dress.

Jean Belin, a young detective at the Sûreté (who would one day be the agency's head), later wrote admiringly of Inspector Jouin, who was leading the effort to find the bandits.

> Jouin . . . had great personal charm—especially for women. . . . Perhaps it was because he had an eye for a pair of pretty ankles that he first stumbled on the track of the nefarious Callemin.
>
> He greatly admired a very attractive young woman who was in the habit of flirting under the trees of the outer boulevards with a commonplace man altogether unworthy of her obvious charms. The couple turned out to be Callemin and his current inamorata.[19]

Jouin followed them home and then called a squad of detectives to stake out the place. When Callemin left the apartment with his new bicycle, he found himself surrounded and swiftly handcuffed by Jouin and the detectives. Though the police found two Browning automatics and ninety-five bullets in his saddlebag, Callemin had not been able to get off a shot. Even so, he taunted his captors as they took him away: "My head's worth a hundred thousand francs, and yours just seven centimes—the price of a bullet." [20]

Garnier had also come to earth in Paris, with another old comrade, in the eighteenth arrondissement, the site of the working-class insurrection of 1871. Compelled to remain inside, he set down on paper some justifications for his actions. "If I became an anarchist," he wrote, "it's because I hated work, which is only a form of exploitation."

Answering the criticism from some anarchist circles that the gang had killed ordinary employees, potential comrades in the struggle, Garnier wrote, "Why kill workers?—They are vile slaves, without whom there wouldn't be the bourgeois and the rich.

"It's in killing such contemptible slaves that slavery will be destroyed." [21]

Bonnot, whose photograph as the mastermind of the gang appeared almost daily in the newspapers, had holed up in the back of a secondhand-clothes shop. Like Garnier, he avidly read *L'Anarchie,* which was still printing provocative sentiments. On April 4, one of its writers lectured the bourgeoisie: "If you apply your wicked laws, then too bad for you; social violence legitimates the most bloody reprisals, and following on from the muffled voice of Brownings, you will hear another, more powerful voice: that of dynamite!" [22]

Bonnot composed a letter in response to sentiments like these, reflecting on what life had brought him: "I am a famous man. My name has been trumpeted to the four corners of the globe. All those people who go through so much trouble to get others to talk about them, yet don't succeed, must be very jealous about the publicity that the press has given my humble self.

"I am not appreciated in this society. I have the right to live, and while your imbecilic criminal society tries to stop me, well too bad for it, too bad for you!"

He recalled some of his life's few happy moments, the times when he made love to Judith in the cemetery at Lyons: "I didn't ask for much. I walked with her by the light of the moon. . . . It was there that I found the happiness I'd dreamed about all my life, the happiness I'd always run after and which was stolen from me each time."

Unlike Garnier, his partner in crime, Bonnot expressed some regrets: "At Montgeron I didn't intend to kill the driver, Mathillet, but merely to take his car. Unfortunately when we signaled him to stop, Mathillet pointed a gun at us and that finished him. I regretted Mathillet's death because he was a prole like us, a slave of bourgeois society. It was his gesture that was fatal.

"Should I regret what I've done? Yes, perhaps, but I will carry on. . . ."[23]

vi

The police were slowly tightening the net around the fugitives. Élie Monier, who had been identified by bank clerks as one of those who had taken part in the Chantilly robbery, was unwise enough to meet one of the editors of *L'Anarchie* for dinner. Since the staff members of the radical paper were under continual surveillance, Monier's cover was blown. Instead of making an immediate arrest, the tail on the newspaper editor followed Monier to his hideout—the Hôtel de Lozère on the boulevard de Menilmontant, near the Père Lachaise Cemetery.

Jouin, the agency's second-in-command, had now been appointed to head the "flying brigade" created to use the motor bandits' own tactics to bring them down. He lost no time in apprehending Monier. In a predawn raid, he led his squad to the hotel, where they burst into Monier's room, catching him asleep. There were two more loaded Brownings on the night table, but Monier was unable to reach them. Jouin triumphantly released the news that yet another member of the gang had been apprehended.

Among Monier's effects were some letters with addresses of other possible hiding places, including the secondhand shop in

Ivry where Bonnot had gone to ground. It was, recalled Belin, "a desolate region of the city . . . dotted with hundreds of tumble-down shacks where criminals, and down and outs, and every kind of undesirable used to live. In this melancholy region of huts and ruined houses . . . was a miserable second-hand clothes store."[24]

Antoine Gauzy, the owner of the shop, was an unlikely anarchist: middle-aged, with a wife and three children to feed. His political inclinations were indicated only by the fact that he had named his youngest child Germinal, after Zola's novel about a coal miner's strike. Unluckily for him, his brother had been a friend of Monier's, which was how Bonnot had come to be staying in one of the tiny rooms above Gauzy's shop. Gauzy had sent his wife and children to the countryside, a wise precaution, though Bonnot said he planned to move on soon.

Four men whose bowler hats marked them as plainclothes policemen arrived while Gauzy was talking to a friend downstairs. Jouin, who led the group, said they had come to search the premises for stolen goods. Leaving one of his men downstairs with the visitor, Jouin led the way to the upper floor. Finding the door to the bedroom locked, he ordered Gauzy to open it. The shutters over the single window were closed, and Jouin, the first one through the door, saw only a vague shape in the darkness, which suddenly stood up and revealed itself as a man. Jouin carried a stick and struck out with it, seemingly stunning Bonnot. But as a second policeman, Inspector Colmar, entered the room, Bonnot managed to pull a small revolver from his pocket. At close range, he shot Jouin three times, once through the neck, killing him. He then turned his weapon on Colmar, who managed to shout, "Attention, c'est Bonnot," before being cut down as well.[25]

The third policeman on the stairway rushed into the room and, he later testified, found three bodies on the floor. Only one was moving: Colmar. He dragged Colmar out of the room and carried him down the narrow stairs, shouting for help.

Bonnot had been lying under Jouin's body and now staggered to his feet, blood flowing from his arm. He made his way across the corridor to the apartment of an old woman who shared the house with Gauzy. Bonnot demanded her bedsheet, planning to lower himself from the window, but she told him she had none. Telling her, "Shut up or I'll burn you," he opened her window, which overlooked a small shed. Bonnot jumped onto its roof, slid into the backyard, and ran down an alley, leaving a trail of blood.[26]

The news electrified Paris. Jouin's superior, Xavier Guichard, was enraged. When he arrived at the scene, he beat Gauzy with his fists, threatening dire consequences if the shopkeeper did not reveal where Bonnot had gone. Of course he could not, even if he had wanted to. However, Guichard now had the support of the government—and the press—in carrying out almost any plan to apprehend the remaining members of the gang. Prime Minister Poincaré visited Colmar in the hospital and authorized an elaborate funeral for Jouin, whom he proclaimed one of France's great heroes. Newspaper editorials urged the police to "shoot first," and orders were given for all detectives to be armed on duty, something that had rarely been authorized in France before.

Guichard started his own campaign of terror, rounding up anyone he could claim was even suspected of anarchist sympathies. His hope was to find someone who would betray the remaining fugitives. Even poor Mme. Gauzy, returning from the countryside with her children, was taken from the train station to police headquarters, where Guichard reportedly told her that her husband was destined for the guillotine and that the police would make sure she had no way of earning a living other than as a prostitute.

For three days, Bonnot continued to elude capture. He made his way down the Seine to Choisy-le-Roi, where a millionaire philanthropist named Alfred Fromentin had donated some property as a refuge for pacifists, anarchists, and others loosely described as libertarians. Jean Dubois, who had sheltered Bonnot and stolen cars with him in the summer of 1911, was still living in what neighbors called Le Nid Rouge ("the Red Nest"). Dubois' garage, which doubled as a chop shop, had already been searched twice by police looking for some trace of the Bonnot Gang.

The garage was still under twenty-four-hour surveillance, and the report that a man had arrived there on the night of April 27, without arousing any barking from a dog Dubois kept, made Guichard suspicious. (Shades of Conan Doyle and "the dog that did not bark in the night-time.") So on the morning of the twenty-eighth, Guichard arrived, personally in charge of sixteen armed detectives. That would not be nearly enough. As it happened, Dubois was an early riser, and they found him working in the yard on a motorcycle. With him was a boy of about six, and the police held their fire as they stealthily approached. As he saw them, Dubois pushed the boy aside and drew a pistol. One of the policemen had trained his gun on the mechanic but failed to release the safety. Dubois shot him through the arm and ran for the garage.

The face of Bonnot—said to be "grinning with rage"—appeared at an upstairs window.[27] Dubois had been forced to take cover behind an automobile in the yard, and Bonnot fired a volley of bullets at the police, trying to give his friend a chance to reach the building. Guichard shouted, "Come out with your hands up. You won't be harmed," to which Dubois responded, "Murderers! Murderers!"[28] He left his shelter and ran for the door, but was hit in the back of the neck as he reached it.

Bonnot had assembled a substantial arsenal of firearms and ammunition and was determined not to be taken without a fight. He returned fire so persistently that Guichard was forced to send for reinforcements, and he got plenty. Local paramilitary Republican Guards arrived, along with a fire brigade and the town mayor. When news of the gunfire spread, civilians began to assemble to gawk at the scene; as the morning wore on, some brought picnic baskets, and others carried pitchforks. Prefect of Police Lépine arrived from the city, bringing with him the investigating magistrate and the public prosecutor for the case. Everyone wanted to be present for the kill. Taxi drivers, whose strike had finally ended, began to bring onlookers from as far away as Paris. According to the newspapers, the crowd would eventually swell to ten thousand people. Movie crews arrived to film the whole affair.

Bonnot gratified the lust for sensation by periodically stepping onto a balcony and firing at anyone who came too near. Once police armed with rifles appeared on the scene (for some reason, the original force had only pistols), they were able to drive Bonnot inside. One eyewitness stated that the outer wall of the house became so punctured with bullet holes that it resembled a pepper mill.

The event was treated as a matter of national security. Lépine went so far as to ask that artillery guns be brought from the fort at Vincennes, but before they appeared, someone produced a cask of dynamite. A lieutenant of the Republican Guard named Fontan declared that he knew how to place the explosives, and the others gladly let him try.

Amazingly, Bonnot was finding time to write some additional material in his notebook. He listed the names of people who had been mentioned in the newspapers as part of the gang, declaring them innocent of any involvement. It is part of his legend that when he ran out of ink, he completed his last testament in his own blood. This one man, a classic loser before he became the Demon Chauffeur, was holding off what was now a force of more than a hundred men.

Lieutenant Fontan ordered a cart filled with mattresses to shield his approach to the house. The cart proved top-heavy, so the mattresses were unloaded and the cart filled with straw. As Fontan pushed the cart toward the house, Bonnot, warned by the noise, released Dubois' dog, which ran out and attacked the guardsman. Fontan drew a pistol and shot the animal.

Finally the guardsman reached the wall of the house, placed the charge of dynamite, lit a fuse, and retreated. Inside, Bonnot made his own mattress barrier and waited for the inevitable—which was painfully delayed. The first fuse fizzled out before reaching the charge. Fontan reapproached the house and lit another. This time, the charge exploded, but with disappointingly small results. More dynamite was procured, and Fontan repeated his actions. Finally, to the delight of the crowd, an enormous explosion destroyed the center portion of the house and set fires in the remainder.

Even then, no one dared approach Bonnot's hiding place, though the crowd began to chant "À mort!" ("Kill him!") to encourage the assembled police and military. Finally the straw-filled cart was called into service again, this time shielding Guichard, Lépine, and a dozen or so other armed men. They dragged Dubois' corpse away from the house and then cautiously made their way to the second floor. Bonnot, amazingly, was still alive. Though he still held a Browning automatic, he was not able to get a shot off. As he cried out, "Bunch of bastards!"[29] the detectives of the Sûreté fired a fusillade at him. Guichard, now believing it was safe to approach, stepped over the body and gave the motor bandit what was intended to be a coup de grâce.

Even so, Bonnot clung to life for another hour, in the backseat of the police car that took him to a Paris hospital, while the police searched his pockets for clues to where the rest of the gang might be hiding. The crowd around the house had to be satisfied with being allowed to trample the body of Dubois.

Two days later, both of the men were placed in an unmarked grave, for even in death they had the capacity to frighten the police—and, perhaps, to inspire others. Guichard, for example, refused to release to the press the contents of Bonnot's notebook, for it contained "a justification for criminal acts."[30]

The anonymous burial of the two anarchists contrasted with the full-blown state funeral held for Inspector Louis Jouin at the Cathedral of Notre-Dame the previous day. Dozens of wreaths were laid upon the catafalque, which was drawn by horses through the streets as a tribute to the brave man who had died to bring the dreaded Bonnot to justice.

In the days that followed, throngs of people visited the ruined house at Choisy. Some came out of curiosity; others showed their feelings by shouting "Vive Bonnot!" (Outraged citizens reported such demonstrations, and a few offenders were sentenced to jail terms of as long as a month.) At movie houses, where newsreel footage of the siege was shown, some in the audience cheered when the figure of Bonnot appeared on the balcony. Though the new editor of *L'Anarchie* played down the death of France's most famous anarchist, an article (signed with the pseudonym "Lionel") declared, "Don't you understand that if there were a hundred Bonnots, a thousand Bonnots, the bourgeois world would be no more than a chapter in history?"[31]

vii

Everyone was aware that there were still active members of the gang at large, primarily Octave Garnier and his friend René Valet, who had taken part in the bank robbery at Chantilly. Guichard was particularly eager to apprehend the man who had taunted him publicly. In May, the two bandits, along with Garnier's lover, Marie, had rented a house in Nogent-sur-Marne, a town to the east of Paris, on the Marne River. Though Garnier had dyed his hair blond and shaved off his mustache, someone recognized him on a bus and reported to the police where he had gotten off. The following day, Guichard, Lépine, and fifty armed men were on their way to Nogent. It took them most of the morning and afternoon to locate the fugitives, and when they approached the house, Marie and Garnier were fixing dinner, while Valet was strolling in the vegetable garden they had planted for themselves. (They followed a vegetarian diet.) Guichard, wearing a red, white, and blue sash as a badge of office, suddenly appeared at the gate and shouted for Valet to surrender. In response, Valet fired a few shots as he retreated to the house. The motor bandits' last stand had begun.

Lépine had deplored the fact that so much force had to be used to bring down Bonnot. In the previous engagement, two detectives had been wounded and the whole affair had turned into a public spectacle. Thus, he offered the duo a chance to surrender. In response, they sent Marie to safety, a signal that they meant to fight to the death. As a further sign of their contempt for society, they set fire to a small pile of banknotes.

Marie told the police that the two men had plenty of arms and ammunition (nine pistols with more than a thousand rounds of bullets), so Guichard and Lépine felt they had to send, once again, for reinforcements—a startling admission that fifty police officers were no match for two members of the gang. By 9:00 P.M., they were in command of what was virtually an army: 250 additional policemen along with dogs, scores of local Republican Guards, 400 elite military Zouaves (infantrymen mostly conscripted from Algeria and Tunisia) dressed in their colorful uniforms of red bloomers, embroidered blue jackets, and fezzes, and finally a company of dragoons. Nogent was a vacation spot, with a casino and beaches, and another huge crowd of civilians assembled. Fortunately for them, the scene was illuminated with a searchlight, scores of flares, and the headlights of police vehicles trained on the house.

No dynamite was immediately available this time, but the Zouaves had brought another fearsome weapon: machine guns. Once they began to fire, the Zouave gunners raked the front of the house from top to bottom. The heavy-caliber ammunition pierced the walls, forcing Garnier and Valet to take shelter in the cellar. Even from there, however, they could still see out and drive back anyone who dared approach. Hoping to end the siege more quickly than the previous one, Guichard equipped some of his men with sheet-metal shields, which unfortunately proved inadequate against the anarchists' pistol shots.

Hours went by, and a supply of an older type of explosive, melinite (picric acid), arrived from the military base at Vincennes. Sappers trained to place combustible materials set off an explosion that shattered windows in nearby homes and virtually demolished the bandits' hideout. Now, using machine-gun fire as cover, making the spotlighted scene an eerie precursor to the trench warfare that would engulf Europe two years later, the Zouaves and the police ran across open ground toward the house. They found the fugitives dazed and bleeding from a variety of wounds. At Guichard's orders, they were summarily executed with a pistol shot through the head. As the bodies were carried from the house, the crowd—still assembled, though it was past midnight—tried to seize and lynch them. Afterward, souvenir seekers entered the bandits' lair and dipped their handkerchiefs in the men's blood.

When Valet's family tried to claim his body, the police declared it was now the property of the state. Both men were buried in the anonymity of the pauper's cemetery, near their comrades.

viii

The deaths of Bonnot, Garnier, and Valet did not bring the affair of the motor bandits to a close. Eighteen other men and three women had been accused by the police of complicity in the gang's crimes. Raymond-la-Science Callemin and André Soudy were of course the principal members of the gang in custody, but the official net also dragged in those who had provided weapons, allowed their homes to be used as hideouts, or merely—as in the case of Victor Serge and his mistress, Rirette Maîtrejean—written articles that encouraged the gang's activities. Besides various specific charges, all were accused of "criminal conspiracy" under one of the so-called Wicked Laws that were passed in 1894 in response to another famous anarchist act: Auguste Vaillant's tossing a bomb onto the floor of the Chamber of Deputies.

Serge, who had earlier written so enthusiastically about the uses of violence, chose to emphasize some of his more moderate statements in his defense. Since the conspiracy evidence against him was strong, considering that he had been part of the communal household that included two of the principal bandits, Callemin and Garnier, Serge had to distance himself from them, as well as from the others who had assisted the robbers. In a letter to his successor as editor of *L'Anarchie,* he wrote, "I am—we are—[he was including Rirette in his defense] disgusted, deeply aggrieved, to see that *comrades*—comrades that I have had affection for since their first and purest passions—could commit things as deplorable as the butchery of Thiais. I am heartbroken to see that the others, all the others, have madly wasted and lost their lives in a pointless struggle, so tragic that, beneath the façade of such desperate courage, they cannot even defend themselves with self-respect." [32]

The trial, with so many defendants, promised to be a long one. Several hundred people were on the witness list, and some seven hundred exhibits entered into evidence, including all firearms that had been recovered. The ominous sight of these weapons, assembled on tables, faced the jury throughout the trial. On the first day, the judge announced that the question of politics was not to enter the deliberations of the trial. But of course virtually everyone in Paris knew of the crimes that the defendants were implicated in.

One of those accused, Marius Medge, was charged with the slayings of the old man and his housekeeper at Thiais. There had been fingerprints left at the murder scene, but apparently they were not distinct enough to incriminate Medge. Bertillon himself was called to the stand to interpret them. He pointed out irregularities in the prints and, with typical convoluted reasoning, said that these proved that the man who left them had been a cook. Unfortunately for Medge, the prosecution was able to produce proof that he had indeed worked as a cook. The jury, only partially convinced, found him guilty but asked the judge to show clemency. As a result, Medge was sentenced to life at hard labor (*la guillotine sèche*, the "dry guillotine").

Ultimately, Callemin, Soudy, Monier, and the unfortunate Dieudonné (who the bank messenger in the first robbery had testified was, after all, the man who shot him) all were sentenced to the guillotine. Most of the others received prison terms; many were sent to Devil's Island, the notorious French penal colony off the coast of South America.

Rather than face Devil's Island, Carouy (who, largely on Bertillon's shaky fingerprint analysis, had been convicted along with Medge of the murders at Thiais) swallowed a cyanide capsule someone in the courtroom had passed to him. He left a note: "Not having known the joys of existence, I shall leave this realm of atoms without regret. When I feel my muscles, when I feel my strength, it's hard to imagine that all this can disappear for ever on the strength of one statement of my guilt. I cannot believe that Monsieur Bertillon can, in cold blood, really dare to send me to my death, because he is obstinate and doesn't wish to admit that he's wrong. Science is playing me a dirty trick."[33] It wasn't the first time Bertillon had condemned a man because he couldn't admit his mistake.

Appeals for the condemned men were presented to the courts and duly rejected. The only hope now was a reprieve from the new president of France, Raymond Poincaré. In view of the intense journalistic outrage at the gang's crimes, it is surprising that Poincaré did in fact commute Dieudonné's sentence to life on Devil's Island.[34] Callemin, Soudy, and Monier were guillotined on April 21, 1913. Despite the fact that it was 4:30 in the morning and a light rain was falling, there was a crowd of spectators that had been steadily gathering since midnight. One of them was Gabriel Astruc, the impresario who had sponsored Serge Diaghilev and the Ballets Russes: "I went with a magistrate friend of mine to the execution of the Bonnot gang. . . . First prisoner. Two steps forward. Plank tilts. Click. Corpse disappears. Three buckets of water. All over. Second prisoner: same business. Third prisoner: same business. An American reporter who had consulted his watch during the triple execution said to my friend: 'You know, monsieur procureur, how long the whole thing lasted? Forty seconds exactly: it's the new record!' "[35] Speed had scored another triumph.

Raymond-la-Science Callemin proved he deserved his nickname by declaring that his last wish was to have his body turned over to the Faculty of Medicine at the University of Paris. That was done. Bertillon's father and the Society for Mutual Autopsy would have approved.

THE THIEF

A year after the *Mona Lisa* vanished, the officials of the Louvre were forced to confront the unthinkable: that she would never return. The blank space on the wall of the Salon Carré had been filled with a colored reproduction of the painting. But that had begun to fade and curl, and people now averted their eyes as they passed it, as if to avoid the reminder of a tragic death.

So one day when the doors to the museum opened, patrons discovered another painting hanging there: also a portrait, but this one of a man, *Baldassarre Castiglione*, by Raphael. Though Raphael, a few years younger than Leonardo, had learned from studying the older man's work, this portrait is markedly different in spirit from *La Joconde*. The sitter is somber, even tired; he looks as if he has not smiled in a long time. Raphael's masterpiece may have reflected the feeling of the curators that even though the space on the wall was now filled, there would be a hole in the museum's soul forever.

i

But was the *Mona Lisa* truly gone for good? Occasionally, stories appeared about sightings of the famous painting. James Duveen, the nephew of Henry J. Duveen, one of London's leading art dealers, later related that his uncle actually had a chance to buy the *Mona Lisa*. The elder Duveen was convinced that the offer was genuine, a hunch that later proved correct.

One morning, Henry J. Duveen was in the Bond Street showrooms . . . when he heard a man arguing with an assistant.

"I won't go away," the fellow was saying. "I've come to see the head of the firm, and see him I will."

The man was creating something of a scene, so my uncle went over.

"What is the trouble?" he asked.

"I must see you alone and at once. It is a very important matter."

Henry J. Duveen, not liking the look of the man, did not take him to his private office but to the far side of the large entrance gallery.

"Well?"

"Will you give me your word of honor that you will never reveal what I am going to tell you?"

My uncle began to think the seedy-looking foreigner was mad and tried to humor him.

"Of course; of course," he murmured.

"If you don't," snarled the Italian, "I and my friends will know how to deal with you. You'd better be careful! Now listen; I have the Gioconda here in London. Will you buy it?"

My uncle stared at him open-mouthed. It was too incredible a thing to grasp all at once. That this anarchistic-looking fellow should—

"Well, what do you say? What's the figure you'll give me?"

Henry J. Duveen suddenly realized that the man was not mad. His brain worked like lightning. He took the only way out: he burst out laughing as though he thought the whole thing was a hoax, and walked away. As my uncle said to me afterwards: "I believed the fellow all right; he had nothing to gain by lying; but I would sooner have gone around with a stick of dynamite in my pocket for the rest of my life than have had any knowledge of that affair!"[1]

ii

Another dealer proved not to be so cautious. Alfredo Geri, owner of the Galleria Borgognissanti in Florence, Italy, was an active dealer in art and antiques. He often placed advertisements in newspapers in several European cities, including Paris, offering to buy old works of art. But he could hardly have imagined what he would be offered in a letter he received in November 1913. The sender, who signed himself "Leonard," claimed to have the *Mona Lisa* in his possession.

At first, Geri thought his correspondent was a crackpot or a hoaxer. But Leonard said he was an Italian who had been "suddenly seized with the desire to return to his country at least one of the many treasures which, especially in the Napoleonic era, had been stolen from Italy."[2] He also mentioned that although he was not setting a specific price, he himself was not a wealthy man and would not refuse compensation if his native country were to reward him.

That struck a note in Geri's heart. He glanced at the return address on the envelope: a post office box in Paris. Probably, Geri thought, the painting had long ago been spirited out of Paris, but just suppose . . . Though Geri was a businessman, he was also a collector, and collectors always live with the hope of finding a treasure among the trash.

Geri took the letter to the most knowledgeable art expert in Florence: Giovanni Poggi, director of the Uffizi Gallery. (Within the Uffizi's collection was a genuine Leonardo: *The Adoration of the Magi.*) Poggi thought following up on the offer was worth a try, but suggested Geri should demand that Leonard bring the painting to Florence, where Poggi could inspect it. Poggi had a document from the Louvre that detailed certain marks that were on the back of the original panel; no forger could be aware of these.

Geri did as Poggi suggested, but Leonard proved to be an elusive figure. More than once, he set a date for his arrival in Florence, and then sent a letter canceling the meeting. Geri assumed that he was a hoaxer after all, until on December 9 he received a telegram saying that Leonard was in Milan and would be in Florence on the following day.

That was inconvenient, for Poggi had gone on a trip to Bologna. Geri sent him an urgent telegram, using oblique language in case someone else should read it: "OUR PARTY COMING FROM MILAN WILL BE HERE WITH OBJECT TOMORROW. NEED YOU HERE. PLEASE RESPOND. GERI."[3] Poggi wired back that he could not arrive by the following day, but would be in Florence the day after that, a Thursday.

Geri prepared to stall. He was well aware that many people had claimed to have, or to know who had, the *Mona Lisa,* and that all these claims had been dead ends. But somehow he had a hunch that Leonard was different. Accordingly, when a thin young man wearing a suit and tie and sporting a handsome mustache arrived at the dealer's gallery the next day, Geri showed him into his office and pulled down the blinds, emphasizing the secret nature of the conversation.

Eagerly—perhaps too much so—Geri asked where the painting was. Leonard replied that it was in the hotel where he was staying. Perhaps because he could not believe that someone would leave such a valuable object in a hotel room, Geri showed him a photographic reproduction of the *Mona Lisa* and asked if this was the painting.

Leonard nodded, with a quizzical look. Didn't everyone know what the *Mona Lisa* looked like?

Geri pressed him further. The original, he asked. You have the original?

According to Geri's account, Leonard replied, "I repeat: we are dealing with the real Gioconda. I have good reason to be sure."[4] Leonard coolly declared that he was certain because he had taken the painting from the Louvre himself. He then gave an abbreviated account of the theft. Interestingly, some of his details were different from those known by the French police to be true. He said, for example, that he had entered the museum on Monday morning with other workers. If that were true, he would have been stopped, for everyone going in was checked against a list; moreover the police had found evidence that someone had stayed overnight in a storage closet from Sunday to the morning of the theft.

Geri was not aware of these discrepancies, but he was curious about one thing. Had Leonard been alone when he stole the painting? he asked. Leonard "was not too clear on that point. He seemed to say yes, but didn't quite do so [but his answer was] more 'yes' than 'no.' "[5]

Eventually the discussion got down to the reward—though here the two men differed in their later accounts. Leonard claimed, "When I came to Florence and was in Geri's presence, these were my exact words: 'I want nothing; I set no price on the restitution I am making to Italy. . . .' Then Geri said to me, 'We'll do things in such a way as to make us all content.' "[6]

Geri, on the other hand, said that when he asked Leonard what kind of reward he had in mind, the thief boldly answered 500,000 lire. That was the equivalent of $100,000 and quite a fortune in those days, though of course the painting itself was valued far higher. Geri, holding his breath, thought that he had better agree, so he said, "That's fine. That's not too high."[7] The important thing was to recover the painting, and he would promise Leonard the sun and the moon if he had to.

Naturally, Geri was eager to see the painting, but he feared he would not be able to determine whether it was genuine without Poggi's help, so he asked Leonard to return the following day at three o'clock. Geri showed the man out, tempted to follow him, not knowing if he would ever see him again.

The next afternoon, with Poggi present, Geri grew anxious when Leonard did not show up at the appointed time. Had he been frightened off by something? The minutes went by and finally the doorbell rang. There stood Leonard, a quarter of an hour late on an errand that could bring him half a million lire!

Geri introduced Poggi, and to his relief, the two men "shook hands enthusiastically, Leonard saying how glad he was to be able to shake the hand of the man to whom was entrusted the artistic patrimony of Florence."[8] As the three of them left the gallery, "Poggi and I were nervous," Geri recalled. "Leonard, by contrast, seemed indifferent."[9]

Leonard took them to the Hotel Tripoli-Italia on the Via de' Panzani, only a few blocks from the Duomo, the magnificent basilica whose dome had towered over the city long before Leonardo da Vinci lived there. Leonard's small room was on the third floor. Inside, he took from under the bed a small trunk made of white wood. When he opened the lid, Geri was dismayed: it was filled with "wretched objects: broken shoes, a mangled hat, a pair of pliers, plastering tools, a smock, some paint brushes, and even a mandolin."[10] Calmly, Leonard removed the items one by one and tossed them onto the floor. Surely, Geri thought, this was not where the *Mona Lisa* had been hidden for the past twenty-seven months. He peered inside but saw nothing more.

Then Leonard lifted what had seemed to be the bottom of the trunk. Underneath was an object wrapped in red silk. Geri held his breath as Leonard took it to the bed and removed the covering. "To our astonished eyes," Geri recalled, "the divine Gioconda appeared, intact and marvelously preserved. We took it to the window to compare it with a photograph we had brought with us. Poggi examined it and there was no doubt that the painting was authentic. The Louvre's catalogue number and stamp on the back of it matched with the photograph."[11]

Geri's heart was pounding, but he forced himself to remain calm, for the most difficult part of the transaction had to be accomplished. He and Poggi explained that the painting had to be taken to the Uffizi Gallery for further tests. Leonard seemed pleased, for he knew that the Uffizi was almost as prestigious an institution as the Louvre itself. Clearly, he expected to go along with them.

The *Mona Lisa* was rewrapped in the red silk, and the three men went downstairs. As they were passing through the lobby, however, the concierge stopped them. Suspiciously, he pointed to the package and asked what it was. He obviously thought it was the hotel's property, but Geri and Poggi, showing their credentials, vouched for Leonard, and the concierge let them pass. Geri remarked later that it had been easier to steal the painting from the Louvre than to remove it from the hotel. "If the guardians of the Louvre had had the same curiosity, never would the Gioconda have come to Florence."[12]

At the Uffizi, Poggi compared sections of the painting with close-up photographs that had been taken at the Louvre. There was a small vertical crack in the upper left-hand part of the panel, matching the one in the photos. Most telling of all was the pattern of *craquelure,* cracks in the paint that had appeared as the surface dried and aged. A forger could make *craquelure* appear on a freshly painted object, but no one could duplicate the exact pattern of the original.

There could be no further doubt: the *Mona Lisa* had been recovered.

Poggi and Geri explained to Leonard that it would be best to leave the painting at the Uffizi. They would have to get further instructions from the government; of course they themselves could not authorize the payment he deserved.

The Uffizi was an awesome setting, and Leonard felt overwhelmed by their arguments. How could he doubt two men of such standing and integrity? He did mention that he was finding it a bit expensive to stay in Florence. Yes, they understood, said the two experts. He would be well rewarded, and soon. They shook his hand warmly and congratulated him on his patriotism.

As soon as he left, Geri and Poggi notified the authorities. Not long after Leonard returned to his hotel room, he answered a knock at the door and found two policemen there to arrest him. He was, they said, quite astonished.

iii

As word spread that the *Mona Lisa* had been found, the first reaction was disbelief. Upon hearing the news, Corrado Ricci, the director of Italy's Department of Fine Arts in Rome, immediately left for Florence so that he could conduct his own tests on the painting. Other art experts converged on the Uffizi, eager to see the work. Of course, just to be present at the examination was a mark of one's importance, so Poggi had more requests than he could handle.

When a reporter telephoned a curator of the Louvre to tell him the news, the Frenchman was at dinner and flatly refused to believe it. He said it was impossible and hung up. The museum itself issued a cautious statement: "The curators of the Louvre . . . wish to say nothing until they have seen the painting. Certain descriptions of details and features give rise to some doubts among them."[13]

Ricci, however, confirmed Poggi's previous judgment that the painting was authentic, and the Italian government made an official announcement to that effect. The French ambassador in Rome made personal calls on the premier and foreign minister of Italy to offer his government's gratitude. It was at the time presumed, but not of course absolutely certain, that the painting would be returned to the Louvre.

When the news reached the Italian Parliament, it interrupted a fistfight on the floor of the Chamber of Deputies. The minister of public education brandished a telegram about the return of the *Mona Lisa,* and the battling deputies surrounded him, clamoring for details. When he reported that the thief had taken the painting under the impression that he was recovering one of the treasures stolen from Italy by Napoleon, some of the deputies nodded. Even those who knew Leonardo himself had taken the painting to France believed that the French armies had seized other works of art during the Napoleonic Wars, for which no reparations had been paid. It seemed only fair that Italy should now keep the painting done by one of its most illustrious sons.

Cooler heads prevailed, and the minister announced later, "The 'Mona Lisa' will be delivered to the French Ambassador with a solemnity worthy of Leonardo da Vinci and a spirit of happiness worthy of Mona Lisa's smile. Although the masterpiece is dear to all Italians as one of the best productions of the genius of their race, we will willingly return it to its foster country . . . as a pledge of friendship and brotherhood between the two great Latin nations."[14] The thought that the two countries were united in their common heritage was significant, for Italy was formally an ally of (non-Latin-speaking) Germany, France's perennial enemy. In 1915, after the outbreak of World War I, Italy joined the fighting on the side of France, in part owing to the fraternal feelings engendered by the *Mona Lisa* affair.

iv

Meanwhile, the man who called himself Leonard was being intensively questioned by the police. He talked freely, for he was still under the impression that he would be acclaimed by Italians when they found out his motive for the theft. He admitted that his real name was Vincenzo Perugia[15] and that he had been born in 1881 in the village of Dumenza, near Lake Como. Having left there as a young man because there were not enough jobs available, he went to France, where he found work as a housepainter and carpenter.

("Pittore," he responded when asked for his occupation—using the word for artist, not merely housepainter.) Yes, he had worked at the Louvre—had, in fact, been one of those who had made the protective box that held the glass covering the painting. Perugia confessed that he had become fascinated by the image: "Many times while working at the Louvre I stopped before daVinci's picture and was humiliated to see it there on foreign soil. I wasn't attached to the Louvre for long, but I remained on friendly terms with my old working companions and I continued to visit the museum, where I was well known. I thought it would be a great thing for Italy were I to present the wonderful masterpiece to her, so I planned the theft." [16]

This news turned the spotlight back to the Sûreté and brought uncomfortable questions for Lépine and Bertillon. It turned out that Bertillon's massive files did contain a record card for Perugia, with fingerprints. He had been arrested twice before: once for attempted robbery, and a second time for carrying a knife. But Bertillon's insistence that his own system was superior to fingerprinting had proved to be a crucial error. He could not match the thumbprint on the *Mona Lisa*'s frame to the one on Perugia's arrest record because the records were not arranged according to fingerprint patterns but by the system of physical measurements called bertillonage. And since the police had no suspect to measure, they could not determine Perugia's identity.

Some reporters recalled that at the time of the theft, all current and recent employees of the Louvre had been called in for questioning. Was that the case with Perugia? The records were checked, producing more embarrassing revelations: Perugia had indeed worked at the Louvre between October 1910 and January 1911, although no one could say for sure if he had really worked on the glass covering for the *Mona Lisa*. Worse yet, when he had not responded to a letter asking him to come in for questioning, a detective named Brunet had gone to Perugia's room and interrogated him. Brunet had even searched the place, finding nothing. If Perugia was telling the truth, the *Mona Lisa* was actually there, in the false-bottomed trunk, during the detective's visit. Brunet had dutifully noted in his report that Perugia had been at work elsewhere on the day the painting was stolen. However, when reporters tracked down Perugia's employer, they learned that his records showed Perugia had been two hours late for work that morning. Perugia confirmed this, saying that after he stole the painting, he took it to his room before reporting for work.

Adding insult to injury as far as the French police were concerned, Perugia's insistence that he was a hero found sympathetic ears, at least in Italy. Every day, people gathered outside the jail in Florence to cheer him. He received gifts of homemade food, wine, cheese, cigarettes, and even money. At the hotel where he had stayed, the proprietor found that the contents of the now-famous trunk were in demand. People offered to buy them as mementoes — even the paint-stained rags Perugia had used to wipe his hands. A reporter for the newspaper *La Nazione* interviewed him in jail, where Perugia protested, "I have rendered outstanding service to Italy. I have given the country back a treasure of inestimable worth, and instead of being thankful, they throw me in jail. It's the height of ingratitude." [17]

After a triumphal tour through Italy, where thousands of people stood in line for a look at the painting, the *Mona Lisa* resumed its old place on the wall of the Salon Carré on January 4, 1914. It had been gone for two years, four and a half months. In the next two days, more than one hundred thousand people filed past, welcoming back one of Paris's icons. Outside, vendors sold postcards, including one that showed La Joconde in a Madonna-like pose, holding a baby. Standing behind her, as if he were a proud new papa, was Perugia.

v

Almost like a father, the man who had kidnapped her was embellishing his story and enjoying the notoriety it brought him. "My work as a house painter brought me in contact with many art-ists," Perugia said. "I always felt that deep in my soul I was one of them. . . . I shall never forget the evening after I had carried the picture home. I locked myself in my room in Paris and took the picture from a drawer. I stood bewitched before 'La Gioconda.' I fell a victim to her smile and feasted my eyes on my treasure every evening, discovering each time new beauty and perversity in her. I fell in love with her." [18]

The police branded Perugia's romantic and patriotic decla-rations as sheer invention. In Paris, detectives had revisited the boardinghouse room where he had stayed, this time giving it a more thorough search. They came up with some interesting finds. First were two notebooks in which Perugia kept a kind of diary. Under a date in 1910 he had made a list of art collectors and deal-ers in the United States, Germany, Italy, and England. Among the collectors were John D. Rockefeller, J. P. Morgan, and Andrew Carnegie. Geri was among the Italians listed. Pretty clearly, Pe-rugia had money on his mind at the very time he was helping to put the *Mona Lisa* inside a protective case—almost a year before the robbery. Perugia tried to deflect the new evidence—and Geri's account of their discussions about money—by claiming he was being a dutiful son: "I was anxious to ensure a comfortable old age for my parents." [19]

Something else the police found in Perugia's room, however, only added to his romantic appeal. This was a bundle of ninety-three love letters, bound with red ribbon, sent to him by a woman who signed herself "Mathilde." Somehow the police, or enterpris-ing reporters (it was never quite clear), developed the story that Perugia had attended a dance where Mathilde had been stabbed by the man who had brought her. Perugia carried her to the house of an old woman, who nursed her back to health. Afterward, Mathilde and Perugia fell passionately in love. The icing on the cake, for the newspapers, was that Mathilde was said to have borne a remark-able resemblance to Mona Lisa.

An intense hunt began to find this mysterious young woman.

Analysis of the letters showed that her French was not very good. From that fact alone, speculation arose that she must be German, and that fueled the idea, never abandoned in some quarters, that the theft had all along been a German plot to embarrass France.

Meanwhile, two detectives from the Sûreté had arrived in Florence to question Perugia. His legal situation was uncertain, for the French government had made no move to extradite him—and never would. It seems possible that the Italian government, recognizing Perugia's popularity, willingly gave the painting back in exchange for France's agreement to allow Perugia to remain in Italy. At any rate, since he freely confessed to the crime, the French detectives were more interested in identifying any accomplices he might have had.

Apparently trying to convince his questioners that he had taken good care of the painting, Perugia said that because he feared it was too cold in his lodgings, he had stored it with a friend named Vincent Lancelotti. That sent French police in search of Lancelotti, another Italian who had come to Paris to find work. Here too they turned up information that proved embarrassing for the French authorities. Shortly after the robbery, Lancelotti had actually been questioned by Magistrate Drioux, and acting on a tip, Drioux had ordered Lancelotti's rooms searched. When nothing was found, Lancelotti was released.

Now the police returned to his apartment house on the rue Bichat, across the street from the Saint-Louis Hospital in the tenth arrondissement. Lancelotti's mistress, Françoise Séguenot, answered the door and said he was out. Asked when he would return, she shouted, "You're not going to start these annoyances again,"[20] and protested that Vincent had already been cleared of any involvement in the theft. The police left but staked out the building and were rewarded a few minutes later when a man with his collar turned up and a cap pulled over his eyes emerged. One of the detectives recognized him as Michael Lancelotti, Vincent's brother. Michael was apparently not the brains of the family, for when the people stopped him, he let slip he was going to the Practical School of Hypnotism and Massage, where his brother was a student. Françoise had told Michael to give Vincent ninety francs and to tell him to take the train to Belgium at once.

The police took the Lancelottis and Séguenot in for questioning. When Vincent heard that Perugia had accused him of hiding the *Mona Lisa,* he vehemently denied it. He admitted knowing Perugia and also acknowledged that he and his brother had gone to the railway station when Perugia left for Italy, but that had been no more than a friendly gesture toward their fellow Italian.

Séguenot was emphatic as well. "I work at home as a washerwoman," she said. "Nothing, however small, could have been brought into our miserable little room without my noticing it immediately. . . . If I had seen [the painting] in Perugia's possession, I would have torn it fom his grasp and rushed it back to the Louvre."[21] In fact, she added under further questioning, "It was only when Perugia was arrested that I even learned that the painting *existed!*" The police official who questioned her expressed some surprise at this, as well he might have, for it seemed unlikely that anyone living in Paris in 1911 could have been oblivious to the theft.

Despite their denials, Magistrate Drioux ordered all three suspects charged with receiving and concealing an art object stolen from a state museum. He released Séguenot and Michael, ordering only Vincent to be held at La Santé Prison.

Those who believed that Perugia could not possibly have acted alone felt that the Lancelotti brothers did more than merely conceal the painting. It was suggested that they could have been his accomplices in physically removing the painting and its heavy frame from the wall of the museum. The argument against this scenario, of course, is that the only two people known to have seen the thief—the plumber who opened the stairway door for him and the passerby who saw him throw away a doorknob outside the museum—both told police that there had been only one man.

In any case, Drioux eventually dropped all charges against the trio when it became clear that Perugia would not be returning to

France to testify against them. His testimony was the only evidence of their involvement, though many accounts of the case since then have mentioned them as coconspirators.

vi

In January 1914, Perugia's hopes of receiving a reward for returning the painting were finally dashed. Alfredo Geri collected the twenty-five thousand francs that had been offered by Les Amis du Louvre, a society of wealthy art lovers, for information leading to the return of the painting. The grateful French government also bestowed upon him its most prestigious decoration, the Légion d'honneur, as well as the title *officier de l'instruction publique*. Geri showed what were perhaps his true colors when he promptly turned around and sued the French government for 10 percent of the value of the *Mona Lisa*. His contention was that a Gallic tradition gave the finder of lost property a reward of one-tenth the value of the object. In the end, a court decided that the *Mona Lisa* was beyond price and that Geri had only acted as an honest citizen should. He received no further reward.

Perugia, meanwhile, was growing depressed in jail. Perhaps it bothered him that Geri collected the reward he had hoped to get, or merely that the authorities insisted on keeping him locked up, not willing to accept him as a hero. Guards reported that he occasionally wept. A psychologist came to see him, but Perugia at first refused treatment, insisting that he wasn't crazy. After a little coaxing, however, he began to discuss his feelings. By the time his trial began on June 4, he was again calm and self-possessed, insisting that he had acted as a patriot.

Since there was no question of guilt, the legal proceedings were more like an inquest intended to establish the truth, if such a thing were possible. Three judges presided in a large room that had been remodeled to provide space for journalists from around the world. The designer of the room had placed on a cushion, in the middle of a semicircle, a massive silver hemisphere that symbolized justice. A cynical journalist remarked that it would not be prudent to allow the defendant to sit too closely to this artistic treasure.

Perugia was handcuffed when he entered the courtroom at 9:00 A.M., but he smiled graciously at the photographers. Cavaliere Barilli, president of the court and head of the three-judge panel, called the proceedings to order. He asked a few questions of Perugia to establish his parentage, the town where he was born, and his occupation. Again, asked if he was a housepainter by trade, Perugia insisted that he was a *pittore,* an artist. The judge asked if he had ever been arrested before, and Perugia's memory failed him. The judge reminded him of the two occasions when he had been arrested in France, once for theft.

With that completed, the court allowed one of Perugia's lawyers to make a motion to dismiss the case because the crime did not occur in Italy and there had been no formal complaint by the French government. Barilli reserved judgment on that matter and resumed his questioning of Perugia. Like everyone else, the judge was curious to learn how this apparently humble man could have carried out the audacious crime. Could Perugia describe what happened on August 21, 1911, when he stole the *Mona Lisa?*

Somewhat eagerly, Perugia asked if he could also tell why he had committed the crime, but the judge told him that he must do that later. For now, he wanted a description of the act itself.

Perugia offered an abbreviated version: He had entered the Louvre through the front door early that Monday, wandered through various rooms, took the *Mona Lisa* from its place on the wall, and left the same way. The judge pointed out that during the pretrial interrogations, Perugia had admitted trying to force the door at the bottom of the little stairwell that led to the Cour du Sphinx. Perugia had no answer for this, and the judge did not press him for one.

It is difficult to understand why Perugia changed his story or even why he did not tell the full truth about how he entered and left the museum, given the fact that he freely confessed to the crime itself. Perhaps he was afraid of implicating others, such as the Lancelotti brothers, or even people who might have helped him in other ways, both before and after the theft. The alibi that he had concocted for himself—that he was a patriot reclaiming one of Italy's treasures—sounded better if he had been the sole actor in the drama.

Now, Perugia was asked why he had stolen the *Mona Lisa*. He responded that all the Italian paintings in the Louvre were stolen works, taken from their rightful home, Italy. When asked how he knew this, he said that when he worked at the Louvre, he had found documents that proved it. He remembered in particular a book with prints that showed "a cart, pulled by two oxen; it was loaded with paintings, statues, other works of art. Things that were leaving Italy and going to France." [22]

Was that when he decided to steal the *Mona Lisa*? Not exactly, Perugia replied. First he considered the paintings of Raphael, Correggio, Giorgione . . . all great masters. "But I decided on the *Mona Lisa*, which was the smallest painting and the easiest to transport."

"So there was no chance," asked the court, "that you decided on it because it was the most valuable painting?"

"No, sir, I never acted with that in mind. I only desired that this masterpiece would be put in its place of honor here in Florence." [23]

Allowed to continue describing his experiences in Paris, Perugia described how the French workers looked down on him. They hid his tools. They mocked him. They put salt and pepper into the wine he drank with his lunch. Finally, they called him "macaroni" and "dirty Italian." The reporters wrote the slurs down, their pencils moving furiously. When that part of Perugia's testimony appeared in print, his popularity at home was secure.

Perhaps thinking that it would be wise not to allow Perugia to turn the proceedings into his personal forum, Barilli played one of the prosecution's trump cards: "Is it true," he asked, "that you tried to sell 'La Gioconda' in England?"

Accounts of the trial say that this was one of the few moments when Perugia lost his composure. He glared around the court-room, clenching his fists as if to do battle with his accusers.

"Me? I offered to sell La Gioconda to the English? Who says so? It's false! Who says so? Who wrote that?"

Barilli pointed out that "it is you yourself who said so, during one of your examinations which I have right here in front of me."

Unable to deny that, Perugia recalled going to England on a pleasure trip with some friends. He saw some postcards of the *Mona Lisa,* and that made him decide to get advice on how he could take the painting to Italy. "I was certainly not going to get this kind of advice in France! Therefore from this same postcard vendor, I got the name of an antiques dealer. That's how I found out about Duveen. At the antiques dealer, I asked how I could take the *Mona Lisa* to Italy, but Duveen didn't take me seriously. I pro-test against this lie that I would have wanted to sell the painting to London. If such a thing had ever been my intention . . . I would have knocked on the door of all the antique dealers and asked for money. . . . But I wanted to take it back to Italy, and to return it to Italy, and that is what I did."[24]

"Nevertheless," said Barilli, "your unselfishness wasn't total—you did expect *some* benefit from restoration."

"Ah benefit, benefit—," Perugia responded, "certainly some-thing better than what happened to me here."[25]

That drew a laugh from the spectators.

The hearing took only two days—quite speedy, reporters noted, for an Italian legal proceeding. It was clear that the judges didn't want the publicity generated by the trial to go on for long. Nor did they tarry over their decision: the next day, Barilli called the court to order and announced a sentence for Perugia of one year and fif-teen days. As Perugia was led away, he was heard to say, "It could have been worse."[26]

It actually got better. The following month, Perugia's attorneys presented arguments for an appeal. This time, the court was more lenient, reducing the sentence to seven months. Perugia had already been incarcerated nine days longer than that since his arrest, so he was released. A crowd had gathered to greet him as he left the courthouse. Someone asked him where he would go now, and he said he would return to the hotel where he had left his belongings. When he did, he found that the establishment's name had changed. No longer was it the Tripoli-Italia; now it was the Hotel La Gioconda—and it was too fancy to allow a convicted criminal to stay there. Perugia's lawyers had to vouch for him before the concierge would give him a room.

Was that the full story? Had the truth of the *Mona Lisa*'s disappearance been revealed? Many people did not think so. Though the romantic tale of the humble Italian workman falling in love with the painting and liberating it for his native country was charming, some felt that such a great theft required a larger explanation, a more elaborate plot—a mastermind, not an ordinary workman. Certainly the Sûreté would have preferred to have been outwitted by a criminal genius instead of having to explain why they had miserably bungled the investigation.

But Paris had many more crimes to offer—including two spectacular murder cases—and though few knew it, the *Mona Lisa* case was not quite closed, either.

CHERCHEZ LA FEMME

It was Alexandre Dumas *père,* in a book called *Les Mohicans de Paris,* who first coined the phrase *cherchez la femme* ("look for the woman") to suggest that at the heart of every crime there was a woman. His dictum made its way into the consciousness of French criminologists, and even Bertillon, who strove for the objectivity of a scientist, when faced with a mystery nevertheless could not resist asking, "Where is the woman?"[1]

The female criminal was the subject of considerable theorizing among social scientists during the Belle Époque. Cesare Lombroso, who argued that criminals were atavistic types—that is, degenerates who had regressed on the scale of evolution—believed that *all* women were biologically inferior to men and hence inherently atavistic.[2] This did not mean that all women would eventually become criminals, but that they were more susceptible than men to influences that could produce aberrant behavior. These influences were as varied as the menstrual cycle, the pressures of urban life, and even the *faits divers* crime stories found in the daily newspapers. Any of these might produce a passionate response that could drive women to criminal acts. So could feminism. In the words of Théodore Joran, a rabid antifeminist, emancipated women acquired "a taste for carnage" because they could no longer contain "the instincts of brutality and savagery that, in [women's] proper state of subordination," were kept under control.[3]

Of course, one result of the belief that women could not control themselves was that courts and juries were frequently more tolerant, not to say forgiving, of women accused of crimes. Ann-Louise Shapiro, a modern feminist author, found that the acquittal rate for women in France was over 50 percent in the 1890s, while only about 30 percent for men. Women criminals sometimes became "celebrities as well as pariahs."[4] The Cours d'Assises were popular places to go for entertainment, and society women were often spectators at the trials of other women. They were known to bring picnic baskets containing canapés, sandwiches, and champagne to consume during recesses. Furthering the trend, many theater companies found that audiences flocked to plays that imitated courtroom dramas.

Shapiro cites a famous case of the 1880s in which Marie Bière, a young actress, shot Robert Gentien, a young man-about-town who had fathered her child. Gentien refused to acknowledge the infant as his own and even when the child died did not attend its funeral. Bière shot him twice in the back as he was out walking with a new mistress. Though she failed to kill him, she was tried for attempted murder. Bière's attorneys showed that Gentien was her first lover, that she resisted his suggestion to have an abortion because she wanted to be the mother of his child, and that she had even attempted suicide in his presence in a vain attempt to win his sympathy. Bière was acquitted by twelve male jurors who wept openly as their verdict was announced.

La Lanterne editorialized that "the jury, in acquitting Mlle. Bière, had performed a useful service."[5] A wittier commentator, in *Le Figaro*, wrote that the defendant "be canonized as Sainte Marie, patron saint of gunsmiths, to whom abandoned women might make pilgrimages to have their revolvers blessed."[6] Gentien was obliged to flee Paris to avoid public opprobrium.

i

The popularity of crime stories, not only the supposedly factual *faits divers* but also the fictional *feuilletons,* was often cited as a cause of female criminality. One social critic, Jules Langevin, stated that "the *roman feuilleton* performs the same ravages in women's brains, perhaps does even graver damage, than does alcohol in the brains of men."[7] Writing in 1902, a Dr. Séverin Icard cited the case of a young woman who regularly came to his office with a bewildering variety of symptoms. Finally, Dr. Icard noticed that the diseases these symptoms indicated were occurring in alphabetical order. Further investigation revealed that the patient had been receiving copies of a medical dictionary, issued in installments, and so developed hysterical symptoms of the disease described in that month's reading.

The sexism went both ways. Two murder cases in the Belle Époque created enormous scandals, not only because the accused in both cases were women of good breeding, but also because they used their femininity to evade responsibility for what seemed like utterly ruthless crimes. Certainly what happened to these two murderers stood in stark contrast to the members of the Bande à Bonnot. And their trials showed that the search for truth—or the attempts to conceal it—could extend even into the courtroom.

ii

The first defendant was Marguerite Steinheil ("Meg" to the newspaper writers), who was already notorious for her role in the sudden death of President Faure in 1899. Long after the event, the story still circulated that Faure had died while in the throes of a passion so intense that his dead fingers were impossible to prize from the hair of the naked young woman whose head was in his lap.

The legend only added a certain piquancy to Meg's reputation. Looking at her husband, who had been forty when he married her in 1890 (she was then twenty-one), one could understand why a woman as beautiful and vibrant as Meg might want to take a lover. Steinheil was timid, balding, and dull. The only reason Meg had married him in the first place was that her recently widowed mother feared that her headstrong young daughter would marry a handsome but penniless young officer she had fallen in love with.

Steinheil, a mediocre academic painter, had no fortune. All he had to offer Meg was a large house in a fashionable cul-de-sac called the impasse Ronsin, in the fifteenth arrondissement, where they settled down after honeymooning in Italy. In June 1891, Meg gave birth to a daughter, Marthe, and soon became bored. All around her she saw people living in luxury, but Steinheil could not afford to give her fine clothes and jewelry. Meg looked for excitement and luxuries outside marriage, using her youth and charm to attract wealthy lovers. Her first was a government prosecutor, Manuel Baudouin. She was with him for four years; during that time she explained the lavish gifts she received by telling Steinheil they were from an Aunt Lily. Meg went to visit her aunt frequently, and it seems likely that if Steinheil was unaware of what was really going on, it was a willful ignorance on his part. At some point, Meg had also made it clear to him that the sexual part of their marriage was over. From then on they slept in separate bedrooms.

Steinheil received fringe benefits from Meg's liaisons when her lovers asked him to paint portraits or other works of art. When Meg became the mistress of President Faure in 1897, Steinheil received a government commission for a large historical painting. His rising income enabled Meg to hold the weekly salons where she presided over three or four hundred guests, including some of the leading social, artistic, and political figures of the time. These included Frédéric-Auguste Bartholdi, the sculptor of the Statue of Liberty; Émile Zola; Hippolyte-François-Alfred Chauchard, the founder of the Louvre *grand magasin* (department store); and Ferdinand de Lesseps, builder of the Suez Canal. It was said that even the Prince of Wales graced her drawing room while on a visit to France.

Steinheil, however, was becoming more of a burden to her. He had begun to need opium to sleep at night, and now in his mid-fifties, he was less and less able to turn out canvasses that Meg could "sell" to her lovers. Thus, in 1905, she took up with Émile Chouanard, a wealthy businessman not much older than she. A man used to having his own way, he quickly tired of the game of meeting her furtively in hotel rooms. Instead, he offered to pay the rent for a villa where they could spend days (and nights) in privacy and comfort. Meg took him up on this and rented a place called the Vert-Logis, forty-five minutes by train from Paris, in the town of Bellevue. Meg signed the lease with the name of a friend but had to share her secret with her longtime maid, Mariette Wolff, who took on the duties of housekeeper at Vert-Logis.

Unfortunately, Chouanard broke off the liaison in November 1907, apparently because Meg had presumptuously tried to influence his choice of a fiancé for his daughter. Not long after, as if to console herself that she was still attractive, Meg fainted while riding the Métro — seemingly to attract a well-dressed young man standing nearby. She had a good eye for men, for he turned out to be the Count Emmanuel de Balincourt. He walked her home and was invited to dinner. Before long, he found himself in her bed at Vert-Logis, which she had kept after the breakup with Chouanard. However, while Balincourt was posing for Steinheil to paint his portrait, he was overcome by guilt at cuckolding the man and broke off the relationship.

Meg was at an age when women who live off their beauty are fearful when they look into the mirror. She also had her daughter, now in her teens, to consider. A husband would one day have to be found for Marthe, and Meg wanted to be able to give her, not only a good dowry, but a respectable family background. Her next lover seemed chosen with those goals in mind. He was Maurice Borderel, a widower with three adolescent children of his own. Borderel, from the Ardennes region, was not a sophisticated Parisian like her other lovers, and soon fell in love with her, assuming the responsibility for paying the rent at Vert-Logis. (Meg was now using the villa as a country home for her family, including her husband, daughter, and mother.)

However, Borderel told Meg frankly that he could not marry her. He did not wish his children to have a stepmother, not even if Meg divorced her husband. He felt that doing so would dishonor his first wife's memory to put a divorcée in her place. Things might be different when his children were older and on their own, another ten years, say. Or perhaps if Meg's husband were to die . . . but Borderel promised nothing.

iii

On Sunday, May 31, 1908, precisely at 6:00 A.M., Rémy Couillard, the Steinheil family's valet, started down from his bedroom on the top floor of the house in the impasse Ronsin. He heard muffled cries coming from the second-floor bedroom that belonged to the Steinheil's daughter Marthe. That seemed strange, for he knew Marthe was at Vert-Logis, where the rest of the family had planned to go that afternoon. Meg's mother, Mme. Japy, had arrived two days earlier and was sleeping in one of the other bedrooms on the second floor. When Couillard investigated, he found Meg bound hand and foot to Marthe's bed, with her nightgown pulled up around her face. Only twenty, Couillard was somewhat transfixed by the sight, until Meg screamed that there were burglars in the house and told him to go for help.

Afraid to leave the room, Couillard threw open the shutters and began to shout. Three people heard him—a neighbor, a night watchman, and a policeman. They rushed into the house and gingerly searched the ground floor for intruders. Finding none, they went upstairs, where Couillard was struggling to free Meg from her bonds. In the two bedrooms next to hers, they discovered more shocking sights: the bodies of Meg's husband and mother, with cords tied around their necks indicating that they had been strangled.

Within hours, an impressive array of law enforcement figures had arrived at the Steinheil residence to investigate, among them Alphonse Bertillon, who personally took photographs of the crime scenes and dusted the house for fingerprints. Also present was Octave Hamard, head of the Sûreté, who arrived with seven assistants in tow to announce that he was taking personal charge of the case. Finally, Magistrate Joseph Leydet, a close friend of the family who was rumored to be one of Meg's lovers, had requested assignment as *juge d'instruction* to assemble evidence and determine what charges should be brought. Clearly, the case was already regarded as more than an ordinary one.

Still distraught, Meg related that she had slept in her daughter's bedroom because she had given her own bed to her mother, who had ailing legs. About midnight she had been awakened by the touch of a cloth on her face. Several people carrying shrouded lanterns were in the room. Three of them were men who wore long black coats; a fourth, carrying a pistol, was a red-haired woman. They demanded to know where Steinheil kept his money, referring to him as "your father," indicating that they knew the layout of the house well enough to know this was normally Marthe's room. After Meg told the intruders where her husband's money was kept, they struck her on the head. When she awoke, she found herself tied and gagged. At last she had been able to spit out the cotton wad they had stuffed in her mouth, and began to call for help.

As word of the murders spread, reporters besieged the house. Hamard told them that it appeared Steinheil had surprised the burglars and been killed. Why Meg's mother, Mme. Japy, had been strangled in her bed was still a mystery — nor was it clear why Meg had been spared, except that she recalled one of the burglars saying, "We don't kill brats," indicating that they had mistaken her for her daughter. The burglars had apparently expected to find the house empty, because the Steinheils had originally planned to go to Vert-Logis the day before. The family remained in Paris only because Mme. Japy's legs were bothering her. As for suspects, Hamard mentioned that many of the male models Steinheil used for his historical paintings had been in the house and knew he kept money there.

iv

The police postponed their questioning of Meg until the following day, to allow her to recover somewhat from her shock. Now she embellished her story, reporting that everyone had gone to bed at 10:00 P.M. after drinking rum toddies that Meg had made to encourage her mother to sleep. She recalled hearing the clock strike midnight just before the burglars appeared in her room. As for the men in long black coats, she now told the police that all the men had beards—one long and black with silver streaks, another red, and the third brown. The man with the long black beard had thin, bony hands. Asked if she recognized any of them, she said that she could not be sure. She added that the woman with red hair appeared to be a *souillon*, a slut.

Bertillon made a report on his findings at the crime scene, which tended to throw doubt on Meg's story. Though rain had fallen heavily that night, there was no sign of water or tracks on the carpets, nor any indication of forced entry. The rope tied around the necks of the two victims had come from a supply of cord in the kitchen. As for the valuables in the house, most of Meg's jewels were still in her room and the silver service in the dining room had been left behind. It was hard to tell how much money might have been taken, but given Steinheil's finances, it hardly seemed enough to justify two murders.

Some evidence was harder to explain. The grandfather clock that Meg heard striking midnight had been stopped at 12:10, and there was a fingerprint on the pendulum that did not seem to match the prints of anyone who lived there. Moreover, two interesting pieces of information turned up that seemed to confirm Meg's story. First, the management of the Hebrew Theater, where actors from eastern Europe presented plays in Hebrew and Yiddish, reported that on the night of May 30, three long black vestments intended for use in a play were found to be missing. Newspapers noted that these matched the description Meg had given of the clothes worn by the male burglars.

A second possible clue turned up the day after the crime, when an employee of the Paris Métro found on the floor of a subway car an invitation to an exhibition of Steinheil's paintings at the impasse Ronsin in April, the month before the murders. On the back of the invitation, someone had written "Guibert, costumier pour théâtres." Inside was the card of Jane Mazeline, an artist in her sixties. Investigation showed that the handwriting on the back did not match Mazeline's, so the Sûreté decided that someone had stolen her invitation to gain entrance to the house, making himself familiar with the layout.

Following up on the Hebrew Theater theft, a detective showed Meg photographs of some of its patrons. One did indeed have a shaggy beard, and she promptly identified him as one of the burglars. It was an American poet and painter, Frederic Harrisson Burlingham, a well-known figure who wandered about the city in sandals. Detectives became excited when they learned he was said to have a red-haired mistress. But unfortunately, Burlingham had an ironclad alibi: he was in Burgundy at the time the murders were committed. Seeing how eagerly the Sûreté had responded to her accusation, however, Meg began casting about for more suspects.

She hired a lawyer, Anthony Aubin, who would make his reputation on this case. Aubin asked Magistrate Leydet to let him inspect the evidence that had been collected so far. This was so irregular a request that Leydet turned him down. Undaunted, Meg sent a letter to L'Écho de Paris declaring that she would conduct her own search for the murderers. Late in November, she found her first candidate: young Rémy Couillard, who had discovered her bound and naked on that fateful Sunday.

According to her, she first became suspicious of him when she needed the address of his parents at a time when he was out on an errand. She looked inside a leather case he had left in his coat, and found a letter he was supposed to have mailed for her. It was addressed to Marthe's fiancé, and shockingly, Couillard, seemed to have opened and read it. She reported this to the Sûreté, which didn't think it suspicious. Meg then enlisted the aid of Henri Barby, an editor at *Le Matin* who had become her confidant. At her urging, Barby searched the leather case again and this time found a pearl wrapped in silk paper. Meg claimed that it was from an art nouveau ring that the burglars had taken.

The Sûreté brought Couillard in for questioning, and he admitted stealing the letter but denied ever having seen the pearl before. If he had been one of the burglars, he said, he could have stolen much more, for he knew secret hiding places that the family used for their valuables.

Meg also claimed that she had received anonymous letters saying that Couillard was in love with her daughter and wanted to break up the engagement. Furthermore, on the morning when he discovered her, she had felt he was tempted to strangle her instead of calling for help.

The police went to search Couillard's room. Meg accompanied them and triumphantly picked up a small diamond from the floor. Here, she announced, was proof he had been in league with the burglars. The police took the hapless valet into custody.

Two days later, on November 25, Meg was called to the Sûreté, where Hamard and Magistrate Leydet were waiting for her. With them were two jewelers and a gemologist. One of the jewelers declared that the pearl Meg had said was in a ring stolen on May 30 had in fact been brought to his shop on June 12—by Meg herself. At her request, he had removed it from the art nouveau ring where it had been mounted. When a picture of the pearl found in Couillard's case appeared in the newspapers, the jeweler recognized it. It had an unusual shape and a distinctively placed hole used to attach it to the ring. The other jeweler, who had made the ring in the first place, confirmed that this was the pearl he had mounted.

It was clear that Meg had deliberately made a false accusation against Couillard and that she now had to be considered a suspect in the murders. Meg called her lawyer, Aubin, who persuaded Leydet to release her. Nonetheless, seven policemen now surrounded her house to keep her from fleeing.

That evening, Meg invited to her home two journalists whose friendship she had cultivated. Supposedly she wanted their advice, but in reality she was preparing a startling new accusation. In tears, she admitted lying about Couillard but then claimed she had done so because she had been threatened by the real culprit—Alexander Wolff, the son of her trusted chambermaid. Wolff, she said, had long resented the Steinheils because he felt they exploited his mother. The only reason Meg had escaped was that he had tied her up with the intention of raping her but had been thwarted from doing so when he heard Couillard approaching. Nevertheless, he had threatened Meg that he would kill her, or tell the Sûreté that she had been his accomplice, if she revealed his name.

She persuaded the police guarding the house to take her to the Sûreté, where Hamard was summoned to hear her latest accusation. Alexander Wolff was arrested and brought in for questioning. Facing Meg, he flatly denied everything she had said, and now she began to waver. Perhaps, she said, the person who had threatened her was only someone who looked like Wolff. Since this was patently absurd, Hamard now began to pressure Meg, bringing Couillard and then Mariette Wolff in to confront her. Finally, Meg was placed under arrest, and everyone else was set free. Magistrate Leydet, presented with the new developments, told her that "by your lies and your concealment of evidence, you have misled justice and placed obstacles in the way of the seizure of the murderers."[8] She was sent to the Santé.

V

Remarkably, at this point the Ministry of Justice took the case away from Leydet and replaced him as *juge d'instruction* with another prosecutor, Louis André. This seemed to be a baffling move, for Leydet had either solved, or was on the brink of solving, the case. André, for his part, acted as if he were starting a new investigation. He ordered the bodies of Steinheil and Mme. Japy exhumed so that they could be autopsied a second time. Bertillon and his assistants were sent back to the house and ordered to check again for fingerprints—something that would seem to have been pointless, considering how many regular residents of the house had been there since the murders.

Mariette Wolff now began to talk to the authorities about Meg's many lovers. To the Sûreté, the most interesting of them was Borderel, who had told Meg he could not marry her if she was a divorced woman. That suggested a motive for her to murder her husband but of course still left the death of her mother an enigma. Here, André's exumation paid off with a valuable clue: the second autopsy found that Mme. Japy had not died of strangulation, despite the rope around her neck. The cause of death was asphyxiation: she had swallowed her dental plate. Because she would not have gone to bed with it in, she must have been placed in her bed by the killers. And of course that gave the lie to Meg's story that everyone had fallen asleep before the crime.

A new witness stepped forward: an attorney who lived on the rue de Vaugirard, which intersects the impasse Ronsin. He had looked out his window around midnight on the night of the murder and saw a car parked at the corner. A man dressed in elegant clothing was standing next to it, smoking a cigar and holding an umbrella. The attorney watched until another man ran out of the *impasse*. The two got into the car and drove off.

On March 13, 1909, Magistrate André formally charged Meg with the premeditated murder of her husband and mother. Legal maneuvering delayed the start of the trial to November 3. There were only one hundred seats allotted for spectators in the Cour d'Assises de la Seine, making it the hottest ticket in town. Women were particularly interested in the trial; wives of foreign ambassadors, countesses, and the mistresses of politicians all pulled strings to obtain places in the courtroom. Marcel Proust astonished his friends by appearing before noon to attend.

The presiding judge, Charles-Bernard de Valles, sat on a raised platform, flanked by two associate judges; all three were clothed in red robes and, with gray beards and solemn faces, looked determined to maintain the dignity of justice. The prosecutor, Paul Trouard-Riolle, also wore a red robe, which did little to conceal his massive girth. Meg's attorney, Aubin, and a colleague wore black robes. Aubin looked every centimeter the well-turned-out barrister, with curly black hair, mustache, and beard. Twelve men were admitted as jurors, ranging from middle-class "proprietors" to a musician, a bricklayer, and a baker. After they were seated, the spectators craned their necks to look at the doorway through which the defendant would be escorted.

A gasp went up at the sight of Meg, dramatically clothed in a black mourning dress and hat. Eleven months in prison had seemed to age her and turn the renowned peach glow of her skin to an unhealthy pallor. Many thought that her features looked harder, coarser than they had been in earlier newspaper pictures. Still, throughout the trial, Meg would become the mistress of the courtroom, skillfully battling the judge and the prosecutor.

Following French judicial practice, the trial began with the presiding judge interrogating the defendant. In theory this procedure was designed to determine the facts, but in this case it was clear that de Valles was going to serve as a prosecutor. He led Meg through a catalog of her lovers. (The scandalous episode with President Faure was not mentioned.) Hadn't she been happy with Steinheil, who had enabled her to create a salon in his house in Paris? He was "a simple man," Meg replied. "Too simple."[9] Hadn't Meg humiliated him? de Valles asked. Meg realized this was a trap and retorted that her husband had known nothing of her extramarital affairs. Nonetheless, she was sorry she had not been a good wife to him. When he fell in love with her, she had been merely a child. As she grew, she wanted lovers—friends—who understood her intellectual needs.

De Valles asked about money. Wasn't that her real reason for taking lovers? Meg denied it, saying that she had never sold herself. Chouanard, who had rented the country villa, was the only one to give her large sums, and that was his choice, not hers.

Meg still insisted that the three black-clad men and the red-haired woman, never found, had committed the crimes. She also tried to excuse the false accusations she had made in the case. She had not been thinking clearly, she said, because the press had persecuted her, making it appear as if she were the murderer. Finding the unmailed letter in Couillard's wallet had made her think he had deceived her on other matters.

After the first day, the newspapers generally gave Meg high marks for successfully parrying de Valles's questions, more by theatrics than by the veracity of her answers. One reporter dubbed her "the Sarah Bernhardt of the Assises."[10]

The examination resumed on the following day, and Meg seemed to have gained confidence. De Valles had discovered that a detective novel, *Les cinq doigts de Birouk* (*The Five Fingers of Birouk*), described a crime very similar to the one in Meg's account of the murders — black-robed burglars and all. The police had found several books by the same author, Louis Ulback, in the Steinheils' library. Did Meg enjoy those novels? She replied that she did, but had never read that particular one.

Various inconsistencies in Meg's story were noted, and she attributed them all to police incompetence. The cotton gag that she said she had spit out to cry for help was found to have no traces of saliva on it. Meg responded that the police had probably picked up the wrong piece of cotton. Why would the burglars strangle Meg's mother and husband with pieces of cord they had cut from a supply in the kitchen? "They told you all of this?" Meg responded as if surprised, drawing laughter from the spectators.[11] Irritated at Meg's riposte, de Valles suggested that she was indeed a cold-hearted killer, for she had murdered her own mother to cover up the fact that her intended victim was her husband. Meg was waiting for this and launched an extended soliloquy about the love she had for her mother.

So it went for three days of examination. Questions from the judge were answered by passionate speeches from Meg. Even the fact that Meg had placed the incriminating pearl in Couillard's case, something she could hardly deny, was brushed aside. "I have been punished enough for that!" she said. "I have been in prison a year for having placed Couillard there for a day." [12]

The prosecutor, Trouard-Riolle, now took command of the case. He was to call some eighty witnesses to testify, most of them experts of various sorts reporting on the physical evidence. Bertillon, for instance, said that he had found ninety-one fingerprints at the crime scene, but that only a fraction of these were clear enough to identify. Much of this testimony was tedious for the jury to sit through.

When the prosecutor summoned young Couillard, however, the jurors sat up to listen. Now serving his required military service and hence decked out in a handsome uniform, Couillard had become a minor celebrity. Vendors outside the court sold postcards with his picture. Nevertheless he made a crucial error describing the scene when he discovered Meg in bed, recalling now that she had been covered by a blanket. This differed from the deposition he had originally given the police, in which he stated that she had been nearly naked. The defense attorney made much of the discrepancy, and Couillard merely replied that his original deposition had been wrong.

He added that Meg had at first told him not to talk about the crime to anyone. In the lively procedure of the French judicial system, Meg was permitted to respond immediately that he was lying. She further demanded to know about the letter he had stolen. Couillard responded that he had forgotten to mail it and countered with the accusation that Meg had instructed him to claim, falsely, that the thieves had stolen some draperies — draperies that never existed. Meg again hotly denied it. On this indecisive note, Couillard was excused.

Three days later, with little testimony of note in the interim, Mariette Wolff came to the stand. There were great expectations:

she was privy to all Meg's secrets and, since Meg had accused Mariette's son, had no reason to be discreet. But Mariette disappointed the prosecutor by suddenly developing a shockingly poor memory.

De Valles once more took over the questioning, leading Mariette through the events leading up to the night of the murders. Nearly all of his questions drew the answer, "I don't remember." Even the night of November 25–26, when Meg had accused Mariette's son of murder, had now become serene in the housekeeper's recollection. Astonishingly, she claimed no one had told her that Meg had accused her son of the murders. Frustrated, the prosecutor dismissed her.

Following her to the stand was Alexander Wolff, the very person who had been the object of Meg's reckless accusations. Did he feel resentment toward her? Not at all, he responded, for it had been an exciting time for him. Clinging to straws, the prosecutor asked if it was true that his sister had provided a watchdog to protect the Steinheil house, and that Meg had sent it away just before the murders. Actually, Alexander said, it was he who had taken the dog back to his sister's: it was a very poor watchdog and would have been of no use. Clearly, for some reason, Meg's housekeeper and her son were not going to incriminate her.

Thwarted, the prosecutor began to call some of Meg's lovers. Chouanard, the most generous of them, had gone on a long trip to avoid testifying. De Balincourt, who had helped Meg home from the Métro, was reluctant to say how deep their involvement had been. Finally, Borderel, the man Meg had supposedly killed her husband in order to marry, came to the stand. As he entered, he turned to Meg and gave her a look that told the spectators he still loved her. He was a sympathetic figure, neither an aristocrat nor a wealthy businessman using power to attract young women, but instead a respectable middle-aged widower who was in search of someone to console him for the loss of his wife. He described an idyllic affair, but one that he had told Meg from the start could not end in marriage. She had seemed content with that. After the murder, when the newspapers had revealed Borderel as Meg's lover, it had shocked his family and neighbors (he was the mayor of a village in the Ardennes), but he had come now to tell the truth as a matter of honor.

He was the last witness for the prosecution and could easily have been the first for the defense, because the impression he left was completely sympathetic to Meg. Her attorney, Aubin, added to that by immediately presenting character witnesses. Relatives testified to Meg's love for her mother and said that she had never tried to get an advance on her inheritance, indicating that she was not in need of money. Aubin then called André Paisant, an attorney who had been a good friend of the Steinheils. He gave a portrait of their marriage that moved many of the spectators to tears. Adolphe Steinheil was an "almost childlike" man, a dreamer, "melancholic, disappointed, beaten, sitting in his big armchair, watching the fall of night." Meg brought joy into his life, "gave him courage, was his inspiration, pawned her jewelry to pay for his extravagances." [13] When Paisant first learned about Meg's lovers, his initial response was to condemn her, but over time his disapproval turned to pity. Hoping to leave the jury with that emotion in mind, Aubin closed his presentation.

The prosecutor, Trouard-Riolle, began his summation with a detailed recounting of the evidence. To most observers, the jury appeared bored and unimpressed. However, as Trouard-Riolle reached the end of a long day, he hinted at spectacular revelations to come. Some of the technical testimony had indicated that it was nearly impossible for one person to have committed the murders. Meg must have had an accomplice, and the prosecutor implied that he would indicate who that person had been on the following day.

The next morning, Trouard-Riolle never specifically named his suspect, but as he gradually filled in the description of her, everyone realized it was Mariette Wolff. As he took the jury through the supposed events of the night of the murder, the prosecutor said that Meg and "this woman" planned to catch Mme. Japy asleep in her bed, tie and gag her, strangle Steinheil, and then tie Meg to the bed. Meg's mother would then be able to confirm Meg's story of burglars. Unfortunately, the gag forced her dentures down her throat and killed her. Trouard-Riolle left the jury with a powerful argument: If there really had been burglar-murderers in the house, why did they not murder Meg and eliminate any possible witness? And why had the clock stopped? Meg had stopped it herself because, Trouard-Riolle declared, like the tell-tale heart of the murder victim in Poe's famous story, it made a noise in the silent house that she could not bear to listen to.

The following day, November 13, Aubin gave the summary for the defense. He pointed out the holes in the prosecution's case, notably that there had been no motive at all for Meg to kill her mother. Nor, he added, was there any convincing reason for her to murder her husband. Meg "was his idol—alas, the idol also of others . . . she was radiant and adorned with all the charms, a bouquet of smiles. Everyone wanted to pluck from the bouquet. So, she was unfaithful." [14] But she was not a murderess.

Aubin pointed out that Mme. Japy would surely have been aware of it if Meg and her female accomplice had bound her. How then could she provide an alibi for them? What really happened, he suggested, was that thieves broke into the house, expecting to find it empty, and then killed Steinheil when he discovered them. Leaving Meg alive, they thought, would throw suspicion on her—and it did.

As his trump card, Aubin brought Meg's daughter, Marthe, to the courtroom for the first time in the trial, seating her behind her mother. Aubin signaled for her to rise: "I call to my side," he said, "this pure and noble child. I want her close to me, stretching her arms appealingly toward you and defending her mother! These two unfortunate beings, how many tears they have already shed, how many tears they will still shed! Ah, gentlemen of the jury, give them the means to console one another and to forget together." [15]

Meg responded to the judge's invitation to make a final statement by dissolving into tears. That was probably her best argument.

In the French system of justice, a unanimous verdict was not required. Seven to five would be enough to convict; six to six would mean acquittal. However, when the jury deliberated till midnight without reaching a verdict, courtroom observers felt it a bad sign for Meg. De Valles asked them to continue their discussions. On three occasions they asked him to explain the penalties for different kinds of verdicts.

At last, at 1:30 in the morning of November 14, the jurors filed into the courtroom. Despite the hour, many spectators had remained to hear the denouement of the drama, and they were not disappointed: the jury announced that it had found Meg not guilty of all charges. Amid the cheers, she fainted.

vi

Meg escaped her notoriety by moving to England, but those who believed in her innocence, as well as those who argued for her guilt, continued to speculate on what really happened at the impasse Ronsin that murderous Sunday night in 1908. Her own memoirs, published in 1912, shed no further light on the crime.

In 1925, however, a man whose credentials as a criminologist could not be questioned, published his own reconstruction of the case. This was Dr. Edmond Locard, now director of the forensic laboratory at Lyons. His book *Le crime et les criminels* had a chapter on methods of strangulation, and he used the Steinheil case to show how one method (manual) might be mistaken for a second (using a cord). In doing so, Locard went much further than simply describing the causes of death of Steinheil and Mme. Japy—he reconstructed the case in such detail that people assumed he had access to hitherto secret sources.

Locard portrayed Meg, in that phase of her life, little better than a high-class streetwalker, saying that she picked up lovers at the Métro exits regularly, pretending to twist "her too-delicate ankle" when a wealthy-looking man came near. Accepting his gallant offer to see her home, she would lead him to the impasse Ronsin, where she made it clear that her husband would look the other way if a romance began. De Balincourt had testified at the trial that this was how he met Meg, and certainly she might have repeated the performance with others.

Locard asked rhetorically, "Is it in this way, or by some intermediary, that one day she makes the acquaintance of an aristocratic foreigner?" [16] He suggested that Meg cultivated this mysterious figure and from time to time obtained money from him. One day, in need of more, Meg calls him to come to the house, but she is not "able to comply with his passionate demands. He feels that he has been duped. Fury. Clamour." Then Steinheil "makes the mistake of poking his worried nose into the business," [17] further arousing the suspicions of the aristocratic foreigner that this is a blackmail scheme. There is a scuffle, and the foreigner takes Steinheil by the throat, only to discover that the artist is even weaker than he looks. His larynx crushed, Steinheil falls to the floor, where the police find him later. As for Meg's unfortunate mother, she investigates the noises she hears, and on seeing Steinheil's body, she swallows her dentures, choking to death.

The foreigner, who Locard later revealed was "a grand-duke, a close relative of the Tsar," [18] has to be protected from scandal. Meg calls "a very high official, who arrives, duly organizes the staging of the scene, and discreetly leaves." [19] He was the person that a neighbor saw leaving the impasse Ronsin, hurrying to a waiting car. Benjamin F. Martin, a modern interpreter of the case, suggests that the high French official was none other than Magistrate Leydet, who then requested appointment as the *juge d'instruction* in the case so that he could manage the investigation to avoid incriminating the foreigner.

In this scenario, Meg had to be willing to endure imprisonment and risk conviction at trial in order to protect this powerful man. Yet just as she had earlier been discreet about the death of President Faure, so she repeated the performance this time. Had she resisted, the wheels of justice would have ground her up. Locard suggested that she was rewarded by a deliberately botched investigation that left too much doubt in the jurors' minds to convict her.

Corroboration for Locard's explanation of the case had to wait until eighteen months after Meg's death in 1954. Armand Lanoux, a French writer and biographer of Zola, revealed "confidential information" that he had received from someone in a position to know the truth. This may have been Roger de Chateleux, the ghost-writer Meg had employed in writing her memoirs. The informant quoted a "Dr. D" who had assisted during the first autopsy of the two bodies. He admitted that Steinheil, without doubt, had been manually strangled and died from a fractured larynx. Mme. Japy had actually expired from a heart attack. Both had ropes placed around their necks to conceal the true causes of death, and the autopsy doctor was part of the cover-up, writing a false report, "not upon what he knew, but upon instructions he had to follow."[20] The mystery would remain.

vii

The second spectacular Belle Époque murder case in which a woman was the central figure required no detection at all. The facts were clear and the defendant admitted them, but the case held a surprise all the same. Was it a crime to march into a man's office and coolly shoot him four times? During the Belle Époque, an age that splintered notions of objectivity in art and science, that all depended on one's point of view.

Henriette Caillaux, née Rainouard, was the second wife of the ambitious politician who had been premier of France at the time the *Mona Lisa* was stolen. A multimillionaire through inheritance, Joseph Caillaux dressed fastidiously, sporting a monocle and spats. Nonetheless, many of his colleagues despised him, not least for his success with women, which he flaunted. He and Henriette had been lovers even while Caillaux was married to his first wife, Berthe. Pressed by Henriette to get a divorce, Caillaux had made it clear that nothing took precedence over his political career. He wrote her frankly that though he hoped "to regain my liberty [through divorce], in no case will I move before the elections." [21] He had also commented indiscreetly on his political policies in other letters to Henriette, and he eventually asked her to return them. When she did, he put them in a desk where his wife later found them. Berthe threatened to divorce him, which would have damaged his chances of re-election to the national legislature. Caillaux wrote her an abject letter of apology, and she relented, giving him back the letters, which he burned. However, without his knowledge, she had made photographic copies.

True to his word to Henriette, Caillaux divorced his wife after the elections of 1910. By the following year, he was once more a happily married man and was able to gain the post of premier.

Caillaux's term as the head of government was controversial. Overriding his own foreign minister, he personally negotiated with German diplomats to defuse what was known as the Agadir Incident. By relinquishing a small part of the French Congo, he obtained Germany's agreement to allow France a protectorate over Morocco. This was a triumph for French diplomacy, yet it made Caillaux unpopular because the French public hated the thought of giving up any territory to the hated Germans, who still occupied the formerly French provinces of Alsace and Lorraine, which had been taken after the war of 1870. It even gave rise to the rumor that the *Mona Lisa* had been stolen by German spies, held hostage to gain an advantage in the negotiations. Caillaux lost his grip on power and was forced to step down as premier in January 1912.

In October 1913, Caillaux's party, the Radicals, elected him as its leader, and two months later he formed a coalition that brought down the current center-right government. Ordinarily, the president of the republic, Raymond Poincaré, would then have asked Caillaux to form a new government as premier, but Poincaré instead turned to Gaston Doumergue, another member of the Radical party. Doumergue became premier but appointed Caillaux minister of finance, a position that Caillaux used to dominate the government. That was another reason Caillaux was so despised by his colleagues. Although his competence at finance was undisputed, he made it clear that he thought others' abilities could not compare with his own.

Nor were his policies popular, though in hindsight it can be seen that France would have done better to follow them. France was in a militaristic mood, and the government had recently increased the required term of military service for young men from two years to three. Generally more cautious about preparing the country for war, Caillaux was considered likely to try to scale back the new law. In addition, he was a strong backer of instituting a graduated income tax, something that was anathema to wealthy Frenchmen and those who served their interests.

Among the latter was Gaston Calmette, the editor of *Le Figaro*, and that newspaper began a campaign to discredit and destroy Caillaux. From December 10, when Caillaux became finance minister, until the middle of March 1914, *Le Figaro* published more than one hundred articles, anecdotes, and cartoons attacking Caillaux. Many leveled accusations of financial impropriety—fraud, conflicts of interests, even embezzlement.

Caillaux's enemies provided Calmette with plenty of ammunition. President Poincaré gave the editor copies of *documents verts* (so called because they were marked with a green bar) that described Caillaux's confidential negotiations with German intermediaries during the Agadir Incident. These were highly secret materials, and Poincaré could not allow Calmette to quote from them because it would be clear who was the source. But Calmette used the information to argue that Caillaux had betrayed France's interests.

In addition, Jean Louis Barthou, the premier who had been turned out of office by Caillaux's party, gave Calmette a document written by a public prosecutor, Victor Fabre. Later known as the Fabre memo, it described how Caillaux, during his term as premier in 1911, had pressured Fabre to postpone the trial of a man who had been accused of selling worthless stock in nonexistent companies. Caillaux's purpose had been to quietly delay the trial till the statute of limitations had passed. Once again, to protect his source, Calmette could not quote from the memo but could merely write about its contents.

Le Figaro's incredible barrage of editorials and articles, vituperative though they were, did little to erode Caillaux's popularity among the voters, so Calmette stepped up his attacks. On March 13, 1914, *Le Figaro* published a letter that Caillaux had written to his first wife, Berthe, back in 1901 when they were carrying on an affair while *she* was still married to another man. This letter was particularly damaging because Caillaux had won favor with his constituents by backing an income tax bill, yet here he confided to Berthe that behind the scenes he had earlier "crushed" the bill while defending it in public. The letter, signed *"Ton Jo"* ("Your Jo") appeared on the front page of *Le Figaro*. Calmette had removed the date to give the impression that it was current, and for good measure he printed beside it a campaign picture that Caillaux had autographed, to show that the handwriting was the same.[22]

The letter was a sensation and became the talk of Paris. Caillaux lamely explained that he had written it thirteen years earlier and that it did not reflect his true sentiments, but the damage was done, and worse might be yet to come. Caillaux assumed, despite Calmette's disavowal, that Berthe was the source of the letter. Now he worried that even though she had promised to turn over all copies of his letters to Henriette, she might have been lying. If the editor published some of those, it would do further damage to Caillaux's career.

This possibility was particularly alarming to Henriette, who thought she was gaining respectability and a position in society by becoming the wife of a man as powerful as Caillaux. Thirty-nine years old and still beautiful, she had already had to endure the many attacks *Le Figaro* had made on her husband; now she feared her own name was about to be dragged in the mud. At the time she had begun her affair with Caillaux, she was married to another man, by whom she had two daughters. She liked to play the role of a gracious hostess, and the revelations in these letters would make her an object of cruel gossip. "To publish these letters or any part of them," she recalled, "would have been to lay out all that was most intimate to me, my most intimate secrets, the secrets I hold most dear and keep most hidden. It would have been to strip me of my honor as a woman."[23] She even claimed to have considered suicide.

On Monday, March 16, *Le Figaro,* now routinely referring to Caillaux as "Jo," continued its relentless campaign, and the editor promised new revelations the following day. At breakfast, Henriette suggested to her husband that he take legal action to stop Calmette. He went off to plead for help from President Poincaré. The president was unsympathetic; he told Caillaux that the editor was a gentleman who would not print personal letters — something that had just been proven untrue.

Meanwhile, at Caillaux's request, the chief justice of the Tribunal de la Seine came to see Henriette. He told her that it was impossible to sue someone for libel before the libel had been published, and in any case a trial would only publicize any scurrilous charges that Calmette made.

When Caillaux returned home, Henriette reported what the chief justice had said. Angry, Caillaux responded, "Since there is nothing else to do, I will take on the responsibility [of dealing with Calmette]. I'll smash his face!"[24] Henriette later testified that "at that moment a cinematographic film . . . flashed before my eyes"[25] in which her husband killed Calmette and was arrested. She began to make the decision to take his place.

After Caillaux left, Henriette called their chauffeur and told him to drive her to Gastinne-Renette, a well-known gunsmith's shop. Henriette was familiar with handguns; her father had insisted that she carry one in her handbag, which she had continued to do after marrying Caillaux. A few months earlier, she had lost it, and now she wanted to find a replacement. The salesman showed her a .32-caliber Smith and Wesson, but Henriette found it hard to pull the trigger. She found more to her liking a Browning automatic, the weapon of choice of the Bonnot Gang and of Picasso. She tried it out at the shooting range in the basement of the store — hitting a cutout figure of a man three out of five times — and decided to purchase it. Back upstairs, she asked the salesman to load the gun for her, but he explained that it was against the law for him to do so. At his direction she loaded it herself, and he cautioned her that to prepare it for firing, she must pull back the slide that would put a bullet into the chamber. A few minutes later, in the backseat of her automobile, she did just that.

After a stop at her bank, where she removed some papers from a safe-deposit box, she returned home. It was around 4:00 P.M. and she was supposed to dress for a reception at the Italian Embassy. Instead, she wrote her husband a note:

> *This morning, when I told you about my meeting with Chief Justice Monier, who had explained to me that in France we have no law to protect us against the calumnies of the press, you replied only that one day you would smash the face of the ignoble Calmette. I understood that your decision was irrevocable. My decision was then taken; it would be I who would render justice. France and the Republic have need of you. I will commit the act. If this letter reaches you, I will have carried out, or tried to carry out, justice. Pardon me, but my patience is at an end. I love you, and I embrace you from the depths of my heart.*
>
> *Your Henriette*[26]

Around five o'clock that afternoon, Henriette arrived at the offices of *Le Figaro* and asked to see the editor. She wore a fur coat and carried a large muff that concealed her hands. After being told that Calmette was out of the office but was expected back within the hour, she handed his secretary a sealed envelope containing her card and said that she would wait. Evidently the staff did not recognize her, and she sat in the anteroom for nearly an hour, speaking to no one.

Calmette finally arrived with his friend the novelist Paul Bourget. He had intended only to pick up some papers and leave, but when he opened the envelope handed to him by his secretary, he showed it to Bourget, who advised him not to see her. Calmette responded that he could not refuse a woman. He entered his office and asked his secretary to send Mme. Caillaux in.

She did not sit, but merely said, "You must know why I am here." Caillaux, standing behind his desk, replied, "But I do not. Please sit down."[27] Instead, she removed her hand from her muff to reveal the pistol and fired six shots at him. Four of them struck their target, and when several employees rushed into the office, they found the editor lying on the floor, blood spurting from his wounds. Several people went to his assistance, and others looked at Henriette, who still held the smoking gun. "Do not touch me!" she told them. "I am a lady. I have my car outside to ride in to the police station."[28] She went downstairs and directed the chauffeur accordingly. Another vehicle took Calmette to a hospital, where he died six hours later. Henriette was quoted as explaining to the police: "There is no justice in France. There is only the revolver."[29]

viii

If Henriette had hoped to save her husband's political career, she only partially succeeded. He was forced to resign his post as finance minister, though he continued to hold his seat in the legislature—indeed, he was reelected a little more than a month after the murder. As for Henriette, bail was not granted in capital cases, and she was given the same cell in Saint-Lazare Prison where Meg Steinheil had been incarcerated. She enjoyed more amenities, however, including a new stove, a lamp, and a foot rug from the warden's own office. She was also permitted to order meals from fine restaurants, and another female prisoner was actually assigned to be her maid.

Those were not the only signs of favoritism. The *juge d'instruction* in the case, Henri Boucard, conducted only a six-week investigation—very brief for a major crime. Of course, Henriette freely admitted killing Calmette, but Boucard uncritically accepted her explanation that she had feared the editor would publish the letters she had written to Caillaux five years earlier—a relevant point because that motive would make this case a *crime passionnel* and increase the likelihood that the jury would find Henriette not guilty.[30] Indeed, as many as one out of three defendants in murder trials claimed that theirs was a crime of passion in order to increase their odds of acquittal.

French jurors were not expected to fully understand the law; they were instructed to reach a verdict based on the "impressions" they received from observing the presentation of the case.[31] These impressions were very often influenced by sympathy, not only for the victim, but also for the perpetrator of the crime.

Louis Proal, one of the era's most esteemed experts on the *crime passionnel,* published a seven-hundred-page book on the subject, in which he regretted the tendency for popular authors to glorify criminals, particularly those who acted out of a sense of honor. "Novels and plays," he wrote, "have so extolled the nobility of crimes of passion and so eloquently justified revenge that juries, quite forgetting the duty they have been summoned to fulfill, fail entirely to defend society and pity, not the victims, but the authors of crimes of this nature."[32] That was certainly what Mme. Caillaux was counting on.

ix

Her trial began on July 20, 1914. Three weeks earlier, far away in the city of Sarajevo, Bosnia-Herzegovina, Gavrilo Princip had shot and killed Archduke Francis Ferdinand, heir to the throne of

Austria-Hungary. The latter event would be the spark that ignited a world war, but the newspapers of Paris devoted most of the space on their front pages to Henriette.

Once more, requests for tickets to the visitor's gallery far outnumbered the available seats. As the trial opened, Henriette entered, clothed in black and wearing a circular hat with tall plumes. It set off her blond hair and fair skin, as did a heavy coating of powder that made her look like a wraith.

Presiding judge Louis Albanel, a close friend of the Caillaux family, was inordinately deferential in his opening interrogation. He asked a few prompting questions and then let Henriette speak for nearly three hours, telling about her life with Caillaux and the anguish that Calmette had brought to her. In contrast to Meg Steinheil, she was dignified rather than emotional. She stressed that as the wife of a minister, she endured along with him the attacks of political enemies. "One day," she testified, "I visited a fashionable *couturier*'s establishment where there were a great many people. One of two ladies seated nearby . . . leaned over to the other and said: 'You see the lady beside me dressed in black? She is the wife of that thief Caillaux.' "[33]

Henriette's greatest fear was that Calmette would print the letters she had written her husband before their marriage. Her father had told her that a woman who took a lover "is a woman without honor," and she dreaded the public disgrace such revelations would bring. Now, of course, everyone knew about the letters, including her nineteen-year-old daughter: "I am obliged to blush in front of her," Henriette said.[34]

She denied that her actions on the day of the murder showed premeditation. When she bought the pistol, she was only replacing the one she had lost. The note she had written to her husband, in which she said, "It would be I who would render justice," meant nothing. "I attached no importance to it,"[35] she said, but it is doubtful that anyone in the courtroom believed her.

The most gripping part of her testimony promised to be her account of the murder, but it was surprisingly dry. Describing how she sat for an hour waiting for Calmette to arrive, she said she thought she heard all around her the newspaper's employees telling jokes about her husband. As she entered the editor's office, "the gun went off all by itself." Henriette paused and said, "I regret it infinitely." With that, she stopped, and Magistrate Albanel had to prompt her to show more remorse, but she merely added, "It was fate. I regret infinitely the unhappiness I have caused."[36]

If the spectators were a little disappointed at her low-key performance, they would be gratified by the rest of the proceedings, in which the trial became a contest between Joseph Caillaux and the murder victim. External events in Serbia, Austria, and Germany were ominously leading toward a general war in Europe, a war that Caillaux had tried to avoid but many other French politicians were willing, even eager, to fight. Nonetheless, all the major Parisian newspapers printed the full transcript of each day's proceedings at the trial—requiring them to add extra pages and often to devote as much as 60 percent of their entire contents to the trial.

Caillaux himself took the stand on the second day, preening and looking as if he were in charge of the proceedings. (Because he was a member of the legislature, he had special privileges: he was allowed to use notes while testifying and did not have to be sworn in.) He began by describing the unhappiness he felt in his first marriage and how he sought relief in the arms of Henriette. In the divorce settlement, Berthe had promised to destroy the letters she had stolen from his desk, but clearly she had not, and when his love letter to *her* (the "Ton Jo" letter) had appeared in *Le Figaro,* he concluded that his letters to Henriette would be next.

Having been accused in *Le Figaro* of "infamy and treason," Caillaux felt entitled to respond, and the judge did not stop him as he launched into a defense of his political career, including the negotiations with Germany during the Agadir Incident. For good measure, he virtually accused Calmette of treason, alleging that *Le Figaro* had ties to German banking interests and had received funds from political parties in Austria-Hungary. As everyone was aware, both these countries were now threatening war against Serbia, an action that would bring a declaration of war by France in a week's time.

The following day, the president of the board of directors of *Le Figaro* contradicted Caillaux's charges against the newspaper and its murdered editor. Pointedly, he said, "The lion attacks the living, the jackal attacks the corpse." One of the lawyers representing the Calmette family[37] added, "I know of no enterprise more shameful than coming before a public audience to profane the tomb one's wife has opened!"[38]

Returning to matters that would seem more relevant to the trial, the court heard a series of witnesses testify about Henriette's emotional state leading up to the murder. The salesman from the gun store said that she was quite calm and, for a woman, showed good markmanship on the test-firing range. Friends of hers, however, stated that they could see that *Le Figaro*'s campaign was affecting her deeply.

The next day, the prosecutor called Caillaux's first wife, Berthe, to the stand. Except for a pair of white gloves, she was dressed in mourning clothes, even though Calmette was no relation to her. Berthe admitted that she had photographic copies made of the eight letters between her husband and Henriette. Labori, the defense attorney, pointed out that the divorce agreement had obliged her to destroy any correspondence, and that Caillaux had paid her generous alimony to ensure her compliance. She denied that, saying that Caillaux had asked for her word of honor that she would destroy the correspondence, and she had refused because *his* word of honor was worthless. She launched into a catalog of grievances against him.

Yet Berthe still insisted that she had not given Calmette the copy of the "Ton Jo" letter that he published, although she admitted that her sister (who had arranged for the photographing of the letters) might have done it. And what, she was asked, of the other letters? Berthe astonished the court by taking a sheaf of photographs from her purse and announcing that she had them right here.

Their appearance set off extended sparring among the lawyers and judge as to whether Berthe should be allowed—or compelled?—to read the letters aloud. Since no one was quite sure how the jury would react to them, only the lawyers for the Calmettes urged that their contents be made public. Finally it was agreed that the defense attorney should read them privately and determine if they were relevant.

Caillaux asked for and was granted permission to respond to Berthe's charges, as if he were the person on trial. He said it had been a mistake for him to marry her, because she was not of the same "stock" as he, even though they had been "perfect friends." Still in the courtroom, Berthe began to shout back at him, "Be quiet! You dishonor yourself!" Caillaux added that he left her because his "dignity" had not permitted him to continue living with her. "I will say nothing more," he added, allowing his listeners to assume the worst about her conduct.[39]

To that, Berthe stood and shouted, "No, I summon you to say everything. I demand it!" He needed no more prompting and, pointing, hit her with the allegation that when she entered his house, she had "not a single centime!" Now, out of concern for her welfare, he had given her nearly half his fortune. "I do not understand what protestations such a woman can raise," he said.[40]

Berthe announced she would no longer respond to Caillaux's insults, and pardoned him. Not to be outdone, he in turn pardoned her. Throughout, the judge had made no move to stop their bickering. That was a mistake, because during the next three days, such outbursts became more common. Caillaux now stood next to his wife at the defendant's rail, as if protecting her or perhaps acknowledging that the trial was as much about him as about her.

Labori returned on the following day and announced that he would read aloud only the three letters written from Caillaux to Henriette. This drew a protest from Charles Chenu, representing the Calmette family, who wanted the jury to hear Henriette's letters as well. The prosecutor suggested that Chenu be allowed to read those letters privately. Berthe, who had returned to see what would happen, declared that all the letters should be read aloud.

This set off a shouting match among the lawyers and Berthe, which finally roused Magistrate Albanel from his permissive mood. He proposed a recess, only to have one of the two assistant judges remark quietly, "Monsieur, you dishonor us!"[41] evidently prompted by Albanel's apparent intention to save the defense attorney from embarrassment.

That became even more obvious with the testimony of the next witness. Postponing the reading of the letters, Magistrate Albanel allowed Caillaux's closest friend in the legislature, Pascal Ceccaldi, to give testimony. It soon became clear that Ceccaldi's only purpose was to smear poor Calmette, saying among other things that the editor had speculated in German stocks and slanted the news coverage in *Le Figaro* to ensure that his stocks would rise. These charges again led to a shouting match that the chief judge allowed to continue unabated.

Ceccaldi's calumnies were interjected into the trial at Caillaux's request. After he finished, the prosecution responded with two character witnesses for the dead man: Henry Bernstein, a young playwright, and Albert Calmette, the editor's brother. Bernstein asked how Caillaux could attack the honor of a man his wife had murdered. It was a taunt Caillaux would not forget. Albert Calmette then related that he had been given the papers his brother carried in his coat. These included all the now-famous documents: the "Ton Jo" letter, the Fabre memorandum, and the *documents verts*. Reading the last of these, Albert realized they were secret state papers and gave them to President Poincaré, who thanked him for "doing his duty." This was an embarrassing revelation, because the government, in order to avoid diplomatic repercussions, had already declared that the *documents verts* were forgeries. Albert Calmette concluded by saying that his brother was an honorable man who would have told Henriette—had she but asked before firing her pistol—that he would never publish her private letters. He turned to Labori, Henriette's defense attorney, and asked if that was true. Embarrassed, because he had known Calmette for years, Labori merely nodded.

The excitement did not end when the court adjourned for the day. In chambers, Magistrate Albanel demanded an apology from the assistant judge who had criticized him. He received it, but in the next morning's *Le Figaro*, Albanel read a report of the incident, along with a statement by the assistant judge saying that he had nothing to apologize for and that he felt Albanel was showing partiality to the defendant. Albanel responded by giving an interview to another newspaper in which he indicated he might have to require satisfaction for this insult. He would not rule out challenging his fellow judge to a duel—in those times, not an empty threat.

The tension only increased on the following day, July 25. The session began with a pointed declaration by Albanel: "More than anyone else in this room I take care to defend my own honor and the honor of the magistrature—despite what anyone may have said."[42] Since many people knew that Albanel had met in his chambers with Émile Bruneau de Laborie, the author of a handbook on dueling, few doubted his words.

The matter of the letters was at last settled, with the agreement that Fernand Labori, the chief defense attorney, would read aloud two of them, from Caillaux to Henriette. They were flowery ("I threw myself toward you with passionate fervor") and contained plans for deceiving Berthe, but they were nonpolitical, indicating that Calmette would not have chosen to publish them. Still, as Caillaux's words became more specific, the letters had an effect. When Labori read the closing of the second letter, "A thousand million kisses all over your adored little body," Henriette fainted.[43]

It might have seemed anticlimactic at this point to bring on doctors to testify about the murder, but this was a trial involving constant diversions. The doctors who had treated Calmette testified that it had been impossible to save him—a conclusion that Labori questioned. Reading from a text, he asserted that it was dangerous to transport patients with severe wounds and argued that once at the clinic, the patient should have received better care. One of the doctors, a professor of surgery, said he had never seen an attorney try "to incriminate the surgeons."[44]

The medical testimony complete, the prosecution rested its case. The next day, before the defense could begin its presentation, Caillaux once more asked, and received, permission to make a statement. This one was truly startling. He flourished what he said was a copy of Calmette's will—by law, a private document. When Magistrate Albanel asked how he had obtained it, Caillaux haughtily declared, "In the same manner by which M. Calmette obtained his copy of the 'Ton Jo' "[45] Despite heated objections by Chenu, Caillaux obtained permission to read it aloud—surely getting his revenge for the publication of the "Ton Jo" letter.

It appeared that Calmette's estate totaled some thirteen million francs. Some of that had accrued from investments, but six million francs had been a gift from Calmette's mistress. Caillaux mocked the memory of a man who would make a fortune in the bedroom. Then he asked rhetorically what kind of person would defend such a man, singling out Henry Bernstein, whose testimony had particularly stung Caillaux. Referring to the playwright, he said, "When one has not fulfilled one's duty to the nation, one is ill-equipped to give certificates of morality to others."[46] The implication was clear—that Bernstein had been a draft dodger.

Chenu was finally able to ask what relevance all this had to the case (the question had seemingly not occurred to Magistrate Albanel). Caillaux responded that "there is something worse than to lose one's life, and that is to save it when one, by turns, attacks women and enriches oneself at their expense."[47] In other words, it was relevant only as character assassination of the man Caillaux's wife had killed.

The defense was then allowed to present its case. It called Dr. Eugène Doyen, another surgeon, who used a diagram of the murder scene to argue that Henriette had aimed her first two shots at the floor, intending only to frighten Calmette. However, the recoil from the pistol tended to bring her arm up at the same time that Calmette was dropping to the floor to shield himself. Unfortunately this brought him into the path of Henriette's fatal bullet.

Chenu was highly indignant at this reconstruction. Having

tried to blame the physicians for Calmette's death, the defense was now saying it was Calmette's own fault for throwing himself into his murderer's range of fire. Chenu demanded that the other physicians be recalled to the stand to refute Doyen's testimony.

The doctors were conferring when the door of the courtroom burst open and Henry Bernstein strode in. He had been informed via telephone of Caillaux's earlier comments. Shouting, "Caillaux! Are you there? Because I do not insult adversaries in their absence!" he marched to the front of the room. With no attempt from the judges' bench to stop him, he began to denounce Caillaux as "a man climbing atop the coffin of his wife's victim in order to speak to you more loudly."[48]

After saying that the *documents verts*—which officially still did not exist—proved that Caillaux was a traitor, Bernstein took up the charge of draft dodging that Caillaux had leveled against him. It was true, he admitted: as a young man serving in the army, he had fled to Belgium after five months of service and only returned to France after a general amnesty. It was, Bernstein said, a mistake of youth. But now he had enlisted in an artillery unit and would be sent into combat should France mobilize for war. "The mobilization may be tomorrow," he pointed out, and he was only about a week too soon. Turning directly to Caillaux, he had a final riposte: "I do not know what day Caillaux leaves for the front, but I must warn him that during a war, he cannot have himself replaced by his wife; he will have to fire himself!"[49] The cheers from the spectators finally forced Albanel to call a recess.

The defense presentation was brief, concluding with testimony from a colonel in an artillery regiment who claimed expertise in ballistics. He was there to confirm Dr. Doyen's analysis. Diagramming the pattern of the six bullets Henriette had fired, he claimed that they moved upward from the floor owing to the involuntary motion of her arm. This proved that she had not meant to kill Calmette and that had he not fallen to get out of her way, she would not have. The jury may have found more authority for this opinion, coming from a military man.

On July 28, Austria-Hungary declared war on Serbia, setting in motion the treaty obligations of other allies on both sides. As France prepared for a war many now saw as inevitable, the lawyers made their final arguments. That evening, the jury began its deliberations, which didn't take long. Five minutes short of an hour later, they announced that by a vote of eleven to one, they had found Henriette Caillaux not guilty of either charge. She and her husband embraced as their friends in the gallery cheered.

The couple's triumph was short-lived. Three days later, on July 31, a student aptly named Raoul Villain shot and killed France's leading pacifist politician, Jean Jaurès. The police feared that someone would make a similar attempt on Caillaux's life because he too was known to prefer negotiations to war. The prefect of police advised him to leave Paris. He and Henriette fled the next morning. It was the first day of August, 1914, the month Europe plunged into the bloodiest war in its history, making the murder of one persistent editor pale into insignificance. The Belle Époque was coming to an end.

THE GREATEST CRIME

Germany declared war on France on August 3, 1914. Most French citizens were elated, feeling that at last they would take revenge for the humiliation inflicted by Germany in 1870. Misia Sert, the wife of a newspaper publisher, who was famous for her Paris salon, recalled thinking, "What luck! Oh God, let there be a war,"[1] when she first heard that Austria had declared war on Serbia six days before. Now, with her wish granted, she took part in the celebration that swept the streets of Paris:

"On the *grands boulevards,* in the midst of a rapturously enthusiastic crowd, I suddenly found myself perched on a white horse behind a cavalry officer. I wound some flowers around the neck of his gala uniform, and the general exaltation was so great that not for a moment did I think it strange. Nor were the officer, the horse, or the crowd around us in any way astonished, for the same sight could be seen all over Paris. Flowers were being sold at every street corner: wreaths, sheaves, bouquets, and loose bunches, which a minute later reappeared on soldiers' caps, on the tips of their bayonets, or behind their ears. People fell into one another's arms; it did not matter who embraced you; you wept, you laughed, you were crushed, you were moved to tears, you were almost suffocated, you sang, you trampled other people's feet, and you felt that you had never been more generous, more noble, more prepared for sacrifice and, in short, more wonderfully happy!"[2]

Within a month's time, the mood had changed drastically. With astonishing speed, German troops had swept through neutral Belgium and into France. By August 26, they had reached the Marne, and an advance cavalry unit captured the race course at Chantilly, a few miles north of Paris. From the top of the Eiffel Tower, people could see the distant German units approaching. Refugees from the countryside poured into the city, and their presence added to the growing panic. On September 2, the government abandoned the capital to relocate in Bordeaux. Among the valuables taken along was the *Mona Lisa,* on its second major journey in two years.

General Joseph Gallieni, commander of the French forces, determined to defend Paris. A map found on the body of the German cavalry officer revealed the enemy's plan, and Gallieni organized his troops to hit the Germans' flank. He commandeered the Parisian taxi fleet to move his troops to the front, and thousands of cabs appeared to accomplish the enormous task of moving an army, in what was called "the miracle of the Marne." The Germans fell back and Paris was never again threatened.

The war, however, dragged on for four years, ultimately resulting in the deaths of eight and a half million soldiers and another twenty million wounded. An uncounted number of civilians died from disease, starvation, and other war-related causes. France alone lost one and a half million men in battle and its aftermath. The war dwarfed any crime, indeed any previous war. It destroyed a generation of young men and brought to an end the optimistic era known in France as "La Belle Époque."

Among the scientific advancements that made this war so terrible was the airplane. Used at first to scout enemy forces, planes then began to carry bombs. (Initally, bombs were merely dropped from open cockpits by pilots.) To counter attacks and observation from the air, military planners started to cover potential targets with cloths to hide them. Later, special paint designs, called camouflage, were used. Naval warfare was also affected by the widespread use of submarines that used periscopes to spot their targets. Ships were painted with geometric patterns in varying colors to create confusion about the ships' size and direction of travel. The French officer credited with inventing camouflage, Guirand De Scévola, explained his inspiration: "In order to totally deform objects, I employed the means Cubists used to represent them."[3]

i

The year 1914 also saw France lose its most prominent criminologist. For more than a year, Alphonse Bertillon had suffered from pernicious anemia, which his doctors told him would be fatal. He felt a continual chill and stayed in a single room where he kept a stove burning day and night. Fatigue dogged him and his vision was going too.

Bertillon worried continually that his identification system would die with him. The news that countries around the world were replacing *bertillonage* with fingerprinting knawed at his spirit and pride. The Argentinian criminologist Juan Vucetich, who was the leading exponent of fingerprinting, had cruelly declared, "I can assure you that in all the years during which we applied the anthropometric system, in spite of all our care, we were unable to prove the identity of a single person by measurements."[4] Later, when Vucetich came to Paris and tried to pay a call, Bertillon kept him waiting for hours in the anteroom of his office, only to open the door, ignore Vucetich's outstretched hand, and declare, "Sir, you have tried to do me a great deal of harm."[5] He slammed the door and that was all Vucetich saw of Bertillon.

Aware that Bertillon was dying, the French government wished to honor his achievements. He had already received the red ribbon of the Legion of Honor for his work, but he desired the rosette of the Legion, which signified a higher distinction. The government offered the rosette on one condition: Bertillon must acknowledge his error regarding the false handwriting analysis of Captain Alfred Dreyfus, now reinstated as an officer. Bertillon is said to have shouted from the bed where he spent his final days: "No! Never! Never!"[6]

He died on February 13, 1914. In his will he ordered that his brain be donated to the Laboratory of Anthropology. Afterward, his wife burned all the letters that he had exchanged with the mysterious Swedish woman with whom he had carried on a love affair years before. In doing so, she ensured that her husband, who had been known for his abhorrence of publicity, would retain his privacy even in death.

Though *bertillonage* was abandoned soon afterward, it has been revived in different form today. Computer programs have been devised to analyze faces and compare them with faces of known criminals. Called biometrics, this system was used in Massachusetts to scan some nine million driver's license photographs to locate a man wanted on rape charges.

Biometrics employs distinctive characteristics at what are called the nodal points of faces. These include the distance between the eyes, the width of the nose, the depth of the eye sockets, chin and jawline patterns — much the same as the system originally devised by Bertillon. Computers allow the use of a much greater number of these than Bertillon employed. One computer program is said to use some eight thousand facial data points.[7]

Facial identification systems have also been used with television cameras to scan crowds at sports events and other places in an attempt to identify terrorists, although it is not known how successful they have been. The use of such systems would be superior to fingerprinting in situations where it is impossible to take the fingerprints of every person involved. Bertillon's insistence that physical features are as definitive a means of identification as fingerprints may yet be confirmed.

ii

Guillaume Apollinaire, who had done so much to popularize and publicize the work of Picasso and others, knew that the war, like the art of his friends, was a profound break with the past. A poem he wrote about an automobile journey he had made just as the war clouds gathered reflected this sense of fracture:

> *The 31st of the month of July 1914[8]*
> *I left Deauville a little before midnight*
> *In Rouveyre's little auto . . .*
> *We said farewell to an entire epoch*
> *Furious giants were casting their shadows over Europe*
>
> *And when after passing that afternoon*
> *Through Fontainebleau*
> *We arrived in Paris*
> *At the moment the mobilization notices were being posted*
> *We understood my friend and I*
> *That the little auto had taken us into an epoch that was New*
> *And then even though we were both grown men*
> *We had nevertheless just been born.[9]*

Apollinaire was essentially a man without a country. France, his adopted homeland, classified him as Russian. In a burst of patriotism, and out of a desire to be born again as a Frenchman, he enlisted in the French army (unlike Picasso, who sat out the war in Paris and Rome, finding new mistresses and finally a wife). Making a pun on his assignment, Apollinaire wrote a friend, "I love art so much that I have joined the artillery." [10]

He did well in the army, winning promotion to sergeant and then, after a transfer to the infantry, becoming a second lieutenant. This new assignment, however, brought him into the trenches, the worst of all places to be in the war. He wrote: "Nine days without washing, sleeping on the ground without straw, ground infested with vermin, not a drop of water except that used to vaporize the gas masks. . . . It is fantastic what one can stand. . . . One of the parapets of my trench is partly made of corpses. . . . There are no head lice, but swarms of body lice, pubic lice. . . . No writer will ever be able to tell the simple horror of the trenches, the mysterious life that is led there."[11]

On March 18, 1916, while reading a copy of a literary magazine to which he regularly contributed, Apollinaire was wounded in the head when an artillery shell landed nearby. If he had not been wearing a helmet, he would have been killed outright, but even so the shrapnel pierced the helmet. Taken to an ambulance, he had pieces of metal (he called the wound "a splinter," but it was more serious) removed from his skull. The doctor thought he would recover quickly, so, as was usual with trench warfare, Apollinaire wasn't immediately evacuated from the combat zone. A week later, however, he grew worse and had to be transported to a hospital in Paris.

By May he was experiencing dizzy spells and paralysis of his left arm. The surgeons decided to do a trepannation — opening his skull to relieve pressure on the brain. Technically, the procedure was a success, for the paralysis and dizziness disappeared. Friends, however, thought Apollinaire had changed in other ways. One of them described him as "irascible and self-absorbed, dull-eyed, heavy-browed — that is what the trepannation had produced. His mouth was distorted with suffering — the same mouth that only a short time before had smiled so broadly as it uttered learned observations, jokes, delightful comments of all kinds."[12]

Fearing that his "cure" would qualify him to be returned to the trenches, a friend found Apollinaire a job in the military offices in Paris — as, of all things, a censor. Given his background, the officer in charge must have found it perfectly appropriate to assign Apollinaire oversight of the literary magazines — which he did, going so far as to censor some of his own work.

Germaine Albert-Birot, the editor of one such magazine, called *Sic,* persuaded Apollinaire to write a play with Cubist sets and costumes. Titled *Les Mamelles de Terésias* ("The Breasts of Terésias"), it is about a woman who becomes a man. Onstage, "Thérèse" performed this transformation when she opened her blouse and gas-filled balloons rose into the air. The most significant thing about the play was its subtitle, *Drame sur-réaliste.* Apollinaire intended *sur-réaliste* to be a synomym for *supernaturaliste,* but in the 1920s, the word was adopted by a group of artists whose work was characterized by fantasy and elements of the subconscious. Surrealists (as they became known), like many younger poets and painters, found Apollinaire's work and spirit an inspiration.

He would, tragically, not be there to enjoy the acclaim. At the beginning of 1918, he contracted pneumonia, which sent him back to the hospital. While there, he learned that the government had turned down his nomination for the Legion of Honor. Despite his status as war hero (he had received the Croix de Guerre), the affair of the stolen statuettes, and the suspicion that he might have had something to do with the theft of the *Mona Lisa,* had not been forgotten.

He did not let the disappointment dampen his zest for love and work. He resumed his former acquaintance with a young, red-haired woman who was completely unconnected with the world of art. The final poem in his last book, *Caligrammes,* was about her. In May they were married in a parish church near his apartment on the Boulevard Saint-Germain. Still producing new work, he began to cough heavily in October. An influenza epidemic would kill millions worldwide during the next year, and Apollinaire was among its first victims. He died on November 9, and two days later, the news arrived of the armistice that ended the war. As friends came to view his body, laid out on a bed in the newlyweds' apartment, crowds thronged the streets, shouting *"À bas Guillaume!"* ("Down with William," referring to the German emperor, Wilhelm II, who was forced to abdicate after the war).

iii

The years since the theft of the *Mona Lisa* had seen Picasso's artistic reputation increase. Kahnweiler arranged for his work to be exhibited in Munich, Berlin, Cologne, Prague, and New York. In March 1914, a group of Parisian investor-collectors held a sale of contemporary paintings it had acquired over the previous ten years. The newspapers covered the event closely. A still-life by Matisse brought 5,000 francs, quite a sum considering that works by Van Gogh and Gauguin went for less. But when a painting from Picasso's rose period, *Family of Saltimbaques,* went under the hammer for 11,500 francs to a buyer from Munich, heads turned in the art world. Picasso would never know poverty again.

Picasso's love life had thrived as well. He broke with Fernande in 1912 after she had an affair with an Italian painter, though some speculated that was a relief to Picasso, who was already in love with Marcelle Humbert, a circus performer whose real name was Eva Gouel. At about the same time, he began to paste objects such as chair caning and newspaper headlines directly onto the canvas, creating (along with Braque, who accompanied him in this as well as cubism) works known as *collages*. Increasingly those headlines reflected violence and the ominous approach of war.

After the war began, Braque, a Frenchman, joined the army, along with many others from the original *bande á Picasso*. Like Apollinaire, Braque was wounded in battle, and when he returned he was no longer as creative as he had been; he and Picasso never worked together again. Kahnweiler, a German, had to leave Paris for the duration of the war, making it difficult for Picasso to sell his work. His mistress, Eva, had been in poor health for some time and died in December 1915. Picasso, with most of his friends gone, now found intellectual stimulation only at the Stein apartment on the rue de Fleurus. Gertrude later wrote, "I very well remember at the beginning of the war being with Picasso on the Boulevard Raspail when the first camouflaged truck passed. It was at night, we had heard of camouflage but we had not yet seen it and Picasso amazed looked at it and then cried out, yes it is we who made it, that is cubism."[13]

Paul Poiret, the fashion designer and friend of Picasso, opened an art gallery on the rue d'Antin in 1916. Criticized because it seemed a frivolous thing to do during wartime, Poiret was defended in the newspaper *L'Intransigéant,* whose critic wrote, "Artists have to live, like other people, and France, more than any other nation, needs art."[14] In need of money, Picasso remounted the rolled-up canvas of his controversial 1907 painting and let Poirot display it. For the first time, it appeared under the title *Les Demoiselles d'Avignon,* a name Picasso is said to have disliked.[15]

That same year, while designing the costumes and scenery for a production of Diaghilev's Ballet Russe, Picasso met a ballerina named Olga Kokhlova, whom he would soon marry. In November 1918, Olga brought the news of Apollinaire's death to Picasso as he was shaving. He put down his razor and began to draw the face he saw in the mirror. He was later to claim it was the last self-portrait he ever made.[16]

iv

The carnage of the war, in which millions died for a cause no one could understand, left disillusionment and cynicism in its wake. Artists, or those who aspired to be artists, felt themselves inadequate to express the emotions the unprecedented horror produced. George Grosz and John Heartfield,[17] two German artists, condemned the "cloud-wandering tendencies of so-called sacred art, whose adherents mused on cubes and gothic while the generals painted in blood."[18]

In the midst of the war, in the city of Geneva in the neutral nation of Switzerland, arose a new form, or theory, of art. Called Dada,[19] it was born at the Cabaret Voltaire, where refugees from other nations often gathered. The idea is generally said to have originated with Tristan Tzara, a Romanian poet, but many others contributed. Dada has been called "a nihilistic creed of disinte-gration, showing the meaninglessness of all western thought, art, morals, traditions."[20] In short, it was a reaction against the civili-zation that had created the war. However, Dada artists made their point through black humor and absurdity. To them, art could be more — or less — than a drawing, a painting, a poem, a play; it might be something "created" at random, or even an event where the actions of the participants, spontaneously generated, are the art. "Everything the artist spits is art," declared Kurt Schwitters, one of the group.[21] The idea spread rapidly, for it appealed to those who felt that traditional art was inadequate in the face of the ulti-mate failure of civilization.

One of those who fell under Dada's influence was Marcel Du-champ, a Frenchman from a family of artists. His cubist painting, *Nude Descending a Staircase,* had created a sensation at the 1913 New York Armory Show, the first major exhibition of modern art in the United States. Inspired by the spirit of Dada, Duchamp be-gan to exhibit "ready-mades," which were manufactured objects that he had transformed into art either by altering them slightly or simply giving them a title and declaring them art. One famous ex-ample was a urinal, turned upside down, that he signed "R. Mutt" and titled *Fountain.*

In 1919, the 400th anniversary of Leonardo's death, Duchamp took an ordinary postcard-sized reproduction of the *Mona Lisa* and drew a mustache and goatee on it. He wrote at the bottom his "title": the letters L.H.O.O.Q. With that alteration, Leonardo's painting made the transition from a masterpiece of Renaissance art to an icon of modernism. Duchamp chose that particular painting to transform — or deface, if you like — because its theft had made it the most famous painting in the world, which it undoubtedly still is. The *Mona Lisa* was the biggest target Duchamp could aim at to show his contempt for what the old, prewar world had called "art."

And the title? Pronounced in French, L.H.O.O.Q. sounds like *Elle a chaud au cul,* which is usually translated as "She has a hot ass." And *that* is what La Gioconda is smiling about.

AFTERWORD:
THE MASTERMIND

In 1932, the American reporter Karl Decker revealed what he said was the true story of the *Mona Lisa*'s theft. Decker was one of the most famous journalists of his time, not only reporting the news but making it as well. His best-known exploit occurred in 1897, when he went to Cuba, then under Spanish rule, and rescued the daughter of a Cuban rebel from jail. Decker smuggled her aboard a ship and brought her back to New York City, where his newspaper, the sensational Hearst-owned *New York Herald,* lionized both its reporter and the beautiful eighteen-year-old Cuban. The exploit was a prelude to the mysterious explosion that sank the American naval ship *Maine* in Havana Harbor the following year, setting off the Spanish-American War.

Thirty-five years later, in the *Saturday Evening Post,* at that time one of the United States' leading weekly magazines, Decker claimed an even bigger scoop: that he knew who masterminded the theft of the *Mona Lisa.* In January 1914, while on assignment in Casablanca, Morocco, Decker had met a longtime acquaintance, a South American called Eduardo who had many aliases but was known to his associates as the Marqués de Valfierno—the "Marquis of the Vale of Hell." He looked the part, wrote Decker: "His admiring associates declared that 'his front was worth a million dollars.' White mustache and imperial [goatee], and a leonine mass of waving white hair, gave Eduardo a distinction that would have taken him past any royal-palace gate in Europe without the troubling necessity of giving his name."[1]

Decker had crossed paths with Valfierno in a number of exotic places and had developed a friendship "based upon the fact that he was one of the few I have known who never bored me." Decker had just returned from a three-month trip to the interior of Morocco and was unaware that a month before, the police had arrested Vincenzo Perugia and recovered the *Mona Lisa*. The marquis spoke of him as "that simp who helped us get the *Mona Lisa*," and of course Decker's curiosity was aroused.[2]

Valfierno made the journalist promise not to publish the story until he gave permission or died. It was the latter event that allowed Decker to reveal what he had been told. Valfierno began by saying that the operation had been several years in the planning. He reminded Decker that in Buenos Aires, the marquis had made a small fortune selling fake artworks that his partner, a Frenchman named Yves Chaudron, turned out. Scanning the newspapers for obituaries of wealthy men, the distinguished-looking Valfierno would approach the widow to ask if she would like to donate a painting to her church as a memorial. At the time, Chaudron specialized in painting fake Murillos—skillfully imitating the seventeenth-century Spanish painter who was famous for his religious scenes—and these were passed off to the widows as genuine.

Valfierno felt that he was performing a civic service. "A forged painting so cleverly executed as to puzzle experts is as valuable an addition to the art wealth of the world as the original," he said. "The aesthetic impression created is the same, and it is only the picture dealer, always a creature of commerce . . . who is really hurt when an imitation is discovered. . . . If the beauty be there in the picture, why cavil at the method by which it was obtained?"[3]

The duo graduated from bilking widows to selling copies of Murillos that they claimed were stolen. Buyers were fooled into thinking that a genuine Murillo, hanging in a church or gallery, was in fact a fake placed there after the original had been filched.

Eventually, "filthy with money," Valfierno and Chaudron felt that the game was getting old, and they sailed for Paris, where, Valfierno said, "Thousands of Corots, Millets, even Titians and Murillos, were being sold in the city every year, all of them fakes, but from my [point of view] this trade seemed cheap and unworthy."[4] He added people to his organization, including an American who was well connected socially. This time, the marquis was more selective in choosing those he wished to fleece, concentrating on wealthy Americans—by nature, more gullible than Europeans—who could pay highly for "masterpieces" that had supposedly been stolen from the Louvre.

Unlike Géry Pieret, who actually stole the Iberian heads he sold to Picasso, the marquis and his gang "never took anything from the Louvre. We didn't have to. We sold our cleverly executed copies, and . . . sent [the buyers] forged documents [that] told of the mysterious disappearance from the Louvre of some gem of painting or world-envied *object d'art*. . . . The documents always stated that in order to avoid scandal a copy had been temporarily substituted by the museum authorities."[5]

Eventually, the marquis peddled the ultimate prize: the *Mona Lisa* itself, in June 1910. Not the genuine article, but a Chaudron-made copy, along with forged official papers that convinced the buyer (an American millionaire) that in order to cover the theft, Louvre officials had hung a copy in the Salon Carré. The buyer, unfortunately, was a little too free in bragging about his new acquisition, and that was why the newspaper *Le Cri de Paris* had printed its article—a year before the actual theft—stating that the *Mona Lisa* had been stolen.

Still, it had been a disturbing experience, one that the marquis was determined to avoid a second time: "The next trip, we decided, there must be no chance for recriminations. We would steal—actually steal—the Louvre *Mona Lisa* and assure the buyer beyond any possibility of misunderstanding that the picture delivered to him was the true, the authentic original."[6]

Of course, he never intended to sell the real painting. "The original would be as awkward as a hot stove," he told Decker. The plan would be to create a copy and ship it overseas before stealing the original. "The customs would pass it without a thought, copies being commonplace and the original still being in the Louvre."[7] After the *Mona Lisa* had been stolen, the imitation could be taken out of storage overseas and sold to a buyer who was convinced he was getting the missing masterpiece.

"We began our selling campaign," recalled Valfierno, "and the first deal went through so easily that the thought, 'Why stop with one?' naturally arose. There was no limit in theory to the fish we might hook. Actually, we stopped with six American millionaires. Six were as many as we could both land and keep hot."[8] Chaudron then carefully produced the six copies, which were in due course sent to America and kept waiting for the proper time to be delivered. Valfierno said that an antique bed made of Italian walnut, "seasoned by time to the identical quality of that on which La Joconde was painted," was broken up to provide the six panels that Chaudron painted on.[9]

Now came what Valfierno thought was the easy part: "Stealing La Joconde was as simple as boiling an egg in a kitchenette," he told Decker. "Our success depended upon one thing—the fact that a workman in a white blouse in the Louvre is as free from suspicion as an unlaid egg. . . . [It] was a uniform that gave [the thief] all the rights and privileges of the museum."[10] Recruiting someone—Perugia—who had actually worked in the Louvre was helpful because he knew the secret rooms and staircases that employees used.

Perugia did not act alone, Valfierno said. He had two accomplices, needed to lift the painting and its heavy protective container and frame from the wall and carry it to a place where it could be removed. Valfierno did not name them, but anyone familiar with the case might have remembered the Lancelotti brothers, whom Perugia had briefly implicated in the heist when he was questioned in Florence.

The one hitch in the plan was that Perugia had failed to test beforehand the duplicate key Valfierno had made for the door at the bottom of the small staircase that Perugia used to make his escape. At the moment he needed it, the key failed to turn the lock. While he was removing the doorknob with a screwdriver, the trio heard footsteps from above, and Perugia's two accomplices hid themselves. The plumber named Sauvet appeared and, seeing only one man in a white smock, had no reason to be suspicious. He opened the door and went on his way, soon followed by Perugia and the other two thieves. At the vestibule, luck was on their side again, for the guard stationed there had abandoned his post temporarily to get a bucket of water to clean the floor.

An automobile waited for the thieves and took them to Valfierno's headquarters, where the gang celebrated "the most magnificent single theft in the history of the world."[11] Now the six copies that had been sent to the United States could be delivered to the purchasers. Because each of the six collectors thought he was receiving stolen merchandise, he could not publicize his acquisition—or even complain should he suspect it wasn't the genuine article. It was, indeed, the perfect crime.

"Chaudron almost died of joy and pride when he learned the prices his work had brought," Valfierno said. "He . . . retired to a country place near Paris and only occasionally does a piece of work for some really great worker in the field of fake-art salesmanship."[12]

Perugia was paid well for his part in the scheme—"enough to take care of him for the rest of his days if he had taken his good fortune with ordinary intelligence." However, he squandered the money on the Riviera, possibly in casinos, and then, knowing where the real *Mona Lisa* was hidden, stole it a second time. The story that he carried it around in his trunk for two years was false. "The poor fool had some nutty notion of selling it," Valfierno told

Decker. "He had never realized that selling it, in the first place, was the real achievement, requiring an organization and a finesse that was a million miles beyond his capabilities." [13]

What about the copies? Decker wanted to know. Someday, speculated Valfierno, all of them would reappear. "Without those, there are already thirty Mona Lisas in the world. That in the Prado Museum is, if anything, superior to the one in the Louvre. Every now and then a new one pops up. I merely added to the gross total." [14]

Perhaps significantly, Decker chose not to publish this sensational story in one of the Hearst publications, even though he was still a Hearst employee. His boss, William Randolph Hearst, was a wealthy man who voraciously collected art—just the sort of person to whom Valfierno might have sold one of the fake *Mona Lisa*s. Hearst Castle, his fabled California estate, was donated to the state of California in 1957, and a curator there in 2005 reported that "there is not—and was not—a copy of Leonardo's *Mona Lisa* at Hearst Castle," although it was impossible to tell if one might have been part of "his larger collection located at various other venues, past and present." [15]

The Decker account is the sole source for the existence of Valfierno and this version of the theft of the *Mona Lisa*. There is no external confirmation for it. Yet it has frequently been assumed to be true by authors writing about the case. True or false? That mystery has yet to be solved.

ACKNOWLEDGMENTS

We want to express our appreciation and thanks to Lyn Nosker and Ellen Hoobler, for their work translating certain books and documents for us. Our thanks also to Dick Nosker, for explaining scientific concepts to us, and to Yohann Thibaudault, for his assiduous research in the Paris Préfecture de Police Museum.

Clearly, we have drawn on the works of many authors, whom we have listed in our bibliography. We owe a particular debt, however, to Dr. Benjamin F. Martin of Louisiana State University and Dr. Edward Berenson of UCLA, whose works have informed our writing of chapter 9; and to Richard Parry, whose comprehensive book on the Bonnot Gang provided the basis of our research for chapter 7.

Our thanks to the staffs of the New York Public Library, the Avery Library, and the Butler Library of Columbia University.

We owe more than we can adequately express to our editor, Geoff Shandler, who initially conceptualized this book and provided many insights and suggestions, and to his assistant, Junie Dahn, who as always was the god in the details.

Finally, our gratitude to our agent, Al Zuckerman, whose support for our work has been unwavering.

NOTES

THEFT

1. There were an estimated 275,000 works in the museum's possession, not all of which were on display.
2. It began as a fortress constructed by Philip Augustus around the year 1190, but many alterations and additions had been made since then.
3. Lawrence Jeppson, *The Fabulous Frauds: Fascinating Tales of Great Art Forgeries* (New York: Weybright and Talley, 1970), 44.

CHAPTER ONE: THE CITY OF LIGHT

1. Vincent Cronin, *Paris on the Eve: 1900–1914* (New York: St. Martin's Press, 1990), 36.
2. Ibid., 35.
3. Malcolm Gee, *Dealers, Critics, and Collectors of Modern Painting: Aspects of the Parisian Art Market between 1910 and 1930* (New York: Garland, 1981), 158.
4. Theodore Dreiser, "Paris," *Century Magazine* 86, no. 6 (October 1913): 910–11.
5. Norma Evenson, *Paris: A Century of Change, 1878–1978* (New Haven: Yale University Press, 1979), 1.
6. Susan Quinn, *Marie Curie: A Life* (New York: Simon and Schuster, 1995), 91.
7. Joshua Zeitz, *Flapper: A Madcap Story of Sex, Style, Celebrity, and the Women Who Made America Modern* (New York: Three Rivers Press, 2006), 129.
8. Theodore Zeldin, *France, 1848–1945: Taste and Corruption* (New York: Oxford University Press, 1980), 23.
9. Nigel Gosling, *The Adventurous World of Paris, 1900–1914* (New York: Morrow, 1978), 18.

10. Zeldin, *France,* 358.
11. Mary Ellen Jordan Haight, *Paris Portraits, Renoir to Chanel: Walks on the Right Bank* (Salt Lake City: Peregrine Smith Books, 1991), 108.
12. Arthur Gold and Robert Fizdale, *Misia: The Life of Misia Sert* (New York: Knopf, 1980), 41.
13. Ibid., 42.
14. Johannes Willms, *Paris: Capital of Europe; From the Revolution to the Belle Epoque,* trans. Eveline L. Kanes (New York: Holmes and Meier, 1997), 335–36.
15. Frankfort Sommerville, *The Spirit of Paris* (London: Black, 1913), 62.
16. Ellen Williams, *Picasso's Paris: Walking Tours of the Artist's Life in the City* (New York: Little Bookroom, 1999), 56.
17. Samuel L. Bensusan, *Souvenir of Paris* (London: Jack, 1911), 51–52.
18. Its name came from the lavender and white lilacs that grew outside.
19. Patrice Higonnet, *Paris: Capital of the World,* trans. Arthur Goldhammer (Cambridge: Belknap Press, 2002), 68.
20. Carolyn Burke, *Becoming Modern: The Life of Mina Loy* (New York: Farrar, Straus and Giroux, 1996), 80.
21. Charles Douglas, *Artist Quarter: Reminiscences of Montmartre and Montparnasse in the First Two Decades of the Twentieth Century* (London: Faber and Faber, 1941), 140.
22. Gino Severini, *The Life of a Painter: The Autobiography of Gino Severini,* trans. Jennifer Franchina (Princeton, NJ: Princeton University Press, 1995), 25.
23. Christopher Green, *Art in France, 1900–1940* (New Haven: Yale University Press, 2000), 150.
24. Cronin, *Paris on the Eve,* 275.
25. Jules Bertaut, *Paris, 1870–1935,* trans. R. Millar (New York: Appleton-Century, 1936), 186.
26. Cronin, *Paris on the Eve,* 284.
27. Ibid., 285.
28. Quinn, *Marie Curie,* 137.
29. Cronin, *Paris on the Eve,* 20.
30. William Fleming, *Art and Ideas,* 6th ed. (New York: Holt, Rinehart and Winston, 1980), 403.
31. Bergson's wife was a cousin of Proust's.
32. Bernice Rose, "Picasso, Braque and Early Film in Cubism" (notes for exhibition at Pace Wildenstein Gallery, New York City, 2007).
33. Jean-Paul Sartre, *The Words,* trans. Bernard Frechtman (New York: Vintage, 1981), 119–25.
34. Fleming, *Art and Ideas,* 400.
35. The Bourbon monarchy; the First Republic established by the Revolution; the Directory; the First Empire under Napoleon Bonaparte; the restoration of the monarchy in 1815; the 1830 revolution that gave France a constitutional monarchy under the Citizen King, Louis-Philippe; the short-lived Second Republic in 1848; and the Second Empire under Napoleon III.
36. Alexander Varias, *Paris and the Anarchists: Aesthetes and Subversives during the Fin-de-Siècle* (New York: St. Martin's Press, 1996), 41–42.

37. Jay Robert Nash, *Encyclopedia of World Crime: Criminal Justice, Criminology, and Law Enforcement* (Wilmette, IL: CrimeBooks, 1990), 633.

38. Richard D. Sonn, "Marginality and Transgression: Anarchy's Subversive Allure," in *Montmartre and the Making of Mass Culture,* ed. Gabriel P. Weisber, 130 (New Brunswick, NJ: Rutgers University Press, 2001).

39. Charles Rearick, *Pleasures of the Belle Époque: Entertainment and Festivity in Turn-of-the-Century France* (New Haven: Yale University Press, 1985), 199.

40. Martin P. Johnson, *The Dreyfus Affair: Honour and Politics in the Belle Époque* (Basingstoke, UK: Macmillan, 1999), 6.

41. Jean-Denis Bredin, *The Affair: The Case of Alfred Dreyfus,* trans. Jeffrey Mehlman (New York: Braziller, 1986), 68.

42. Ibid., 68.

43 Ann-Louise Shapiro, *Breaking the Codes: Female Criminality in Fin-de-Siècle Paris* (Stanford, CA: Stanford University Press, 1996), 2.

44 Sanche de Gramont, *The French: Portrait of a People* (New York: Putnam's, 1969), 390.

45. The French pronounce the term *apache* as "ah POSH."

46. Daniel Gerould, *Guillotine: Its Legend and Lore* (New York: Blast Books, 1992), 179.

47. Mel Gordon, *The Grand Guignol: Theatre of Fear and Terror,* rev. ed. (New York: De Capo Press, 1997), 22.

48. Agnes Peirron, "House of Horrors," http://www.GrandGuignol.com/history.htm.

49. John Ashbery, "Introduction of Marcel Allain and Pierre Souvestre's *Fantômas,*" in *Selected Prose,* ed. Eugene Richie, 185 (Ann Arbor: University of Michigan Press, 2004).

50. Ibid., 185.

CHAPTER TWO: SEARCHING FOR A WOMAN

1. Jürgen Thorwald, *The Century of the Detective,* trans by Richard Winston and Clara Winston (New York: Harcourt, Brace, and World, 1965), 85.

2. Seymour Reit, *The Day They Stole the Mona Lisa* (New York: Summit Books, 1981), 78.

3. Francis Steegmuller, *Apollinaire: Poet among the Painters* (New York: Farrar, Straus, 1963), 188–89.

4. Milton Esterow, *The Art Stealers* (New York: Macmillan, 1966), 107.

5. The French version of *La Gioconda,* an Italian name for the *Mona Lisa,* referring to the fact that the subject of the painting is thought to be the wife of Francesco del Giocondo.

6. Molly Nesbit, "The Rat's Ass," *October* 56 (Spring 1991): 13–14.

7. Steegmuller, *Apollinaire,* 188.

8. Aaron Freundschuh, "Crime Stories in the Historical Landscape: Narrating the Theft of the Mona Lisa," *Urban History* 33, no. 2 (2006): 281.

9. E. E. Richards, *The Louvre* (Boston: Small, Maynard, 1912), 96.

10. *Los Angeles Times,* August 26, 1911.

11. About twice the annual wage of a skilled worker at the time.

12. Esterow, *Art Stealers,* 101.

13. Donald Sassoon, *Becoming Mona Lisa: The Making of a Global Icon* (San Diego: Harcourt, 2001), 174.

14. Freundschuh, "Crime Stories," 286.

15. Barbara Gardner Conklin, Robert Gardner, and Dennis Shortelle *Encyclopedia of Forensic Science: A Compendium of Detective Fact and Fiction* (Westport, CT: Oryx Press, 2002), 282–83.

16. Esterow, *Art Stealers,* 117.

17. Steegmuller, *Apollinaire,* 187–88.

18. Freundschuh, "Crime Stories," 287.

19. Ibid., 285.

20. "A Hint to Mr. Morgan," *New York Times,* January 18, 1912.

21. *Los Angeles Times,* September 6, 1911.

22. *New York Times,* March 3, 1912.

23. Darian Leader, *Stealing the Mona Lisa: What Art Stops Us From Seeing* (New York: Counterpoint, 2002), 66.

24. Max Brod, ed., *The Diaries of Franz Kafka,* vol. 2, *1914–1923,* trans. Martin Greenberg with the cooperation of Hannah Arendt (New York: Schocken, 1949), 276.

25. Sassoon, *Becoming Mona Lisa,* 179.

26. Nesbit, "Rat's Ass," 7.

27. Ibid., 179,

28. Théophile Homolle, director of the national museums, had been fired shortly after the theft.

29. Contemporary photographs show four hooks at the space on the wall where the painting had hung.

30. Hanns Zischler, *Kafka Goes to the Movies,* trans. Susan H. Gillespie (Chicago: University of Chicago Press, 2003), 49–51.

31. Esterow, *Art Stealers,* 102.

32. *New York Times,* October 1, 1911.

33. Ibid.

34. Esterow, *Art Stealers,* 108.

35. *New York Times,* October 1, 1911.

36. Ibid.

37. *Mona* is a diminutive of *Madonna,* used as a term of respect for a married woman.

38. The sitter in the *Mona Lisa* appears to have no eyebrows.

39. Renaud Temperini, *Leonardo da Vinci at the Louvre* (Paris: Éditions Scala, 2003), 56.

40. Roy McMullen, *Mona Lisa: The Picture and the Myth* (Boston: Houghton Mifflin, 1975), 116.

41. Sassoon, *Becoming Mona Lisa,* 39.

42. Temperini, *Leonardo da Vinci,* 56.

43. Sassoon, *Becoming Mona Lisa,* 26.

44. Ibid., 27.

45. Ibid., 61.

46. Ibid., 54.

47. Ibid., 89.

48. Ibid., 95.
49. Ibid., 110.
50. Ibid., 111.
51. Walter Pater, "Leonardo da Vinci," in *Three Major Texts,* ed. William E. Buckley (New York: New York University Press, 1986), 149.
52. Sigmund Freud, *Leonardo da Vinci and a Memory of His Childhood,* trans. Alan Tyson (New York, Norton, 1964), 65.
53. Ibid., 69.
54. Freud presumes that Leonardo, as a homosexual, had an unhappy erotic life. No one seriously argues this today.
55. Ibid., 77.
56. Sassoon, *Becoming Mona Lisa,* 108.
57. Steegmuller, *Apollinaire,* 188.
58. *Boston Daily Globe,* September 10, 1911.
59. Freundschuh, "Crime Stories," 287.
60. Pater, "Leonardo da Vinci," 150.

CHAPTER THREE: SYMPATHY FOR THE DEVIL

1. Steegmuller, *Apollinaire,* 182 (see chap. 2, n. 3).
2. R. D. Collins, *The Origins of Detective Fiction: A Brief History of Crime and Mystery Books,* http://www.classiccrimefiction.com/historydf.htm.
3. Vidocq, François-Eugène, *Memoirs of Vidocq: Master of Crime* (Edinburgh: AK Press, 2003), 1.
4. Ibid., 1.
5. Ibid., 7.
6. Ibid., 57.
7. Ibid., 192.
8. Ibid., 185.
9. Julian Symons, *Bloody Murder: From the Detective Story to the Crime Novel; A History,* 2nd ed. (London: Pan Books, 1992), 37.
10. Joseph Geringer, *Vidocq: Convict Turned Detective Magnifique: Police Spy,* http://www.crimelibrary.com/gangsters_outlaws/cops_others/vidocq/3.html.
11. The brand was "TF," for *travaux forcés,* forced work.
12. Geringer, *Vidocq,* http://www.crimelibrary.com/gangsters_outlaws/cops_others/vidocq/4.html.
13. Vidocq, *Memoirs,* 204.
14. Ibid., 368.
15. Alfred Morain, *The Underworld of Paris: Secrets of the Sûreté* (London: Jarrolds, 1929), 233–34.
16. Vidocq, *Memoirs,* xiii.
17. Geringer, *Vidocq,* http://www.crimelibrary.com/gangsters_outlaws/cops_others/vidocq/7.html.
18. Honoré de Balzac, *Père Goriot,* trans. Burton Raffel (New York: Norton, 1994), 39.
19. Ibid., 90.
20. Edward Berenson, *The Trial of Madame Caillaux* (Berkeley: University of California Press, 1992), 216.

21. According to Poe's biographer Arthur Hobson Quinn, Poe took the name of his fictional detective from Marie Dupin, the heroine of a story that appeared in a collection titled "Unpublished Passages in the Life of Vidocq, the French Minister of Police." Published in the magazine *Burton's* from September to December 1838 and signed J. M. B., these stories capitalized on Vidocq's fame and portrayed him in action capturing criminals. *Edgar Allan Poe: A Critical Biography* (Baltimore: Johns Hopkins University Press, 1998), 310–11.
22. A. E. Murch, *The Development of the Detective Novel* (Port Washington, NY: Kennikat Press, 1968), 68.
23. Quinn, *Edgar Allan Poe,* 430.
24. Symons, *Bloody Murder,* 46.
25. Keith Parkins, *Edgar Allan Poe,* http://www.huerka.clara.net/art/poe.htm.
26. Edmund Wilson, *Axel's Castle: A Study in the Imaginative Literature of 1870–1930* (New York: Scribner's, 1959), 12.
27. Ibid., 12.
28. Parkins, *Edgar Allan Poe,* 4.
29. *New York Times,* December 13, 1991.
30. Parkins, *Edgar Allan Poe,* 2–3.
31. LeRoy Lad Panek, *An Introduction to the Detective Story* (Bowling Green, OH: Bowling Green State University Popular Press, 1987), 71.
32. Janet Pate, *The Book of Sleuths* (Chicago: Contemporary Books, 1977), 18.
33. Ibid., 18.
34. Henry Douglas Thomson, *Masters of Mystery: A Study of the Detective Story* (1931; repr., New York: Dover, 1978), 96.
35. Ibid., 101.
36. Ibid., 102.
37. Gaboriau, Émile, *Monsieur Lecoq,* ed. and intro. E. F. Bleiler (New York: Dover, 1975), v.
38. Murch, *Detective Novel,* 12.
39. J. Kenneth Van Dover, *You Know My Method: The Science of the Detective* (Bowling Green, OH: Bowling Green State University Popular Press, 1994), 24.
40. Jean-Marc Lofficier and Randy Lofficier, *Shadowmen: Heroes and Villains of French Pulp Fiction* (Encino, CA: Black Coat Press, 2003), 231.
41. Ibid., 233.
42. Pierre Souvestre and Marcel Allain, *Fantômas* (New York: Morrow, 1986), 80.
43. Ibid., 11.
44. Robin Walz, *Pulp Surrealism: Insolent Popular Culture in Early Twentieth-Century Paris* (Berkeley: University of California Press, 2000), 62.

CHAPTER FOUR: SCIENCE VS. CRIME

1. Shapiro, *Breaking the Codes,* 41 (see chap. 1, n. 43).
2. Nash, Jay Robert, *Encyclopedia of World Crime* (Wilmette, IL: History, Inc., 1999), 1868.
3. Gerould, *Guillotine,* 96 (see chap. 1, n. 46).
4. Ibid., 96.
5. Nash, *Encyclopedia of World Crime,* 1868.
6. Ibid., 1868.

7.   Canler would later serve as head of the Sûreté himself and write his memoirs, which were suppressed by the authorities for being too frank. They were published seventeen years after his death.
8.   Higonnet, *Paris,* 79 (see chap. 1, n. 19).
9.   Nash, *Encyclopedia of World Crime,* 1869.
10. The Cour d'Assises assembled to hear specific cases; it usually consisted of a three-judge panel and nine jurors.
11   Gerould, *Guillotine,* 96.
12. The *Memoirs,* published posthumously, met with acclaim. Stendhal, Hugo, Flaubert, and Dostoevsky were all fascinated with the man, particularly his sense of himself as a genius warring against society. Dostoevsky later published Lacenaire's memoirs in Russian in a magazine he edited, and he used him as a model for Raskolnikov, the double murderer in *Crime and Punishment.* Lacenaire also served as the model for the character Montparnasse in Victor Hugo's *Les misérables.* The 1943 movie *Children of Paradise,* regarded as one of the peaks of French cinema, includes a character named Lacenaire, who is loosely based on the real person.
13. Gerould, *Guillotine,* 97.
14. Nash, *Encyclopedia of World Crime,* 1869.
15   Thorwald, *Century of the Detective,* 275 (see chap. 2, n. 1).
16. Ibid., 276.
17. Jay Robert Nash, *Look for the Woman* (New York: Evans, 1981), 236.
18. Ibid., 237.
19. Ibid., 237.
20. Ibid., 240.
21. Ibid., 242.
22. Ibid., 243.
23   Ibid., 244.
24. Thorwald, *Century of the Detective,* 285.
25. Ibid., 286.
26. Nash, *Look for the Woman,* 244.
27. Ibid., 245.
28. Lassiter Wren, *Master Strokes of Crime Detection* (Garden City, NY: Doubleday, Doran, 1929), 70.
29. Ibid., 75–76.
30. Ibid., 93.
31. Shapiro, *Breaking the Codes,* 40.
32. Colin Wilson and Damon Wilson, *The Giant Book of True Crime* (London: Magpie Books, 2006), 389–90.
33. Thorwald, *Century of the Detective,* 46.
34. Shapiro, *Breaking the Codes,* 18.
35. Ibid., 40.
36. Yvonne Deutsch, ed., *Science against Crime* (New York: Exeter Books, 1982), 72.
37. Thorwald, *Century of the Detective,* 128.
38. Ibid., 131.
39. Ibid., 117.

40. Henry B. Irving, *A Book of Remarkable Criminals* (London: Cassell, 1918), 310.
41. Ibid., 318.
42. Nash, *Encyclopedia of World Crime,* 122.
43. Thorwald, *Century of the Detective,* 137.
44. Coincidentally, Bram Stoker's novel *Dracula,* about a bloodsucking vampire, was published in the year Vacher was caught.
45. "The Ripper Is Dead," *Iowa State Press,* January 30, 1899, http://www.casebook.org/press_reports/iowa state_press/990130.htm.
46. Ibid.
47. Ibid.
48. Timothy B. Smith, "Assistance and Repression: Rural Exodus, Vagabondage, and Social Crisis in France, 1880–1914," *Journal of Social History* 32, no. 4 (Summer 1999): 822.
49. Angus McLaren, *The Trials of Masculinity: Policing Sexual Boundaries, 1870–1930* (Chicago: University of Chicago Press, 1997), 160.
50. Matt K. Matsuda, *The Memory of the Modern* (New York: Oxford University Press, 1996), 141.
51. Jean Belin, *Secrets of the Sûreté: The Memoirs of Commissioner Jean Belin* (New York: Putnam's, 1950), 7–8.
52. "Paris Slayer Wore Armored Sleeves," *New York Times,* January 16, 1910.
53. Ibid.
54. James Morton, *Gangland: The Early Years* (London: Time Warner Paperbacks, 2004), 531.
55. Hans Gross (1847–1915) was an Austrian judge whose 1893 handbook for examining magistrates, police officials, etc., was a milestone in the field of criminalistics, the application of science to crime investigation.
56. Henry Morton Robinson, *Science versus Crime* (Indianapolis: Bobbs-Merrill, 1935), 201.
57. "Locard's Exchange Principle," http://en.wikipedia.org/wiki/Locard's_exchange_principle.

CHAPTER FIVE: THE MAN WHO MEASURED PEOPLE

1. Jennifer Michael Hecht, *The End of the Soul: Scientific Modernity, Atheism, and Anthropology in France* (New York: Columbia University Press, 2003), 165.
2. Ibid., 148.
3. Ibid., 148.
4. Jennifer Michael Hecht, "French Scientific Materialism and the Liturgy of Death: The Invention of a Secular Version of Catholic Last Rites (1876–1914)," *French Historical Studies* 20, no. 4 (Fall 1997): 709.
5. Ibid., 971.
6. He came up with the concept of the cephalic index—the breadth of the head above the ears expressed as a percentage of its length from forehead to back.
7. Brian Baker, "Darwin's Gothic Science and Literature in the Late Nineteenth Century," in *Literature and Science: Social Impact and Interaction,* ed. John H. Cartwright and Brian Baker, 212 (Santa Barbara, CA: ABC-CLIO, 2005).
8. Fingerprinting was still in the future.

9. Henry T. F. Rhodes, *Alphonse Bertillon: Father of Scientific Detection* (New York: Greenwood, 1968), 91.
10. Colin Beavan, *Fingerprints: The Origins of Crime Detection* (New York: Hyperion, 2001), 83.
11. Rhodes, *Alphonse Bertillon,* 88.
12. Ibid., 95.
13. Ibid., 218.
14. Robinson, *Science versus Crime,* 142 (see chap. 4, n. 56).
15. Matsuda, *Memory of the Modern,* 136 (see chap. 4, n. 50).
16. Ibid., 136.
17. Hecht, *End of the Soul,* 164.
18. Thorwald, *Century of the Detective,* 28 (see chap. 2, n. 1).
19. Ibid., 29.
20. Ibid., 30.
21. Gerould, *Guillotine,* 195 (see chap. 1, n. 46).
22. Thorwald, *Century of the Detective,* 31.
23. George Dilnot, *Triumphs of Detection: A Book about Detectives* (London: Bles, 1929), 108.
24. Ibid., 108–9.
25. Ibid., 109–10.
26. In the Conan Doyle story "The Naval Treaty," Dr. Watson summarizes a talk with Holmes: "His conversation, I remember, was about the Bertillon system of measurements, and he expressed his enthusiastic admiration of the French savant."
27. Harry Ashton-Wolfe, *The Forgotten Clue: Stories of the Parisian Sûreté with an Account of Its Methods* (New York: Houghton Mifflin, 1930), 115.
28. Ibid., 115–16.
29. Ibid., 116.
30. Ibid., 117.
31. Ibid., 118.
32. Ibid., 120.
33. Ibid., 123.
34. Ibid., 127–28.
35. Their daughter interviewed Alphonse late in his life and wrote a favorable biography of him.
36. Hecht, *End of the Soul,* 63.
37. Bredin, *Affair,* 74 (see chap. 1, n. 41).
38. Ibid., 74.
39. Louis L. Snyder, *The Dreyfus Case: A Documentary History* (New Brunswick, NJ: Rutgers University Press, 1973), 190.
40. Bredin, *Affair,* 262.
41. Snyder, *Dreyfus Case,* 303.
42. Nash, *Encyclopedia of World Crime,* 306 (see chap. 1, n. 37).
43. Colin Evans, *Casebook of Forensic Detection: How Science Solved 100 of the World's Most Baffling Crimes* (New York: Wiley, 1996), 95.
44. Thorwald, *Century of the Detective,* 83.
45. Nash, *Encyclopedia of World Crime,* 351.

46. Ida Tarbell, "Identification of Criminals: The Scientific Method in Use in France," *McClure's Magazine* 2, no. 4 (March 1894): 165–66.

47. Ibid., 160.

48. Ibid., 169.

49. Michelle Perrot, ed., *A History of Private Life,* vol. 4, *From the Fires of Revolution to the Great War* (Cambridge, MA: Belknap Press, 1990), 473.

50. Katherine Blackford, "An Afternoon with Bertillon," *Outlook* 100, no. 7, (February 24, 1912): 427–28.

51. Rhodes, *Alphonse Bertillon,* 193.

CHAPTER SIX: THE SUSPECTS

1. Steegmuller, *Apollinaire,* 168 (see chap. 2, n. 3).

2. Ibid., 168.

3. Ibid., 168.

4. Ibid., 169.

5. Ibid., 170.

6. Ibid., 170.

7. Arianna Stassinopoulos Huffington, *Picasso: Creator and Destroyer* (New York: Avon, 1989), 58.

8. Ibid., 77.

9. Steegmuller, *Apollinaire,* 125.

10. Ibid., 126.

11. Huffington, *Picasso,* 80.

12. Ibid., 85.

13. Roger Shattuck, *The Banquet Years: The Origins of the Avant Garde in France, 1885 to World War I,* rev. ed. (New York: Vintage, 1968), 254.

14. Ibid., 256.

15. Robert Tombs, "Culture and the Intellectuals," in *Modern France, 1880–2002,* ed. James McMillan, 181 (New York: Oxford University Press, 2003).

16. Although the ancient Greek Democritus of Abdera posited atoms as fundamental elements of matter in the fifth century B.C.E., his idea was not generally accepted for more than two thousand years.

17. Eric Temple Bell, *Men of Mathematics* (New York: Simon and Schuster, 1965), 526.

18. Arthur I. Miller, *Einstein, Picasso: Space, Time and the Beauty That Causes Havoc* (New York: Basic Books, 2001), 103–4.

19. Linda Dalrymple Henderson, *The Fourth Dimension and Non-Euclidian Geometry in Modern Art* (Princeton, NJ: Princeton University Press, 1983), 38.

20. In the book, he also dies in 820 places simultaneously.

21. Patricia Dee Leighten, *Re-ordering the Universe: Picasso and Anarchism, 1897–1914* (Princeton, NJ: Princeton University Press, 1989), 63.

22. Ibid., 53.

23. Ibid., 58.

24. Ibid., 65.

25. Huffington, *Picasso,* 83.

26. Ibid., 86.

27. Ibid., 88.
28. Ibid., 89.
29. Ibid., 89.
30. Ibid., 89–90.
31. Leighten, *Re-ordering the Universe*, 87.
32. Steegmuller, *Apollinaire*, 166.
33. The name Avignon, later applied to the painting, was said by André Salmon to refer to a particular street in Barcelona, the carrer d'Avinyó (Avignon in French), but Picasso denied that this was true, and his biographer John Richardson confirms that the carrer d'Avinyó was quite respectable.
34. Dan Franck, *The Bohemians: The Birth of Modern Art, Paris 1900–1930*, trans. Cynthia Hope LeBow (London: Weidenfeld and Nicolson, 2001), 132–33.
35. Jarry died in November 1907, apparently without having seen the painting.
36. Leighten, *Re-ordering the Universes*, 90.
37. Steegmuller, *Apollinaire*, 191.
38. Franck, *Bohemians*, 102.
39. Lael Wertenbaker and the editors of Time-Life Books, *The World of Picasso, 1881–1973* (Alexandria, VA: Time-Life Books, 1980), 54.
40. Henderson, *Fourth Dimension*, 80.
41. William R. Everdell, *The First Moderns: Profiles in the Origins of Twentieth-Century Thought* (Chicago: University of Chicago Press, 1997), 248.
42. Ibid., 248.
43. George Heard Hamilton, *Painting and Sculpture in Europe, 1880–1940*, The Pelican History of Art (Baltimore: Penguin Books, 1972), 238.
44. Everdell, *First Moderns*, 249.
45. John Richardson, with the collaboration of Marilyn McCully, *A Life of Picasso*, vol. 2, *1907–1917* (New York: Random House, 1996), 211.
46. Fernande Olivier, *Picasso and His Friends*, trans. Jane Miller (New York: Appleton-Century, 1965), 133.
47. Ibid., 139.
48. Steegmuller, *Apollinaire*, 167.
49. Ibid., 173.
50. Olivier, *Picasso and His Friends*, 148.
51. Steegmuller, *Apollinaire*, 173.
52. Ibid., 174
53. Ibid., 175.
54. Ibid., 177.
55. Ibid., 176.
56. Ibid., 176.
57. Ibid., 211.
58. Ibid., 212.
59. Ibid., 217.
60. Olivier, *Picasso and His Friends*, 148–49.
61. Ibid., 149.
62. Steegmuller, *Apollinaire*, 218–19.
63. Ibid., 213.

64. Ibid., 207.
65. Ibid., 207–08.
66. He was Polish.
67. Willard Bohn, *Apollinaire and the International Avant-Garde* (Albany: State University of New York Press, 1997), 6.

CHAPTER SEVEN: THE MOTOR BANDITS

1. Richard Parry, *The Bonnot Gang* (London: Rebel Press, 1987), 35.
2. Victor Serge, *Memoirs of a Revolutionary, 1901–1941,* trans. and ed. Peter Sedgwick (Oxford: Oxford University Press, 1980), 30.
3. Ibid., 18.
4. Ibid., 38–39.
5. Ibid., 39.
6. Ibid., 40.
7. Serge, *Memoirs,* 32–33.
8. Parry, *Bonnot Gang,* 70.
9. Ibid., 79.
10. Ashton-Wolfe, *Forgotten Clue,* 51–52 (see chap. 5, n. 27).
11. Serge, *Memoirs,* 20–21.
12. Parry, *Bonnot Gang,* 90.
13. Serge, *Memoirs,* 35.
14. Parry, *Bonnot Gang,* 97.
15. Ibid., 101.
16. Ibid., 111.
17. Ibid., 111.
18. Maurice Leblanc, "The Most Amazing True Crime Story Ever Told: The Auto-Bandits of Paris," *New York Times,* May 5, 1912.
19. Belin, *Secrets of the Sûreté,* 29–30 (see chap. 4, n. 51).
20. Parry, *Bonnot Gang,* 123.
21. Ibid., 125.
22. Ibid., 125.
23. Ibid., 126.
24. Belin, *Secrets of the Sûreté,* 31–32.
25. Harry, Ashton-Wolfe, *Crimes of Violence and Revenge* (Boston: Houghton Mifflin, 1929), 115.
26. Parry, *Bonnot Gang,* 128.
27. Ashton-Wolfe, *Crimes,* 116.
28. Ibid., 116.
29. Parry, *Bonnot Gang,* 136.
30. Ibid., 137.
31. Ibid., 139.
32. Ibid., 150.
33. Ibid., 160.
34. Thirteen years later, in 1928, he escaped and made his way to Brazil, where the authorities refused to extradite him to France. His wife had never ceased her attempts to prove his innocence, and a year later he received a pardon.
35. Gerould, *Guillotine,* 129 (see chap. 1, n. 46).

CHAPTER EIGHT: THE THIEF

1. James Henry Duveen, *Art Treasures and Intrigue* (Garden City, NY: Doubleday, Doran, 1935), 316–17.
2. Reit, *Day They Stole*, 134 (see chap. 2, n. 2).
3. Ibid., 135.
4. Ibid., 136.
5. Ibid., 137.
6. Ibid., 168.
7. Ibid., 137.
8. Esterow, *Art Stealers*, 147 (see chap. 2, n. 4).
9. Ibid., 147.
10. Ibid., 147.
11. Ibid., 147.
12. Ibid., 148.
13. Reit, *Day They Stole*, 143.
14. Esterow, *Art Stealers*, 149–50.
15. The last name is spelled Perruggia on the Bertillon card in police files, but most authorities regard that as an error.
16. *New York Times*, December 13, 1913.
17. Reit, *Day They Stole*, 142.
18. Esterow, *Art Stealers*, 150.
19. Ibid., 150.
20. Jérôme Coignard, *Loin du Louvre: Le vol de la Joconde* (Paris: Éditions Olbia, 1998), 121. Trans. Lyn Nosker.
21. Reit, *Day They Stole*, 155.
22. Ibid., 163.
23. Coignard, *Loin du Louvre*, 126.
24. Ibid., 127.
25. Reit, *Day They Stole*, 165.
26. Esterow, *Art Stealers*, 169.

CHAPTER NINE: CHERCHEZ LA FEMME

1. Irving Wallace, "France's Greatest Detective," *Reader's Digest*, February 1950, 106.
2. Lucia Zedner, "Women, Crime and Penal Responses: A Historical Account," in *History of Criminology*, ed. Paul Rock, 339 (Aldershot, UK: Dartmouth, 1994).
3. Berenson, *Trial of Madame Caillaux*, 268–69 (see chap. 3, n. 20).
4. Shapiro, *Breaking the Codes*, 14 (see chap. 1, n. 43).
5. Ibid., 38.
6. Ibid., 38.
7. Ibid., 34.
8. Benjamin F. Martin, *The Hypocrisy of Justice in the Belle Epoque* (Baton Rouge: Louisiana University Press, 1984), 35.
9. Ibid., 46.
10. Ibid., 48.
11. Ibid., 49.

12. Ibid., 52.
13. Ibid., 63–64.
14. Ibid., 66.
15. Ibid., 68.
16. Ernest Dudley and Marguerite Steinheil, *The Scarlett Widow* (London: Muller, 1960), 192.
17. Ibid., 193.
18. Ibid., 197.
19. Ibid., 193.
20. Ibid., 194.
21. Berenson, *Trial of Madame Caillaux*, 63.
22. Even in the rough-and-tumble world of French journalism, it was an unwritten rule that the foibles of politicians' personal lives were off limits. Calmette had to defend his decision to print the "Ton Jo" letter. He published a statement: "This is the first time in my thirty years of journalism that I am publishing a private, intimate letter, against the wishes of its author, its owner, or its receiver. My dignity experiences true suffering at this act." Martin, *Hypocrisy of Justice*, 170.
23. Berenson, *Trial of Madame Caillaux*, 23.
24. Martin, *Hypocrisy of Justice*, 172.
25. Berenson, *Trial of Madame Caillaux*, 24.
26. Martin, *Hypocrisy of Justice*, 173.
27. Ibid., 151–52.
28. Ibid., 152.
29. James Trager, *The Women's Chronology: A Year-by-Year Record from Prehistory to the Present* (New York: Holt, 1994), 400.
30. Boucard ignored the possibility that Henriette wanted to prevent Calmette from publishing other documents, such as the Fabre memo, because that would have shown a more political motive on her part.
31. Berenson, *Trial of Madame Caillaux*, 35.
32. Ibid., 33.
33. Alister Kershaw, *Murder in France* (London: Constable, 1955), 94.
34. Martin, *Hypocrisy of Justice*, 180–81.
35. Ibid., 181.
36. Ibid., 181.
37. French law permitted them to take part in the criminal trial, in addition to the prosecution and defense attorneys.
38. Martin, *Hypocrisy of Justice*, 185.
39. Ibid., 191.
40. Ibid., 191.
41. Berenson, *Trial of Madame Caillaux*, 173.
42. Ibid., 171.
43. Ibid., 208–09.
44. Martin, *Hypocrisy of Justice*, 197.
45. Ibid., 198.
46. Ibid., 199.
47. Ibid., 199.

48. Ibid., 200.
49. Ibid., 201.

CHAPTER TEN: THE GREATEST CRIME

1. Gold, Arthur, and Robert Fizdale, *Misia: The Life of Misia Sert* (New York: Knopf, 1980), 162.
2. *Ibid.*
3. Miller, Arthur I., *Insights of Genius: Imagery and Creativity in Science and Art* (New York: Copernicus, 1996), 419.
4. Nash, Jay Robert, *Encyclopedia of World Crime* (Wilmette, IL: CrimeBooks, 1990), 35.
5. *Ibid.*
6. *Ibid.*
7. Liptak, Adam, "Driver's License Emerges as Crime-Fighting Tool, but Privacy Advocates Worry," *New York Tiimes*, February 17, 2007.
8. Forgetting the month later, Apollinaire wrote "August 1914."
9. Steegmuller, Francis, *Apollinaire: Poet Among the Painters* (New York: Farrar, Straus, 1963), 233.
10. *Ibid.*, 235.
11. *Ibid.*, 249.
12. *Ibid.*, 259.
13. Kern, Stephen, *The Culture of Time and Space 1880–1918* (Cambridge, MA: Harvard University Press, 2003), 302.
14. Kluver, Billy, *A Day with Picasso: 24 Photographs by Jean Cocteau* (Cambridge, MA: MIT Press, 1997), 65.
15. The painting was not sold to anyone until 1924, when the Paris couturier Jacques Doucet purchased it.
16. Brassai, *Picasso and Company,* trans. Francis Price (Garden City, NY: Doubleday, 1966), 119.
17. Heartfield's original name was Helmut Herzfeld, which he changed during the war as a protest to anti-British propaganda.
18. Betin, Wolfgang, et al., trans. Clare Krojzl, *A History of German Literature from the Beginnings to the Present Day,* 4th ed. (London: Routledge, 1993), 452.
19. The name has a variety of explanations. One is that it was a French word for "hobby-horse." Another was that it was Russian for "yes, yes," meant sarcastically.
20. Rookmaaker, H. R., *Modern Art and the Death of a Culture* (London: InterVarsity Press, 1970), 130.
21. Lynton, Norbert, *The Story of Modern Art* (Ithaca, NY: Cornell University Press, 1980), 127.

AFTERWORD: THE MASTERMIND

1. Karl Decker, "Why and How the Mona Lisa Was Stolen," *Saturday Evening Post,* June 25, 1932.
2. Ibid., 14.
3. Ibid., 15.

4. Ibid., 89.
5. Ibid., 89.
6. Ibid., 89.
7. Ibid., 89.
8. Ibid., 89.
9. Ibid., 91.
10. Ibid., 89.
11. Ibid., 91.
12. Ibid., 91.
13. Ibid., 91.
14. Ibid., 91.
15. Jana Seely, e-mail message to authors, September 26, 2005.

BIBLIOGRAPHY

Abel, Richard. *The Ciné Goes to Town: French Cinema, 1896–1914*. Berkeley: University of California Press, 1994.

———. "The Thrills of *Grand Peur*: Crime Series and Serials in the Belle Époque." *Velvet Light Trap*, no. 37 (1996).

Allaby, Michael, and Derek Gjertsen. *Makers of Science*. 5 vols. New York: Oxford University Press, 2002.

Allen, Grant. *Paris*. Boston: Page, 1901.

Allwood, John. *The Great Exhibitions*. London: Studio Vista, 1977.

Antliff, Mark, and Patricia Leighten. *Cubism and Culture*. The World of Art Library. London: Thames and Hudson, 2001.

Apollinaire, Guillaume. *Apollinaire on Art: Essays and Reviews, 1902–1918*. Edited by LeRoy C. Breunig. New York: Viking Press, 1972.

———. *Selected Writings of Guillaume Apollinaire*. Edited by Roger Shattuck. New York: James Laughlin, 1948.

Ashbery, John. *Selected Prose*. Edited by Eugene Richie. Ann Arbor: University of Michigan Press, 2004.

Ashton-Wolfe, Harry. *Crimes of Violence and Revenge*. Boston: Houghton Mifflin, 1929.

———. "The Debt of the Police to Detective Fiction, Part 1." *Illustrated London News*, February 20, 1932.

———. "The Debt of the Police to Detective Fiction, Part 2." *Illustrated London News*, February 27, 1932.

———. *The Forgotten Clue: Stories of the Parisian Sûreté with an Account of Its Methods*. Boston: Houghton Mifflin, 1930.

———. *Strange Crimes, Culled from the Archives of the Paris Sûreté*. London: Hurst and Blackett, 1932.

Atalay, Bülent. *Math and the Mona Lisa: The Art and Science of Leonardo da Vinci*. New York: Smithsonian Books, 2006.

Baker, Brian. "Darwin's Gothic Science and Literature in the Late Nineteenth Century." In *Literature and Science: Social Impact and Interaction,* by John H. Cartwright and Brian Baker. Santa Barbara, CA: ABC-CLIO, 2005.

Baker, Phil. *The Book of Absinthe: A Cultural History.* New York: Grove Press, 2001.

Balzac, Honoré de. *A Harlot High and Low.* Translated with an introduction by Rayner Heppenstall. Baltimore: Penguin, 1970.

———. *Père Goriot.* Translated by Burton Raffel. New York: Norton, 1994.

Barzun, Jacques. *Classic, Romantic, and Modern.* Boston: Little, Brown, 1961.

———. *From Dawn to Decadence: 500 Years of Western Cultural Life, 1500 to the Present.* New York: HarperCollins, 2000.

Baumer, Franklin L. *Modern European Thought: Continuity and Change in Ideas, 1600–1950.* New York: Macmillan, 1977.

Baxter, John. *We'll Always Have Paris: Sex and Love in the City of Light.* New York: HarperCollins, 2006.

Beavan, Colin. *Fingerprints: The Origins of Crime Detection.* New York: Hyperion, 2001.

Beirne, Piers. "Adolphe Quetelet and the Origins of Positivist Criminology." In *The Origins and Growth of Criminology,* edited by Piers Beirne. Aldershot, UK: Dartmouth, 1994.

Belin, Jean. *Secrets of the Sûreté: The Memoirs of Commissioner Jean Belin.* New York: Putnam's, 1950.

Bell, Eric Temple. *Men of Mathematics.* New York: Simon and Schuster, 1965.

Benjamin, Walter, and Hannah Arendt. *Illuminations.* New York: Schocken Books, 1969.

Bensusan, Samuel L. *Souvenir of Paris.* London: Jack, 1911.

Berenson, Edward. *The Trial of Madame Caillaux.* Berkeley: University of California Press, 1992.

Bergson, Henri. *Selections from Bergson.* Edited by Harold Atkins Larrabee. New York: Appleton-Century-Crofts, 1949.

Bertaut, Jules. *Paris, 1870–1935.* Translated by R. Millar. New York: Appleton-Century, 1936.

Beutin, Wolfgang. *A History of German Literature: From the Beginnings to the Present Day.* 4th ed. London: Routledge, 1993.

Bianco, Margery Williams. *Paris.* London: Black, 1910.

Bicknell, Ethel E. *Paris and Her Treasures.* New York: Scribner's, 1912.

Biddiss, Michael Denis. *The Age of the Masses: Ideas and Society in Europe since 1870.* Harmondsworth, UK: Penguin Books, 1977.

Blackford, Katherine M. H. "An Afternoon with Bertillon." *Outlook* 100, no. 7 (February 24, 1912).

Bohn, Thomas W., Richard L. Stromgren, and Daniel H. Johnson. *Light and Shadows: A History of Motion Pictures.* Port Washington, NY: Alfred, 1975.

Bohn, Willard. *Apollinaire and the International Avant-Garde.* Albany: State University of New York Press, 1997.

Boorstin, Daniel J., and Daniel J. Boorstin Collection (Library of Congress). *The Creators.* New York: Vintage Books, 1993.

Brandon, Ruth. *Surreal Lives: The Surrealists, 1917–1945*. New York: Grove Press, 1999.

Brassaï. *Picasso and Company*. Garden City, NY: Doubleday, 1966.

Bredin, Jean-Denis. *The Affair: The Case of Alfred Dreyfus*. Translated by Jeffrey Mehlman. New York: Braziller, 1986.

Brown, Blanche R. *Five Cities: An Art Guide to Athens, Rome, Florence, Paris, London*. Garden City, NY: Doubleday, 1964.

Bryson, Bill. *A Short History of Nearly Everything*. New York: Broadway Books, 2003.

Bulliet, Clarence Joseph. *The Significant Moderns and Their Pictures*. New York: Covici, 1936.

Burchell, S. C., and Time-Life Books. *Age of Progress*. Great Ages of Man: A History of the World's Cultures. Amsterdam: Time-Life International, 1966.

Burgess, Gelett. "The Wild Men of Paris." *Architectural Record* 27, no. 5 (1910): 401–14.

Burke, Carolyn. *Becoming Modern: The Life of Mina Loy*. New York: Farrar, Straus and Giroux, 1996.

Butler, Christopher. *Early Modernism: Literature, Music and Painting in Europe, 1900–1916*. Oxford: Clarendon Press, 1994.

Cabanne, Pierre. *Pablo Picasso: His Life and Times*. New York: Morrow, 1977.

Canaday, John. *Mainstreams of Modern Art*. New York: Holt, 1959.

Canler, Louis, and Jacques Brenner. *Mémoirs de Canler, ancien chef du service de Sûreté*. Paris: Mercure de France, 1968.

Carter, William C. *Proust in Love*. New Haven: Yale University Press, 2006.

Caruchet, William. *Ils ont tué Bonnot: Les révélations des archives policières*. Paris: Calmann-Lévy, 1990.

Charney, Leo, and Vanessa R. Schwartz. *Cinema and the Invention of Modern Life*. Berkeley: University of California Press, 1995.

Chipp, Herschel Browning, Peter Howard Selz, and Joshua Charles Taylor. *Theories of Modern Art: A Source Book by Artists and Critics*. Berkeley: University of California Press, 1968.

Cline, Barbara Lovett. *Men Who Made a New Physics: Physicists and the Quantum Theory*. New York: New American Library, 1965.

Cobb, Peter. "Forensic Science." In *Crime Scene to Court: The Essentials of Forensic Science*, edited by Peter White. Cambridge: Royal Society of Chemistry, 1998.

Cobban, Alfred. *A Modern History of France*. Vol. 3, *1871–1962*. Baltimore: Penguin, 1967.

Cocteau, Jean. *My Contemporaries*. Translated by Margaret Crosland. Philadelphia: Chilton, 1968.

Coignard, Jérôme. *Loin du Louvre: Le vol de la Joconde*. Paris: Éditions Olbia, 1998.

Cole, Robert. *A Traveller's History of Paris*. 3rd ed. Traveller's History. New York: Interlink Books, 2005.

Conklin, Barbara Gardner, Robert Gardner, and Dennis Shortelle. *Encyclopedia of Forensic Science: A Compendium of Detective Fact and Fiction*. Westport, CT: Oryx Press, 2002.

Conrad, Peter. *Modern Times, Modern Places*. New York: Knopf, 1999.

Cowles, Virginia. *1913: An End and a Beginning*. New York: Harper and Row, 1967.

Cragin, Thomas. *Murder in Parisian Streets: Manufacturing Crime and Justice in the Popular Press, 1830–1900*. Lewisburg: Bucknell University Press, 2006.

Cronin, Vincent. *Paris on the Eve: 1900–1914*. New York: St. Martin's Press, 1990.

Crump, Thomas. *A Brief History of Science*. New York: Carroll and Graf, 2002.

Curie, Eve. *Madame Curie: A Biography*. Translated by Vincent Sheehan. Garden City, NY: Doubleday, 1937.

d'Archimbaud, Nicholas, and Bruno de Cessole. *Louvre: Portrait of a Museum*. New York: Stewart, Tabori and Chang, 1998.

Darmon, Pierre. *Marguerite Steinheil, ingénue criminelle?* [Paris]: Perrin, 1996.

Davenport, William W. *The Seine: From Its Source, to Paris, to the Sea*. New York: McGraw-Hill, 1968.

Decker, Karl. "Why and How the Mona Lisa Was Stolen." *Saturday Evening Post*, June 25, 1932.

Delacourt, Frédéric. *L'affaire Bande à Bonnot*. Paris: De Vecchi, 2006.

Derfler, Leslie. *The Dreyfus Affair*. Westport, CT: Greenwood Press, 2002.

Deutsch, Yvonne, ed. *Science against Crime*. New York: Exeter, 1982.

Dilnot, George. *Triumphs of Detection: A Book about Detectives*. London: Bles, 1929.

Douglas, Charles. *Artist Quarter: Reminiscences of Montmartre and Montparnasse in the First Two Decades of the Twentieth Century*. London: Faber and Faber, 1941.

Dreiser, Theodore. "Paris." *Century Magazine* 86, no. 6 (October 1913).

Duby, Georges, and Robert Mandrou. *A History of French Civilization*. New York: Random House, 1966.

Dudley, Ernest, and Marguerite Steinheil. *The Scarlett Widow*. London: Muller, 1960.

Duncan, Martha Grace. *Romantic Outlaws, Beloved Prisons: The Unconscious Meanings of Crime and Punishment*. New York: New York University Press, 1996.

DuParcq, Georges. *Crime Reporter*. New York: McBride, 1934.

Duveen, James Henry. *Art Treasures and Intrigue*. Garden City, NY: Doubleday, Doran, 1935.

Eco, Umberto, and Alastair McEwen. *History of Beauty*. New York: Rizzoli, 2004.

Edwards, Samuel. *The Vidocq Dossier: The Story of the World's First Detective*. Boston: Houghton Mifflin, 1977.

Eksteins, Modris. *Rites of Spring: The Great War and the Birth of the Modern Age*. New York: Anchor Books, 1990.

Esterow, Milton. *The Art Stealers*. New York: Macmillan, 1966.

Evans, Colin. *The Casebook of Forensic Detection: How Science Solved 100 of the World's Most Baffling Crimes*. New York: Wiley, 1996.

Evenson, Norma. *Paris: A Century of Change, 1878–1978*. New Haven: Yale University Press, 1979.

Everdell, William R. *The First Moderns: Profiles in the Origins of Twentieth-Century Thought*. Chicago: University of Chicago Press, 1997.

Faux dans l'art et dans l'histoire. Paris: Grand Palais, 1955.

Fleming, William. *Art and Ideas*. 6th ed. New York: Holt, Rinehart and Winston, 1980.

Fosdick, Raymond B. "The Passing of the Bertillon System of Identification." *Journal of the American Institute of Criminal Law and Criminology* 6, no. 3 (September 1915): 363–69.

Franck, Dan. *The Bohemians: The Birth of Modern Art, Paris 1900–1930*. Translated by Cynthia Hope LeBow. London: Weidenfeld and Nicolson, 2001.

Freud, Sigmund. *Leonardo da Vinci and a Memory of His Childhood*. New York: Norton, 1964.

Freundschuh, Aaron. "Crime Stories in the Historical Landscape: Narrating the Theft of the Mona Lisa." *Urban History* 33, no. 2 (2006).

Gaboriau, Émile. *Monsieur Lecoq*. New York: Dover, 1975.

Galison, Peter. *Einstein's Clocks, Poincaré's Maps: Empires of Time*. New York: Norton, 2003.

Garde, Serge, Rémi Gardebled, and Valérie Mauro. *Guide du Paris des faits divers du moyen-âge à nos jours*. Paris: Cherche Midi, 2004.

Gay, Peter. *Modernism: The Lure of Heresy; From Baudelaire to Beckett and Beyond*. New York: Norton, 2008.

Gee, Malcolm. *Dealers, Critics, and Collectors of Modern Painting: Aspects of the Parisian Art Market between 1910 and 1930*. Outstanding Dissertations in the Fine Arts. New York: Garland, 1981.

Gerould, Daniel Charles. *Guillotine: Its Legend and Lore*. New York: Blast Books, 1992.

Gersh-Nešic, Beth S. *The Early Criticism of André Salmon: A Study of His Thoughts on Cubism*. New York: Garland, 1991.

Gide, André. *The Journals of André Gide, 1889–1949*. New York: Vintage Books, 1956.

Giroud, Françoise. *Marie Curie: A Life*. New York: Holmes and Meier, 1986.

Gold, Arthur, and Robert Fizdale. *Misia: The Life of Misia Sert*. New York: Knopf, 1980.

Golding, John. *Cubism: A History and an Analysis, 1907–1914*. Rev. American ed. Boston: Boston Book and Art Shop, 1968.

———. "The Demoiselles d'Avignon." *Burlington Magazine* 100, no. 662 (1958): 154–63.

Goldsmith, Barbara. *Obsessive Genius: The Inner World of Marie Curie*. London: Weidenfeld and Nicolson, 2005.

Goldwater, Robert John, and Marco Treves. *Artists on Art: From the XIV to the XX Century*. New York: Pantheon Books, 1972.

Gordon, Mel. *The Grand Guignol: Theatre of Fear and Terror*. Rev. ed. New York: Da Capo Press, 1997.

Gosling, Nigel. *The Adventurous World of Paris, 1900–1914*. New York: Morrow, 1978.

Gramont, Sanche de. *The French: Portrait of a People*. New York: Putnam's, 1969.

Green, Christopher. *Art in France, 1900–1940*. New Haven, CT: Yale University Press, 2000.

Greenwall, Harry J. *Paris Calling: Stories and Anecdotes of Twenty-Five Years in the French Capital*. London: Hurst and Blackett, 1932.

Gribbin, John R. *The Scientists: A History of Science Told through the Lives of Its Greatest Inventors.* New York: Random House, 2003.

Gribbin, John R., and Mary Gribbin. *Almost Everyone's Guide to Science: The Universe, Life, and Everything.* New Haven: Yale Nota Bene/Yale University Press, 2000.

Gribble, Leonard R. *Famous Feats of Detection and Deduction.* Garden City, NY: Doubleday, Doran, 1934.

Grierson, Francis Durham. *The Compleat Crook — in France.* London: Butterworth, 1934.

———. *Famous French Crimes.* London: Muller, 1959.

Guilbert, Yvette, and Harold Simpson. *Yvette Guilbert: Struggles and Victories.* London: Mills and Boon, 1910.

Gunning, Tom. "A Tale of Two Prologues: Actors and Roles, Detectives and Disguises in Fantômas, Film and Novel." *Velvet Light Trap,* no. 37 (Spring 1996).

Haight, Mary Ellen Jordan. *Paris Portraits, Renoir to Chanel: Walks on the Right Bank.* Salt Lake City: Peregrine Smith Books, 1991.

———. *Walks in Gertrude Stein's Paris.* Salt Lake City: Peregrine Smith Books, 1988.

Haine, W. Scott. *The World of the Paris Café: Sociability among the French Working Class, 1789–1914.* Baltimore: Johns Hopkins University Press, 1999.

Halasz, Nicholas. *Captain Dreyfus: The Story of Mass Hysteria.* New York: Simon and Schuster, 1968.

Hale, Oron J. *The Great Illusion, 1900–1914.* The Rise of Modern Europe. New York: Harper and Row, 1971.

Hall, Peter Geoffrey. *Cities in Civilization: Culture, Innovation, and Urban Order.* London: Weidenfeld and Nicolson, 1998.

Hamilton, George Heard. *Painting and Sculpture in Europe, 1880–1940.* The Pelican History of Art. Baltimore: Penguin Books, 1972.

Harriss, Joseph A. "Seeking Mona Lisa." *Smithsonian* 30, no. 2 (May 1999).

Harvey, David. *The Conditions of Postmodernity: An Enquiry into the Origins of Cultural Change.* Oxford: Blackwell, 1989.

Hecht, Jennifer Michael. *The End of the Soul: Scientific Modernity, Atheism, and Anthropology in France.* New York: Columbia University Press, 2003.

———. "French Scientific Materialism and the Liturgy of Death: The Invention of a Secular Version of Catholic Last Rites (1876–1914)." *French Historical Studies* 20, no. 4 (Fall 1997).

Heisenberg, Werner. *Physics and Philosophy: The Revolution in Modern Science.* New York: Harper, 1958.

Henderson, Linda Dalrymple. *The Fourth Dimension and Non-Euclidean Geometry in Modern Art.* Princeton, NJ: Princeton University Press, 1983.

Herbert, Rosemary. *The Oxford Companion to Crime and Mystery Writing.* New York: Oxford University Press, 1999.

Higonnet, Patrice. *Paris: Capital of the World.* Translated by Arther Goldhammer. Cambridge: Belknap Press, 2002.

Hoffmann, Stanley, and Harvard University, Center for International Affairs. *In Search of France: The Economy, Society, and Political System in the Twentieth Century.* New York, NY: Harper and Row, 1965.

Holmes, Diana, and Carrie Tarr. *A "Belle Epoque"?: Women in French Society and Culture, 1890–1914.* New York: Berghahn Books, 2006.

Horne, Alistair. *The Fall of Paris: The Siege and the Commune, 1870–1871.* Garden City, NY: Anchor Books, 1967.

———. *Seven Ages of Paris.* New York: Vintage Books, 2004.

Huddleston, Sisley. *Paris Salons, Cafés, Studios.* New York: Blue Ribbon Books, 1928.

Huer, Jon. *The Great Art Hoax: Essays in the Comedy and Insanity of Collectible Art.* Bowling Green, OH: Bowling Green State University Popular Press, 1990.

Huffington, Arianna Stassinopoulos. *Picasso: Creator and Destroyer.* New York: Avon Books, 1989.

Hughes, H. Stuart. *Consciousness and Society: The Reorientation of European Social Thought, 1890–1930.* Rev. ed. New York: Vintage Books, 1977.

Hunter, Sam. *Modern French Painting, 1855–1956.* New York: Dell, 1956.

Hussey, Andrew. *Paris: The Secret History.* London: Viking, 2007.

Hutchings, Peter. *The Criminal Spectre in Law, Literature and Aesthetics: Incriminating Subjects.* London: Routledge, 2001.

Hutton, Patrick H., Amanda S. Bourque, and Amy J. Staples. *Historical Dictionary of the Third French Republic, 1870–1940.* 2 vols. Historical Dictionaries of French History. New York: Greenwood Press, 1986.

Irving, Henry B. *A Book of Remarkable Criminals.* London: Cassell, 1918.

Jay, Mike, and Michael Neve. *1900: A Fin-De-Siècle Reader.* New York: Penguin Books, 1999.

Jeppson, Lawrence. *The Fabulous Frauds: Fascinating Tales of Great Art Forgeries.* New York: Weybright and Talley, 1970.

Joll, James. *The Anarchists.* Boston: Little, Brown, 1964.

Jones, Colin. *Paris: Biography of a City.* New York: Viking, 2005.

Jones, David Arthur. *History of Criminology: A Philosophical Perspective.* Contributions in Criminology and Penology. Westport, CT: Greenwood Press, 1986.

Kafka, Franz, and Max Brod. *The Diaries of Franz Kafka.* Vol. 2, *1914–1923.* New York: Schocken Books, 1949.

Karl, Frederick Robert. *Modern and Modernism: The Sovereignty of the Artist, 1885–1925.* New York: Atheneum, 1988.

Kalifa, Dominique. "Crime Scenes: Criminal Topography and Social Imagining in Nineteenth Century Paris." *French Historical Studies* 27, no. 1 (Winter 2004).

Kennedy, Randy. "Which Picasso and Braque Went to the Movies." *New York Times,* April 15, 2007.

Kern, Stephen. *The Culture of Time and Space, 1880–1918.* Cambridge, MA: Harvard University Press, 2003.

Kershaw, Alister. *Murder in France.* London: Constable, 1955.

Klüver, Billy. *A Day with Picasso: Twenty-Four Photographs by Jean Cocteau.* Cambridge, MA: MIT Press, 1997.

Knapp, Bettina. *This Was Yvette.* New York: Holt, Rinehart, and Winston, 1964.

Kritzman, Lawrence D., Brian J. Reilly, and M. B. DeBevoise. *The Columbia History of Twentieth-Century French Thought.* New York: Columbia University Press, 2006.

La Cour, Tage, and Harald Mogensen. *The Murder Book: An Illustrated History of the Detective Story.* New York: Herder and Herder, 1971.

Lacenaire, Pierre François, and Monique Lebailly. *Mémoires de Lacenaire: Avec ses poèmes et ses lettres.* Paris: Éditions Albin Michel, 1968.

Lane, Brian. *The Encyclopedia of Forensic Science.* London: Magpie Books, 2004.

Lartigue, Jacques-Henri. *Diary of a Century.* New York: Viking Press, 1970.

Laux, James Michael. *In First Gear: The French Automobile Industry to 1914.* Montreal: McGill-Queen's University Press, 1976.

Leader, Darian. *Stealing the Mona Lisa: What Art Stops Us from Seeing.* New York: Counterpoint, 2002.

Leblanc, Maurice. *Arsène Lupin, Super-Sleuth.* New York: Macaulay, 1927.

———. "The Most Amazing True Crime Story Ever Told: The Auto Bandits of Paris." *New York Times,* May 5, 1912.

Leighten, Patricia Dee. *Re-ordering the Universe: Picasso and Anarchism, 1897–1914.* Princeton, NJ: Princeton University Press, 1989.

Lemaître, Georges Édouard. *From Cubism to Surrealism in French Literature.* Cambridge, MA: Harvard University Press, 1941.

Levenstein, Harvey A. *Seductive Journey: American Tourists in France from Jefferson to the Jazz Age.* Chicago: University of Chicago Press, 1998.

Lightman, Alan P. *The Discoveries: Great Breakthroughs in 20th Century Science.* New York: Pantheon Books, 2005.

Locard, Edmond. *La police et les méthodes scientifiques.* Paris: Éditions Rieder, 1934.

———. "The Police Methodology of Sherlock Holmes." Translated 1942 by John Hugh Holla (typescript at New York Public Library Research Collection). *La Revue Hebdomadaire,* année 31, tome 2 (February 1922).

———. *Le fiancé de la guillotine (Lacenaire).* Paris: Éditions de la flamme d'or, 1954.

Locard, Edmond, and Robert Corvol. *Mémoires d'un criminologiste.* Paris: Fayard, 1957.

Lofficier, Jean-Marc, and Randy Lofficier. *Shadowmen: Heroes and Villains of French Pulp Fiction.* Encino, CA: Black Coat Press, 2003.

Logan, Guy B. H. *Rope, Knife and Chain: Studies of English, French, and American Crimes.* London: Stanley Paul, 1930.

Longstreet, Stephen. *We All Went to Paris: Americans in the City of Light, 1776–1971.* New York: Macmillan, 1972.

Lucas, Netley. *Criminal Paris.* London: Hurst and Blackett, 1926.

Luhan, Mabel Dodge. *European Experiences.* New York: Harcourt, Brace, 1935.

Lynton, Norbert. *The Story of Modern Art.* Ithaca, NY: Cornell University Press, 1980.

MacDonald, John F. "Paris and Mme. Steinheil." *Fortnightly Review* 92 (December 1909.)

Mackworth, Cecily. *Guillaume Apollinaire and the Cubist Life.* New York: Horizon Press, 1963.

Mailer, Norman. *Portrait of Picasso as a Young Man: An Interpretative Biography.* New York: Atlantic Monthly Press, 1995.

Mandell, Richard. *Paris 1900.* Toronto: University of Toronto Press, 1967.

March, Harold. *The Two Worlds of Marcel Proust*. New York: Barnes, 1961.

Marquis, Alice Goldfarb, and Marcel Duchamp. *Marcel Duchamp: The Bachelor Stripped Bare; A Biography*. Boston: MFA Publications, a division of the Museum of Fine Arts, 2002.

Marriner, Brian. *On Death's Bloody Trail: Murder and the Art of Forensic Science*. New York: St. Martin's Press, 1993.

Martin, Benjamin F. *Crime and Criminal Justice under the Third Republic: The Shame of Marianne*. Baton Rouge: Louisiana State University Press, 1990.

———. *The Hypocrisy of Justice in the Belle Epoque*. Baton Rouge: Louisiana State University Press, 1984.

Martin Du Gard, Roger. *Jean Barois*. New York: Viking Press, 1949.

Martin, Marianne W. *Futurist Art and Theory, 1900–1915*. Oxford: Clarendon Press, 1968.

Mason, Raymond. *At Work in Paris: Raymond Mason on Art and Artists*. New York: Thames and Hudson, 2003.

Masur, Gerhard. *Prophets of Yesterday: Studies in European Culture, 1890–1914*. New York: Macmillan, 1961.

Matsuda, Matt K. *The Memory of the Modern*. New York: Oxford University Press, 1996.

Maurois, André. *Proust: Portrait of a Genius*. New York: Harper, 1950.

McLaren, Angus. *The Trials of Masculinity: Policing Sexual Boundaries, 1870–1930*. The Chicago Series on Sexuality, History, and Society. Chicago: University of Chicago Press, 1997.

McLeave, Hugh. *Rogues in the Gallery: The Modern Plague of Art Thefts*. Boston: Godine, 1981.

McMillan, James F. *Dreyfus to De Gaulle: Politics and Society in France, 1898–1969*. London: Arnold, 1985.

McMullen, Roy. *Mona Lisa: The Picture and the Myth*. Boston: Houghton Mifflin, 1975.

Mellow, James R. *Charmed Circle: Gertrude Stein and Company*. New York: Praeger, 1975.

Miller, Arthur I. *Einstein, Picasso: Space, Time and the Beauty That Causes Havoc*. New York: Basic Books, 2001.

———. *Insights of Genius: Imagery and Creativity in Science and Art*. New York: Copernicus, 1996.

Morain, Alfred. *The Underworld of Paris: Secrets of the Sûreté*. London: Jarrolds, 1929.

Morton, James. *Gangland: The Early Years*. London: Time Warner Paperbacks, 2004.

Murch, A. E. *The Development of the Detective Novel*. Port Washington, N.Y.: Kennikat Press, 1968.

Murphy, Bruce. *The Encyclopedia of Murder and Mystery*. New York: St. Martin's Minotaur, 1999.

Museum of Modern Art (New York, NY), and Alfred Hamilton Barr. *Masters of Modern Art*. Garden City, NY: Doubleday, 1958.

Nash, Jay Robert. *Encyclopedia of World Crime: Criminal Justice, Criminology, and Law Enforcement*. Wilmette, IL: CrimeBooks, 1990, 1999.

———. *Look for the Woman: A Narrative Encyclopedia of Female Poisoners, Kidnappers, Thieves, Extortionists, Terrorists, Swindlers, and Spies, from Elizabethan Times to the Present*. New York: Evans, 1981.

Nesbit, Molly. "The Rat's Ass." *October* 56 (Spring 1991): 6–20.

Olivier, Fernande. *Loving Picasso: The Private Journal of Fernande Olivier*. New York: Abrams, 2001.

———. *Picasso and His Friends*. New York: Appleton-Century, 1965.

Osterburg, James W., and Richard H. Ward. *Criminal Investigation: A Method for Reconstructing the Past*. Cincinnati: Anderson, 1992.

Paléologue, Maurice. *An Intimate Journal of the Dreyfus Case*. New York: Criterion Books, 1957.

Panek, LeRoy Lad. *An Introduction to the Detective Story*. Bowling Green, OH: Bowling Green State University Popular Press, 1987.

Parry, Richard. *The Bonnot Gang*. London: Rebel Press, 1987.

Parsons, Ernest Bryham. *Pot-Pourri Parisien*. London: Argus, 1912.

Pate, Janet. *The Book of Sleuths*. Chicago: Contemporary Books, 1977.

Pater, Walter. *The Renaissance: Studies in Art and Poetry*. New York: Mentor, 1959.

Paul, Robert S. *Whatever Happened to Sherlock Holmes: Detective Fiction, Popular Theology, and Society*. Carbondale: Southern Illinois University Press, 1991.

Perrot, Michelle, ed. *A History of Private Life*. Vol. 4, *From the Fires of Revolution to the Great War*. Cambridge, MA: Belknap Press, 1990.

Pflaum, Rosalynd. *Grand Obsession: Madame Curie and Her World*. New York: Doubleday, 1989.

Poincaré, Henri. *Science and Hypothesis*. New York: Dover, 1952.

Poincaré, Raymond, and George Arthur. *The Memoirs of Raymond Poincaré, 1914*. London: Heinemann, 1929.

Porter, Dennis. *The Pursuit of Crime: Art and Ideology in Detective Fiction*. New Haven: Yale University Press, 1981.

Quinn, Arthur Hobson. *Edgar Allan Poe: A Critical Biography*. Baltimore: Johns Hopkins University Press, 1998.

Quinn, Susan. *Marie Curie: A Life*. New York: Simon and Schuster, 1995.

Read, Herbert Edward. *A Concise History of Modern Painting*. New York: Praeger, 1959.

Rearick, Charles. *Pleasures of the Belle Époque: Entertainment and Festivity in Turn-of-the-Century France*. New Haven: Yale University Press, 1985.

Reit, Seymour. *The Day They Stole the Mona Lisa*. New York: Summit Books, 1981.

Rhodes, Henry T. F. *Alphonse Bertillon: Father of Scientific Detection*. New York: Greenwood, 1968.

———. *Clues and Crime: The Science of Criminal Investigation*. London: Murray, 1933.

———. *Some Persons Unknown: Being an Account of Scientific Detection*. London: Murray, 1931.

Richards, E. E. *The Louvre*. Boston: Small, Maynard, 1912.

Richardson, John, and Marilyn McCully. *A Life of Picasso*. Vol. 1, *1881–1906*. New York: Knopf, 1991.

———. *A Life of Picasso*. Vol. 2, *1907–1917*. New York: Random House, 1996.

Richardson, John, Public Education Association of the City of New York., and M. Knoedler and Co. *Picasso: An American Tribute [Exhibition] April 25– May 12, 1962 [for the Benefit of the Public Education Association]*. New York: Public Education Association, 1962.

Roberts, Mary Louise. *Disruptive Acts: The New Woman in Fin-De-Siècle France.* Chicago: University of Chicago Press, 2002.

Robinson, Henry Morton. *Science versus Crime.* Indianapolis: Bobbs-Merrill, 1935.

Rookmaaker, H. R. *Modern Art and the Death of a Culture.* Downers Grove, IL: Inter-Varsity Press, 1970.

Rothstein, Edward. "A Case for Sherlock: The Double Helix of Crime Fiction." *New York Times,* March 4, 2000.

Rudorff, Raymond. *The Belle Epoque: Paris in the Nineties.* New York: Saturday Review Press, 1973.

Sachs, Samuel, II. "Fakes and Forgeries." Minneapolis Institute of Arts, 1973.

Saferstein, Richard. *Criminalistics: An Introduction to Forensic Science.* 2d ed. Englewood Cliffs, NJ: Prentice-Hall, 1981.

Salmon, André. *Souvenirs sans fin, deuxième époque (1908–1920).* Paris: Gallimard, 1956.

———. *Souvenirs sans fin, troisième époque (1920–1940).* Paris: Gallimard, 1961.

Sannié, Charles. *Eléménts de police scientifique.* Paris: Hermann et Cie, 1938.

Sartre, Jean-Paul. *The Words.* Translated by Bernard Frechtman. New York: Vintage Books, 1981.

Sassoon, Donald. *Becoming Mona Lisa: The Making of a Global Icon.* San Diego: Harcourt, 2001.

Saunders, Edith. *The Mystery of Marie Lafarge.* London: Clerke and Cockeran, 1951.

Sayre, Henry M. *A World of Art.* 2nd ed. Upper Saddle River, NJ: Prentice Hall, 1997.

Scharf, Aaron. *Art and Photography.* Baltimore: Penguin, 1974.

Schmitz, E. Robert. *The Piano Works of Claude Debussy.* New York: Duell, 1950.

Schüller, Sepp. *Forgers, Dealers, Experts: Strange Chapters in the History of Art.* New York: Putnam, 1960.

Schütt, Sita A. "French Crime Fiction." In *The Cambridge Companion to Crime Fiction*, edited by Martin Priestman. Cambridge: Cambridge: University Press, 2003.

Schumacher, Claude. *Alfred Jarry and Guillaume Apollinaire.* Basingstoke: Macmillan, 1984.

Seigel, Jerrold E. *Bohemian Paris: Culture, Politics, and the Boundaries of Bourgeois Life, 1830–1930.* New York: Penguin Books, 1987.

Serge, Victor. *Memoirs of a Revolutionary, 1901–1941.* Translated and edited by Peter Sedgwick Oxford: Oxford University Press, 1980.

Settegast, Mary. *Mona Lisa's Moustache: Making Sense of a Dissolving World.* Grand Rapids, MI: Phanes Press, 2001.

Severini, Gino. *The Life of a Painter: The Autobiography of Gino Severini.* Translated by Jennifer Franchina, Princeton, NJ: Princeton University Press, 1995.

Seymour-Smith, Martin. *Guide to Modern World Literature.* Vol. *two, Dutch, Finnish, French and Belgian, German, Scandinavian.* London: Hodder and Stoughton, 1975.

Shapiro, Ann-Louise. *Breaking the Codes: Female Criminality in Fin-De-Siècle Paris.* Stanford, CA: Stanford University Press, 1996.

Shattuck, Roger. *The Banquet Years: The Arts in France, 1885–1918; Alfred Jarry, Henri Rousseau, Erik Satie, Guillaume Apollinaire.* New York: Vintage, 1968.

———. *Proust's Binoculars: A Study of Memory, Time, and Recognition in A la recherche du temps perdu.* New York: Vintage Books, 1967.

Shlain, Leonard. *Art and Physics: Parallel Visions in Space, Time, and Light.* New York: Morrow, 1991.

Singer, Barnett. *Modern France: Mind, Politics, Society.* Seattle: University of Washington Press, 1980.

Skinner, Cornelia Otis. *Elegant Wits and Grand Horizontals: A Sparkling Panorama Of "La Belle Epoque," Its Gilded Society, Irrepressible Wits and Splendid Courtesans.* Boston: Houghton Mifflin, 1962.

Slosson, Edwin Emery. *Major Prophets of To-Day.* Freeport, NY: Books for Libraries Press, 1968.

Smith, Frank Berkeley. *How Paris Amuses Itself.* New York: Funk and Wagnalls, 1903.

Smith, Timothy B. "Assistance and Repression: Rural Exodus, Vagabondage, and Social Crisis in France, 1890–1914." *Journal of Social History* 32, no. 4, (Summer 1999).

Snyder, Louis L. *The Dreyfus Case: A Documentary History.* New Brunswick, NJ: Rutgers University Press, 1973.

Soderman, Harry, and John J. O'Connell. *Modern Criminal Investigation.* London: Bell, 1935.

Sommerville, Frankfort. *The Spirit of Paris.* London: Black, 1913.

Sonn, Richard David. *Anarchism and Cultural Politics in Fin De Siècle France.* Lincoln: University of Nebraska Press, 1989.

Souvestre, Pierre, and Marcel Allain. *Fantômas.* New York: Morrow, 1986.

Steegmuller, Francis. *Apollinaire: Poet among the Painters.* New York: Farrar, Straus, 1963.

Stein, Gertrude. *The Autobiography of Alice B. Toklas.* New York: Vintage Books, 1960.

Stewart, R. F. *And Always a Detective: Chapters on the History of Detective Fiction.* North Pomfret, VT: David and Charles, 1980.

Storey, Mary Rose, and David Bourdon. *Mona Lisas.* New York: Abrams, 1980.

Storm, John. *The Valadon Drama: The Life of Suzanne Valadon.* New York: Dutton, 1959.

Symons, Julian. *Bloody Murder: From the Detective Story to the Crime Novel.* 2nd ed. London: Pan Books, 1992.

Sypher, Wylie. *Rococo to Cubism in Art and Literature.* New York: Vintage Books, 1963.

Tallack, Peter. *The Science Book.* London: Cassell, 2001.

Tarbell, Ida. "Identification of Criminals: The Scientific Method in Use in France." *McClure's Magazine* 2, no. 4 (March 1894).

Temperini, Renaud. *Leonardo Da Vinci at the Louvre.* Paris: Éditions Scala, 2003.

Thiher, Allen. *Fiction Rivals Science: The French Novel from Balzac to Proust.* Columbia: University of Missouri Press, 2001.

Thomson, Henry Douglas. *Masters of Mystery: A Study of the Detective Story.* 1931. Reprint, New York: Dover, 1978.

Thorwald, Jürgen. *The Century of the Detective.* Translated by Richard Winston and Clara Winston. New York: Harcourt, Brace, and World, 1965.

———. *Crime and Science: The New Frontier in Criminology.* Translated by Richard Winston and Clara Winston. New York: Harcourt, 1967.

Tombs, Robert. "Culture and the Intellectuals." In *Modern France, 1880–2002,* edited by James McMillan. New York: Oxford University Press, 2003.

Tomkins, Calvin, and Time-Life Books. *The World of Marcel Duchamp, 1887–1968.* Rev. ed. New York: Time-Life Books, 1974.

Trager, James. *The Women's Chronology: A Year-by-Year Record from Prehistory to the Present.* New York: Holt, 1994.

Tuchman, Barbara Wertheim. *The Proud Tower: A Portrait of the World before the War, 1890–1914.* New York: Macmillan, 1966.

Tulard, Jean, and Alfred Fierro. *Almanach de Paris: Tome 2, de 1789 à nos jours.* Paris: Encyclopaedia universalis, 1990.

Van Dover, J. Kenneth. *You Know My Method: The Science of the Detective.* Bowling Green, OH: Bowling Green State University Popular Press, 1994.

Varias, Alexander. *Paris and the Anarchists: Aesthetes and Subversives during the Fin-de-Siècle.* New York: St. Martin's Press, 1996.

Vasari, Giorgio. *The Lives of the Artists: A Selection.* Hammondsworth, UK: Penguin Books, 1977.

Vidocq, François-Eugène. *Memoirs of Vidocq: Master of Crime.* Edinburgh: AK Press, 2003.

Vollard, Ambroise. *Recollections of a Picture Dealer.* New York: Hacker Art Books, 1978.

Wallace, Robert, and Time-Life Books. *The World of Leonardo, 1452–1519.* Rev. ed. New York: Time-Life Books, 1975.

Walz, Robin, and NetLibrary Inc. *Pulp Surrealism: Insolent Popular Culture in Early Twentieth-Century Paris.* Berkeley: University of California Press, 2000.

Watson, Peter. *Ideas: A History of Thought and Invention, from Fire to Freud.* New York: HarperCollins, 2005.

———. *The Modern Mind: An Intellectual History of the 20th Century.* New York: HarperCollins, 2001.

Weber, Eugen. *France, Fin De Siècle.* Cambridge, MA: Belknap Press, 1986.

———. *A Modern History of Europe: Men, Cultures, and Societies from the Renaissance to the Present.* New York: Norton, 1971.

———. *My France: Politics, Culture, Myth.* Cambridge, MA: Belknap Press 1991.

Weisberg, Gabriel P. *Montmartre and the Making of Mass Culture.* New Brunswick, NJ: Rutgers University Press, 2001.

———. "The Urban Mirror: Contrasts in the Vision of Existence in the Modern City." In *Paris and the Countryside: Modern Life in Late 19th-Century France.* Portland, ME: Portland Museum of Art, 2006.

Wertenbaker, Lael Tucker, and Time-Life Books. *The World of Picasso, 1881–1973.* Rev. ed. Alexandria, VA: Time-Life Books, 1980.

Weston, Norman. "The Crime Scene." In *Crime Scene to Court: The Essentials of Forensic Science,* edited by Peter White. Cambridge: Royal Society of Chemistry, 1998.

Williams, Ellen. *Picasso's Paris: Walking Tours of the Artist's Life Life in the City.* New York: Little Bookroom, 1999.

Williams, John. *Heyday for Assassins.* London: Heinemann, 1958.

Williams, Roger Lawrence. *Manners and Murders in the World of Louis-Napoleon.* Seattle: University of Washington Press, 1975.

Willis, F. Roy. *Western Civilization: An Urban Perspective.* Lexington, MA: Heath, 1973.

Willms, Johannes. *Paris: Capital of Europe; From the Revolution to the Belle Epoque.* Translated by Eveline L. Kanes. New York: Holmes and Meier, 1997.

Wilson, Colin, and Damon Wilson. *The Giant Book of True Crime.* London: Magpie Books, 2006.

Wilson, Edmund. *Axel's Castle: A Study in the Imaginative Literature of 1870–1930.* New York: Scribner's, 1959.

Wilton, George Wilton. *Fingerprints: History, Law and Romance.* London: Hodge, 1938.

Wolf, John B. *France, 1814–1919: The Rise of a Liberal-Democratic Society.* New York: Harper and Row, 1963.

Wraight, Robert. *The Art Game Again!* London: Frewin, 1974.

Wright, Willard Huntington. "The Great Detective Stories." In *The Art of the Mystery Story,* edited by Howard Haycraft. New York: Simon and Schuster, 1946.

Wren, Lassiter. *Master Strokes of Crime Detection.* Garden City, NY: Doubleday, Doran, 1929.

Wright, Gordon. *Between the Guillotine and Liberty: Two Centuries of the Crime Problem in France.* New York: Oxford University Press, 1983.

Zedner, Lucia. "Women, Crime and Penal Responses: A Historical Account." *In History of Criminology,* edited by Paul Rock. Aldershot, UK: Dartmouth, 1994.

Zeitz, Joshua. *Flapper: A Madcap Story of Sex, Style, Celebrity, and the Women Who Made America Modern.* New York: Three Rivers Press, 2006.

Zeldin, Theodore. *France, 1848–1945: Ambition and Love.* New York: Oxford University Press, 2003.

———. *France, 1848–1945: Politics and Anger.* New York: Oxford University Press, 1979.

———. *France, 1848–1945: Intellect and Pride.* New York: Oxford University Press, 1980.

———. *France, 1848–1945: Anxiety and Hypocrisy.* New York: Oxford University Press, 1981.

———. *France, 1848–1945: Taste and Corruption.* New York: Oxford University Press, 1980.

Zischler, Hanns. *Kafka Goes to the Movies.* Translated by Susan H. Gillespie. Chicago: University of Chicago Press, 2003.

Zweig, Stefan. *The World of Yesterday: An Autobiography.* Lincoln, NE: University of Nebraska Press, 1964.

INDEX

ABOUT THE AUTHORS

Dorothy and Thomas Hoobler are a married couple who have written numerous books together, including *The Monsters* and the Edgar Award–winning *In Darkness, Death*. They live in New York City.